CAMBRIDGESHIRE
LIBRARIES

REFERENCE
AND
INFORMATION
SERVICE

CAMBRIDGE REFERENCE LIBRARY

............................LIBRARY

The Lyle official ARTS *review*

While every care has been taken in the compiling of information contained in this volume the publishers cannot accept any liability for loss, financial or otherwise, incurred by reliance placed on the information herein.

702. REF.
CAMBRIDGESHIRE
LIBRARIES
A814947
21 FEB 1980

Converted at the rate of exchange on the day of sale.

REFERENCE LIBRARY

SBN 902921-91-6

Copyright © Lyle Publications '79
Glenmayne, Galashiels, Scotland.

Printed by Apollo Press
Dominion Way, Worthing, Sussex, England.

Bound by Newdigate Press, Vincent Lane,
Dorking, Surrey, England.

Distributed in the U.S.A. by
Apollo, 391 South Road (U.S.9),
Poughkeepsie, New York 12601.

The Lyle official ARTS review 1980

COMPILED BY JENNIFER KNOX

EDITED BY TONY CURTIS

Auction Acknowledgements

Aldridge's of Bath, *130-132 Walcot Street, Bath.*
Andrew, Hilditch & Son, *19 The Square, Sandbach, Cheshire.*
Australian Art Auctions, *P. O. Box 50, Sutherland, Australia.*
Australian Art Auctions, *11 Trade Winds Place, Kareela, Australia.*
Richard Baker & Baker, *9 Hamilton Street, Birkenhead.*
Bonham's, *Montpelier Galleries, Montpelier Street, London.*
Bracketts, *27-29 High Street, Tunbridge Wells, Kent.*
Butler & Hatch Waterman, *High Street, Tenterden, Kent.*
Christie's, *8 King Street, St. James', London.*
Christie's, *502 Park Avenue, New York, N.Y. 10022.*
Dacre, Son & Hartley, *1/5 The Grove, Ilkley, West Yorkshire.*
Dee & Atkinson, *The Exchange, Driffield, East Yorkshire.*
Edmiston's, *164 Bath Street, Glasgow.*
Elliot & Green, *40 High Street, Lymington, Hants.*
J. Entwistle & Co., *The Galleries, Kingsway, Lytham St. Annes, Lancs.*
Geering & Colyer, *Highgate, Hawkhurst, Kent.*
Graves, Son & Pilcher, *71 Church Road, Hove, Sussex.*
Gribble, Booth & Taylor, *West Street, Axminster, Devon.*
James Harrison, *35 West End, Hebden Bridge, West Yorkshire.*
Heathcote Ball & Co., *47 New Walk, Leicester.*
J. W. Hilam (Auctioneers), *53 Springfield Road, Gorleston-on-Sea.*
Husseys, *Alphinbrook Road, Alphington, Exeter.*
G. A. Key, *Market Place, Aylsham, Norfolk.*
King & Chasemore, *Station Road, Pulborough, West Sussex.*
Lalonde Bros. & Parham, *71 Oakfield Road, Bristol.*
W. H. Lane & Son, *Morrab Road, Penzance, Cornwall.*

Laurence & Martin Taylor, *63 High Street, Honiton, Devon.*
Lawrence of Crewkerne, *19b Market Street, Crewkerne, Somerset.*
Manchester Auction Mart, *2/4 Atkinson Street, Manchester.*
Messenger, May & Baverstock, *93 High Street, Godalming, Surrey.*
Morphets of Harrogate, *4/6 Albert Street, Harrogate.*
Mortons Auction Exchange Inc., *643 Magazine Street, New Orleans, L.A. 70190.*
Alfred Mossop & Co., *Loughrigg Villa, Kelsick Road, Ambleside, Cumbria.*
Neales of Nottingham, *192 Mansfield Road, Nottingham.*
D. M. Nesbit & Co., *7 Clarendon Road, Southsea.*
Osmond Tricks & Son, *Regent Street Salerooms, Clifton, Bristol.*
Outhwaite & Litherland, *Kingsway Galleries, Fontenoy Street, Liverpool.*
Phillips, *The Old House, Knowle, Solihull.*
Christian Rosset, *29 Rue du Rhone, 3e Etage, Geneve, Switzerland.*
Russell, Baldwin & Bright, *Leominster Salerooms, Leominster.*
Andrew Sharpe & Partners, *2 The Grove, Ilkley, West Yorkshire.*
Sotheby's, *34/35 New Bond Street, London.*
Sotheby Bearne, *Rainbow Salerooms, Torquay.*
Sotheby's Belgravia, *19 Matcomb Street, London.*
Sotheby's (Hong Kong), *P. O. Box 83, Hong Kong.*
Sotheby, Parke Bernet, *New York.*
Spear & Sons, *The Hill, Wickham Market, nr. Woodbridge, Suffolk.*
Henry Spencer & Sons, *20 The Square, Retford, Notts.*
D. L. Staniland, *3 Kingsway House, Doncaster.*
Wallis & Wallis, *Regency House, 1 Albion Street, Lewes, Sussex.*
Warner, Sheppard & Wade, *16/18 Halford Street, Leicester.*
Woolley & Wallis, *Castle Street, Salisbury.*

ACKNOWLEDGEMENTS

The publishers wish to thank the following for their assistance in the production of this volume.

Marjorie Clark May Mutch Alison Morrison Pamela Grant Nicky Park Lynn Hall Janice Moncrieff Carmen Milivoyevich

CAMBRIDGE REFERENCE LIBRARY

Introduction

This is the sixth edition of the Lyle Official Arts Review. The 1980 edition contains details of many thousands of oil paintings, watercolours and drawings, covering a wide spectrum of what is available on the market today. There are over 2,500 illustrations of selected pictures computed from auction results gathered over the past year.

Every entry is listed alphabetically under the Artist's name for easy reference and includes a description of the picture, its size, medium, auctioneer and the price fetched.

As regards authenticity of the works listed, this is often a delicate matter and throughout this book the conventional system has been observed:

The full Christian name(s) and surname of the artist denote that, in the opinion of the auctioneer listed, the work is by that artist.

The initials of the Christian name(s) and the surname denote that, in the opinion of the auctioneer listed, the work is of the period of the artist and may be wholly or partly his work.

The surname only of the artist denotes that, in the opinion of the auctioneer listed, the work is of the school or by one of the followers of the artist or painted in his style.

The word 'after' associated with the surname of the artist denotes that, in the opinion of the auctioneer listed, the picture is a copy of the work of the artist. The word 'signed' associated with the name of the artist denotes that, in the opinion of the auctioneer listed, the work bears a signature which is the signature of the artist.

The word 'bears signature' or 'traces of signature' denote that, in the opinion of the auctioneer listed, the work bears a signature or traces of a signature that may be that of the artist.

The word 'dated' denotes that the work is dated and, in the opinion of the auctioneer listed, was executed at that date.

ARTS REVIEW

The year 1980 makes a good point for surveying the last decade of the Art Market.

Who would have believed ten years ago that prints, once dusty and disregarded on the back shelves of antique shops, would now be demanding sales of their own in the big auction houses and fetching unprecedented prices?

Who would have believed that 'genre' pictures would be all the rage? Who would have believed that damaged, unattributed still lives would be making prices reserved for known artists only?

The story of ten years of picture buying and selling underlines the fact that the art fanciers have had to spread their nets wider than they ever imagined to find saleable items. Critics often complain that the art world, more than any other facet of the collecting market, is too often subject to swings and cycles like the stock market. The belief of some collectors that "you should put it into pictures" has turned art into a type of commodity and the fashions that have swept through the market over the past decade can be as clearly charted as the oscillations of stocks and shares.

On the whole however, investors have been fortunate for prices have climbed steadily – but there have been some exceptions. Modern art, riding on the top of the wave ten years ago, took a severe dip and is only now beginning to show an upward climb. More recently the works of Constable have been suffering from a crisis of confidence among buyers because of the revelation that some of the pictures, long believed to be by Constable, were actually done by his son – surely a mistake on the part of a painter to give his son the same initials as himself!

Another frisson swept the collecting market when the activities of Tom Keating were discovered and worried art experts began looking again at their Palmers.

But there were few dips and hollows in art as an investment over the past ten years. It is still considered a highly desirable way of spending your money and most people who bought wisely ten years ago must today be sitting with an increase in their investment which greatly outweighs inflation. Over the past year there have been several pictures coming back into the market and showing by their new prices just how much their value has increased. New records for old favourites are continually being made – only to be re-broken again within weeks or months. The art market is a healthy market and, once again, investors are advised to back their hunches. "If you like it, buy it," is the safest advice that anyone can be given.

London is still the capital of the world as far as picture buying and selling is concerned – with the big auction houses leading the field in volumes of sales. During 1978 Britain exported £129.9 million of fine art, an increase of five per cent over the previous year. Exports of pictures to the U.S.A. came to £44.6 million – an increase of twenty per cent; to Switzerland £23.3 million; to Germany £10.8 million; to Holland £4.7 million; to Japan £4.7 million; to Canada £2.0 million and to Australia £2.0 million. Only two of those figures show a drop from the previous year's trading – Holland and Canada alone bought fewer pictures. The biggest increase, thirty-three per cent, was to Germany and this was accounted for by the heavy buying of Germans at the von Hirsch sales.

Old Masters continue to lead the field as far as price is concerned. When Christie's sold Italian Old Masters in 1979 they made prices that astonished even the auctioneers – A Madonna and Child by Giulio Cesare Pocaccini which was once in the collection of King Charles I made the astonishing price of £150,000 although Christie's had estimated it at a mere £30,000. In Bonham's December Old Master sale a pair of paintings of the life of Christ by the Spaniard Juan de Nisa Valdes Leal made £25,000 against an estimate of between £1,500 and £3,000. In New York at Sotheby Parke Bernet in January

"Christ in the House of Martha and Mary" – Leal *(Bonham's)*
$49,500 £25,000

1979, a floral still life by the elder Brueghel which had once belonged to Napoleon's brother the King of Spain, sold for £205,000. And, also in New York but at Christie's, another still life by the Dutch artist Balthasar Van Der Ast set up a new record for that artist by selling for £147,631 almost £8,000 more than the previous record. A younger Jan Breughel river landscape was knocked down by telephone at Christie's Old Master sale in March to a Belgain buyer for £160,000.

Another highly priced field was Old Master drawings where German, Dutch and Flemish examples continued to make high prices. A chalk drawing of a man's head by Watteau made £10,000. A sketch of his son by Liotard made £60,000.

Other consistent money spinners have been Impressionist and Post Impressionist works and a list of the prices made by some of these artists over the previous twelve months only proves the point that art is a good investment.

When Sotheby's sold the Barlow Collection in London in April 1979 several interesting comparisons, with prices paid for the pictures just over ten years ago, were made. For example

"La Grande Guerre" – Rene Magritte *(Sotheby's)* $221,760 £112,000

Etude pour "Les Joueurs de Cartes" – Paul Cezanne *(Sotheby's)*
$732,600 £370,000

Corot's 'Venus au Bain' painted in 1873 sold for £57,350 in 1961 but in 1979 it made £240,000. Other high prices recorded included £370,000 for Cezanne's 'Les Joueurs de Cartes'; Chagall's 'Le Cirque Mauve' painted in 1961 made £115,000 and Magritte's 'Le Grande Guerre' made £112,000, three times its estimate.

At Christie's April sale of Impressionist and Modern paintings several new records were made – a Fantin Latour still life with flowers and fruit made a new record at £55,000 and Albert Marquet's 'Les Quais du Louvre' set a new record for him at £20,000. In the same sale a Van Gogh pencil sketch was knocked down for £18,000. At other sales during the year German and Japanese buyers dominated the scene bidding for Impressionist, Modern and Contemporary paintings. They paid £75,000 for a Munch painting of two sisters; £78,000 for a Renoir, 'La Conversation'; £75,000 for a Derain landscape; and £42,000 for Chagall's 'Etude pour La Sainte Chapelle'. A Kandinski watercolour was also sold for £18,000.

In July Christie's brought off another "collection coup" by selling one of the finest collections of Impressionist and Post Impressionist work which has come onto the market since the 1960's. The pictures belonged to Mr Hans Mettler of Switzerland and included works by Toulouse Lautrec, estimated to sell for a quarter of a million pounds; Van Gogh, Matisse, Cezanne,

"Venus au Bain" – Jean-Baptiste-Camille Corot *(Sotheby's)*
$475,200 £240,000

Pissarro, Redon and Bonnard. The sale brought in well over £2 million.

Of course, sales of pictures by artists that are household names only made up part of the market. Other areas where great interest was shown was in still lives which have now been rising steadily in price for the past two years. Things have now reached the stage that even unsigned pictures in doubtful condition are making amazing prices, not only in London, but all over the country and in America.

At Hove, in Graves, Son and Pilcher's saleroom, an 1930's still life by the hitherto little known painter Harold Clayton sold for £1,200. In Bonham's a still life by an artist catalogued as G.

Spadino sold for £3,000. At Christie's, prices kept on going up the scale when an Abraham Mignon floral still life set up a new Mignon record at £19,000. At Sotheby's the modern artist Laurence Biddle's still life sold for £1,500. Another record was made when £13,000 was paid for a still life with fruit by Edward Ladell. The trend was reflected in America where a buyer at Christie's in New York paid £81,052 for a still life by Jan Van Der Hamar Y Leon, painted about 1622. In April, Sotheby's sold a still life by Balthasar Van Der Ast for £90,000.

Another growing vogue is still for Victorian 'genre' pictures – a field that people either love or hate. Every picture "tells a story" and the titles are mini plots on their own. Favourites like Charles Gogin's 'The Dolls' Tea Party' (£1,400 at Sotheby's) and 'The Cardinals' Chess Game' by Zoffoli (£1,200 at Bonham's) always finds buyers. Other 'genre' pictures sold during the year included 'Oliver Cromwell Searching His Uncle's House For Arms' by Arthur

"Still Life Of Fruit" – Edward Ladell *(Sotheby's Belgravia)*
$26,260 £13,000

"A Christmas Story" – Sir John Everett Millais *(Sotheby's Belgravia)*
$7,920 £4,000

"The Garden Of Idleness" – Sir Edward Coley Burne-Jones *(Sotheby's Belgravia)*
$30,690 £15,500

David McCormick (£800); 'Bonnie Kilmeny' by John Faed (£1,600); Henry Brooker's 'Tea With Grandmother' (£2,800); 'An Amusing Story' by Stephano Novo (£2,600); 'Feeding the Hungry After the Lord Mayor's Banquet' by Adrian Marie (£18,000); 'The Billet Doux' by John William Godward (£6,000, a record) and the awful 'Uncle Tom and Eva' an unsigned oil on panel which was presented to Mr Beeton, husband of the famous cook, by Harriet Beecher Stowe, author of Uncle Tom's Cabin and which sold this year for £1,350 in spite of having little to recommend it artistically.

The school of 'genre' flourished during the Victorian age and all Victorian painters have come into their own and been high in price this year. The one hundred and fiftieth anniversary of the birth of Millais was in 1979 and buyers commemorated the occasion by bidding his pictures to high prices. At Sotheby's March sale of Victorian paintings £33,000 was paid for Millais' 'The Huguenot'; £27,000 for his 'Red Riding Hood'; £26,000 for 'Esther' and £4,000 for a watercolour entitled 'Christmas Story' which Millais originally sold for £42. At Christie's sale of English watercolours a Millais' drawing sold for £9,000. Other famous Victorian names like Burne Jones also did well during 1979 – his drawings for 'The Garden of Idleness' sold for £15,500. High prices were also recorded for Atkinson Grimshaw's 'The Docks at Liverpool' – £20,000; his 'Hull Docks at Night' made £12,000 at Christie's in February, and for 'The Lumber Cart' by Henry John Boddington, £8,000, a record.

Perhaps the biggest success story recently has been the rise in popularity of Edgar Hunt and his ilk; farmyard scenes are top of the pops with many collectors. It is doubtful if this new vogue has anything to do with the desire to return to the simple life, but it seems that no painting with hens and chickens, rabbits and goats can fail to do well. Edgar Hunt popped up here and there throughout the year, always making good prices. 'Poultry in a Barn', painted by Hunt in 1910, sold for £8,000. A picture of rabbits and pigeons by Hunt made £3,200 at Bonham's and a pair of 'Henscapes' by him made £4,800 at Phillips. The record Hunt price however, was for a picture of donkeys and a goat which sold for £9,500 at Sotheby's in March.

Other painters who have zoomed to popularity on the "back to the land" boom have been R. Stone, four of whose hunting pictures sold for £1,450; Archibald Thorburn, a watercolour of ptarmigans in the snow by him sold for £2,600; and the Herrings. A painting of ducks by Herring Senior and a farrier's shop by Herring Junior realised £4,500 each. The popular painter, Sir George Clausen's picture 'Binding the Sheaves' was knocked down at £7,500 and a landscape with cattle by Ramsey Richard Reinagle made £1,600 at Aldridge's of Bath.

Hunting pictures too kept up their established popularity and four Henry Alken's made £23,000 while John Ferneley's portrait of a chestnut horse made £11,000. A Munnings' study of a saddling enclosure was sold at Christie's for £3,800.

This nostalgia for country life and the past was also echoed in a strong

"Queen Victoria's Spaniel 'Dash'" – Sir Edwin Henry Landseer *(Sotheby's)*
$7,524 £3,800

trend towards sentimentality – how else could a Landseer portrait of Queen Victoria's simpering spaniel "Dash" have made the unlikely price of £3,800 at Sotheby's Scone Palace sale in the spring? Birket Foster too cashed in on the trend towards "pretty" pictures and his work was much in demand in the salerooms. At Newcastle a Birket Foster only six and a quarter inches by four and a quarter inches sold for £750 and a watercolour by him, entitled 'The Hayfield' fetched £8,500 at Sotheby's. Other idealised works sold included George Sheridan Knowles' 'Figures in an Old English Garden' (£5,200); William Stephen Coleman's 'Fisherman's Children' (£1,700) and Mrs Helen Allingham's two attractive portraits of children which made £500. The sentimental trend appeared again in the steady climb to popularity of the Russian artist Alexei Alexeivitsch Harlamoff – a typical work by him like 'The Flower Girls' sold this year for £25,000 but as recently as 1976 it would have been lucky to have fetched £8,000.

As usual there has been noticeably high prices made for "local" favourite painters in different parts of the country – Scotland has stayed faithful to Peploe and to the rather specialised taste of Hornel. Peploe established an astonishing record of £13,500 this year when Christie's and Edmiston's in Glasgow sold 'Pink Roses' for more than double the estimate. Sickert made a record £21,000 and Hornel's 'The Locket' sold for the record £10,500 at Phillips in Edinburgh. Other local Scottish favourites included Joseph Crawhall, Robert Gemmel Hutchison and John

MacWhirter whose 'View of Edinburgh from Arthur's Seat' made £1,500. A William MacTaggart sold in Glasgow made over £11,000.

Local man, George Turner's 'View of Tonge' sold at Edgbaston for £1,500; a Thomas Smythe painting of Playford Hall, Suffolk, sold at Ipswich for £4,200 and the Cornish favourite, Elizabeth Stanhope Forbes' 'Girls In A Wood' made £700 on her native ground. Even amateur painters are now coming into their own and it might be worth collectors' while to start looking out for good examples of this sort of work which was once disregarded completely. Take encouragement from the price of £4,500 recently recorded at Sotheby's for one hundred and forty botanical plates done by amateur artist Elizabeth Harvey of Deal around 1830.

Every year has its favourite painter and apart from Millais, 1979 seems to have been enamoured of the Norwegian painter, Munch. A Munch woodcut entitled 'Frauen am Melresufer' was bought for £41,000 by Rijks Museum in Amsterdam this year. At Christie's, a Munch watercolour sold for £27,000 and at Sotheby's a lithograph and woodcut established a Munch record in England by making £46,000. Another painter whose name kept appearing in catalogues through the year was George Chinnery, the Irish painter who worked in India and China in the late 18th and early 19th century and whose marriage portrait of one of his pupils and his wife made £30,500 this year. Two Chinese blacksmiths painted by Chinnery sold for £7,000 and an album of drawings by him sold for £4,400 at Sotheby's. His view of Whampoa Harbour made £2,750 at Sotheby's New York saleroom.

The high interest which has been shown in English watercolours for some time showed no slackening through 1979. A Lear sketch of Corfu made £3,900 at Bonham's and the watercolours of George Weatherhill, a Whitby painter whose work used to sell about £90 a pair, hit the price of £620 for two at Phillips this year. A Turner sketchbook sold for £17,000 and a record price of £1,400 for a Walter Greaves' watercolour of Whistler in his studio was paid at Christie's. Gainsborough's 'Cart In A Wooded Landscape' sold for £13,000 and a Thomas Rowlandson of Brighton Pavilion made £6,800. There was also strong interest in more obscure watercolour painters like Louis Rayner whose views of Chester made £4,600 for nine and the rising Charles Harrington, one of whose works sold for £290 at Phillips. A 19th century album of watercolours of people and places by John Scarlett Davis made £10,000 at Christie's.

Most authorities say that buyers with an eye for future investment ought now to be looking for good prints. This is still mainly a home market with eighty per cent of the prints sold remaining in the U.K. There are certain categories of prints of course that will always demand a foreign following – the Swiss love landscapes of Switzerland, the Germans like sporting prints. It is interesting to note that over the past three years prices for good, decorative prints have doubled, trebled and quadrupled and seem set fair to go up even more. British prints, say the specialists, are still undervalued and buyers should remember that a good Gilray impression which could be picked up ten years ago for £2, will today fetch over £100 and in another few years

"Les Animaux du Desert" – Karel Appel *(Sotheby's)* $30,690 £15,500

should double that again. Topographical prints have always demanded a big following, especially on the Continent. Among the prices recorded this year is £8,500 for a pair of mezzotints by J. G. Laminitt; £800 for shepherds by William Ward after Morland and £3,000 for thirty-eight coloured engravings of oxen by George Garrard dating from about 1800.

German and Japanese buyers appeared too in the print sales, snapping up two "pearls" – Picasso's Vollard Suite which went to a German buyer at Sotheby's for £105,000 and Picasso's Saltimbanques Suite which went to a Japanese for £42,500. There is also a very big market for 19th and 20th century prints in the U.S.A. where they are eagerly sought after by collectors.

Buyers abroad and in America also seem to be showing increased interest in Contemporary art. An Yves Klein, whose previous record set up in 1974 was £26,250, sold for £43,000 to a foreign buyer this year, and a Swiss collector paid the record of £15,500 for Karl Appel's 'Les Animaux Du Desert'. An American college bought Roy Lichtenstein's 'Modern Paintings No 1' for £28,000 and four cartoon drawings done by David Hockney when he was only a child prodigy of ten made £1,000 at Sotheby's. However, apart from that, Modern British paintings seem to be slow in picking up in price and Ben Nicholson's 'Feb 62 Mantua' was sold for only £6,500 this year.

Taken over all however, the art market seems to be in a very healthy condition and the advice of most experts to would-be collectors is to look for good amateur work – in particular botanical or topographical drawings and watercolours – and especially to hunt for prints. Pictures that once would have fetched only a couple of pounds in the local antique shop are now fetching sums that would make their original sellers blanche. It is almost a licence to print money, if you will excuse the pun!

LIZ TAYLOR

H. VAN AACHEN – The Madonna And Child With Saints And Angels – on metal – 11¼ x 8¼in.
(Sotheby's) **$1,707** **£880**

H. VON AACHEN – The Adoration Of The Shepherds – 23½ x 18in.
(Christie's) **$2,522** **£1,300**

H. VAN AACHEN – The Entombment Of Christ – on panel – 10½ x 8in.
(Sotheby's) **$1,261** **£650**

SEAN O'MAOIS AARAIN – A Hunchback Traveller Surrounded By Dancing Leprechauns – signed and dated '44 – pen and brown ink and watercolour – recto; Figure Standing – pencil, pen and brown ink on watercolour – verso – 11½ x 15½in.
(Sotheby's) **$107** **£55**

NICOLAS AARTMAN I – A Tower On A Beach With Fisherfolk And Vessels At Sea – signed and dated 1756 – black chalk and grey wash – 17 x 23cm.
(Christie's) **$614** **£320**

JOHN ABSOLON – 'Light And Shade' – signed and titled – 9¾ x 6¾in.
(Lawrence) **$247** **£130**

ADAM – The 'Triton', A Trawler – 22 x 35in.
(Sotheby's Belgravia)
$396 **£200**

JOSEPH DENOVAN ADAM – Still Life Of Peaches And Grapes – signed – 9½ x 13in.
(Sotheby's) **$594** **£300**

JOSEPH DENOVAN ADAM – Cattle And Poultry In A Barn, In A Winter Landscape – signed – 8 x 11½in.
(Christie's) **$621** **£320**

JOSEPH DENOVAN ADAM – A Highland Bull – signed – on board – 16 x 18½in.
(Sotheby's Belgravia) **$48** **£25**

JOSEPH DENOVAN ADAM – January, An Old Strathearn Street – 33½ x 43in.
(Sotheby's) **$576** **£300**

HENRY WILLIAM ADAMS – Winter – signed – 47½ x 72in.
(Sotheby's Belgravia)
$1,188 **£600**

JOHN CLAYTON ADAMS – Harvesting – signed and dated 1880 – 36 x 50in.
(Sotheby's Belgravia)
$7,042 **£3,500**

JOSEPH FRANZ ADOLPH – A Hunting Still Life Of A Dead Hare And Birds In A Landscape – signed and dated 1701 – canvas on panel – 15½ x 13¼in.
(Christie's) **$1,649** **£850**

GEORGE RUSSELL, Called AE – Coastal Scene With Two Girls By Moonlight – signed with monogram – 19½ x 25½in.
(Sotheby's) **$2,231** **£1,150**

GEORGE RUSSELL, Called AE – Two Ladies By The Shore – signed – 16 x 21in.
(Sotheby's) **$776** **£400**

GEORGE RUSSELL, Called AE – Trysting Place – signed with monogram – pen and ink and coloured chalk – 8¼ x 11¼in.
(Sotheby's) **$330** **£170**

VAN AELST – Roses And Other Flowers On A Ledge – 16¾ x 13½in.
(Christie's) **$2,522** **£1,300**

J. VAN AELST – Still Life, Spring And Summer Flowers Including Roses, Tulips, Morning Glory And Blossoms In A Green Glass Vase – signed and dated 1876 – oil – on panel – 40 x 30cm.
(Henry Spencer & Sons) **$277** **£140**

PIETER COECK VAN AELST – The Holy Family, The Virgin, Seated Beneath A Tree, On Her Knee The Infant Christ Holding A Bird And An Apple – 33 x 25½in.
(Sotheby's) **$26,460** **£13,500**

P. COECK VAN AELST – Landscape With The Rest On The Flight – on panel – 36½ x 47½in.
(Sotheby's) **$27,440** **£14,000**

PIETER AERTSEN – The Procession To Calvary – on panel – 45 x 65in.
(Sotheby's) **$27,440 £14,000**

PIETER AERTSEN – A Fishwife And An Old Man – on panel – 66 x 29½in.
(Sotheby's) **$4,312 £2,200**

JOHN MACDONALD AIKEN – Portrait Of The Artist And His Wife – signed and dated 1910 – 70½ x 44in.
(Sotheby's) **$5,760 £3,000**

A. AIKMAN – Landscape With Girl Picking Flowers – 50 x 59cm.
(Edmiston's) **$601 £310**

G. AIKMAN – Extensive Coastal Landscape, With Fishing Boats On The Shore, Figures Unloading The Catch Into Carts – signed – 29.5 x 50cm.
(Henry Spencer & Sons) **$356 £180**

GEORGE W. AIKMAN – Arran From The Cumbrae – signed and inscribed – 23½ x 35½in.
(Sotheby's) **$249 £130**

GEORGE W. AIKMAN – The Poem – signed and dated 1882 – 9½ x 6¼in.
(Sotheby's Belgravia)
$67 £35

JAMES ALFRED AITKEN – An Autumn Evening – signed – 9¼ x 13¼in.
(Sotheby's) **$329** **£170**

JAMES ALFRED AITKEN – On A Canadian River – signed – watercolour – 23 x 15½in.
(Sotheby's) **$79** **£40**

JAMES ALFRED AITKEN – Lobster Fishing – signed – 10 x 14in.
(Sotheby's) **$388** **£200**

JEAN ANTOINE CONSTANTIN D'AIX – An Extensive Landscape With A Town Near A Lake; and A Landscape With A Distant Tower – pen and grey ink, grey wash – 26.2 x 37.8cm.
(Christie's) **$614** **£320 Pair**

PIETRO ALAMANNA *(Active 1475; ca. 1497)* – The Madonna And Child Enthroned – signed – gold ground – on panel – 44½ x 20in.
(Sotheby's) **$75,240** **£38,000**

ALBANI – Saint Catherine – on marble – 8½ x 7½in.
(Christie's) **$277** **£140**

ALBANO – Diana Called To The Chase: Diana Seated Under A Canopy Being Aroused By Her Attendants, Trees Beyond oil – 38.5 x 59cm.
(Henry Spencer & Sons) **$562** **£290**

FREDERICK JAMES ALDRIDGE – Beating To Wind'ard – signed – 14 x 21in.
(Sotheby's Belgravia) **$178** **£90**

FREDERICK JOHN ALDRIDGE – On A Venetian Canal; On The Seine – signed – one heightened with bodycolour – 14½ x 7in.
(Sotheby's Belgravia) **$233** **£120 Pair**

EDWIN J. ALEXANDER – Mannikins In A Cage – signed with monogram – gouache – on linen – 17½ x 8¾in.
(Sotheby's) **$384** **£200**

GEORGE ALEXANDER – Valley Of The Wye, An Extensive View – signed with monogram and dated 1887 – watercolour – 19½ x 29in.
(Neales of Nottingham) **$101** **£56**

LENA ALEXANDER – Mixed Flowers In Jug – 52 x 42cm.
(Edmiston's) **$136** **£70**

LENA ALEXANDER – Roses In Jar – pastel – 51 x 42cm.
(Edmiston's) **$237** **£122**

W. S. ALFRED – The 'Earl Of Zetland', A Three-Masted Brig – signed, inscribed and dated 1884 – 23½ x 35½in.
(Sotheby's Belgravia) **$713** **£360**

THEODORE ALIGNY – Paysage A La Fontaine Antique – signed and dated 1840 – pen and indian ink – 8¼ x 6¼in.
(Sotheby's) **$228** **£120**

DAVID ALISON – Portrait Of A Mother And Her Three Daughters – signed and dated 1919 – 40 x 30in.
(Sotheby's) **$537** **£280**

HENRY Y. ALISON – On The West Coast – signed – 33½ x 43in.
(Sotheby's) **$182** **£95**

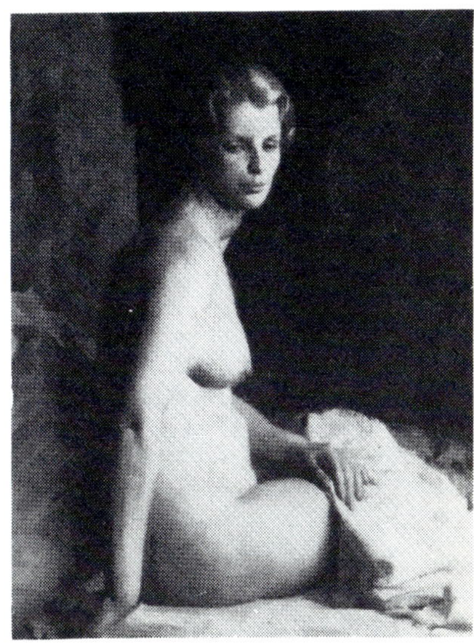

HENRY Y. ALISON – A Portrait Of The Artist's Wife – 39½ x 29½in.
(Sotheby's) **$422** **£220**

H. ALKEN – Drawing Cover – on panel – 6 x 8¼in.
(Christie's) **$1,067** **£550**

H. ALKEN – The Meet – on panel – 6 x 8¼in.
(Christie's) **$1,455 £750**

HENRY ALKEN, JNR. – Taking The Water – Huntsmen At Full Gallop Crossing An Open Brook – signed – heightened with white – 9¼ x 14½in.
(Sotheby's) **$679 £350**

E. ALLAGRAIN – An Italianate River Landscape With Women Laundering – 49¼ x 60in.
(Christie's) **$2,328 £1,200**

A. ALLAN – Merchiston Castle School, Edinburgh – watercolour – 7 x 10in.
(Outhwaite & Litherland)
$61 £30 Pair

ARCHIBALD RUSSELL WATSON ALLAN – A Farmyard – signed – 23½ x 19in.
(Sotheby's Belgravia) **$250 £130**

H. ALLAN – The Thames At Hampton – signed – 15½ x 25½in.
(Sotheby's Belgravia)
$356 £180

M. ALLAN – Evening On The Thames At Sonning; Henley-On-Thames – signed, inscribed on the reverse – 16 x 24in.
(Sotheby's Belgravia)
$665 £350 Pair

ROBERT WEIR ALLAN – The Herring Fleet At Boddam – signed, inscribed on a label on the reverse – 20 x 29in.
(Sotheby's) **$998 £520**

ALLAN – Country Pursuits – 27 x 49in.
(Sotheby's Belgravia)
$418 £220

CHARLES F. ALLBON – Warwick Castle – signed, inscribed and dated '94 – heightened with white – 8 x 11½in.
(Sotheby's Belgravia) **$107 £55**

JOHN ALLCOT – Shipping in Sydney Harbour – signed – oil on board – 23 x 28cm.
(Australian Art Auctions)
$398 £207

WALTER H. ALLCOTT – A North Italian Town – signed and dated 1915 – 14 x 18in.
(Sotheby's Belgravia) **$78 £40**

FRANCESCO ALLEGRINI – Christ Preaching – red chalk – 22.8 x 40.6cm.
(Christie's) **$384 £200**

HELEN ALLINGHAM – A Mother And Child On A Path Outside A Thatched Cottage – signed – watercolour – 11¼ x 9¼in.
(Christie's) **$1,358 £700**

HELEN ALLINGHAM – 'Old Cottages, Bucks.' – signed – 10¾ x 8¼in.
(Messenger May Baverstock)
$1,932 £960

HELEN ALLINGHAM – 'Michaelmas Daisies, Munstead Wood, Godalming' – signed – 12¾ x 9¾in.
(Messenger May Baverstock)
$1,851 £920

THOMAS ALLOM – Inverness From The West – pencil and brown wash – 4½ x 7in.
(Christie's) **$97 £50**

DENIS VAN ALSLOOT – An Ice Carnival With Numerous Figures Skating On The Moat Outside The Walls Of Antwerp – on panel – 23 x 43in.
(Christie's) **$115,200 £60,000**

DENIS VAN ALSLOOT – A Carnival On The Ice Outside Antwerp – on panel – 28½ x 48in.
(Sotheby's) **$66,640 £34,000**

ABBEY ALSTON – A Watcher In The Night – signed and dated 1903 – 28 x 18in.
(Christie's) **$1,649 £850**

RUDOLPHE VON ALT – Ein Kaffeehaus Im Garten – signed and dated '864 – pencil and watercolour – 6 x 8in.
(Sotheby's) **$1,710 £900**

FRITZ B. ALTHAUS – A Border Castle – signed and dated 1902 – 9½ x 13½in.
(Sotheby's Belgravia)
$58 £30

AMERICAN SCHOOL – Trompe L'Oeil Of An Envelope – inscribed and dated 1905 – watercolour and bodycolour – 6¼ x 8¼in.
(Sotheby's) **$512 £220**

AMERICAN SCHOOL, mid 19th century – Figures On A Road In The Mountains – watercolour – 13¼ x 9¼in.
(Sotheby's) **$28 £14**

AMERICAN SCHOOL, late 19th century – Portraits Of Putaski And Kosciuszko – oil on canvas – 10 x 7¾in.
(Sotheby's) **$591 £300 Pair**

AMIGONI – Rinaldo And Armida – 25 x 19in.
(Christie's) **$1,843 £950**

AMIGONI – Venus And Cupid, In The Foreground Of A Landscape – 13¼ x 6¾in.
(Sotheby's) **$737 £380**

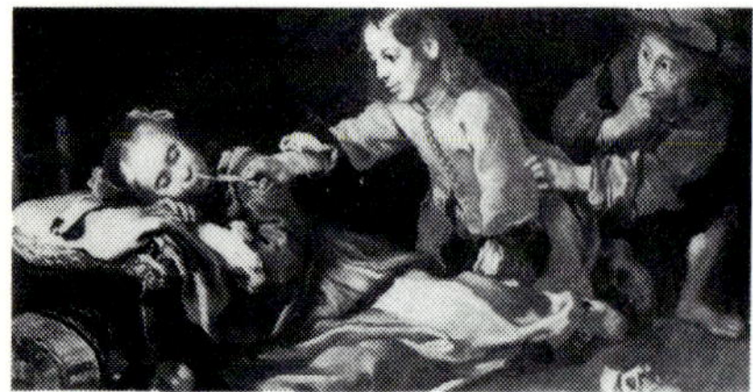

A. AMOROSI – A Boy Teasing A Sleeping Girl – 28½ x 54½in.
(Christie's) **$4,268 £2,200**

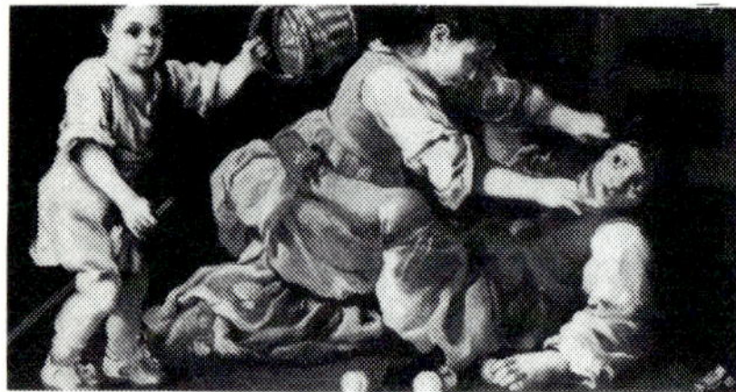

A. AMOROSI – Children Quarrelling In An Interior – 28 x 55in.
(Christie's) **$4,268 £2,200**

ANTONIO AMOROSI – Portrait Of A Boy, Wearing Classical Style Costume, Small Half Length, Holding A Coin – 16 x 12¼in.
(Christie's) **$960 £500**

ANTONIO AMOROSI – A Peasant Family In An Interior With A Woman Spanking A Girl – 41½ x 54½in.
(Christie's) **$13,440 £7,000**

ALEXANDER ANDERSON, Attributed to – Last Thoughts Of Home, A Young Lady Sits With All Her Possessions At A Port – signed – oil on canvas – 23½ x 29½in.
(Sotheby's) **$1,143 £580**

ROBERT ANDERSON – An Irish Cabin, Connemara – signed – 9¼ x 12¾in.
(Sotheby's) **$1,125 £580**

J. B. ANDERSON – Still Life And Fruit – 39 x 50cm.
(Edmiston's) **$252** **£130**

W. ANDERSON – 'Fishing Boats In Harbour' – signed – oil – 18½ x 26in.
(Dacre, Son & Hartley) **$643** **£320**

W. ANDERSON – Shipping In An Estuary With Figures In A Rowing Boat In The Foreground – watercolour – 11¼ x 16¼in.
(Christie's) **$504** **£260**

WILLIAM ANDERSON, After J. H. Koekkoek – "On The Scheldt", Holland – oil on wood panel – 7½ x 9½in.
(Morphets of Harrogate) **$1,125** **£580**

JURIAAN ANDRIESSEN – A Classical Landscape With Figures Near A Fountain – signed and dated 1794 on the reverse – watercolour heightened with white – 42 x 33.3cm.
(Christie's) **$1,536** **£800**

CLEMENT AUGUSTE ANDRIEUX – Les Soldats Et Le Maire – signed – pencil and watercolour heightened with white – 8½ x 11½in.
(Sotheby's) **$342** **£180 Pair**

PIETRO ANGELETTI – Portrait Of Pius VI, Half Length, Holding A Letter – indistinctly signed – 31¼ x 24¾in.
(Christie's) **$729** **£380**

P. ANGILLIS – A Wooded Landscape With Peasants Shearing Sheep By Cottages – indistinctly dated – on panel – 9¾ x 14¼in.
(Christie's) **$2,910** **£1,500**

RICHARD ANSDELL – The Final Struggle – signed and dated 1884 – 35½ x 71in.
(Sotheby's) **$1,089** **£550**

RICHARD ANSDELL – A Gordon Setter Bitch With Her Puppies – signed and dated 1840 – 24 x 29in.
(Sotheby's) **$4,356 £2,200**

RICHARD ANSDELL – A Highlander In His Croft – signed and dated 1840 – 27½ x 35½in.
(Sotheby's) **$3,264 £1,700**

R. ANSDELL – The Gamekeeper – inscribed – 31 x 24in.
(Sotheby's) **$1,584 £800**

RICHARD ANSDELL And JOHN PHILLIP – The Fair At Seville – signed and dated 1857 and 8 – 44 x 66in.
(Sotheby's Belgravia)
$6,036 £3,000

MAUD ANSELL – Rural Cottages, Sunset – signed – 19½ x 29½in.
(Sotheby's Belgravia)
$171 £90 Pair

G. VAN ANSTELL – Ducks Resting Beside A Pond – signed – oil on canvas – 16 x 12in.
(Morphets of Harrogate)
$297 £150

HENRICUS JOSEPHUS ANTONISSEN – A Wooded River Landscape With Peasants Fishing, Cattle And Sheep At Rest On A Bank, And A House Beyond – signed and dated 1775 – 26 x 36in.
(Christie's) **$12,480 £6,500**

BIAGIO DI ANTONIO, Circle of – Marcus Furius Camillus Recapturing Rome From The Gauls: A Cassone Panel – on panel – 15¾ x 50¼in.
(Sotheby's) **$15,520 £8,000**

ANTWERP SCHOOL, circa 1630 – The Temptation Of Saint Anthony, In A Southern Landscape – on metal – 6¾ x 9in.
(Sotheby's) **$1,358 £700**

ANTWERP SCHOOL, 17th century – Achilles Among The Daughters Of Lycomedes – 34 x 46in.
(Sotheby's) **$2,376 £1,200**

APOLLO AND DAPHNE LEGEND, The Master of the *(Active at end of XV century)* – The Annunciation – on panel – circular – diameter 31½in.
(Sotheby's) **$39,600 £20,000**

KAREL APPEL – Tete – signed – oil on canvas – 23¼ x 19in.
(Sotheby's) **$3,762 £1,900**

LOUIS APPIAN – Le Port De Collioure – signed and dated '19 – pen and ink and watercolour – 4¼ x 7in.
(Sotheby's) **$608 £320**

JOHN CHARLES ARDAGH – View From The Top Of Majuba, Showing Troop Deployments At Charlestown, Volksrust, Lang's Nelk And Prospect – signed, inscribed and dated 1902 on the reverse – watercolour – 10 x 22in.
(Sotheby's) **$49 £25**

ARELLANO – A Still Life Of Flowers In A Sculptured Urn, On A Wooden Ledge – 19½ x 15¾in.
(Sotheby's) **$1,980 £1,000**

ARMFIELD – Studies Of Dogs – on board – 9 x 12in.
(Sotheby's Belgravia) **$109 £55 Three**

EDWARD ARMFIELD – Around The Cauldron; Terriers Ratting – both signed – 11½ x 15¼in.
(Sotheby's Belgravia)
$1,536 £800 Pair

EDWARD ARMFIELD – Retrievers – signed – 11½ x 15½in.
(Sotheby's Belgravia) **$460** **£240**

G. ARMFIELD – A Desperate Struggle – 19½ x 23½in.
(Sotheby's Belgravia) **$194** **£100**

G. ARMFIELD – Terriers – on board – 5 x 5½in.
(Sotheby's Belgravia) **$42** **£22**

GEORGE ARMFIELD – An Intruder – signed – 8 x 12½in.
(Sotheby's Belgravia) **$480** **£250**

GEORGE ARMFIELD – Spaniels Putting Up A Pheasant; Terriers Attacking A Fox – signed – on panel – 7½ x 10½in.
(Sotheby's Belgravia)
$752 **£380 Pair**

GEORGE DENHOLM ARMOUR – Plunging His Great Antlers In – signed – heightened with white – 13 x 10in.
(Sotheby's Belgravia)
$211 **£110**

MARY ARMOUR – Autumn, Milngavie – 31 x 49cm.
(Edmiston's) **$369** **£190**

JOHN ARMSTRONG – Abstract Composition – signed and dated '60 – tempera on board – 16¼ x 10¼in.
(Sotheby's) **$198** **£100**

GIUSEPPE CESARI, IL CAVALIERE D'ARPINO – The Expulsion From Paradise – on copper – 19 x 13¾in.
(Christie's) **$2,688** **£1,400**

D'ARPINO – The Last Supper – on panel – 8¾ x 13in.
(Christie's) **$737** **£380**

JACQUES D'ARTHOIS – An Extensive River Landscape With Muleteers – 63½ x 95in.
(Christie's) **$10,560** **£5,500**

JACQUES D'ARTHOIS – An Extensive Wooded Landscape With A Lake – 36¾ x 40½in.
(Christie's) **$3,492** **£1,800**

THOMAS MORRIS ASH – Cattle Watering By A River – signed – 15½ x 23½in.
(Sotheby's Belgravia) **$570** **£300**

SIR WILL ASHTON – Mount Kosciusko, New South Wales, Australia – signed, inscribed on the reverse – oil on canvas – 19 x 25in.
(Sotheby's) **$1,281** **£650**

SIR WILL ASHTON – Afternoon Light – Marbella, Spain – signed, inscribed on the reverse – oil on board – 15¼ x 19in.
(Sotheby's) **$256** **£130**

REGINALD ASPINWALL – Cottages By The Sea – signed and dated 1889 – 9¾ x 14in.
(Sotheby's Belgravia) **$115** **£60 Pair**

JAN ASSELYN – Travellers Halted By An Inn, Near The Porta Maggiore, Rome – 18 x 20½in.
(Sotheby's) **$10,067** **£5,500**

SAMUEL ATKINS – Man O'War Setting Out; Sailing Vessel Becalmed – pen and grey ink and watercolour – 5 x 6¼in.
(Sotheby's) **$679** **£350 Pair**

SAMUEL ATKINS – Leaving Harbour In Heavy Seas – signed – pen and black ink, watercolour – 11 x 15¼in.
(Sotheby's) **$1,164** **£600**

SAMUEL ATKINS – H.M.S. Endymion Commanded By Captain The Hon. Charles Paget Rescuing A French Two-Decker – signed – pen and black ink, watercolour – 11 x 15¼in.
(Sotheby's) **$1,649** **£850**

ROBERT ATKINSON – A Cottage Orchard – indistinctly signed – 19¼ x 29¼in.
(Sotheby's Belgravia) **$768** **£400**

JAMES AUMONIER – On The Downs – signed – 11½ x 15½in.
(Sotheby's Belgravia) **$218** **£110**

WINIFRED AUSTEN – Brent Geese – watercolour – 32 x 49cm.
(Edmiston's) **$660** **£340**

AUSTRALIAN SCHOOL – Lady With A Parasol – oil on board – 37 x 37cm.
(Australian Art Auctions) **$208** **£106**

ONOFRIO AVELLINO – Saint Catherine Of Siena Before An Altar – on copper – 8¾ x 6¾in.
(Christie's) **$537** **£280**

ALBERT W. AYLING – The Cockle Gatherer – watercolour – 24¾ x 18½in.
(Outhwaite & Litherland) **$303** **£150**

ALBERT AYLING – Looking For Trout, Glen Conway, North Wales – signed, inscribed on a label on the reverse – 16 x 11in.
(Sotheby's Belgravia) **$49** **£25**

GEORGE AYLING – Moonrise And Mist – signed – 10 x 14in.
(Lawrence) **$103** **£54**

GIOVANNI BATTISTA GAULLI, IL BACICCIO, Circle of – Two Studies Of A Putto Holding A Riband – black chalk, pen and brown ink, brown wash heightened with white on light brown paper – 16.9 x 21.2cm
(Christie's) **$288** **£150**

J. DE BACKER – The Last Judgment – on panel – 35 x 28¾in.
(Christie's) **$1,067** **£550**

J. DE BACKER – The Last Judgment – on copper – circular – diameter 32¾in.
(Christie's) **$10,670** **£5,500**

LUDOLF BACKHUIZEN – Dutch Smallships In A Stormy Sea Off The Coast – 24½ x 31in.
(Christie's) **$19,200** **£10,000**

GIOVANNI BAGLIONI – The Coronation Of A Female Saint – inscribed – pen and brown ink – 11.9 x 11.1cm.
(Christie's) **$480** **£250**

THOMAS BAINES – Indian Elephants Carrying Guns In Abyssinia – signed, and signed, inscribed and dated 1868 on the reverse – oil on canvas – 11½ x 17¾in.
(Sotheby's) **$2,758** **£1,400**

NATHANEIL HUGHES JOHN BAIRD – 'The Old Fisherman's Cottages, Dawlish' – oil – 14 x 24in.
(Husseys) **$252** **£130**

WILLIAM BAPTISTE BAIRD – Young Chicks With A Cock And Hen – signed – oil on canvas – 9¼ x 12½in.
(Sotheby's) **$985** **£500**

WILLIAM BAPTISTE BAIRD – The Dovecot – signed and dated 1875 – oil on canvas – 9¼ x 7in.
(Sotheby's) **$749 £380**

OLIVER BAKER – A Country Churchyard – 14 x 22in.
(Sotheby's Belgravia) **$153 £80**

SAMUEL HENRY BAKER – Temple Balsall – signed – heightened with white – 15 x 21¾in.
(Sotheby's Belgravia)
$466 £240

SAMUEL HENRY BAKER – Cader Idris From The Mawdda: Extensive River Landscape With Figures, A Horse And Cart And Cattle Near Small Boats Drawn Up On The River Bank, Buildings Among Trees, And Mountains Beyond – signed and inscribed oil – 27 x 41cm.
(Henry Spencer & Sons) **$465 £240**

THOMAS BAKER OF LEAMINGTON – Fishing By A Stream – signed and dated 1864 – 12 x 17½in.
(Sotheby's Belgravia)
$1,235 £650

THOMAS BAKER Of Leamington – Saggy's Barn, Leamington: Cattle Resting By A River, A Large House Among Trees Beyond – signed and dated 1863 – oil on panel – 18.5 x 31cm.
(Henry Spencer & Sons)
$2,910 £1,500

THOMAS BAKER Of Leamington – Cattle Resting And Grazing In A Pasture Under A Cloudy Summer Sky – signed and dated 1861 – oil on canvas – 30 x 25cm.
(Henry Spencer & Sons)
$737 £380

T. BAKER – Cattle – oil – on panel – 7¼ x 11¾in.
(Elliot & Green)
$827 £420

WILLIAM GEORGE BAKER – Lake Manapouri, New Zealand – signed and inscribed – oil on canvas – 11¼ x 16½in.
(Sotheby's) **$473 £240**

LUDOLF BAKHUIZEN – Sailing Ships In A Stormy Sea, A Rowing Boat With Several Men And Cargo Approaching A Barge – dated 1690 – 20 x 28½in.
(Sotheby's) **$16,830 £8,500**

BALE – Still Life Of Grapes – on board – 24 x 19in.
(Sotheby's Belgravia)
$153 £80

BALE – Still Life Of Fruit – 15½ x 19½in.
(Sotheby's Belgravia)
$86 £45

J. BALE – Thames River Scenes – one signed – on board – 14 x 32in..
(Sotheby's Belgravia)
$172 £90 Pair

T. C. BALE – Still Life Of Fruit – 17½ x 21½in.
(Sotheby's Belgravia)
$323 £170

THOMAS CHARLES BALE – Still Lives Of Fruit And A Bird's Nest On A Ledge – one signed with monogram – 11½ x 15¼in.
(Sotheby's Belgravia)
$1,811 £900 Pair

H. VAN BALEN – Apollo And Marsyas – on copper – 11¼ x 14in.
(Christie's) **$1,455 £750**

VAN BALEN And VAN KESSEL – The Marriage Feast Of Peleus And Thetis – on panel – 20½ x 29in.
(Christie's) **$10,670 £5,500**

HENDRICK VAN BALEN – Christ Blessing The Little Children – signed and dated 1632 – on panel – 24 x 38½in.
(Sotheby's) **$6,336 £3,200**

ANTONIO BALESTRA, Circle of – The Guardian Angel, The Angel In A White Robe And Red Drapery' – 68 x 48in.
(Sotheby's) **$4,900 £2,500**

A. BALESTRA – Apollo And The Muses – 38¾ x 53in.
(Sotheby's) **$3,564 £1,800**

JOHN BALLANTYNE – King James I Of Scotland And The Unruly Barons – signed and dated 1859, inscribed on a label on the reverse – 40 x 68½in.
(Sotheby's) **$1,920** **£1,000**

ALEX. BALLINGALL – Fishing Boats At Sea And At Rest – watercolour – 49 x 74cm.
(Edmiston's) **$330** **£170 Pair**

ALEXANDER BALLINGALL – Old Man Of Stoer – watercolour – 50 x 32cm.
(Edmiston's) **$25** **£13**

P. BALTEN – A Market In A Town Square – on panel – 31 x 67in.
(Christie's) **$53,760** **£28,000**

J. O. BANKS – Homeward Bound – signed – 40 x 65in.
(Sotheby's Belgravia)
$7,646 **$3,800**

JOHN JAMES BANNATINE – Sunshine And Shadow – signed – 15½ x 23½in.
(Sotheby's Belgravia)
$134 **£70**

JOSEPH VINCENT BARBER – Cockermouth Castle, Cumberland – inscribed – 7¼ x 10in.
(Sotheby's) **$273** **£140**

MARCIANO A. BAPTISTA – A View Of Hong Kong Seen From Morrison Hill – watercolour – 17 x 24½in.
(Sotheby's (Hong Kong) Ltd.)
$1,406 **£710**

E. R. BARCHUS – Mount Hood, Oregon – signed, inscribed on reverse – oil on panel – 9½ x 11½in.
(Sotheby's) **$128** **£65**

JOHN RANKINE BARCLAY – A Mediterranean Market Town – bears signature – 12 x 18in.
(Sotheby's Belgravia)
$86 **£45**

D. BARENDSZ – Portrait Of A Gentleman, Bust Length, Wearing Black Dress And A White Ruff – on panel – 24 x 29in.
(Christie's) **$1,455** **£750**

GEORGE BARKER – Breakers On The Coast – signed – heightened with bodycolour – 14 x 21in.
(Sotheby's Belgravia) **$153** **£80**

G. W. BARKER – The American Clipper 'Lightning' In Full Sail – signed – oil on canvas – 15½ x 19¼in.
(Sotheby's) **$197** **£100**

JOSEPH JOHN BARKER – Upon The Misty Moor – signed – 17½ x 23½in.
(Sotheby's) **$460** **£240**

JOHN JOSEPH BARKER – Driving Sheep – inscribed, inscribed on the stretcher – 13½ x 20½in.
(Sotheby's Belgravia) **$288** **£150**

JOHN JOSEPH BARKER – Gleaners; The Midday Rest – both signed – 29½ x 24½in.
(Sotheby's Belgravia)
$1,152 £600 Pair

JOHN JOSEPH BARKER – To Pastures New – signed – 29½ x 24in.
(Sotheby's Belgravia) **$422 £220**

WINIFRED V. BARKER – The Pursuit Of The Soul – signed – heightened with body-colour – 11 x 8in.
(Sotheby's Belgravia) **$171 £90**

JAMES MacDONALD BARNSLEY – Sailing Barges In Venice – signed and dated 1887 and one inscribed – 9¼ x 12½in.
(Sotheby's) **$256 £130 Two**

BAROCCI – The Supper At Emmaus – 27 x 22½in.
(Christie's) **$213 £110**

BAROCCI – St. Theresa In Ecstasy – circular – diameter 66½in.
(Christie's) **$679 £350**

BAROCCI, After – The Annunciation – 41 x 32in.
(Sotheby's) **$621 £320**

BAROCCIO – The Adoration Of The Shepherds. With The Child Christ In The Manger And With Mary, Joseph, Shepherds And Angels; Cherubim In Glory Above – oil on arch-topped panel – 31 x 18cm.
(Henry Spencer & Sons)
$446 £230

F. BAROCCIO – 'The Annunciation' – 12 x 8in.
(Messenger May Baverstock)
$704 £350

M. E. BARRATT – Raindrops – signed with initials and inscribed – 10½ x 8in.
(Sotheby's Belgravia) **$89 £45**

FRANCIS PHILIP BARRAUD – A Meet Near A Country House – signed – watercolour – 12½ x 17½in.
(Christie's) **$165 £85**

HENRY BARRAUD – Lady's Bay Hunter, Bridled And Wearing Side-Saddle, Standing By A Stone Archway – signed – oil on canvas – 62 x 75cm.
(Henry Spencer & Sons)
$2,475 £1,250

HENRY BARRAUD – A Grey Hunter In A Horse Box – signed – 17¾ x 24in.
(Christie's) **$2,328 £1,200**

WILLIAM BARRAUD – Terriers Baiting Rats In A Stable – signed and dated 1840 – 13¾ x 17¼in.
(Christie's) **$931 £480**

GEORGE BARRET – A Classical River Landscape, With Tivoli On A Hill To The Right, Figures In The Foreground – 43½ x 34½in.
(Sotheby's) **$8,316 £4,200**

GEORGE BARRET, JNR. – Figures Resting Above A Lake In An Italian Landscape – watercolour – 7¼ x 10in.
(Christie's) **$116 £60**

BARRY – A Lion Hunt – 8 x 10in.
(Christie's) **$218 £110**

WILLIAM HENRY BARTLETT – Ballananick, Ireland – 9 x 14in.
(Sotheby's Belgravia) **$24** **£12**

TADDEO DI BARTOLO *(ca. 1362-1422)* – The Madonna And Child – on panel – 29¾ x 21in.
(Sotheby's) **$108,900** **£55,000**

BACCIO DELLA PORTA, FRA BARTOLOMMEO – Christ And The Woman Of Samaria (recto) – pen and brown ink; Studies Of The Madonna And Child And A Standing Man (verso) – pen and brown ink, brown wash – 13.5 x 9.6cm.
(Christie's) **$15,360** **£8,000**

MARY E. BASHAM – Still Life Of Game – signed and dated 1886 – 19½ x 29½in.
(Sotheby's Belgravia) **$250** **£130**

BASSANO – The Mocking Of Christ – 30 x 40in.
(Christie's) **$291** **£150**

FRANCESCO BASSANO – Landscape With Peasants And Cattle – 26½ x 42¾in.
(Sotheby's) **$4,356** **£2,200**

FRANCESCO DA PONTE, Called Francesco Bassano The Younger – The Mocking Of Christ – 44½ x 66½in.
(Christie's) **$5,760** **£3,000**

G. BASSANO – The Three Fates, Spinning In A Lamplit Interior – 30½ x 39in.
(Sotheby's) **$1,089** **£550**

L. BASSANO – Portrait Of A Gentleman, Three-Quarter Length, Wearing A Black Fur-lined Coat, Seated At A Table – 45 x 39in.
(Christie's) **$951** **£480**

B. VAN BASSEN And C. VAN POELENBURGH – The Interior Of A Church, With Saint Peter And A Beggar In The Foreground – on panel – 22¼ x 32¼in.
(Christie's) **$1,552** **£800**

BARTHOLOMEUS VAN BASSEN – The Interior Of A Church, Seen From The West End – on panel – 17 x 22¾in.
(Sotheby's) **$3,880** **£2,000**

BARTHOLOMEUS VAN BASSEN – The Interior Of A Cathedral, Seen From The North-West, With A Gentleman Entering Through A Classical Portico – on panel – 15x 21¼in.
(Sotheby's) **$5,820** **£3,000**

STEPHEN JOHN BATCHELDER – Leafy June, Barton Broad – signed and dated 1885 and inscribed – 21 x 29½in.
(Lawrence) **$1,596** **£840**

DAVID BATES – The Isle Of Bute – signed and dated 1863 – on board – 11 x 16¾in.
(Christie's) **$621** **£320**

DAVID BATES – A Cooling Stream – signed and dated 1879 – 23¼ x 35¼in.
(Sotheby's Belgravia) **$1,811** **£900**

DAVID BATES – By-Ways In Shakespeare's Country, Behind The Village, Welford – signed and dated 1902, inscribed on the reverse – 11½ x 17½in.
(Sotheby's Belgravia) **$2,178** **£1,100**

DAVID BATES – After Work, Ambleside – signed, inscribed on the reverse – 17 x 23½in.
(Sotheby's Belgravia) **$4,024** **£2,000**

DAVID BATES – Welsh Landscape With Two Children And A Dog By A River, Other Figures In The Distance – signed and dated – 20 x 36in.
(Woolley & Wallis) **$2,613** **£1,250**

BATES – Tinkers – on board – 8½ x 13½in.
(Sotheby's Belgravia) **$257 £130**

DAVID BATES – River Landscape With Waterfall – signed and dated – 11 x 15½in.
(Woolley & Wallis) **$439 £210**

FREDERICK DAVENPORT BATES – Portrait Of An Arab Girl Seated On A Stone Verandah, A Basket Of Apples At Her Side, Buildings Beyond – signed and dated 1895 – oil on board – 44 x 24cm.
(Henry Spencer & Sons) **$485 £250**

BATONI – Studies Of Putti – red chalk – 168 x 182mm.
(Christie's) **$38 £20**

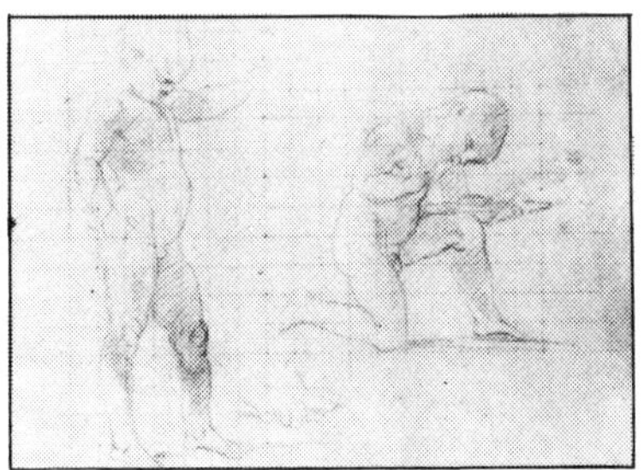

POMPEO GIROLAMO BATONI – Studies Of A Boy Standing And Another Kneeling – red chalk, squared – 14.7 x 20.3cm.
(Christie's) **$768 £400**

POMPEO GIROLAMO BATONI – Portrait Of John Woodyeare, Three-Quarter Length, Wearing The Uniform Of The King's Own Third Hussars – bears signature and the date Rome 1750 – 38½ x 28¼in.
(Christie's) **$21,120 £11,000**

POMPEO GIROLAMO BATONI – Portrait Of Princess Benedetto Giustiniani, nee Cecilia Mahony, Seated Half Length, Wearing A White Dress And Blue Sash And Ribbons – signed and dated 1785, and bears inscription – 29 x 24in.
(Christie's) **$32,640 £17,000**

POMPEO GIROLAMO BATONI – The Madonna And Child Appearing To Saint Camillo – on copper – 13¼ x 11in.
(Christie's) **$6,144** **£3,200**

POMPEO GIROLAMO BATONI – The Immaculate Conception – on copper – 17½ x 12½in.
(Christie's) **$2,880** **£1,500**

POMPEO GIROLAMO BATONI – Saint Bartholomew, Half Length – bears inscription on an old label on the reverse – 28¼ x 23½in.
(Christie's) **$6,144** **£3,200**

ARTHUR BATT – Highland Cattle – signed and dated '90 – on board – 8 x 6in.
(Sotheby's Belgravia) **$230** **£120**

WALTER WHALL BATTIS – A South African Landscape With A Small Settlement Beneath A Belt Of Hills – signed and dated 1929 – watercolour – 8½ x 21½in.
(Sotheby's) **$118** **£60**

P. A. BAUDOUIN – A Lady Drowsing In A Boudoir; A Lady With A Pet Dog – 11½ x 9½in.
(Sotheby's) **$7,920** **£4,000 Pair**

F. L. BAUER – A Parakeet – watercolour heightened with white – 21¼ x 16½in.
(Christie's) **$388** **£200**

F. L. BAUER – A Salmon Crested Cockatoo – watercolour heightened with white – 29½ x 22in.
(Christie's) **$1,552** **£800**

F. L. BAUER – A Green Winged Macaw – watercolour and bodycolour – 29½ x 22in.
(Christie's) **$970** **£500**

BAXTER – Poise – 11½ x 9in.
(Sotheby's Belgravia) **$95** **£48**

CHARLES BAXTER – The Fair Fruit Bearer – 23½ x 19½in.
(Christie's) **$1,843** **£950**

CHARLES BAXTER – Flora – 21 x 17in.
(Christie's) **$679** **£350**

EVELYN BAXTER – Still Life – signed – oil on board – 15 x 20cm.
(Australian Art Auctions) **$92** **£47**

WALTER BAYES – Boulogne Market Scene – signed and dated '97 – on panel – 12¾ x 16in.
(Sotheby's) **$792** **£400**

WALTER BAYES – Stronghold – signed with initials – on board – 29½ x 45¼in.
(Sotheby's) **$554** **£280**

JAMES BAYNES – Landscape – Spring Sunshine – 11 x 16¼in.
(Sotheby's) **$291** **£150**

THOMAS MANN BAYNES – A View On The Thames At London Bridge, With A Paddle Steamer In The Foreground And St. Paul's Beyond – signed – on panel – 12½ x 32¼in.
(Christie's) **$1,843** **£950**

G. BAZZANI – Perseus And Adromeda – bears initials – 29 x 39½in.
(Christie's) **$1,843** **£950**

JAMES PRINSEP BEADLE – The Royal Hussars And The Household Cavalry – signed – 27 x 51in.
(Christie's) **$1,552** **£800**

ARTHUR BEATTIE – An Extensive Italianate Wooded River Landscape, With Ruins And Cattle Beyond; and A Frozen River Landscape With A Water-Mill And Figures On The Ice – 27½ x 35½in.
(Christie's) **$1,940** **£1,000 Pair**

E. BEATTIE – Miller's Castle, Bootle, Lancashire, 1879 – watercolour – 9¾ x 14in.
(Outhwaite & Litherland) **$141** **£70**

DAVID BEATTY – Sailing Vessels – oil – 10 x 12in.
(Husseys) **$198** **£100**

LADY DIANA BEAUCLERK – A Goat-herd, Young Women And Putti Resting Beneath A Tree – watercolour heightened with white – 29 x 21¾in.
(Christie's) **$427** **£220**

LADY DIANA BEAUCLERK – Putti Gambolling With A Lion – watercolour heightened with white – 14¼ x 17¾in.
(Christie's) **$272** **£140**

EDOUARD DE BEAUMONT – L'Heure Du Coucher – signed and inscribed – pencil and watercolour, heightened with white – 7¾ x 6½in.
(Sotheby's) **$475** **£250**

RICHARD BEAVIS – Olive Groves Outside Florence – signed and dated 1874 indistinctly inscribed on the stretcher – 13½ x 20½in.
(Sotheby's Belgravia) **$436** **£220**

RICHARD BEAVIS – Shores Of The Adriatic: Fishermen Preparing For Sea – signed and dated 1877 – 23 x 36in.
(Sotheby's Belgravia) **$1,811** **£900**

RICHARD BEAVIS – A Rocky Wooded Landscape With A Fisherman – indistinctly signed – on board – 9¾ x 12in.
(Christie's) **$233** **£120**

ROSA BEBB – Comfortable Circumstances; The Onlookers See Most Of The Game – both signed, one dated 1914, both inscribed on the reverse – 11 x 17in.
(Sotheby's Belgravia) **$1,056** **£550 Pair**

EDMUND BECKER – Windsor Castle From Romney Island – pen and grey and brown ink, grey wash – 7 x 10¼in.
(Christie's) **$49** **£25**

RICHARD BRYDGES BEECHEY – Picking Up A Lame Duck; and Off To The Wreck – inscribed and dated '90 – on board – 12¼ x 16¼in.
(Sotheby's) **$4,462** **£2,300 Two**

RICHARD BRYDGES BEECHEY – A View Of Poole Beg Lighthouse On South Wall, Dublin, With Figures And Shipping – signed, inscribed on the reverse and dated 1869 – 9½ x 14½in.
(Sotheby's) **$5,820** **£3,000**

JOHN BEER – The Stirring Finish For The Goodwood Cup, 1908 – signed and inscribed – gouache – 9 x 13½in.
(Sotheby's Belgravia) **$162** **£85**

JOHN BEER – The Derby On A Rainy Day: The Finish; and Returning After The Race – signed, inscribed and dated 1891 – watercolour heightened with white – 10½ x 14½in.
(Christie's) **$126** **£65 Pair**

SIR MAX BEERBOHM – Mr. Balfour – signed and inscribed – a frieze – pencil and watercolour – 11¾ x 15¾in.
(Sotheby's) **$2,376** **£1,200**

ABRAHAM BEERSTRAATEN – A Southern Port – signed and dated 1655 – 32¾ x 42¾in.
(Sotheby's) **$12,610** **£6,500**

BEERSTRATEN – A Frozen River Landscape With Skaters And Buildings Beyond – 29½ x 39½in.
(Christie's) **$8,316** **£4,200**

A. BEERSTRATEN – Mediterranean Rocky Coastal Scene With Moored Galleons And Figures Ashore, A Castle Towering Above – bears signature – oil – 28 x 40in.
(James Harrison) **$1,568** **£750**

J. BEERSTRATEN – A Galleon Arriving In A Southern Port, Mountains To The Right, A Ruined Town Beyond – 31½ x 53½in.
(Sotheby's) **$1,386** **£700**

J. A. BEERSTRATEN – A Frozen Winter Landscape With Skaters And Buildings Beyond – 29½ x 20in.
(Christie's) **$5,820** **£3,000**

O. BEERT – A Still Life Of Oysters On A Pewter Plate, Pastries In A Chinese Bowl, A Dish Of Chestnuts With Glasses Of Wine On A Table – 32½ x 44½in.
(Christie's) **$21,120** **£11,000**

SYBRAND VAN BEEST – A View In The Hague – signed and dated 1646 – on panel – 24¼ x 33¼in.
(Sotheby's) **$21,340** **£11,000**

ABRAHAM HENDRIK VAN BEESTEN – Allegories Of Labour And Abundance – signed and dated 1767 – grisailles – 48½ x 41in. and 49½ x 41½in.
(Christie's) **$2,328** **£1,200 Pair**

BEGA – A Peasant Family At Table – on panel – 15¾ x 19in.
(Christie's) **$1,067** **£550**

CORNELIS PIETERSZ. BEGA – The Interior Of An Inn With A Peasant Dancing To The Music Of A Violin – signed – on panel – 14¼ x 15¾in.
(Sotheby's) **$8,316** **£4,200**

KARL JOSEPH BEGAS – Die Heilige Elizabeth Von Ungarn Und Die Armen Leute – signed with monogram and dated 1823 – watercolour – 12½ x 10¾in.
(Sotheby's) **$2,090** **£1,100**

ABRAHAM JANSZ. BEGEYN – Peasants With Cattle, Sheep And Goats In An Extensive Italianate Landscape – signed and dated 1663 – 17¼ x 19½in.
(Christie's) **$2,328** **£1,200**

A. BEGYN – A Southern Landscape With Herdsmen, The Ruins Of A Tower To The Right – 24½ x 29½in.
(Sotheby's) **$3,168** **£1,600**

STEFANO DELLA BELLA – A Horse – black chalk, pen and brown ink – 95 x 133mm.
(Christie's) **$171** **£90**

CHARLES ALPHONSE PAUL BELLAY – Portrait D'Homme – signed, dated and inscribed 1894 – chalk – 10 x 7½in.
(Sotheby's) **$143** **£75**

WILLIAM DE BELLEROCHE – Pommes de Terre – signed and dated 1962 – coloured chalk and watercolour, heightened with bodycolour – 20¾ x 27in.
(Sotheby's) **$50** **£25**

J. A. BELLEVOIS – Sailing Vessels In A Choppy Sea – on panel – 14 x 19in.
(Christie's) **$1,164** **£600**

BERNARDO BELLOTTO, Follower of – Elegant Figures On The Terrace Of A Villa – 45¼ x 37½in.
(Sotheby's) **$7,128 £3,600**

FREDERIC MARTLETT BELL-SMITH – Emerald Lake, New Field, British Columbia – signed, inscribed on an old label on the reverse – watercolour – 11½ x 17¾in.
(Sotheby's) **$512 £260**

BELVEDERE – Tulips And Other Flowers In A Vase – 24½ x 18½in.
(Christie's) **$291 £150**

BEMBO – The Madonna And Child Enthroned With Donors, A Garden Beyond – on panel – 27½ x 19in.
(Sotheby's) **$9,900 £5,000**

J. G. VON BEMMEL – River Landscape With A Peasant Family On A Path, Conversing With Travellers – on metal – 7 x 9in.
(Sotheby's) **$6,336 £3,200 Four**

MARCO BENEFIAL – Portrait Of A Man, Thought To Be Bonaventura Lamberti, Bust Length, Wearing An Open Shirt – bears signature and dated 1708 – 18½ x 15½in.
(Christie's) **$864** **£450**

MARCO BENEFIAL – The Betrayal Of Christ – a sketch – 15½ x 12¾in.
(Christie's) **$864** **£450**

FRANK MOSS BENNETT – This To Win – signed and dated 1926 – 15 x 20in.
(Sotheby's Belgravia)
$4,224 **£2,200**

FRANK MOSS BENNETT – Crossbow Men At Practice – signed and dated 1928, inscribed on the reverse – 14 x 20in.
(Sotheby's Belgravia)
$806 **£420**

FRANK MOSS BENNETT – 'The Discussion' – signed and dated 1920 – oil on canvas – 34 x 50cm.
(King & Chasemore)
$3,072 **£1,600**

FRANK MOSS BENNETT – Late But Welcome – signed and dated 1948 – on board – 14¾ x 19½in.
(Sotheby's Belgravia)
$4,024 **£2,000**

W. BENNETT – A Figure In A Cart On A Road Above A Ford – watercolour – 10¼ x 14¼in.
(Christie's) **$233** **£120**

WILLIAM BENNETT – A View From A Wooded Hill Across A Plain – watercolour – 13½ x 21¼in.
(Christie's) **$126** **£65**

WILLIAM BENNETT – In A Glade Near Sevenoaks, Kent; A Lane In Kent – one signed and dated 1853 – 12¼ x 18in.
(Sotheby's) **$970** **£500 Pair**

AMBROSIUS BENSON, Follower of – The Madonna And Child Enthroned – 33¾ x 27½in.
(Sotheby's) **$2,574** **£1,300**

JOHN BENSON – A Perspective Of The Proposed Great Southern And Western Railway Terminus At Cork – pen and ink and grey wash – 16 x 38½in.
(Sotheby's) **$737** **£380**

JOSEPH AUSTIN BENWELL – The Gate Of Ephriam, Jerusalem – signed and dated 1864, inscribed on the reverse – heightened with white – 16½ x 21in.
(Sotheby's Belgravia) **$504** **£260**

BERCHEM – Studies Of Cattle And Lambs – 11½ x 19¼in.
(Sotheby's) **$679** **£350**

BERCHEM – Cattle And A Milkmaid In An Extensive Italianate Landscape – on panel – 9½ x 11½in.
(Christie's) **$873** **£450**

BERCHEM – A Southern Landscape, Cattle, Sheep And A Goat By A Stream, A Couple To The Right – on panel – 10 x 13½in.
(Sotheby's) **$233** **£120**

NICOLAES BERCHEM – An Ambush In A Mountain Pass – signed and dated 1668 – 39½ x 53½in.
(Sotheby's) **$21,560** **£11,000**

GERRIT BERCKHEYDE – A Street Scene With Performing Actors – signed – 18¾ x 22in.
(Christie's) **$7,372** **£3,800**

FRANK ERNEST BERESFORD – Selling Jacob Into Slavery – signed and dated 1904 – 12 x 18¼in.
(Sotheby's Belgravia) **$211** **£110**

SCHOOL OF BERGAMO, early 17th century – Portrait Of A Man, Half Length, His Right Hand Resting On A Book – 28 x 23½in.
(Sotheby's) **$563** **£290**

AMBROGIO DI STEFANO DA FOSSANO, Called Il Bergognone *(Active 1481–1523(?))* – The Madonna And Child – on panel – 33¾ x 24¾in.
(Sotheby's) **$71,280 £36,000**

ANTOINE BERJON – Campanulas – coloured chalk on grey paper – 474 x 320mm.
(Christie's) **$114 £60**

J. BERKLEY – A Proposal – inscribed – 11½ x 14½in.
(Sotheby's Belgravia) **$307 £160**

JOHN ARCHIBALD ALEXANDER BERRIE – Friar's Crag, Derwentwater – signed – heightened with bodycolour – 7¼ x 17½in.
(Sotheby's Belgravia) **$107 £55**

JEAN-VICTOR BERTIN – Paysage Italien: L'Abbaye Et Ses Religieux – signed – watercolour – 14½ x 18in.
(Sotheby's) **$752 £380**

B. BESCHEY – A River Landscape, A Ferry And Other Small Vessels On A River – on panel – 10 x 13¾in.
(Sotheby's) **$9,408 £4,800**

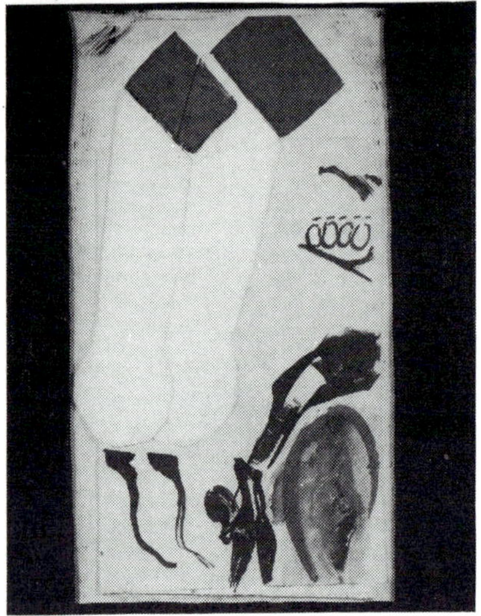

JOSEPH BEUYS – Das Medium – signed – pencil, oil, gouache and collage on paper and glass – 28¾ x 21in.
(Sotheby's) **$12,870 £6,500**

JOSEPH BEUYS – Lumen I – signed and dated '57, signed and dated 1957 on the reverse – collage, pencil and brown wash on paper – 17¾ x 24¾in.
(Sotheby's) **$2,376 £1,200**

JOSEPH BEUYS – Halbakt – signed and dated 1956 on the reverse – pencil and gouache on paper – 8¾ x 13in.
(Sotheby's) **$5,940** **£3,000**

JOSEPH BEUYS – Kopf Vor Hand – signed – pencil and gouache on paper – 8¼ x 11¾in.
(Sotheby's) **$3,366** **£1,700**

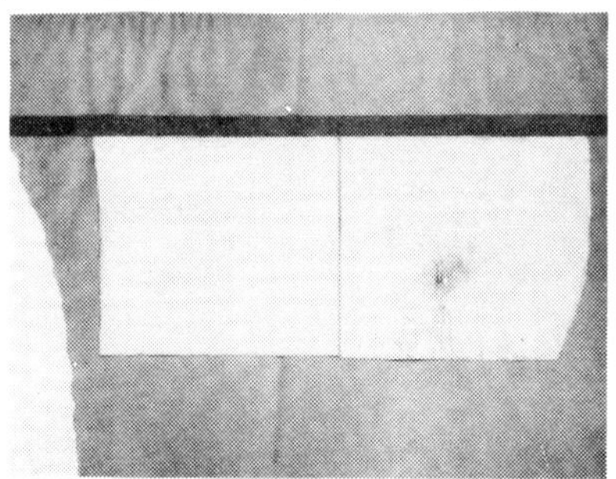

JOSEPH BEUYS – Bienen – signed and dated 1954 – pencil, stain and collage on paper – 19¾ x 25½in.
(Sotheby's) **$5,148** **£2,600**

W. R. BEVERLEY – Figures And A Boat On The Sea Shore – pencil and watercolour – 5¼ x 6¾in.
(Christie's) **$97** **£50**

PIETRO BIANCHI – Saint Anthony Abbot, Reading In A Shrine – on copper – 13¾ x 10¼in.
(Christie's) **$730** **£380**

BEYEREN – A Still Life Of Flowers, Fruit, Game And Fish, All On A Table, A Landscape Beyond – 27 x 33in.
(Sotheby's) **$873** **£450**

LORENZO DI BICCI *(Active 1370; 1427)* – The Madonna And Child With Saints – on panel – 46¼ x 27in.
(Sotheby's) **$79,200** **£40,000**

LAWRENCE BIDDLE – Still Life – Flowers In A Vase – signed – oil – 11½ x 17½in.
(Woolley & Wallis)
$1,212 **£580**

JACOB BILTIUS – A Still Life Of Dead Birds And A Hen With A Cat By A Wicker Basket On A Draped Table – 30½ x 24½in.
(Christie's) **$1,940** **£1,000**

FRANK BINDLEY – The Gardener's Daughter – signed and dated '78 – 29½ x 19½in.
(Sotheby's Belgravia) **$806** **£420**

R. WARD BINKS – A Spaniel Flushing Duck – signed – heightened with bodycolour – 13 x 15¾in.
(Sotheby's Belgravia) **$499** **£260**

R. WARD BINKS – 'Rani', a dachshund – signed, inscribed and dated 1935 – heightened with bodycolour – 14¼ x 10¼in.
(Sotheby's Belgravia) **$86** **£45**

DAVID BINNS – A Break In The Weather – signed and dated '74 – heightened with bodycolour – 20 x 29in.
(Sotheby's Belgravia) **$188** **£95**

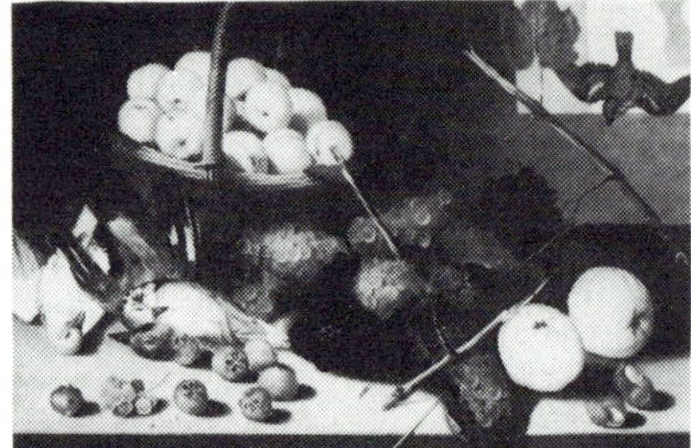

PETER BINOIT – A Still Life Of Fruit – on panel – 23 x 34¼in.
(Sotheby's) **$13,720** **£7,000**

SAMUEL JOHN LAMORNA BIRCH – A Woodland Stream – signed and dated 1895 – 16 x 12in.
(Sotheby's Belgravia) **$247** **£130**

SAMUEL JOHN LAMORNA BIRCH – The Peel Moat, Stockport – signed, inscribed and dated 1900 – 14½ x 10½in.
(Sotheby's Belgravia) **$342** **£180**

SAMUEL JOHN LAMORNA BIRCH – A Haunt Of Ancient Peace, The Forss River, Thurso – signed – 30 x 38in.
(Sotheby's) **$2,178** **£1,100**

SAMUEL JOHN LAMORNA BIRCH – 'April Showers At St. Erth Church' – oil on canvas – 12 x 15½in.
(W. H. Lane & Son) **$659** **£340**

S. LAMORNA BIRCH – "Coastal Scene" – signed – watercolour drawing – 5¼ x 9in.
(J. Entwistle & Co.) **$23** **£12**

S. J. LAMORNA BIRCH – Scottish Lake And Mountain Scene – signed and dated 1924 – watercolour – 14 x 20in.
(Husseys) **$291** **£150**

WILLIAM MINSHALL BIRCHALL – H.M.S. Undaunted & Co. – signed, inscribed and dated 1914 – watercolour heightened with white – 11 x 17¾in.
(Christie's) **$136** **£70**

GEOFFREY BIRKBECK – A Roman Garden – signed and inscribed – 20½ x 14in.
(Sotheby's) **$83** **£42**

HENRY BIRTLES – A Summer Afternoon In The Country – signed and dated 1862 – 19½ x 29¼in.
(Sotheby's Belgravia) **$5,634** **£2,800**

BISON – Studies Of A Relief In The Neo-Classical Taste And An Architectural Capriccio – pen and brown ink – 184 x 273mm.
(Christie's) **$76** **£40**

BISON – The Grand Canal, Venice; and The Riva Degli Schiavone – 5½ x 8½in.
(Christie's) **$3,298** **£1,700 Pair**

G. B. BISON – Capriccios Of Figures By Classical Arches – 6¼ x 5in.
(Christie's) **$873** **£450 Pair**

EUGENE DE BLAAS – A Punch And Judy Show In A Convent – signed twice – black chalk and watercolour heightened with white – 376 x 587mm.
(Christie's) **$950** **£500**

ANDREW BLACK – A Hill Road, Glenfinlas – signed, inscribed on a label on the reverse – 11 x 21in.
(Sotheby's) **$238** **£120**

ANDREW BLACK – Trawlers, St. Monance – signed – on panel – 11 x 15in.
(Sotheby's) **$317** **£160**

ANDREW BLACK – Morning In A Village – signed and dated 1880 – 13½ x 9½in.
(Sotheby's) **$288** **£150**

ANDREW BLACK – An East Coast Harbour, Return Of The Boats – signed, inscribed and dated 1884 – 33 x 61in.
(Sotheby's) **$576** **£300**

DOROTHY ISABEL BLACKHAM – Cottages In County Mayo – signed with monogram – on panel – 11½ x 15¼in.
(Sotheby's) **$126** **£65**

THOMAS BROMLEY BLACKLOCK – The Duffer's Caddy – signed, inscribed and dated 1895 – 15½ x 11½in.
(Sotheby's) **$1,113** **£580**

WILLIAM KAY BLACKLOCK – Rural Scene With Many Figures Turning And Loading Hay On To Carts In A Meadow – signed and dated 1916 – oil on canvas – 55.5 x 76cm.
(Henry Spencer & Sons) **$1,386** **£700**

WILLIAM KAY BLACKLOCK – A Summer's Day – signed – on panel – 10 x 13½in.
(Sotheby's) **$792** **£400**

WILLIAM K. BLACKLOCK – 'Summer Time', A Young Girl Picking Berries, A Lady And Small Child Seated On The Banks Of A River, Watching Her – signed – 29.5 x 39.5cm.
(Henry Spencer & Sons) **$1,287** **£650**

JOHN BLAIR – Neidpath Castle; and Leader Haughs – signed and inscribed – 21 x 28in.
(Sotheby's) **$752** **£380 Pair**

BLAKE – A Spaniel With Game – on panel – 8½ x 12in.
(Sotheby's Belgravia) **$153** **£80**

LOUIS NICOLAS VAN BLARENBERGHE, Attributed to – A Dutch Coast Scene, With Fishermen Inspecting And Selling Their Catch On The Beach – gouache – paper on panel – 7½ x 10in.
(Sotheby's) **$1,386** **£700**

DR. CHARLES BLATHERWICK – Storm Passing Over The Arran Moors, Glen Ashdale In The Distance – signed and dated 1876 – 24 x 40in.
(Lawrence) **$114** **£60**

GERRIT CLAESZ. BLEKER – The Reconciliation Of Jacob And Laban – signed and dated 1634 – on panel – 25¼ x 44½in.
(Christie's) **$19,200** **£10,000**

DANIEL DE BLIECK – Figures In The Garden Of A Palace – signed and dated 1645 – 15 x 23¼in.
(Sotheby's) **$2,178** **£1,100**

ABRAHAM VAN BLIJENBERCH – Portrait Of A Gentleman, Bust Length, Wearing A Black Doublet And A White Collar – on panel – 24½ x 19¾in.
(Sotheby's) **$1,881** **£950**

DOUGLAS PERCY BLISS – Summer In The Hebrides – signed and dated '35, inscribed on the reverse – 30 x 40½in.
(Sotheby's) **$337** **£170**

ABRAHAM BLOEMAERT – The Baptism Of Christ – signed and dated 1646 – 33 x 46¾in.
(Christie's) **$38,400** **£20,000**

VAN BLOEMEN – An Italianate Wooded River Landscape With Figures And Cattle In The Foreground – 11½ x 16¾in.
(Christie's) **$317** **£160**

PIETER VAN BLOEMEN – Horsemen, Horses, A Goat And A Dog In A Stable – 18¼ x 24¼in.
(Christie's) **$2,328** **£1,200**

PIETER VAN BLOEMEN – A Farrier Shoeing A Horse – 15½ x 19in.
(Christie's) **$2,522** **£1,300**

PIETER VAN BLOEMEN – A Fountain In A Southern Town With A View Of A Rotunda; A Capriccio With The Farnese Hercules – signed in monogram – 16¼ x 23¾in.
(Sotheby's) **$10,670** **£5,500 Pair**

J. F. VAN BLOEMEN – An Italianate Wooded Landscape With Figures On A Path – 14 x 18in.
(Christie's) **$2,134** **£1,100**

JAN BLOM – An Ornamental Park Landscape – 29 x 24in.
(Sotheby's) **$1,358** **£700**

CHARLES BLOMFIELD – The White And Pink Terraces, New Zealand – signed with initials and one dated 1885 – oil on canvas – 9½ x 13¼in.
(Sotheby's) **$2,167** **£1,100 Two**

PIETER DE BLOOT – An Assembly Of Peasants By A Farm – signed with initials – on copper – 3¾ x 6¼in.
(Christie's) **$3,492 £1,800**

HUARDER BLY – Village Scene – signed – woodblock – 16 x 18cm.
(Australian Art Auctions) **$10 £5**

ERNEST BOARD – The Arrival – signed – 21¼ x 16¾in.
(Sotheby's Belgravia) **$61 £32**

FAUSTINO BOCCHI – A Nocturnal Fantasy – signed – on slate – 16½ x 13in.
(Sotheby's) **$21,560 £11,000**

MELCHIOR BOCKSBERGER, Circle of – Studies Of Animals, Including A Unicorn, An Elephant, A Camel, A Giraffe, A Porcupine And Many Others – pen and brown ink, brown wash heightened with white on brown preparation – 27.1 x 41.7cm.
(Christie's) **$1,728 £900**

J. B. BODEN – A Country Track – signed and dated 1872 – heightened with white – 10 x 14in.
(Sotheby's Belgravia) **$139 £70**

EDWIN H. BODDINGTON – An Extensive River Landscape, With Cattle Watering And A Barge Beyond – signed and dated 1857 – 23½ x 37¼in.
(Christie's) **$2,328 £1,200**

EDWIN H. BODDINGTON – The Ferry – bears a signature and date – 19½ x 31½in.
(Sotheby's Belgravia) **$2,012 £1,000**

HENRY JOHN BODDINGTON – A Wooded River Landscape With Children Fishing – signed – 31 x 42in.
(Christie's) **$3,880 £2,000**

HENRY JOHN BODDINGTON – A Ferry On The Yare At Sunset – 17¾ x 23¾in.
(Christie's) **$1,940 £1,000**

HENRY JOHN BODDINGTON – A View On The Isle Of Wight – signed and dated 1838 – on panel - 23¾ x 32½in.
(Christie's) **$9,700 £5,000**

HENRY JOHN BODDINGTON – On The Barmouth Waters, North Wales, Midday – signed and dated 1855, inscribed on a label on the reverse – 19 x 32½in.
(Sotheby's Belgravia) **$3,420 £1,700**

HENRY JOHN BODDINGTON – A View On The Isle Of Wight – 24¼ x 29¼in.
(Christie's) **$6,208 £3,200**

E. BOEHM – Well-Wooded River Landscape With Two Men On A Track, Hills In The Distance – signed – oil on canvas – 106 x 90cm.
(Henry Spencer & Sons) **$1,624 £820**

J. BOECKHORST – The Four Seasons – 46 x 35in.
(Sotheby's) **$6,930 £3,500 Four**

BOGDANI – Ornamental Fowl In A Landscape – 31 x 49½in.
(Sotheby's) **$3,298 £1,700**

J. BOGDANY – A Basket Of Strawberries, Grapes, Peaches And A Nest, On A Ledge – 17¼ x 14in.
(Christie's) **$970 £500**

FRANK BOGGS – Les Martigues – signed – watercolour – 29 x 43cm.
(Christian Rosset) **$290** **£144**

LOUIS LEOPOLD BOILLY – Portrait Of A Gentleman, Small Bust Length, Wearing Brown Dress – 8¼ x 6in.
(Christie's) **$2,910** **£1,500**

FRANCOIS BOITARD – A Man Offering Tribute To An Enthroned Queen – signed – pen and grey ink, grey wash – 400 x 257mm.
(Christie's) **$80** **£42**

HANS BOL – Market Day In A Dutch Town With A Large Church And A Clock Tower – bodycolour – 8.3 x 11.9cm.
(Christie's) **$3,648** **£1,900**

BOLOGNESE SCHOOL, 17th century – Study Of A Bishop Saint, recto; Studies Of Drapery And A Hand, verso – the verso inscribed – red chalk – 277 x 153mm.
(Christie's) **$86** **£45**

BOLOGNESE SCHOOL, 17th century – A Boy Carrying A Basket Of Carrots And A Money Box With Initials – red chalk – 25.8 x 10.7cm.
(Christie's) **$921** **£480**

BOLOGNESE SCHOOL, 17th century – Studies Of The Head Of A Bearded Old Man – inscribed, inscribed on the reverse – red chalk on blue paper – 204 x 260mm.
(Christie's) **$181** **£95**

BOLOGNESE SCHOOL, 18th century – Women Sacrificing (recto); Alexander And Diogenes (verso) – black chalk, the verso with pen and grey ink – 27 x 21.8cm.
(Christie's) **$268** **£140**

DAVID BOMBERG – Carmencita, 1954 – signed and dated – on board – recto; Portrait Of A Woman, 1954 – signed and dated – verso – 28 x 23¼in.
(Sotheby's) **$832** **£420**

DAVID BOMBERG – Monastery Of St. George Hodjava, Wady Kelt – signed – 12½ x 9in.
(Sotheby's) **$1,584** **£800**

WILLIAM JOSEPH J. C. BOND – Bidston, Cheshire – oil – 11½ x 17¾in.
(Outhwaite & Litherland) **$465** **£230**

WILLIAM JOSEPH J. C. BOND – Coastal Scene – watercolour – 3 x 10in.
(Outhwaite & Litherland) **$444** **£220**

SIR MUIRHEAD BONE – My Brother's Workshop – pen and ink – 30 x 22cm.
(Edmiston's) **$446** **£230**

SIR MUIRHEAD BONE – San Silvestro, Rome – silverpoint drawing – 27 x 12cm.
(Edmiston's) **$291** **£150**

GEORGE R. BONFIELD – Shipping In A Cove At Dusk – signed with initials – oil on canvas – 11½ x 17¾in.
(Sotheby's) **$1,379** **£700**

BONIFAZIO – The Madonna And Child With Saint Catherine And The Infant Saint John The Baptist – 24 x 19¾in.
(Christie's) **$330** **£170**

WILLIAM BONNAR – From 'The Gentle Shepherd' – on panel – 16¾ x 20½in.
(Christie's) **$5,044** **£2,600**

ALESSANDRO BONVICINO, Studio of, Called Moretto Da Brescia – The Mystical Marriage Of Saint Catherine – 29 x 33¼in.
(Sotheby's) **$1,513** **£780**

E. C. BOOTH – 'On The Shore Near Sandsend'; and 'Fisherfolk Near Whitby' – signed and dated 1890 – watercolour – 13 x 20in.
(Morphets of Harrogate) **$194** **£100 Pair**

R. BOOTHS – Monument At Toba Hill, Pakistan, Erected To The Memory Of Captain La Touche And Five Sepoys – signed – watercolour – 9¼ x 17in.
(Sotheby's) **$24** **£12**

EDWARD BOREIN – The Pony Express Carrying United States Mail Across The Plains – signed – pen and black, ink, black and light brown washes, heightened with white on grey paper – 21 x 27in.
(Sotheby's) **$14,775** **£7,500**

AUGUSTE BORGET – Interior Of A Barber's Shop, Canton – signed and inscribed – pencil, heightened with white – 4 x 5¼in.
(Sotheby's (Hong Kong) Ltd.)
$647 £327

AUGUSTE BORGET – A Chinese Beachcomber, Macao – signed, inscribed and dated 1839 – pencil, heightened with white – 4¼ x 5¼in.
(Sotheby's (Hong Kong) Ltd.)
$758 £383

AUGUSTE BORGET – Chinese Figures Outside Dwellings, Macao – signed and inscribed – pencil – 7¼ x 11in.
(Sotheby's (Hong Kong) Ltd.)
$691 $349

AUGUSTE BORGET – A Barber At Macao – signed and inscribed – pencil, heightened with white – 4¼ x 5½in.
(Sotheby's (Hong Kong) Ltd.)
$693 £350

AUGUSTE BORGET – Sampans On The Shore, Macao – inscribed and indistinctly dated – pencil – 6¾ x 10¼in.
(Sotheby's (Hong Kong) Ltd.)
$756 £382

AUGUSTE BORGET – Fisherfolk By A Sampan On The South Coast, Hong Kong – signed, inscribed and dated 1838 – pencil – 4½ x 7¼in.
(Sotheby's (Hong Kong) Ltd.)
$972 £491

AUGUSTE BORGET – A Fruit Seller Near A Restaurant, Macao – inscribed and dated 1839 – pencil – 7¼ x 11in.
(Sotheby's (Hong Kong) Ltd.)
$1,190 £601

AUGUSTE BORGET – A Chinese Village With Figures And Sampans Outside A Temple In The Foreground – 13 x 20in.
(Sotheby's (Hong Kong) Ltd.)
$6,924 £3,497

AUGUSTE BORGET – A Group Of Chinese Figures Paying Homage To The Dead In A Mountain Landscape – 13 x 20in.
(Sotheby's (Hong Kong) Ltd.)
$5,193 £2,623

BORGOGNONE – A Cavalry Skirmish – 6 x 8¾in.
(Christie's) **$693** **£350**

GUGLIELMO CORTESE, Called Il Borgognone – Portrait Of Monsignore Fabrizio Paolucci, Half Length, Holding A Sheet Of Paper – 31 x 23¼in.
(Christie's) **$5,760** **£3,000**

BERNARD LOUIS BORIONE – L'Artiste Et Son Mecene – signed – pencil and watercolour – 7¼ x 5½in.
(Sotheby's) **$494** **£260**

BORSTALL – The 'Elbe', In Heavy Seas – 25¼ x 35½in.
(Sotheby's Belgravia) **$436** **£220**

E. BOSCH – Dickens Interior Scene, Oliver Twist Learning How To Pick Pockets – oil on board – 9 x 11¼in.
(Richard Baker & Baker) **$4,656** **£2,400**

BOSCH, Follower of – The Expulsion From Eden – on panel – 13¼ x 10½in.
(Christie's) **$3,880** **£2,000**

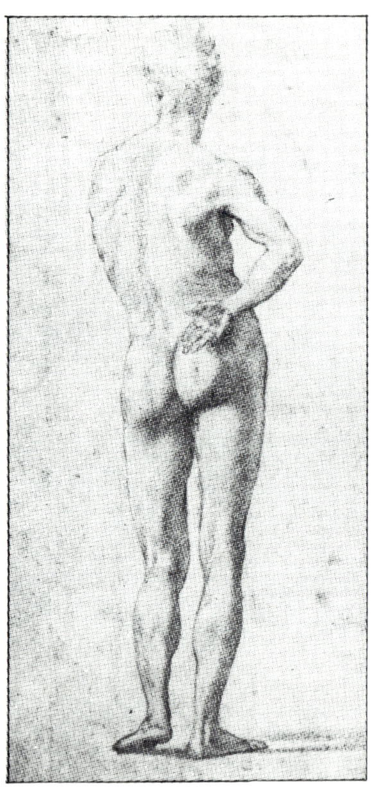

ANDREA BOSCOLI – A Nude Youth Seen From The Back – red chalk – 39.8 x 21.7cm.
(Christie's) **$614** **£320**

F. BOSELLI – Still Life Paintings Of Fowl And Game, On A Ledge – 19 x 25½in.
(Sotheby's) **$660** **£340 Pair**

AMBROSIUS BOSSCHAERT The Younger – Flowers In A Glass Beaker – on copper – 17¾ x 13¼in.
(Sotheby's) **$93,120 £48,000**

J. BOTH – An Italianate Wooded River Landscape With Peasants On A Path – bears signature – on panel – 27¼ x 35¾in.
(Christie's) **$3,880 £2,000**

J. BOTH – A Southern River Landscape With Fishermen By The Shore – 48½ x 49in.
(Sotheby's) **$5,148 £2,600**

JOHN WILLIAM BOTTOMLEY – The Day's Bag – signed and dated 1855 – on board – 13½ x 19½in.
(Christie's) **$776 £400**

F. BOUCHER – Study Of A Female Nude – black, brown and white chalk on blue paper – 194 x 155mm.
(Christie's) **$133 £70**

F. BOUCHER – A Lady On A Sofa Surprised By A Girl And A Young Man – 31 x 25in.
(Christie's) **$6,790 £3,500**

FRANCOIS BOUCHER *(1703-1770)* – 'Le Billet Doux' – signed – 122¾ x 73½in.
(Sotheby's) **$227,700 £115,000**

FRANCOIS BOUCHER *(1703-1770)* – Landscape With Figures On A Bridge By A Tower – signed – 32 x 56¼in.
(Sotheby's) **$148,500 £75,000**

FRANCOIS BOUCHER *(1703-1770)* – Landscape With A Stone Bridge And A Villa – signed – 23½ x 30in.
(Sotheby's) **$63,360 £32,000**

FRANCOIS BOUCHER – Venus With Two Amorini – inscribed – red and white chalk on buff paper – 24.9 x 35.8cm.
(Christie's) **$6,144 £3,200**

FRANCOIS BOUCHER – A Wooded Landscape With A Farmstead – signed – red chalk – 18 x 29.7cm.
(Christie's) **$4,608 £2,400**

BOUCHER – Putti Teasing Sleeping Cupid – 48 x 37½in.
(Christie's) **$1,746 £900**

BOUCHER – Classical Maiden With Magnifying Glass, Landscape Background – oil on canvas – 29 x 38¼in.
(Lalonde Bros. & Parham)
$594 £300

BOUCHER, Studio of – A Nymph Of Diana Waking A Companion In A Wooded Landscape – 34½ x 45¼in.
(Christie's) **$7,296 £3,800**

BOUCKHORST – Portrait Of A Woman In A Ruff – pen and brown ink – 141 x 120mm
(Christie's) **$42 £22**

BOUGH – Fishing Village – watercolour – 28 x 43cm.
(Edmiston's) **$194 £100**

BOUGH – Beached Fishing Boats – on panel – 7¾ x 9½in.
(Sotheby's Belgravia)
$115 **£60**

SAMUEL BOUGH – Stirling Castle From The River Forth – signed and dated 1857 – 19½ x 27¾in.
(Sotheby's) **$1,426** **£720**

SAMUEL BOUGH – Dunbarton Road – signed and dated 1875 – heightened with white – 13 x 17½in.
(Sotheby's) **$574** **£290**

SAMUEL BOUGH – Rochester – pencil and watercolour – 19¼ x 27½in.
(Christie's) **$873** **£450**

SAMUEL BOUGH – Wrack Gatherers – signed and dated 1876 – 13 x 20¼in.
(Sotheby's Belgravia)
$576 **£300**

SAMUEL BOUGH – Dover – watercolour – 19¼ x 27½in.
(Christie's) **$776** **£400**

SAMUEL BOUGH – Lindisfarne – signed, inscribed and dated 1867 – heightened with white – 18 x 24in.
(Sotheby's) **$921** **£480**

S. BOUGH – A Moonlit Harbour – inscribed – 15½ x 24in.
(Sotheby's Belgravia)
$307 **£160**

GEORGE HENRY BOUGHTON – The Vision At The Martyr's Well – signed – 64 x 40in.
(Sotheby's Belgravia)
$1,911 **£950**

GEORGE HENRY BOUGHTON – Falling Leaves – signed with monogram and dated 1871 – 23¼ x 21½in.
(Sotheby's Belgravia)
$2,817 **£1,400**

GEORGE HENRY BOUGHTON – Wales Before The Cave Of Belarius – signed – 66 x 53in.
(Sotheby's Belgravia) **$644** **£320**

GEORGE HENRY BOUGHTON – Expectancy – signed – on panel – 20¼ x 12in.
(Sotheby's Belgravia) **$845** **£420**

CORNELIS BOUMEESTER – A Dutch Man-Of-War In A Mediterranean Harbour – monochrome – on panel – 28½ x 42½in.
(Sotheby's) **$8,730** **£4,500**

J. BOURNE – Figures Near Stone Buildings In The Lake District – watercolour – 14½ x 22in. and smaller.
(Christie's) **$68** **£35 Two**

P. BOUT – An Italianate Wooded River Landscape With Cattle And Drovers By A Bridge – 8¾ x 11½in.
(Christie's) **$1,552** **£800**

P. BOUT And A. F. BOUDEWIJNS – A Southern Landscape With Peasants Returning From Market – 22 x 27in.
(Sotheby's) **$6,336** **£3,200**

PAUL EMILE BOUTIGNY – Cavaliers Russes – signed – brush and wash – 12¼ x 8¼in.
(Sotheby's) **$48** **£25**

F. BOUTTATS – The Element Water – on panel – 10½ x 14½in.
(Sotheby's) **$1,164** **£600**

AUGUSTUS JULES BOUVIER – The Jewel Seller – signed – heightened with body-colour – 30 x 23in.
(Sotheby's Belgravia)
$614 **£320**

G. BOWMAN – By A River – signed and dated 1906 – 29 x 49in.
(Sotheby's Belgravia)
$139 **£70**

R. A. BOXER – The Clipper 'Indian Empire' In Full Sail Out At Sea – signed and dated '97, inscribed – oil on board – 18 x 24in.
(Sotheby's) **$630** **£320**

DAVID BOYD – Children at the River – signed – oil on canvas – 44 x 59cm.
(Australian Art Auctions)
$1,170 **£610**

GEORGE BOYLE – A Country Evening – signed – on panel – 10 x 14in.
(Sotheby's Belgravia)
$345 **£180**

GEORGE A. BOYLE – A Walk In The Woods; Cattle At A Pool – signed, one dated 1879 – on panel – 10 x 8in.
(Sotheby's Belgravia)
$422 **£220 Pair**

GEORGE A. BOYLE – Cattle In Marshland – signed – on panel – 9¼ x 13½in.
(Sotheby's Belgravia)
$380 **£200 Pair**

GEORGE A. BOYLE – By An Estuary; A Wooded Pond; Cattle By A Wood – two signed – on panel – two 9½ x 13½in. and one 6½ x 13¼in.
(Sotheby's Belgravia)
$570 **£300 Three**

GEORGE A. BOYLE – Cattle By A River – signed, inscribed on the reverse – on board – 9 x 11in.
(Sotheby's Belgravia)
$171 **£90**

HERCULES BRABAZON BRABAZON – An Open Landscape At Sunset – signed with initials – watercolour – 9¼ x 13¼in.
(Christie's) **$155** **£80**

HERCULES BRABAZON BRABAZON – A Moorish Town – signed with initials – pencil and touches of coloured chalk on grey paper – 6½ x 10in.
(Christie's) **$136** **£70**

R. BRACKENBERG – A Peasant Wedding Feast – bears another signature – on panel – 15¾ x 13½in.
(Christie's) **$4,554** **£2,300**

BASIL BRADLEY – Supper Time On The Farm, Buckinghamshire – dated 1878 – oil – 25¼ x 44¾in.
(Outhwaite & Litherland)
$5,858 **£2,900**

HELEN BRADLEY – Family Round The Bonfire – signed, signed and dated 1974 on the reverse – linen on board – 16¼ x 20¼in.
(Sotheby's) **$3,960** **£2,000**

HELEN BRADLEY – Miss Carter And The Bank Manager With An Umbrella – signed, signed and dated 1975 on the reverse – linen on board – 12 x 8in.
(Sotheby's) **$2,574** **£1,300**

HELEN BRADLEY – Chadwick's Hat Shop – signed, inscribed and dated 1973 on the reverse – canvas on board – 16 x 20in.
(Sotheby's) **$4,752** **£2,400**

WILLIAM BRADLEY – Rowing Boats On The Thames – signed and dated 1887 – heightened with bodycolour – 22¾ x 34¾in.
(Sotheby's Belgravia) **$854** **£440**

W. HANLEY BRAITHWAITE – Friends – signed – 33 x 43in.
(Sotheby's Belgravia) **$855** **£450**

RICHARD BRAKENBURG – The Procuress – bears signature – on panel – 6 x 4½in.
(Christie's) **$970** **£500**

RICHARD BRAKENBURGH – Atalanta And Meleager, Who Presents Her With The Head Of The Calydonian Boar, In A Wooded Landscape – 27½ x 34½in.
(Sotheby's) **$1,164** **£600**

L. BRAMER – A Potentate Bestowing Arms – on panel – 17¼ x 15¼in.
(Christie's) **$931** **£480**

FRANK BRAMLEY – The Pergola – signed and dated 1911 – 13¾ x 10in.
(Sotheby's Belgravia) **$178** **£90**

A. BRANDEIS – The Rialto Bridge, Venice – signed – on panel – 16 x 22cm.
(King & Chasemore) **$864** **£450**

A. BRANDEIS – St. Mark's Square, Venice – signed – on panel – 16 x 22cm.
(King & Chasemore) **$1,113** **£580**

A. BRANDEIS – A Venetian Canal Scene – signed – on panel – 16 x 22cm.
(King & Chasemore) **$1,248** **£650**

GIACINTO BRANDI – The Vestal Virgin Tuccia – 47 x 67¼in.
(Sotheby's) **$4,704** **£2,400**

J. F. BRANEGAN – Off Whitby; On The Lincolnshire Coast – signed, inscribed and dated '92 – heightened with bodycolour – 9¾ x 18in.
(Sotheby's Belgravia) **$77** **£40 Pair**

SIR FRANK BRANGWYN – Hollyhocks – dated 1890 – 49½ x 31½in.
(Sotheby's) **$1,782** **£900**

SIR FRANK BRANGWYN – Ships At Sea – signed and dated 1889 – on board – 7¾ x 11in.
(Sotheby's) **$792** **£400**

MELCHIOR BRASSAUW – A Porcelain Vendor – 5½ x 5½in.
(Sotheby's) **$1,782** **£900**

DE BRAY – The Crucifixion – 47½ x 69in.
(Christie's) **$1,067** **£550**

SALOMON DE BRAY – Portrait Of A Little Girl – on panel – 7¼ x 5¾in.
(Sotheby's) **$2,744** **£1,400**

W. A. BREAKESPEARE – A Young Ophelia – 17 x 12¾in.
(Sotheby's Belgravia) **$144 £75**

WILLIAM A. BREAKESPEARE – The Young Falconer – signed – on panel – 9 x 5½in.
(Christie's) **$1,746 £900**

A. DE BREANSKI – A View On The River – signed and dated '91 – on panel – 6½ x 9in.
(Sotheby's Belgravia) **$144 £75**

ALFRED DE BREANSKI – 'Autumn', A River Landscape – signed and dated 1870 – 23½ x 39½in.
(Christie's) **$1,067 £550**

ALFRED DE BREANSKI – Cattle At A Stream – signed and dated '82 – heightened with bodycolour – 20¼ x 29in.
(Sotheby's Belgravia) **$456 £240**

ALFRED DE BREANSKI – At Bettws-y-Coed, North Wales – signed – oil – 24 x 36in.
(Phillips) **$3,267 £1,650**

ALFRED DE BREANSKI – Anglers On The Dee, Near Balmoral – signed – 23 x 36in.
(Sotheby's) **$5,940 £3,000**

ALFRED DE BREANSKI – 'At Cookham, Evening' – signed and dated 1878-9 – 15 x 22½in.
(Messenger May Baverstock) **$624 £310**

ALFRED DE BREANSKI – 'At Sunrise', Cattle By A Meandering River – signed, inscribed on reverse – oil – 24 x 39in.
(Heathcote Ball & Co.) **$4,326 £2,150**

ALFRED DE BREANSKI – The Brander Pass To Loch Awe; The Vale Of Shiel – signed – 19 x 29¼in.
(Sotheby's Belgravia) **$7,645 £3,800 Pair**

ALFRED DE BREANSKI – The Call Of The Highlands – signed – 43 x 63in.
(Sotheby's) **$7,680 £4,000**

ALFRED DE BREANSKI – A Mountain Pass – signed, and signed and inscribed on the reverse – 29½ x 49½in.
(Christie's) **$6,790 £3,500**

ALFRED DE BREANSKI – The Balvaig Stream – signed, inscribed on the reverse – 15¼ x 23½in.
(Sotheby's Belgravia) **$3,521 £1,750**

ALFRED DE BREANSKI, JNR. – Cattle By A Highland Loch – one signed – 19½ x 29½in.
(Sotheby's Belgravia) **$608 £320 Pair**

ALFRED DE BREANSKI, JNR. – Deganwy From Conway, North Wales – signed, inscribed on the reverse – 11½ x 17½in.
(Sotheby's Belgravia) **$192 £100**

ALFRED FONTEVILLE DE BREANSKI – Early Morning On The River Wey – signed – 15½ x 23½in.
(Christie's) **$1,455 £750**

ALFRED FONTVILLE DE BREANSKI – In A Perthshire Valley; Evening In A Welsh Valley – signed, inscribed on the reverse – 20 x 30in.
(Sotheby's) **$2,496 £1,300 Pair**

ALFRED FONTVILLE DE BREANSKI – 'Haddon Hall, Derbyshire' – signed – oil – 30 x 40in.
(Bonham's) **$2,772 £1,400**

ALFRED FONTVILLE DE BREANSKI – The Head Of A Highland Loch – signed, inscribed on the reverse – 19 x 29½in.
(Sotheby's) **$1,386 £700**

ALFRED FONTVILLE DE BREANSKI – Cattle In The Highlands – signed – 23½ x 36in.
(Sotheby's Belgravia) **$693** **£350**

D. DE BREANSKI – Fishing Vessels Becalmed – 29½ x 49in.
(Sotheby's Belgravia) **$384** **£200**

GUSTAVE DE BREANSKI – Returning To Port; A Quiet Harbour – signed, one indistinctly inscribed – 24 x 36in.
(Sotheby's Belgravia)
$988 **£520 Pair**

GUSTAVE DE BREANSKI – Trawlers – signed and inscribed on the reverse – on board – 10 x 12½in.
(Sotheby's Belgravia) **$285** **£150**

BREDAEL – A Cavalry Engagement In A Landscape – canvas on board – 20½ x 30in.
(Christie's) **$776** **£400**

BREDAEL – A Quay On A River With Figures, And A Castle Beyond – 14 x 19in.
(Christie's) **$2,328** **£1,200**

VAN BREDAEL – Cattle And Sheep With Figures By Classical Ruins – 33½ x 45¼in.
(Christie's) **$1,584** **£800**

J. F. VAN BREDAEL – The Tower Of Babel – 35½ x 44½in.
(Christie's) **$2,134** **£1,100**

K. VAN BREDAEL – A Cavalry Engagement In A Wooded Landscape – bears signature – on copper – 8¾ x 12½in.
(Christie's) **$1,067** **£550**

PIETER VAN BREDAEL – A Cattle Market In An Extensive Southern Landscape – signed – 26¾ x 33¾in.
(Sotheby's) **$10,864** **£5,600**

B. BREENBERGH – An Extensive Classical Landscape, With Travellers, Donkeys And Camels By A Ruin – on panel – 15½ x 20¼in.
(Christie's) **$1,261** **£650**

BREKELENKAM – A Kitchen Interior With A Maid Scouring Pots – 18½ x 15¾in.
(Sotheby's) **$1,746** **£900**

Q. G. VAN BREKELENKAM – A Domestic Interior – on panel – 32¼ x 27½in.
(Christie's) **$1,455** **£750**

QUIRINGH VAN BREKELENKAM – A Woman Asleep By A Spinning-Wheel – signed and dated 1662 – on panel – 14 x 9¾in.
(Sotheby's) **$7,840** **£4,000**

QUIRYN GERRITSZ. VAN BREKELENKAM – An Old Man Gutting Fish In An Interior – signed and dated 1660 – on panel – 18 x 14½in.
(Christie's) **$7,372** **£3,800**

SCHOOL OF BRESCIA, 16th century – Portrait Of A Man, Three-Quarter Length, In Black – 42½ x 33¼in.
(Sotheby's) **$1,746** **£900**

BRETLAND – Four Sporting Dogs In An Extensive Rolling Landscape – oil on canvas – 50 x 76cm.
(Henry Spencer & Sons) **$756** **£390**

BRETT – Ecclesbourne, Hastings – bears signature and date, inscribed and dated 1881 on the stretcher – 11½ x 19½in.
(Sotheby's Belgravia) **$211** **£110**

JOHN BRETT – Forest Cove, Cardigan Bay – signed and dated 1883 – 15 x 29½in.
(Sotheby's Belgravia) **$5,835** **£2,900**

JOHN BRETT – The Isle Of Arran From Farland Head – signed and dated 1886 – 15 x 29½in.
(Sotheby's Belgravia) **$4,024** **£2,000**

HENRY CHARLES BREWER – The Transept, Beauvais – signed and inscribed – 28 x 19in.
(Sotheby's Belgravia) **$384** **£200**

CAREL BREYDAEL – A Battle Skirmish In A Southern Landscape – signed and dated 1714 – on panel – 8 x 9¼in.
(Sotheby's) **$2,910** **£1,500**

FREDERICK LEE BRIDELL – A Classical Idyll – signed and dated 1860 – on board – 39 x 23in.
(Sotheby's Belgravia) **$1,408** **£700**

FREDERICK LEE BRIDELL – A Mountainous Wooded Landscape With Travellers By A Lake – signed and dated 1851, and signed on a label on the reverse – 19¼ x 23¼in.
(Christie's) **$1,358** **£700**

SIR OSWALD WALTER BRIERLY – A Paddle Steamer In Milford Sound, New Zealand – signed – watercolour, heightened with white – 11¼ x 17½in.
(Sotheby's) **$1,734** **£880**

BRIGHT – By A Norfolk Windmill – bears signature and date – on panel – 7¼ x 9¼in.
(Sotheby's Belgravia) **$143 £75**

HENRY BRIGHT – A Woman With A Pitcher Outside A Cottage Near Ipswich, Suffolk – signed – watercolour – 16¼ x 12¼in.
(Christie's) **$213 £110**

PAUL BRIL – The Temptation Of Saint Anthony – on copper – 7¾ x 9¾in.
(Christie's) **$14,400 £7,500**

PAUL BRIL – Saint John On Patmos, Visiting The Gospel On A Craggy Island – on panel – 17¾ x 26in.
(Sotheby's) **$5,820 £3,000**

BRIL – A Coastal Landscape With Christ On The Road To Emmaus – on metal – 6¾ x 8½in.
(Sotheby's) **$776 £400**

BRILL – An Extensive River Landscape – inscribed with monogram and inscribed on the reverse – pen and brown ink – 214 x 342mm.
(Christie's) **$152 £80**

FRED BRINDLE – Baslow, Derbyshire – signed – 8½ x 11½in.
(Sotheby's Belgravia) **$72 £38**

BRISTOL SCHOOL – A Stream In A Wooded Mountain Landscape – brown wash – 9 x 13in.
(Christie's) **$35 £18**

EDMUND BRISTOW – Cottage Interior, With Game On A Table, A Spaniel Stands By A Brass Pan And Wicker Basket, A Cat Looks In At The Open Window – signed and dated 1834 – oil on panel – 38 x 30cm.
(Henry Spencer & Sons) **$5,626 £2,900**

C. E. BRITTAN – The Secretary Bird Standing Amongst Grasses, A Snake At The Bird's Feet – inscribed on the reverse – watercolour – 36½ x 25in.
(Sotheby's) **$79 £40**

SAMUEL FREDERICK BROCAS – Figures And Cattle By A Lake In The Mourne Mountains – signed – 10½ x 16in.
(Sotheby's) **$621 £320**

MODESTO BROCOS – La Senorita – signed – watercolour – 15 x 10½in.
(Sotheby's) **$315 £160**

WILLIAM BROCAS – Waiting For The Immigrant Ship: A Family With Their Possessions By A Quay – signed and dated 1842 – 27¼ x 35¼in.
(Sotheby's) **$14,356** **£7,400**

J. G. BROCKENHURST, Attributed to – Sir Samuel Peyton, Son Of Thomas Peyton, Three-Quarter Length, In Black Coat, With White Collar And Cuffs – dated 1632 – oil on canvas – 42 x 32in.
(Spear & Sons) **$1,509** **£750**

GERALD BROCKHURST – Head Of A Girl – signed – red chalk – 13¾ x 10in.
(Sotheby's) **$1,386** **£700**

WILLIAM BROMLEY – The Young Dentist – signed and dated 1872 – 11½ x 9¾in.
(Christie's) **$1,164** **£600**

J. G. VAN BRONCKHORST – Christ Preaching In The Wilderness – inscribed – pen and brown ink, grey wash – 11.4 x 15.2cm.
(Christie's) **$211** **£110**

C. BRONTE – Orpheus And Euridice – signed and dated 1882 – arched top – 24 x 17in.
(Sotheby's Belgravia)
$192 **£100**

BROOKS – Portrait Of A Gentleman – 36 x 28in.
(Sotheby's Belgravia)
$86 **£45**

THOMAS BROOKS – The Milkmaid – 20 x 16in.
(Sotheby's Belgravia)
$805 **£400**

BROOME – A Thames Hay Barge – 23 x 19½in.
(Sotheby's Belgravia)
$133 **£70**

ROBERT BROUGH – In An Oriental Garden – canvas on panel – 11½ x 13½in
(Sotheby's) **$499** **£260**

ROBERT BROUGH – Portrait Of Kathleen Crombie – signed with monogram and inscribed – 13½ x 9½in.
(Sotheby's) **$1,980 £1,000**

BROUWER – The Sense Of Smell – bears signature – on panel – 14 x 10¾in.
(Christie's) **$1,584 £800**

SIR ARNESBY BROWN – 'September', Landscape With Ploughman At Aldeby, Norfolk – signed – oil on canvas – 15½ x 19¾in.
(J. W. Hilham) **$3,169 £1,575**

SIR ARNESBY BROWN – 'The Smug And Silver Trent' – signed – oil on canvas – 15½ x 19¾in.
(J. W. Hilham) **$1,006 £500**

SIR ARNESBY BROWN – 'The Watch Tower' At Salthouse – signed – oil on canvas – 15½ x 19½in.
(J. W. Hilham) **$2,213 £1,100**

A. K. BROWN – Ardmore On The Clyde – dated 1889 – watercolour – 7 x 15cm.
(Edmiston's) **$50 £26**

FREDERICK MAY BROWN – Still Life Of Delphiniums In A Jug – signed and dated 1912 – 30¼ x 22¼in.
(Sotheby's Belgravia)
$31 £16

G. BROWN – Still Life Of Peaches – signed – 17½ x 23½in.
(Sotheby's Belgravia)
$79 £40

JOHN GEORGE BROWN – 'The Cavalier' – signed – oil on canvas – 18½ x 10in.
(Morton's Auction Exchange, Inc.)
$1,500 £761

J. MICHAEL BROWN – Evening – signed – 13½ x 17½in.
(Sotheby's) **$518 £270**

R. AUSTEN BROWN – 'Sailing Boats At Harbour Wall' – signed – watercolour – 16½ x 12½in.
(Dacre, Son & Hartley)
$121 £60

TAYLOR BROWN – Ballantrae – signed, inscribed on a label on the reverse – 24½ x 31½in.
(Sotheby's) **$1,152** **£600**

WILLIAM BEATTIE BROWN – A Castle Keep – signed and dated 1876 – 7½ x 11in.
(Sotheby's) **$218** **£110**

WILLIAM BEATTIE BROWN – Findhorn Village, Sundown, Morayshire – signed and inscribed – 19½ x 29½in.
(Sotheby's) **$691** **£360**

WILLIAM BEATTIE BROWN – Cornfield, Strath Spey – inscribed – 11 x 17½in.
(Sotheby's) **$960** **£500**

WILLIAM BEATTIE BROWN – Spring In Flanders – signed, inscribed and dated 1888 – 11½ x 19in.
(Sotheby's Belgravia) **$96** **£50**

W. J. BROWN – The Grounds Of A Country House – indistinctly signed – 12½ x 18½in.
(Sotheby's Belgravia) **$99** **£50**

WILLIAM MARSHALL BROWN – Dinnertime – signed – 8½ x 11in.
(Sotheby's) **$1,089** **£550**

WILLIAM MARSHALL BROWN – Duck Pond – signed, inscribed on a label on the reverse – 11 x 15in.
(Sotheby's) **$475** **£240**

WILLIAM MARSHALL BROWN – Gathering Cockles – signed – 6 x 9in.
(Sotheby's) **$891** **£450**

WILLIAM MARSHALL BROWN – Portrait Of James Dunn Of Edinburgh, Keeper of the Royal Seal of Scotland – signed and dated 1893 – 23½ x 17½in.
(Sotheby's Belgravia) **$34** **£18**

HABLOT KNIGHT BROWNE – You Over! – pencil and coloured washes – signed and inscribed – 7½ x 11in.
(Sotheby's Belgravia) **$158** **£80**

MABEL BROWNE – At Whitby – signed with initials, inscribed on the reverse – canvas – on panel – 10½ x 7½in.
(Sotheby's Belgravia) **$30** **£16**

TOM BROWNE – The New Milking Stool – signed and inscribed – pen and ink and grey wash – 13½ x 10in.
(Sotheby's Belgravia) **$61** **£32**

VINCENT BALFOUR BROWNE – A Mallard – heightened with white – 13½ x 20in.
(Sotheby's) **$257** **£130**

PELEG FRANKLIN BROWNELL – By The River In Early Spring – signed with monogram and dated '28 – oil on board – 10½ x 15in.
(Sotheby's) **$906** **£460**

GEORGE WASHINGTON BROWNLOW – Going To The Hustings – signed and dated '58 – 9½ x 13½in.
(Sotheby's) **$891** **£450**

WILLIAM BLAIR BRUCE – A Council Of Three, Young Native Boys Lying On A Beach – signed and dated 1885 – oil on canvas – 9¼ x 12¾in.
(Sotheby's) **$1,260** **£640**

JAN BRUEGHEL The Elder – An Extensive Wooded Landscape With A Tower, A Mill And Peasants Loading A Wagon In The Foreground – on panel – circular – diameter 8¼in.
(Christie's) **$61,440** **£32,000**

JAN BRUEGHEL The Elder – A Wooded Village, With Peasants By A Waterway – on copper – 4 x 6½in.
(Christie's) **$46,080 £24,000**

JAN BRUEGHEL The Elder – A Wooded Estuary With A Ferry With Fishermen Unloading And Selling Their Catch At A Mooring Place And A Village Beyond – signed and dated 1612 – on copper – circular – diameter 8½in.
(Christie's) **$130,560 £68,000**

JAN BRUEGHEL The Younger – A River Landscape – on copper – 15¼ x 24½in.
(Sotheby's) **$116,400 £60,000**

JAN BRUEGHEL – The Four Elements: Earth, Ceres Receiving Fruit And Flowers From Putti; Water, A Naiad, Holding A Cornucopia Filled With Shells And Coral, To Whom A Putto Brings Water In A Shell; Air, A Woman With A Bunch Of Feathers And An Astrolabe, Before Her Birds Of Many Kinds; Fire, Vulcan Bringing An Embossed Silver Shield To Venus – on copper – 15¾ x 22in.
(Sotheby's) **$54,320 £28,000 Four**

PETER BRUEGHEL The Elder, Circle of – Trees On The Banks Of A Swollen River – pen and brown ink – 22.7 x 32.6cm.
(Christie's) **$5,376 £2,800**

P. BRUEGHEL The Younger – A Wedding Dance In A Landscape – on panel – 28¼ x 43¾in.
(Sotheby's) **$29,100 £15,000**

PIETER BRUEGHEL The Younger – The Return From Kermesse, With Peasants Dancing In The Foreground, A Piper By A Tree, Peasants Brawling And Numerous Figures Feasting And Dancing, With A Distant Avenue – signed – on panel – 16 x 28½in.
(Christie's) **$499,200 £260,000**

PIETER BRUEGHEL The Younger – The Egg Dance – on panel - 26 x 41in.
(Christie's) **$80,640 £42,000**

BRUEGHEL – A Wooded Landscape With Peasants – on copper – oval – 3½ x 4½in.
(Christie's) **$417 £210**

BRUEGHEL – A Maypole Dance In A Village Beside A River – 11 x 13in.
(Sotheby's) **$1,358 £700**

SCHOOL OF BRUGES, mid 16th century – The Madonna And Child – on panel – 9¼ x 16½in.
(Sotheby's) **$5,544 £2,800**

BRUGES SCHOOL, 17th century – Portrait Of A Nun, Said To Be Mary Elizabeth Timperley Of The Order Of The Blue Nuns Of Bruges – inscribed – 39½ x 30in.
(Sotheby's) **$194 £100**

LE BRUN, After – Mary Magdalene, Seated At Her Toilette, On The Terrace Of A Palace In A White And Floral-Patterned Silk Dress – bears initials – on panel – 19 x 13½in.
(Sotheby's) **$990 £500**

FRANCOIS BRUNGRY – 'Romance Nouvelle' – signed – oil on canvas – 45 x 38cm.
(King & Chasemore) **$7,128 £3,600**

CHARLES BRYANT – Ships Entering Harbour – signed and dated '24 – oil on board – 23 x 70cm.
(Australian Art Auctions)
$433 £221

G. F. BUCHANAN – Culzean Castle, Firth Of Clyde – signed and dated '83 – 19 x 29in.
(Sotheby's) **$317 £160**

PETER BUCHANAN – A View Over An Estuary – signed – 13½ x 21½in.
(Sotheby's) **$158 £80**

JOHN BUCKLER – Wells Cathedral From The North-East – signed and dated 1841 – pencil and watercolour – 17 x 25½in.
(Sotheby's) **$485 £250**

J. E. BUCKLEY – A Hawking Party Outside An Old House – signed and dated 1871 – watercolour heightened with white – 17¼ x 26¼in.
(Christie's) **$116 £600**

ERNEST PILE BUCKNALL – In A Kentish Village – signed – 19 x 29in.
(Sotheby's Belgravia)
$346 £180

FREDERICK BUCKSTONE – Campsie Glen, Near Glasgow; Brathay Bridge, Grassmere – signed and dated 1882, inscribed on the reverse – 15½ x 23½in.
(Sotheby's) **$499 £260 Pair**

ZANETTO BUGATTO, After – The Sforza Altarpiece – on panel – 22¼ x 34½in.
(Sotheby's) **$9,700 £5,000**

GIULIO BUGIARDINI – The Madonna And Child With St. John – 28 x 21½in.
(Sotheby's) **$2,772 £1,400**

JEAN-EUGENE BULAND – Portrait De Vieillard – signed and dated 1890 – charcoal, red and white chalk – 11½ x 9in.
(Sotheby's) **$118 £62**

EDITH BULLOCK – Shepherd And Sheep In A Landscape – signed – on panel – 12 x 15½in.
(Christie's) **$582 £300**

KATE ELIZABETH BUNCE – The Guard – signed with monogram – 30 x 18in.
(Christie's) **$485** **£250**

EDGAR BUNDY – 'Not Convinced' – signed – 19½ x 29½in.
(Sotheby Bearne) **$3,007** **£1,550**

JOHN WHARLTON BUNNEY – Venice: Sunset Over The Salute – signed and dated 1880 and inscribed and dated on an old label on the reverse – watercolour on grey paper – 6 x 9in.
(Christie's) **$330** **£170**

RUPERT BUNNY – Landscape, South Of France – oil on board – 25 x 14cm.
(Australian Art Auctions) **$218** **£111**

PACINO DA BUONAGUIDA, Attributed to – St. John The Evangelist In A Red Robe Edged With Gold, Holding A Book With A Red Cover – inscribed – gold ground – on panel – 22 x 13¾in.
(Sotheby's) **$9,800** **£5,000**

JOHN BAGNOLD BURGESS – A Senorita – signed and dated 1880 – on panel – 12 x 9½in.
(Sotheby's Belgravia) **$1,911** **£950**

JOHN BAGNOLD BURGESS – A Mediterranean Beauty – signed and dated 1875 – on panel – 7½ x 9½in.
(Christie's) **$1,045** **£550**

AVERIL MARY BURLEIGH – Motherhood – signed – 15 x 11½in.
(Sotheby's Belgravia) **$672** **£350**

SIR EDWARD COLEY BURNE-JONES – The Failure Of Sir Lancelot – black, white, and brown chalk on brown paper – 20 x 22in.
(Sotheby's Belgravia) **$5,030** **£2,500**

SIR EDWARD COLEY BURNE-JONES – Santa Maria Virgo – inscribed – coloured chalks – 67½ x 22in.
(Sotheby's Belgravia) **$17,102 £8,500**

SIR EDWARD COLEY BURNE-JONES – Santa Dorothea – inscribed – coloured chalks – 67½ x 22in.
(Sotheby's Belgravia) **$19,114 £9,500**

SIR EDWARD COLEY BURNE-JONES – Saint Agnes – mixed media – 37 x 15½in.
(Sotheby's Belgravia) **$5,231 £2,600**

SIR EDWARD COLEY BURNE-JONES, Attributed to – A Portrait Study Of A Young Girl – inscribed – oil on canvas – 60 x 50cm.
(King & Chasemore) **$1,683 £850**

ALEXANDER HOHENLOHE BURR – The Monkey And The Magnet – signed – 14 x 17¾in.
(Sotheby's) **$921 £480**

ALEXANDER HOHENLOHE BURR – Feeding Rabbits – bears signature – 16½ x 12in.
(Sotheby's) **$864 £450**

JOHN BURR – The Sick Child – signed and dated 1833 – 59½ x 47¼in.
(Christie's) **$1,164 £600**

O. BURRELL – Maternal Pride – signed and dated 1851 – 11¼ x 15¼in.
(Sotheby's Belgravia) **$342 £180**

BURROWS – A Wooded Lane – on panel – 6¼ x 8¾in.
(Sotheby's Belgravia) **$288 £150**

CHARLES THOMAS BURT – River Landscape With An Angler And Ghillie – signed – 23 x 38½in.
(Sotheby's) **$3,564 £1,800**

REUBEN BUSSEY – An Extensive Landscape With Figures Opening Canal Lock Gates In The Foreground, Their Horses Tethered Close-By – signed and dated 1837 – oil on canvas – 12 x 16in.
(Neales of Nottingham) **$99 £50**

MILDRED ANNE BUTLER – The Home Garden – signed, inscribed verso – watercolour – 14 x 20in.
(Sotheby's) **$388 £200**

HAROLD BYRN – Ballerina – signed – watercolour – 18 x 21cm.
(Australian Art Auctions) **$41 £21**

BYZANTINE SCHOOL – The Madonna; and Christ The Redeemer – on copper – oval – 4 x 3¼in.
(Christie's) **$272 £140 Two**

JAMES CADENHEAD – A Midsummer Morning – signed with monogram – 28¼ x 37¼in.
(Sotheby's) **$436** **£220**

GIUSEPPE CADES – The Return Of The Prodigal Son – diameter 7in.
(Christie's) **$1,056** **£550**

H. CAFE – Herding The Flock Homewards – signed – 15½ x 11½in.
(Sotheby's Belgravia) **$178** **£90**

THOMAS CAFE, JNR. – River Landscapes With A Lock And Barges – one signed – watercolour, one heightened with white – 10 x 14½in. and smaller.
(Christie's) **$116** **£60 Pair**

M. CAFFI – Still Life Of Flowers In A Sculptured Urn, On A Wooden Ledge – 27¼ x 30½in.
(Sotheby's) **$6,534** **£3,300**

HECTOR CAFFIERI – Pelargoniums In A Lustre Ware Jug By A Basket – signed and dated 1872 – watercolour and bodycolour – 10¼ x 14½in.
(Christie's) **$136** **£70**

WALTER WALLOR CAFFYN – A Peaceful River – signed and dated 1890 – 11½ x 17½in.
(Sotheby's Belgravia)
$768 **£400**

CHARLES WILLIAM CAINE – Whispering Steps; and Hassan's House, Baghdad – signed – pen and brown ink and watercolour – 14¾ x 9¾in.
(Sotheby's) **$217** **£110 Pair**

JOHN CAIRNEY – Garnqueen Loch – signed and dated 1878, inscribed on the reverse – 9 x 13in.
(Sotheby's) **$188** **£95**

FRANCESCO DEL CAIRO – Solomon And The Queen Of Sheba – 55 x 70½in.
(Sotheby's) **$6,208** **£3,200**

PHILIP HERMOGENES CALDERON – The Orphans – signed and dated 1870 – 26 x 19½in.
(Christie's) **$1,261** **£650**

WILLIAM FRANK CALDERON – Dinner – signed, inscribed on the reverse – 23 x 33in.
(Sotheby's Belgravia)
$2,213 **£1,100**

CHARLES CALLCOTT – Mending The Net – signed with monogram – 13½ x 11½in.
(Sotheby's Belgravia)
$297 **£150**

GEORGE CALLOW – Day And Night Shipping Scenes – 40 x 30cm.
(Edmiston's) **$640** **£330 Pair**

JOHN CALLOW – 'A Breezy Day' – signed and dated 1869 – oil on canvas – 29½ x 49in.
(W. H. Lane & Son) **$3,492** **£1,800**

JOHN CALLOW – Fishing Smacks Off Garleston Pier – 18 x 32in.
(Christie's) **$970** **£500**

JOHN CALLOW -- Fishing Boats Returning To Port After A Gale – signed, inscribed on the reverse – 29½ x 49in.
(Sotheby's Belgravia) **$2,012** **£1,000**

J. CALLOW – Shipping Off The Coast – 11½ x 21in.
(Sotheby's Belgravia) **$304** **£160**

WILLIAM CALLOW – Innsbruck – signed – 17¾ x 13¾in.
(Sotheby's) **$1,649** **£850**

WILLIAM CALLOW – Schloss Weilburg On The Lahn – signed, inscribed and dated '71 – pencil and watercolour – 9¾ x 13½in.
(Sotheby's) **$970** **£500**

CALRAET – Horsemen Fording A Stream – on panel – 13½ x 15½in.
(Christie's) **$1,125** **£580**

ABRAHAM CALRAET – A Hen, Sitting On Her Nest, In A Basket – on panel – 24¾ x 18½in.
(Sotheby's) **$5,148** **£2,600**

EDWIN SHERWOOD CALVERT – In A Farmyard – signed and dated 1902 – 12½ x 15½in.
(Sotheby's) **$806** **£420**

FREDERICK CALVERT – Fishing Vessels Offshore – 19¼ x 29½in.
(Christie's) **$873** **£450**

SAM CALVERT – Haddon Hall – signed, inscribed on the reverse – 19 x 29½in.
(Sotheby's Belgravia)
$133 **£70**

CAMBIASO – Time With A Putto On A Cloud – pen and brown ink – 184 x 234mm.
(Christie's) **$114** **£60**

CAMERON – The Stinchar Near Ballantrae – watercolour – 26 x 36cm.
(Edmiston's) **$272** **£140**

SIR DAVID YOUNG CAMERON – The Mountain Pool – signed, inscribed – 17½ x 29½in.
(Sotheby's) **$1,632** **£850**

SIR D. Y. CAMERON – Ruthven Castle – 20 x 25cm.
(Edmiston's) **$640** **£330**

SIR D. Y. CAMERON – Landscape With Mountain In Distance – pencil – 22 x 37cm.
(Edmiston's) **$85** **£44**

SIR D. Y. CAMERON – Killundine, Sound Of Mull – watercolour – 14 x 27.5cm.
(Edmiston's) **$378** **£195**

DUNCAN CAMERON – A Cornfield On The Coast – signed – 12 x 17½in.
(Sotheby's) **$317** **£160**

DUNCAN CAMERON – A Crofter's Harvest – signed, inscribed on a label on the reverse – 19 x 29in.
(Sotheby's) **$792** **£400**

DUNCAN CAMERON – Stirling Castle – signed – 11½ x 17½in.
(Sotheby's) **$268** **£140**

DUNCAN CAMERON – Looking Down A River – signed – 23½ x 35in.
(Sotheby's) **$326** **£170**

DUNCAN CAMERON – On The Tay Near Stanley – signed – 19 x 29½in.
(Sotheby's) **$576** **£300**

DUNCAN CAMERON – The Calm Before The Storm – signed – 11½ x 17½in.
(Sotheby's Belgravia) **$192** **£100**

CAMPAGNOLA – An Extensive Landscape At Dawn With A Sleeping Man – inscribed on the reverse – black chalk, pen and brown ink, grey and blue wash – 243 x 333mm.
(Christie's) **$152** **£80**

J. H. CAMPBELL – A View In Co. Wicklow With A River And Cottages, Hills In The Distance – 12½ x 16in.
(Sotheby's) **$317** **£160**

TOM CAMPBELL – Foulds, Moss Side – signed – 13½ x 20in.
(Sotheby's) **$198** **£100**

TOM CAMPBELL – Arran – signed – heightened with bodycolour – 14 x 21in.
(Sotheby's) **$307** **£160**

TOM CAMPBELL – Sheep By A Highland Loch – signed – 23½ x 36in.
(Sotheby's) **$672** **£350**

TOM CAMPBELL – Pastoral Scene – watercolour – 27 x 37cm.
(Edmiston's) **$140** **£72**

T. CAMPBELL – Outside A Country Cottage – 13½ x 17in.
(Sotheby's Belgravia) **$86** **£45**

CAMPHUYSEN – A Wooded River Landscape With Travellers On A Path – on panel – 22¼ x 16¼in.
(Christie's) **$475** **£240**

CAMPIDOGLIO – A Bowl Of Flowers And A Basket Of Flowers In A Landscape – 21½ x 43½in.
(Christie's) **$621** **£320**

GEORGE BRYANT CAMPION – Lake Lucerne – signed – heightened with bodycolour – 27½ x 45¼in.
(Sotheby's Belgravia) **$805** **£400**

GEORGE BRYANT CAMPION – Figures And A Pony Beside A Highland Loch – signed with initials – pencil and watercolour heightened with white – 8¼ x 13¾in.
(Christie's) **$126** **£65**

FREDERICO DEL CAMPO – Scenes In Venice – oil on panel – 5 x 8in.
(W. H. Lane & Son)
$4,416 **£2,300 Pair**

VINCENZO CAMUCCINI – The Finding Of Romulus And Remus – 17 x 25¼in.
(Christie's) **$3,456** **£1,800**

CANADIAN SCHOOL – A Young Indian Girl Winding Wool – signed and dated 1910 and inscribed on the reverse – oil on canvas – 45½ x 31½in.
(Sotheby's) **$356** **£180**

CANADIAN SCHOOL, late 19th century – Canadian Prospectors Paddling Downstream In A Canoe – oil on canvas – 10¾ x 15¾in.
(Sotheby's) **$512** **£260**

CANALETTO – A View Of The Piazzetta, Venice, Looking North – 32½ x 50¼in.
(Sotheby's) **$2,328** **£1,200**

CANALETTO – A View Of Charing Cross – 24 x 30½in.
(Christie's) **$873** **£450**

CANALETTO – Venice: The Grand Canal And Santa Maria Della Salute – 27¾ x 43¼in.
(Sotheby's) **$10,088** **£52,000**

ANTONIO CANALE, Called Canaletto *(1697-1768)* – Venice: The Colleoni Statue And The Church Of SS. Giovanni And Paolo – 16¼ x 13¼in.
(Sotheby's) **$79,200** **£40,000**

ANTONIO CANALE, Called Canaletto *(1697-1768)* – Venice: The Molo And The Entrance To The Grand Canal – 70½ x 101in.
(Sotheby's) **$356,400** **£180,000**

ANTONIO CANALE, Called Canaletto *(1697-1768)* – Venice: The Bacino Di San Marco – 23 x 36½in.
(Sotheby's) **$237,600** **£120,000**

ANTONIO CANALE, Called Canaletto *(1697-1768)* – Venice: Santa Maria Della Salute – 18¼ x 15in.
(Sotheby's) **$110,880 £56,000**

GIUSEPPE CANELLA – A Street Scene In Rome – signed and dated 1830 – bodycolour – 187 x 228mm.
(Christie's) **$798 £420**

P. CANDIDO – The Death Of Cleopatra – 48½ x 40in.
(Sotheby's) **$5,544 £2,800**

ANTONIO CANOVA – Four Young Women Dancing – grisaille – 26 x 44¾in.
(Christie's) **$7,296 £3,800**

POLIDORO CALDARA DA CARAVAGGIO, Circle of – A Scene From The Story Of Niobe – pen and brown ink, brown wash heightened with white on blue paper – 19.7 x 42.1cm.
(Christie's) **$460 £240**

J. W. CAREY – A View Of Portora, Enniskillen – signed, dated 1917 and inscribed – heightened with bodycolour – 10¼ x 31¼in.
(Sotheby's) **$330 £170**

CARLEVARIS – A Caprice View Of A Southern Port – 38 x 50in.
(Sotheby's) **$7,524 £3,800**

GEORGE F. CARLINE – 'Go On In Virtuous Seed Sowing' – signed, inscribed and signed again on the reverse – 51¼ x 33¼in.
(Christie's) **$970 £500**

GEORGE F. CARLINE – A Harvest Landscape With A Woman And Children In The Foreground – signed – on panel – 7½ x 11in.
(Christie's) **$1,746 £900**

GIOVANNI BATTISTA CARLONE – The Assumption Of The Magdalen, St. Mary Magdalene – 67 x 47¾in.
(Sotheby's) **$1,650 £850**

JOHN WILSON CARMICHAEL – A Wooded Landscape With A Figure On A Path – signed on a letter on the reverse – on panel – 8 x 6in.
(Christie's) **$349 £180**

JOHN WILSON CARMICHAEL – Scarborough Beach – signed and dated 1864 – 17½ x 31½in.
(Sotheby's Belgravia)
$4,225 £2,100

J. W. CARMICHAEL – "St. Michael's Mount, Cornwall", A Tall-Masted Sailing Ship And A Fishing Boat In Choppy Waters – oil on canvas – 24 x 30in.
(Morphets of Harrogate)
$1,746 £900

ANTHONY CARO – Head Of A Man – signed and dated 1956 – monotype – 23 x 17¾in.
(Sotheby's) **$495 £250**

CARON – A Classical Warrior With A Bow pen and brown ink, grey wash on brown paper – 17.4 x 10.3cm.
(Christie's) **$124 £65**

CAROSELLI – Saint Cecilia, Playing The Cello Accompanied By A Musical Angel – on panel – 16¾ x 13¼in.
(Sotheby's) **$931 £480**

CARRACCI – Portrait Of The Artist, Head And Shoulders – 16 x 10¾in.
(Christie's) **$1,164 £600**

CARRACCI – The Martyrdom Of Saint Stephen – 45¾ x 34¾in.
(Christie's) **$427 £220**

AGOSTINO CARRACCI, Circle of – Trees On A Rocky Outcrop Above A Lake – dated 1641 – pen and brown ink – 31.1 x 20.5cm.
(Christie's) **$365 £190**

ANNIBALE CARRACCI, Attributed to – Portrait Of A Nobleman – oil on panel – 21 x 18½in.
(Morton's Auction Exchange, Inc.)
$1,550 £782

ANNIBALE CARRACCI – The Butcher's Shop – 23½ x 28¼in.
(Christie's) **$499,200 £260,000**

ROBERT CARRICK – Picking Flowers – signed and dated 1887 – heightened with white – 14 x 17in.
(Sotheby's) **$515 £260**

ROSALBA CARRIERA – Portrait Of Lord Sidney Beauclerk, Half Length, In Grey Velvet Coat, Lined In Pink, Embroidered Grey Waistcoat And White Lace Stock - pastel on blue paper – 54.2 x 41.2cm.
(Christie's) **$21,120 £11,000**

LOUIS ROBERT CARRIER-BELLEUSE – Deux Danseuses – signed – pastel – 39 x 31½in.
(Sotheby's) **$1,520 £800**

DORA CARRINGTON – Ted At The Violin, A Study Of The Artist's Family – pencil – 10¾ x 12in.
(Sotheby's) **$356 £180**

DORA CARRINGTON – Ship's Bell And Rope – pencil and sepia wash – 5¾ x 7in.
(Sotheby's) **$396 £200**

HENRY BARLOW CARTER – Fishing Boats Off Whitby In Stormy Weather – signed and dated 1860 – watercolour – 6½ x 9¼in.
(Christie's) **$252 £130**

SAMUEL JOHN CARTER – Tigers Resting – signed, inscribed and dated 1867 – 15½ x 28¼in.
(Christie's) **$737 £380**

F. CASANOVA – The Aftermath Of A Battle, In The Foreground A Mounted Soldier And Another Attend To A Fallen Horse And Rider – bears signature and dated 1771 – on panel – 16½ x 20in.
(Sotheby's) **$1,683 £850**

JACOPO DEL CASENTINO – The Madonna And Child Enthroned With Saint Francis, Another Male Saint And Four Angels – on gold ground panel – 9½ x 6in.
(Christie's) **$7,372 £3,800**

CASOLANI – The Pieta – black chalk and brown wash on brown paper – 247 x 193mm.
(Christie's) **$105 £55**

EDMOND CASTAN – The Reading Lesson, Depicting Interior Scene With Mother Figure Rocking Cradle And Attending Young Daughter With Book – signed and dated 1872 – oil on panel – 10½ x 8½in.
(Richard Baker & Baker)
$8,342 £4,300

GUSTAVE CASTAN – Fontaine Dans Un Sous-Bois – oil on board – 35 x 45cm.
(Christian Rosset) **$811 £403**

CASTEELS – Poultry In Landscapes – on copper – 7¾ x 10¼in.
(Christie's) **$1,261 £650 Pair**

P. CASTEELS – A Chorus Of Birds, Perched On A Tree-top – 43¼ x 70¼in.
(Sotheby's) **$4,356 £2,200**

CASTELLI – The Adoration Of The Magi; and The Presentation Of The Virgin In The Temple – bears indistinct signature – 13½ x 19½in.
(Christie's) **$1,746 £900 Pair**

G. B. CASTIGLIONE – The Animals Entering The Ark, In A Landscape – 53 x 77in.
(Sotheby's) **$3,960 £2,000**

CATLIN, After – Black Hawk And Followers In Balls And Chains – inscribed and dated 1832 – pen and brown ink, watercolour – 6½ x 10½in.
(Sotheby's) **$512 £260**

JACOB CATS – A Herdsman Under A Cliff Overlooking A Valley – signed and dated 1779 on the reverse – pen and brown ink, grey wash – 17.7 x 24.6cm.
(Christie's) **$1,248 £650**

CHARLES CATTERMOLE – A Hawking Party – signed – watercolour heightened with white – 5¾ x 17¾in.
(Christie's) **$146 £75**

CHARLES CATTERMOLE – Worshippers Arriving At The Entrance To An Abbey – signed – watercolour – 5¾ x 17¾in.
(Christie's) **$107 £55**

GEORGE CATTERMOLE – Viola And Olivia In 'Twelfth Night' – signed with a monogram – 16½ x 21½in.
(Sotheby's Belgravia) **$192 £100**

E. CATTS – Well-Wooded River Landscape, With A Cottage Among Trees, A Fisherman In A Coat, Buildings On The Far Shore – signed – oil on canvas – 48 x 73cm.
(Henry Spencer & Sons) **$223 £115**

LOUIS DE CAULLERY – The Building Of The Tower Of Babel – on panel – 22 x 32¾in.
(Sotheby's) **$27,440 £14,000**

LOUIS DE CAULLERY – The Piazza San Marco, Venice; A Caprice View Of A City – on panel – 18½ x 30¼in.
(Sotheby's) **$10,780 £5,500 Two**

L. DE CAULLERY – A Festival In Rome – on panel – 22½ x 35¾in.
(Sotheby's) **$6,790** **£3,500**

L. DE CAULLERY – A Contest Between The Fishermen's Guild And The Butcher's Guild In A Town Street – on panel – 27½ x 41¼in.
(Christie's) **$14,400** **£7,500**

JULES CAVAILLES – Matinee a Cannes – signed – oil on canvas – 82 x 66cm.
(Christian Rosset) **$2,551** **£1,268**

ANTONION CAVALLUCCI – Portrait Of Saint Benedict Joseph Labre, Small Half Length – 22½ x 17¼in.
(Christie's) **$7,680** **£4,000**

PETER LA CAVE – A Beached Fishing Boat With Fishermen Attending To Their Nets – signed and dated – 11 x 11¾in.
(Lawrence) **$61** **£32**

PETER LA CAVE – Keswick Bridge And A Distant View Of Skiddaw, Cumberland – inscribed – pen and black ink and watercolour – 8 x 10¾in.
(Sotheby's) **$776** **£400**

PETER LA CAVE – Telling The Table – signed and dated 1799 – pen and brown ink and watercolour – 15 x 20¾in.
(Sotheby's) **$780** **£400**

PETER LA CAVE – Travellers On A Road – pen and black ink, watercolour – 4¼ x 5½in.
(Sotheby's) **$878** **£450 Three**

PETER LA CAVE – A Herdsman And Cow Near A House – pen and grey ink and watercolour – 7½ x 10¾in.
(Christie's) **$87** **£45**

JEAN-CHARLES CAZIN – A L'Entree Du Village – signed and inscribed – charcoal on beige paper – 10½ x 9in.
(Sotheby's) **$162** **£85**

SEBASTIANO CECCARINI – Portrait Of A Cardinal, Bust Length – 21¾ x 20¼in.
(Christie's) **$864** **£450**

GASPARE CELIO – Portrait Of A Jesuit, Small Three-Quarter Length, At An Altar – indistinctly signed and dated 1603, and bears inscription on the reverse – on copper – 13¾ x 10in.
(Christie's) **$576** **£300**

G. CESARI – The Assumption Of The Virgin, With Saints Beneath – on panel – 33 x 27in.
(Christie's) **$970** **£500**

CORNELIUS JOHNSON, Janssens Van Ceulen – Portrait Of A White-Bearded Man – on panel – 30½ x 25in.
(Sotheby's) **$3,920** **£2,000**

JOHN CHALMERS – Ailsa From The Shore – signed, inscribed on a label – 15½ x 21in.
(Sotheby's) **$268** **£140**

JOHN JAMES CHALON – Cattle In A Hill Meadow; Driving The Cattle Home – signed and dated 1833 and 1834 – 12½ x 16¼in.
(Sotheby's) **$546** **£280 Pair**

GEORGE CHAMBERS – A Shipwreck Off Mont Saint Michel – signed and dated 1838 – on panel – 19¾ x 23¾in.
(Christie's) **$3,686** **£1,900**

PHILIPPE DE CHAMPAGNE – Portrait Of Francois Lotin De Charny Conseiller Du Parlement, Bust Length – 25¼ x 20¼in.
(Christie's) **$12,480** **£6,500**

CHAMPAIGNE – L'Abbe Seguier – grey wash – 290 x 199mm.
(Christie's) **$49** **£26**

BENJAMIN CHAMPNEY – 'Waterbury, Vermont' – signed – oil on canvas – 22 x 36in.
(Morton's Auction Exchange, Inc.) **$1,800** **£913**

CHARLES CHAPLIN – Portrait de Femme – signed – oil on canvas – 23½ x 19¼in.
(Sotheby's) **$322** **£160**

CONRAD WISE CHAPMAN – Harvesters In The Campagna – inscribed and dated 1867 on the reverse – oil on board – 10 x 14in.
(Sotheby's) **$788** **£400**

E. CHARLEMONT – Interior Scene With Lady Holding A Brass Ewer – signed and dated 1884 – oil on canvas – 17½ x 16in.
(The Manchester Auction Mart.) **$1,408** **£700**

E. CHARLEMONT, 19th century – A Head And Shoulders Study Of The Young David – oil on canvas – 19¾ x 14¼in.
(The Manchester Auction Mart.) **$322** **£160**

NICOLAS TOUSSAINT CHARLET – Le Petit Voyageur – signed and inscribed – pencil and coloured crayons – 7 x 5in.
(Sotheby's) **$418** **£220**

JOHN CHARLTON – Farmyard Scene With A Grey Mare And Bay Foal Standing On The Cobbled Yard With A Dog, A Cat, Chickens And Other Birds, A Cow In A Byre, And Trees Beyond – monogrammed and dated 1873 – oil on canvas – 85 x 110cm.
(Henry Spencer & Sons) **$3,267** **£1,650**

PIERRE PUVIS DE CHAVANNES – Tete De Profil – pen and indian ink – 3 x 2¾in.
(Sotheby's) **$198** **£100**

E. CHESTER – Still Lives Of Fruit And Flowers – all signed – on board – 11¾ x 7¾ and 7¾ x 11¾in.
(Sotheby's Belgravia) **$61** **£32 Four**

NICHOLAS CHEVALIER – The Taj At Agra – signed and dated 1870, inscribed – pen and brown ink, watercolour, heightened with white – 5½ x 8¼in.
(Sotheby's) **$433 £220**

GIUSEPPE BARTOLOMEO CHIARI – Time Revealing Truth – 67½ x 57½in.
(Christie's) **$2,496 £1,300**

CHINESE SCHOOL, 19th century – Two Ladies In An Interior – on reverse of glass – 19¼ x 13½in.
(Sotheby's (Hong Kong) Ltd.)
$974 £492

CHINESE SCHOOL, circa 1820 – A Mandarin, Half Length, Wearing A Fur Trimmed Coat And Hat, Holding An Arrow – watercolour, heightened with bodycolour and gold – 13¼ x 8½in.
(Sotheby's (Hong Kong) Ltd.)
$606 £306

CHINESE SCHOOL, circa 1830 – The Waterfront At Canton Showing The Austrian, American, British And Dutch Flags – 16 x 23¼in.
(Sotheby's (Hong Kong) Ltd.)
$6,924 £3,497

CHINESE SCHOOL, 19th century – Portrait Of A Mandarin, Seated Half Length – canvas on board – 42 x 30in.
(Sotheby's (Hong Kong) Ltd.)
$607 £306

CHINESE SCHOOL, circa 1810 – Whampoa Anchorage From Dane's Island, With American, Austrian, Dutch And British Shipping – 15 x 20in.
(Sotheby's (Hong Kong) Ltd.)
$2,499 £1,262

CHINESE SCHOOL, circa 1880 – Hong Kong Harbour With British Naval And Merchant Ships At Anchor – 12¼ x 28in.
(Sotheby's (Hong Kong) Ltd.)
$3,463 £1,749

CHINESE SCHOOL, circa 1840 – Portrait Of A Woman Wearing A Blue Dress Seated By A Table – 14 x 11½in.
(Sotheby's (Hong Kong) Ltd.)
$433 £219

CHINESE SCHOOL, circa 1810 – The Waterfront At Canton, Showing The Austrian, American, British And Dutch Flags – 17¾ x 23in.
(Sotheby's (Hong Kong) Ltd.)
$7,789 £3,934

CHINESE SCHOOL, 19th century – A View Of Whampoa Anchorage Seen From Dane Island, With British And French Shipping At Anchor And Junks Under Sail – 17½ x 30¼in.
(Sotheby's (Hong Kong) Ltd.)
$2,595 £1,311

CHINESE SCHOOL, circa 1900 – A View Of Hong Kong By Night – 9 x 20in.
(Sotheby's (Hong Kong) Ltd.)
$497 £251

CHINESE SCHOOL, 19th century – An Extensive View Of The Praya Grande, Macao – 17½ x 30¼in.
(Sotheby's (Hong Kong) Ltd.)
$4,544 £2,295

CHINESE SCHOOL, 19th century – A Mandarin Officer And His Entourage In A Landscape – on reverse of mirrored glass – 17 x 23¼in.
(Sotheby's (Hong Kong) Ltd.)
$432 £218

CHINESE SCHOOL, circa 1830 – An Extensive View Of Macao From The South – 18 x 23¾in.
(Sotheby's (Hong Kong) Ltd.)
$2,380 £1,202

CHINESE SCHOOL – Princess Scindwaty, A British Packet Ship, Leaving Hong Kong, E. Roy Master – inscribed and dated 1860 – 17½ x 23in.
(Sotheby's (Hong Kong) Ltd.)
$518 £262

CHINESE SCHOOL, 19th century – Portraits Of Young Chinese Ladies, Three-Quarter Length, Standing Holding Sprigs Of Flowers – 15½ x 12¼in.
(Sotheby's (Hong Kong) Ltd.)
$6,492 £3,279 Two

CHINESE SCHOOL, 19th century – Flowers And Birds – inscribed – on reverse of glass – 19¼ x 13in.
(Sotheby's (Hong Kong) Ltd.)
$434 £219

CHINESE SCHOOL, circa 1840 – A View Of Part Of The Waterfront, Canton – 23½ x 19½in.
(Sotheby's (Hong Kong) Ltd.)
$1,190 £601

CHINESE SCHOOL, mid 19th century – Processions Outside Temples – 8¼ x 11in.
(Sotheby's (Hong Kong) Ltd.)
$4,328 £2,186 Pair

CHINESE SCHOOL, 19th century – Portrait Of A Mandarin Seated, Full Length, Wearing Blue Robes – gouache – 31½ x 19¼in.
(Sotheby's (Hong Kong) Ltd.)
$822 £415

CHINESE SCHOOL, circa 1890 – M.S.S. Machiak, Flying The American Flag, Underway Off The Coast Of China – 25¼ x 34¼in.
(Sotheby's (Hong Kong) Ltd.)
$758 £383

CHINESE SCHOOL, circa 1850 – A Scholar In An Interior Reading A Book – 17 x 13½in.
(Sotheby's (Hong Kong) Ltd.)
$519 £262

CHINESE SCHOOL, circa 1840 – Portrait Of A Mandarin, Half Length – 22¾ x 17½in.
(Sotheby's (Hong Kong) Ltd.)
$865 £437

CHINESE SCHOOL, 19th century – Study Of An Empress – watercolour – 34 x 23in.
(Morton's Auction Exchange, Inc.)
$470 £237

G. CHINNERY – Portrait Of W. W. Wood, Half Length, Writing In A Book On A Table – 9¼ x 7¾in.
(Sotheby's (Hong Kong) Ltd.)
$1,297 £655

G. CHINNERY – Portrait Of A Gentleman, Seated, Three-Quarter Length, Wearing A Dark Suit – 10¾ x 9in.
(Sotheby's (Hong Kong) Ltd.)
$1,514 £765

G. CHINNERY – A Joss House, The Inner Harbour, Macao – 11¾ x 19¾in.
(Sotheby's (Hong Kong) Ltd.)
$4,110 £2,076

G. CHINNERY – A Riverside Temple, Junks And Sampans In The Foreground – 11¾ x 19¾in.
(Sotheby's (Hong Kong) Ltd.)
$2,596 £1,311

GEORGE CHINNERY – Portrait Of A Gentleman Said To Be The Artist As A Young Man, Half Length, Wearing A Black Coat – 8¾ x 7¼in.
(Sotheby's (Hong Kong) Ltd.)
$3,676 £1,857

GEORGE CHINNERY – Cattle With A Farmhand By A River – 5½ x 7in.
(Sotheby's) **$1,164 £600**

GEORGE CHINNERY – Portrait Of A Young Man, Three-Quarter Length, Seated By A Table Holding A Book – 11¼ x 9¾in.
(Sotheby's (Hong Kong) Ltd.)
$3,894 £1,967

GEORGE CHINNERY – Two Indian Figures Outside A Dwelling, One Smoking A Hookah Pipe – inscribed and dated '18 – pencil – 6¼ x 9in.
(Sotheby's (Hong Kong) Ltd.)
$390 £197

GEORGE CHINNERY – Portrait Of Captain Henry Gribble, Half Length, Seated Wearing A Dark Coat – 9 x 7¾in.
(Sotheby's (Hong Kong) Ltd.)
$6,058 £3,060

GEORGE CHINNERY – A Woman Holding A Child – pen and sepia ink – 4½ x 4in.
(Sotheby's (Hong Kong) Ltd.)
$649 £328

GEORGE CHINNERY – Study Of A Sleeping Baby – inscribed and dated 1823 – pen and black ink – 5 x 4¾in.
(Sotheby's (Hong Kong) Ltd.)
$97 £49

GEORGE CHINNERY – Cattle Watering By A Bend In The River – 4½ x 7¾in.
(Sotheby's) **$815 £420**

CHINNERY – Chinese River, Stream And Coast Scenes – 45 x 58cm.
(Edmiston's) **$194 £100 Pair**

CHINNERY – A Chinese Coastal View, With A Dwelling In The Foreground – 5½ x 4½in.
(Sotheby's (Hong Kong) Ltd.)
$562 £284

JAMES ELDER CHRISTIE – Near Larbie Beg, Arran – signed – canvas on panel – 11 x 14½in.
(Sotheby's) **$576 £300**

CHRISTO – Houston Mastaba – Stacked Oil Drums – signed, inscribed and dated 1965-70 – pencil and coloured crayons – 36½ x 65½in.
(Sotheby's) **$15,840 £8,000**

CHRISTO – Yellow Store Front – signed, inscribed and dated 1965-66 – oil and mixed media on wood – 29 x 24in.
(Sotheby's) **$6,138** **£3,100**

THOMAS CHURCHYARD – Figures In A Boat On A River In A Wooded Landscape – watercolour – 6 x 8in.
(Christie's) **$252** **£130**

CIGNANI – The Personification Of Poetry – 35 x 29¾in.
(Christie's) **$737** **£380**

GIANBETTINO CIGNAROLI – The Adoration Of The Shepherds – 11½ x 8¼in.
(Christie's) **$1,067** **£550**

LODOVICO CARDI, IL CIGOLI – The Penitent Magdalen – 21¼ x 17in.
(Christie's) **$3,880** **£2,000**

CIMAROLI – Italianate Wooded River Landscapes With Figures – on panel – oval – 12 x 13¾in.
(Christie's) **$1,552** **£800**

GIOVANNI BATTISTA CIPRIANI – Cephalus And Procris – black chalk, pen and black ink, brown wash – 183 x 243mm.
(Christie's) **$152** **£80**

CLAESSINS – Saint Luke Painting The Virgin – on panel – circular – diameter 11¾in.
(Christie's) **$1,455** **£750**

GEORGE CLARE – Still Life Of Primulas – on board – 6¾ x 9¾in.
(Sotheby's Belgravia) **$384** **£200**

GEORGE CLARE – Still Life Of Flowers By A Bank – on board – 5 x 10in.
(Sotheby's Belgravia) **$95** **£50**

OLIVER CLARE – Still Lives Of Fruit By Mossy Banks – both signed – 6 x 7¾in.
(Sotheby's Belgravia)
$1,632 **£850 Pair**

OLIVER CLARE – A Peach, Plums And Raspberries – signed – 10½ x 8¼in.
(Christie's) **$737** **£380**

OLIVER CLARE – 'Still Life – Plums, Greengages And Strawberries' – signed – oil on canvas – 7 x 10in.
(Lalonde Bros. & Parham) **$218** **£110**

VINCENT CLARE – Still Life Of Apples And Grapes – signed – 19 x 23in.
(Sotheby's Belgravia) **$3,420** **£1,700**

VINCENT CLARE – A Basket Of Grapes, Plums And Peaches By A Mossy Bank – signed – 19¼ x 23¼in.
(Christie's) **$1,843** **£950**

VINCENT CLARE – Still Lives Of Fruit And Flowers By A Bank – signed and inscribed on the reverse – 9 x 13in.
(Sotheby's Belgravia) **$456** **£240 Pair**

VINCENT CLARE – Still-life: Plums, Peaches And Grapes On A Mossy Bank; And Primroses, Lilac And Apple Blossom – signed – oil on canvas – 17 x 24cm.
(Henry Spencer & Sons) **$1,901** **£980 Pair**

VINCENT CLARE – Still Lives Of Fruit And Flowers – both signed – 9½ x 7½in.
(Sotheby's Belgravia) **$864** **£450 Pair**

JAMES CLARK – Kilchurn Castle, Loch Awe – signed and dated 1867 – 29 x 49in.
(Sotheby's) **$960** **£500**

LOUIS E. CLARK – The Liane, Pas De Calais, France – signed, inscribed – 14 x 18in.
(Sotheby's Belgravia) **$83** **£42**

M. A. CLARK – A Springer Spaniel – signed – oil on canvas – 10 x 14in.
(Andrew, Hilditch & Son) **$293** **£140**

O. T. CLARK – Warwick Castle In Landscape – oil – 20 x 30in.
(Husseys) **$243** **£125**

WILLIAM CLARK – Ships Becalmed Off The Scottish Coast – signed and dated 1870 – 11½ x 19½in.
(Sotheby's) **$1,824** **£950**

W. H. CLARKE – By A Lake – signed and dated 1920 – 24½ x 30in.
(Sotheby's) **$576** **£300**

SIR GEORGE CLAUSEN – Blonde – signed – 17½ x 13½in.
(Sotheby's) **$891** **£450**

SIR GEORGE CLAUSEN – A Young Dutch Girl On A Seashore – signed and dated 1876 – 18 x 14½in.
(Christie's) **$3,800** **£2,000**

SIR GEORGE CLAUSEN – Searchlights – signed – 9½ x 14in.
(Sotheby's Belgravia) **$172** **£90**

P. J. CLAYS – The Royal Yacht Coming Into Harbour After A Gale – signed and dated 1839 – on panel – 17 x 23½in.
(Sotheby's Belgravia) **$1,509** **£750**

PAUL JEAN CLAYS – Fishing Boats In Harbour – signed – black chalk and grey wash – 153 x 263mm.
(Christie's) **$456** **£240**

J. HUGHES CLAYTON – Cemeas Bay, Anglesey – signed – heightened with white – 10 x 14in.
(Sotheby's Belgravia) **$69** **£35**

JAMES HUGHES CLAYTON – Cottages – watercolour – 11 x 17¾in.
(Outhwaite & Litherland) **$505** **£250 Pair**

T. HUGHES CLAYTON – Drying The Sails, Camis Bay, Anglesey, North Wales – watercolour – 10 x 14in.
(G. A. Key) **$158** **£80**

JOOS VAN CLEEVE – The Crucifixion – on panel – 22 x 19¼in.
(Christie's) **$28,800** **£15,000**

VAN CLEEVE – An Infant Boy, Small Full Length, Seated On A Cushion, Eating Cherries – on panel – 13¾ x 10½in.
(Christie's) **$1,358** **£700**

ROBERT CLEMINSON – Retrievers – signed – 35 x 27in.
(Sotheby's) **$515** **£260**

R. CLEMINSON – Dogs On A Moor – bears signature – 36 x 28in.
(Sotheby's) **$317** **£160**

JACQUES LOUIS CLERISSEAU – Warriors In A Ruined Basilica – signed and dated 1761 – black chalk, grey wash heightened with white – 57.5 x 43.6cm.
(Christie's) **$1,632** **£850**

CLERISSEAU – Rome With Fireworks On Castel Sant' Angelo – watercolour and body-colour – 352 x 423mm.
(Christie's) **$114** **£60**

C. VAN CLEVE – The Nativity, The Virgin Adoring The Infant Christ Who Lies On The Skirt Of Her Red Cloak – on panel – 40½ x 31in.
(Sotheby's) **$7,840** **£4,000**

VAN CLEVE – The Christ Child And The Infant Saint John Embracing – on panel – 14 x 19in.
(Sotheby's) **$310** **£160**

J. VAN CLEVE – The Death Of Lucretia, Who Is Seated Wearing A Scarlet Cloak – on panel – 20¾ x 15¼in.
(Sotheby's) **$1,552** **£800**

JOOS VAN CLEVE, After – Portrait Of An Elderly Man, Bust Length, Wearing A Black Silk Robe With Black And Gold Brocade Collar And Black Hat – on panel – 24 x 17in.
(Sotheby's) **$1,584** **£800**

MARTEN VAN CLEVE – The Massacre Of The Innocents – on panel – 27¾ x 41¾in.
(Sotheby's) **$41,160** **£21,000**

EDWARD C. CLIFFORD – Ribbons And Lace – signed – on board – 17½ x 7½in.
(Sotheby's Belgravia)
$3,018 **£1,500**

CLOUET – Portrait Of Charles VII Of France, Bust Length, Wearing A Plumed Cap – on panel – 16½ x 13in.
(Christie's) **$126** **£65**

CLOUET – Portrait Of A Young Lady, Small Bust Length, Wearing A Ruff And An Embroidered Dress – on panel – 10½ x 8¼in.
(Christie's) **$931** **£480**

ALFRED CLINT – Jersey – signed – 23½ x 35in.
(Sotheby's Belgravia) **$5,633** **£2,800**

CLUETT – The 'Naiad', A Battle Cruiser – inscribed and dated 1890 – heightened with white – 9¼ x 13¼in.
(Sotheby's Belgravia) **$15** **£8 Three**

VICTOR COBB – Canberra 1913 – watercolour – 19 x 36cm.
(Australian Art Auctions) **$29** **£15**

VICTOR COBB – River Vista – signed – pencil drawing – 22.5 x 30cm.
(Australian Art Auctions) **$35** **£18**

FREDERICK SIMPSON COBURN – Horses Drawing Logs In The Laurentian Hills, Quebec – signed and dated '24 – oil on canvas – 14½ x 17½in.
(Sotheby's) **$5,910** **£3,000**

COCCORANTE – Italianate Wooded Landscapes With Classical Ruins – 11¾ x 7½in.
(Christie's) **$1,188** **£600 Pair**

LEONARDO COCCORANTE – A Landscape With A Roman Ruin, Figures On The Steps Of A Ruined Classical Building With Doric Columns; A Ship In A Storm, A Ship In Rough Sea Driving Towards A Shore – both signed in monogram – 24 x 18¾in.
(Sotheby's) **$6,790** **£3,500 Pair**

CODAZZI – The Flight Into Egypt – canvas on board – 17 x 21¾in.
(Christie's) **$776** **£400**

CODAZZI – A View Of A Classical Palace – 29¼ x 38¼in.
(Sotheby's) **$970** **£500**

V. CODAZZI – A Capriccio Of A Classical Ruin With Soldiers – 23 x 28¾in.
(Christie's) **$2,716** **£1,400**

V. CODAZZI – Mediterranean Port Scenes – 28 x 38in.
(Sotheby's) **$4,356** **£2,200 Pair**

V. CODAZZI – A Southern Landscape With Travellers Halted Outside An Inn, Beside The Ruins Of A Classical Temple – 26¼ x 19¾in.
(Sotheby's) **$2,970** **£1,500**

JAN COELENBIER – A Coastal Landscape With Figures On The Shore – bears monogram – on panel – 15¾ x 12¼in.
(Sotheby's) **$2,134** **£1,100**

COELLO – Portrait Of Philip II Of Spain, Standing Three-Quarter Length, Wearing A Brown Brocade Doublet and Ermine-Trimmed Cloak – 34 x 29in.
(Christie's) **$495** **£250**

M. COFFERMANS – The Education Of The Virgin – on panel – 12¾ x 10in.
(Christie's) **$6,208** **£3,200**

ELLEN COLE – Country Views – both signed – 23 x 11in.
(Sotheby's Belgravia)
$460 **£240 Pair**

GEORGE COLE – Extensive Surrey Summer Landscape – signed, inscribed and dated 1859 on reverse – oil on canvas – 13 x 19in.
(Bonham's) **$6,336** **£3,200**

GEORGE COLE – Homeward Bound – 16 x 24in.
(Sotheby's Belgravia)
$3,018 **£1,500**

GEORGE VICAT COLE – Cattle By A Highland River – signed with monogram and dated 1879 – heightened with white – 17 x 26in.
(Sotheby's Belgravia)
$268 **£140**

GEORGE VICAT COLE – Fields And A Wood On A Hillside – signed with monogram – watercolour – 8¼ x 13½in.
(Christie's) **$107** **£55**

J. W. COLE – Portraits Of Hunters – signed and dated '64 – 19½ x 23½in.
(Sotheby's Belgravia)
$570 £300 Pair

REX VICAT COLE – The Lollards' Tower, Lambeth Palace – signed, inscribed on a label on the reverse – 35 x 47½in.
(Sotheby's Belgravia)
$1,811 £900

REX VICAT COLE – The Old Barn – signed and dated 1932, inscribed on the reverse – 33 x 44in.
(Sotheby's Belgravia)
$1,006 £500

REX VICAT COLE – Whitehall From St. James's – signed, inscribed on a label on the reverse – 35½ x 53in.
(Sotheby's Belgravia)
$3,420 £1,700

V. COLE – Cornfield Near Getley, Worcestershire – bears monogram, inscribed on the reverse – 15½ x 23½in.
(Sotheby's Belgravia)
$384 £200

S. COLEIRAE – South American Gauchos Herding Cattle – indistinctly signed – watercolour – 25½ x 36¼in.
(Sotheby's) $108 £55

WILLIAM STEPHEN COLEMAN – Playtime – signed – on panel – 17½ x 11½in.
(Sotheby's Belgravia)
$1,811 £900

WILLIAM STEPHEN COLEMAN – Fairies – both signed – one heightened with white – circular – diameter 17in.
(Sotheby's Belgravia) **$730** **£380 Pair**

WILLIAM STEPHEN COLEMAN – Nature's Jewels – signed – heightened with bodycolour – 12 x 8in.
(Sotheby's Belgravia) **$475** **£250**

SAMUEL DAVID COLKETT – A Wooded River Landscape With A Shepherd And Sheep – on panel – 9¼ x 13½in.
(Christie's) **$931** **£480**

JOHN COLLETT – Six Studies – Five Of Birds, And One Of An Ermine – pen and black ink and watercolour – each drawing 3 x 4¾in.
(Sotheby's) **$780** **£400**

JOHN COLLETT – Studies Of Birds – pen and black ink and watercolour – 3 x 4¾in.
(Sotheby's) **$780** **£400 Six**

ARTHUR BEVAN COLLIER – Salisbury From The Avon – signed and dated 1899, inscribed on a label – 23½ x 39½in.
(Sotheby's Belgravia) **$456** **£240**

ARTHUR BEVAN COLLIER – Holly Street Mill, Chagford – dated '88 and inscribed on the reverse – 17½ x 11½in.
(Sotheby's Belgravia) **$95** **£50**

EVERT COLLIER – A 'Vanitas' Still Life – 29 x 23¼in.
(Sotheby's) **$7,372** **£3,800**

EVERT COLLIER – A Still Life With Books And A Globe – signed on a letter, inscribed – 29 x 24¾in.
(Sotheby's) **$5,880** **£3,000**

EVERT COLLIER – A Vanitas Still Life With A Globe And Musical Instruments – signed and dated 1669, inscribed – on panel – 12 x 10¼in.
(Sotheby's) **$7,128** **£3,600**

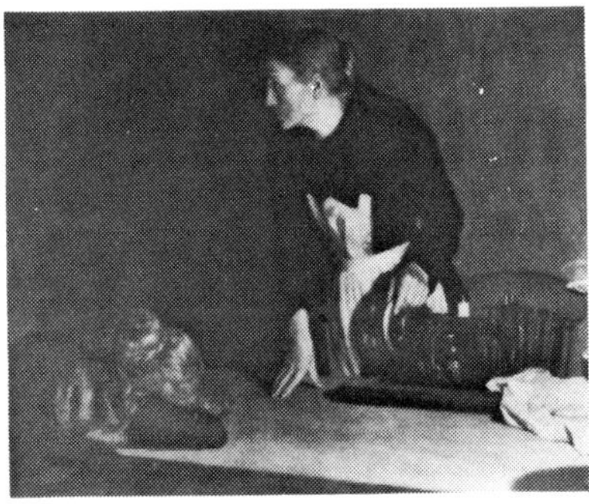

JOHN COLLIER – Trouble – 39 x 47in.
(Sotheby's Belgravia) **$2,414** **£1,200**

THOMAS F. COLLIER – Still Life Of Apples And Grapes – signed and dated 1874 – 11 x 15in.
(Sotheby's Belgravia) **$245** **£130**

W. COLLINGWOOD – The Matterhorn – 38 x 28½in.
(Sotheby's Belgravia) **$456** **£240**

COLLINS – A Fisherman And His Family On The Beach – 7½ x 11½in.
(Sotheby's Belgravia) **$422** **£220**

WILLIAM COLLINS – View On The Brent – signed and inscribed on the reverse – 13¾ x 16½in.
(Christie's) **$1,164** **£650**

W. COLLINS, After – Happy As A King – 7¼ x 9in.
(Sotheby's Belgravia) **$77** **£40**

ROBERT COLLINSON – A Quiet Dell – signed with monogram and dated 1862 and inscribed on the reverse – paper on canvas – 8 x 10¾in.
(Christie's) **$1,940** **£1,000**

CONCA – Saint Barbara – canvas on cardboard – circular – diameter 6¼in.
(Christie's) **$485** **£250**

S. CONCA – A Capriccio Of Mercury, Psyche And Cupid – on gold ground panel – 24¼ x 21½in.
(Christie's) **$1,746** **£900**

SEBASTIANO CONCA – Venus Appearing At The Forge Of Vulcan – pen and brown ink, brown wash heightened with white – diameter 43.8cm.
(Christie's) **$2,880** **£1,500**

SEBASTIANO CONCA – The Martyrdom Of Saint Erasmus – signed and dated 1729 – 28¾ x 24in.
(Christie's) **$2,688** **£1,400**

SEBASTIANO CONCA – An Academy Study Of A Male Nude As Bacchus – oil on paper on board – 18¼ x 13in.
(Christie's) **$730** **£380**

TOMMASO CONCA – The Visitation – 35½ x 28¾in.
(Christie's) **$1,344** **£700**

NICHOLAS CONDY – Boats In Cawsand Bay, Cornwall – inscribed on the reverse – watercolour and bodycolour – 4¼ x 3½in.
(Christie's) **$504** **£260**

D. DE CONINCK – A Boar Hunt – 67 x 102in.
(Christie's) **$5,044** **£2,600**

WILLIAM CONOR – My Mother – signed – coloured chalks on buff paper – 16½ x 12½in
(Sotheby's) **$1,125** **£580**

E. P. CONSTABLE – On The Cornish Coast – signed – 23 x 35in.
(Sotheby's Belgravia) **$194** **£100**

J. CONSTABLE – 'Brampton Village, Suffolk' – signed with initials – pencil and grey wash drawing – 7¾ x 4¾in.
(Manchester Auction Mart) **$545** **£270**

JOHN CONSTABLE – Cattle By A Pond, A Child Talking To A Maid, A Cottage Behind A Wooden Fence – pencil on paper – 7¼ x 9¼in.
(Sotheby's) **$1,940** **£1,000**

JOHN CONSTABLE – Flatford Meadows – inscribed and dated 1827 – 8¾ x 13in.
(Sotheby's) **$2,328** **£1,200**

CONSTABLE – Tulse Hill, Norwood – inscribed and dated 1832 – pencil – 6½ x 10¼in.
(Christie's) **$54** **£28**

H. CONSTANZ. – 'The Winning Card' – signed – oil on canvas – 15 x 19½in.
(Morton's Auction Exchange, Inc.) **$650** **£328**

LE CONTE – York – 22 x 29in.
(Sotheby's Belgravia) **$125** **£65**

CONTINENTAL SCHOOL, 19th century – 'Mediterranean Port' – oil on canvas – 27½ x 35½in.
(W. H. Lane & Son) **$291** **£150**

C. H. COOK – Three Irishmen, One Playing The Bagpipes, Another A Fiddle, And A Third Dancing A Jig And Twirling A Shillelagh, In A Country Lane – signed and dated 1883 – oil on canvas – 42 x 50cm.
(Henry Spencer & Sons) **$614 £310**

E. WAKE COOK – 'Ponte-Vecchio, Florence' – signed – watercolour – 15¼ x 21½in.
(Lalonde Bros. & Parham) **$549 £280**

JOSHUA COOK, JNR. – Still Life Of Fruit – signed – oval – 19 x 23½in.
(Sotheby's Belgravia) **$182 £950**

WILLIAM COOK – A Rocky Cove – signed with monogram and dated '82 – watercolour heightened with white – 12½ x 20¼in.
(Christie's) **$155 £80**

WILLIAM COOK OF PLYMOUTH – Bedruthan Steps, North Cornwall – signed with monogram and dated '87 – watercolour heightened with white – 25 x 39in.
(Christie's) **$213 £110**

EDWARD WILLIAM COOKE – Santa Lucia, Port Of Cartagena, East Coast Of Spain – signed and dated 1865 – 14½ x 22¾in.
(Sotheby's Belgravia) **$6,036 £3,000**

EDWARD WILLIAM COOKE – Venetian Fishing Craft Off The Lido – signed and dated 1858, and signed and inscribed on an old label on the reverse – 24½ x 40in.
(Christie's) **$8,730 £4,500**

EDWARD W. COOKE – 'Dutch Shipping In The Zuyder Zee' – signed and dated 1863 – oil – 23½ x 17½in.
(Phillips) **$2,178 £1,100**

E. W. COOKE, 19th century – Italian Landscape With Ruins – oil on board – 12 x 15½in.
(Butler & Hatch Waterman) **$503 £250**

E. W. COOKE – Fisherfolk Cooking Lobsters On A Beach – on panel – 6¾ x 23½in.
(Christie's) **$970 £500**

ISAAC COOKE – The Evening Light, Stable Hills, Derwentwater – signed – 29½ x 47½in.
(Sotheby's Belgravia) **$570 £300**

ISAAC COOKE – Shooting Grouse – signed – 11 x 20in.
(Sotheby's Belgravia)
$69 £35

HUBERT COOP – A Coastal Landscape With Fisherfolk And Beached Fishing Boats – signed – 31 x 55in.
(Lawrence) **$361 £190**

A. COOPER – An Unofficial Gathering – 14 x 19¼in.
(Sotheby's Belgravia) **$323 £170**

ABRAHAM COOPER – A Sportsman's Rest – signed with monogram and dated 1854 – on board – 9½ x 12in.
(Sotheby's) **$768 £400**

HENRY COOPER – Ben Scoust; Near Ardoula, North Harris – signed – heightened with bodycolour – 11 x 17¾in.
(Sotheby's Belgravia)
$57 £30 Pair

PHYLLIS M. COOPER – The Speedster; Little Mother – signed – heightened with bodycolour – 9 x 13in.and 17¾ x 11½in.
(Sotheby's Belgravia)
$34 £18 Two

THOMAS SIDNEY COOPER – Cattle Resting On The Banks Of A River, Trees And Buildings Beyond, Under A Cloudy Summer Sky – 30 x 55cm.
(Henry Spencer & Sons)
$634 £320

THOMAS SIDNEY COOPER – Canterbury Meadows – signed and dated 1897 – 20 x 28in.
(Christie's) **$1,261 £650**

THOMAS SIDNEY COOPER – Cows In A Meadow – signed and dated 1897 – on board – 24 x 17¾in.
(Christie's) **$1,067 £550**

THOMAS SIDNEY COOPER – An Approaching Storm – signed and dated 1892 – 29 x 49in.
(Sotheby's Belgravia)
$9,054 £4,500

THOMAS SIDNEY COOPER – Where Sheep May Safely Graze – signed, indistinctly inscribed and dated '69 – on panel – 17½ x 23¼in.
(Sotheby's Belgravia)
$3,420 £1,700

THOMAS SIDNEY COOPER – Cattle Watering At A Pond – signed and dated '67 – on board – 9½ x 11½in.
(Christie's) **$1,164 £600**

THOMAS SIDNEY COOPER – Cattle And Sheep By An Estuary – signed and dated 1857 – 17¼ x 23½in.
(Sotheby's Belgravia)
$2,012 £1,000

T. S. COOPER – Sheep In A River Landscape – bears signature and the date 1876 – 15½ x 19½in.
(Christie's) **$291 £150**

THOMAS SIDNEY COOPER – Cattle And Sheep On The Sussex Marshes – signed and dated 1872 – oil – 30 x 43in.
(Laurence & Martin Taylor)
$7,524 £3,600

T. S. COOPER – Cattle By A River – signed and dated 1877 – 29 x 47in.
(Sotheby's Belgravia) **$891 £450**

WILLIAM SIDNEY COOPER – Cattle In A Meadow – signed and dated 1904 – 29½ x 19½in.
(Sotheby's Belgravia) **$1,056 £550**

WILLIAM SIDNEY COOPER – An Extensive Wooded Landscape With Sheep In The Foreground – signed and dated 1893 – 19¼ x 29¼in.
(Christie's) **$1,552 £800**

WILLIAM SIDNEY COOPER – Home From Pasture – signed and dated 1907 – 14 x 9¾in.
(Sotheby's Belgravia) **$230 £120**

COOPER – Cattle In A Pasture – on panel – 7½ x 14½in.
(Sotheby's Belgravia) **$266 £140**

COOPER – Cattle Watering At A Stream – signed – oil on canvas – 18 x 35in.
(D. M. Nesbit & Co.) **$291 £150**

COOPER – Sheep And Cattle Resting – bears signature and date – 15¼ x 23½in.
(Sotheby's Belgravia) **$422 £220**

ADRIAEN COORTE – A Still Life Of Shells, Four Exotic Sea-Shells On A Marble Ledge – signed and dated 1698 – paper on panel – 11½ x 8¾in.
(Sotheby's) **$47,040 £24,000**

JOHN SINGLETON COPLEY – Portrait Of Mrs George Turner, Head And Shoulders – pastel – 22¼ x 16½in.
(Sotheby's) **$60,140 £31,000**

HAROLD COPLIMAN – An Indian Girl – signed – grey wash – 14¾ x 9¾in.
(Sotheby's) **$256 £130 Two**

C. COPPINI – Studies Of Dead Birds – signed and dated 1875 – oil on panel – 8½ x 7in.
(Morphets of Harrogate) **$297 £150 Pair**

HIERONYMUS HASTNER, IL CORAZŻA – Italianate River Landscapes With Fisherfolk – both inscribed on the reverse – 25 x 36in.
(Christie's) **$11,520 £6,000 Pair**

EDWARD HENRY CORBOULD – One Way Or The Other – signed, inscribed and dated 1889, inscribed on a label on reverse – heightened with white – 17 x 23in.
(Sotheby's Belgravia) **$503 £250**

EDWARD HENRY CORBOULD – Mountain Solitude – signed and dated 1838 – 19½ x 15in.
(Sotheby's) **$233 £120**

GINO CORELLI – View Of Naples And Bay With Vesuvius In The Background – signed – oil on panel – 16½ x 8½in.
(Lalonde Bros. & Parham) **$396 £200**

CORREGGIO, After – Venus Playing With Cupid Beneath A Tree, A Satyr Steals Cupid's Quiver And Arrows – oil on canvas – 151 x 106cm.
(Henry Spencer & Sons) **$307 £155**

EDOUARD CORTES – Parisienne Street Scene With Notre Dame In The Background – signed – oil on canvas – 13 x 18in.
(Morton's Auction Exchange, Inc.) **$2,300 £1,162**

DOMENICO CORVI, Studio of – Portrait Of Cardinal York, Small Half Length – 15½ x 11in.
(Christie's) **$768 £400**

C. COSBORN – Paraselenre And Lunar Halos – signed, inscribed and dated 1857 – oil on board – 8 x 13in.
(Sotheby's) **$177 £90**

JAN COSSIERS – A Gypsy Fortune Teller, Reading The Palm Of A Young Dandy In A White And Gold Brocade Silk Suit – 39¼ x 55¼in.
(Sotheby's) **$3,762 £1,900**

PLACIDO COSTANZI – Justice And Temperance Triumphant Over Deceit – 24¼ x 29¼in.
(Christie's) **$2,880 £1,500**

RICHARD COSWAY – A Young Girl In A White Muslin Dress Standing By A Pillar – pencil with blue and pink crayon – 12½ x 8½in.
(Sotheby's) **$873 £450**

ROBERT COTHIED – Us And Them – signed with monogram and dated 1880 – 27¼ x 38¾in.
(Sotheby's Belgravia) **$2,414 £1,200**

FREDERICK GEORGE COTMAN – A Mill Stream – signed and dated 1889 – 13½ x 10½in.
(Sotheby's Belgravia) **$480 £250**

FREDERICK GEORGE COTMAN – Tower Church From Northgate Road – signed and dated 1869 – heightened with bodycolour – 15 x 21in.
(Sotheby's Belgravia)
$198 £100

JOSEPH JOHN COTMAN – Evening On The Yare – signed and dated 1877 – pencil and watercolour – 13 x 19in.
(Sotheby's) **$3,298 £1,700**

JOHN JOSEPH COTMAN – Throwing Pebbles From A Bridge – signed and dated 1876 – 10¾ x 15in.
(Sotheby's) **$310 £160**

JOHN JOSEPH COTMAN – A View At Thorpe With Whitlingham Church In The Distance – signed – watercolour – 6¾ x 13¼in.
(Christie's) **$873 £450**

JOHN SELL COTMAN – The Quay, Yarmouth, Norfolk – pencil and brown wash – 7¼ x 12¼in.
(Sotheby's) **$485 £250**

HORATIO HENRY COULDERY – A Sumptuous Repast – signed – 20 x 33in.
(Sotheby's Belgravia)
$768 £400

JACQUES COURTIN – Portrait Of An Elegant Lady In A Villa Garden, Three-Quarter Length – signed and dated 1729 – 45½ x 34½in.
(Sotheby's) **$2,134 £1,100**

G. COURTOIS – Studies Of Putti, recto and verso – red chalk – 205 x 282mm.
(Christie's) **$133 £70**

J. LE COUTEUR – A Male Nude Kneeling, His Head Bowed – inscribed '1819' – black and white chalk on grey paper – 267 x 372mm.
(Christie's) **$95 £50**

J. VAN COUVER – 'De Outdebrug, Holland' – signed – on canvas – 71 x 56cm.
(King & Chasemore)
$1,152 £600

ROBERT McGOWN COVENTRY – Dordrecht Harbour – signed – 8¾ x 11¾in.
(Lawrence) **$209 £110**

ROBERT McGOWN COVENTRY – After Rain, Loch Lomond – signed and dated 1884, inscribed on a label on the reverse – 39 x 59½in.
(Sotheby's) **$634 £320**

A. G. COWARD – 'Off To The Fishing Grounds', Scottish Coastal Scene – signed – oil on board – 9¾ x 13¼in.
(J. W. Hilham) **$322 £160**

WILLIAM COWEN – Lake Albano, Near Rome; The Convent Of San Francesco At Aquapendente; and An Extensive View Of Como, Italy – signed and signed, inscribed and dated 1827 on the reverse – on panel – 8½ x 12½in.
(Christie's) **$2,328 £1,200 Three**

DAVID COX – Valle Crucis Abbey, North Wales – signed and dated 1835 – 7 x 11in.
(Sotheby's) **$1,261** **£650**

DAVID COX – Inverary Castle, Argyll – signed – blue crayon and watercolour – 7½ x 10in.
(Sotheby's) **$1,008** **£520**

DAVID COX – Hardwick Hall, Derbyshire – Evening – signed – 10¾ x 15¾in.
(Sotheby's) **$1,649** **£850**

D. COX – 'Woodland And Stream Scene With Anglers' – signed – watercolour drawing – 22½ x 16¾in.
(J. Entwistle & Co.) **$50** **£26**

DAVID COX – Landscape With Trees – watercolour – 8 x 10½in.
(W. H. Lane & Son) **$288** **£150**

DAVID COX – The Water Mill, An Old Thatched Water Mill Among Trees – signed – watercolour – 23 x 34cm.
(Henry Spencer & Sons) **$386** **£195**

GARSTIN COX – Cornish Coast Scape – Summer – oil on canvas – 20 x 24in.
(W. H. Lane & Son)
$250 **£130**

RAYMOND COXON – Portrait Of Sir Jacob Epstein – signed and dated 1948 – 23½ x 19½in.
(Sotheby's) **$436** **£220**

COYPEL – Lot And His Daughters – 32 x 40in.
(Christie's) **$466** **£240**

A. COYPEL – Saint Cecilia In Glory – 41¾ x 49½in.
(Christie's) **$970** **£500**

NOEL-NICOLAS COYPEL – The Adoration Of The Shepherds – 51¼ x 38¼in.
(Christie's) **$46,560** **£24,000**

ALEXANDER COZENS – In Calabria, Mountain Over A Bay With Buildings Among Trees – inscribed 16' – grey and brown washes on tinted paper – 8¾ x 11½in.
(Sotheby's) **$4,850 £2,500**

CRAESBEECK – A Quack In A Village – on panel – 9 x 14in.
(Christie's) **$369 £190**

JOOS VAN CRAESBEECK – Elegant Figures In A Landscape – on panel – 15 x 10¾in.
(Christie's) **$2,716 £1,400**

JOHN HUMBERT CRAIG – The Blue Hills Of Antrim On The Coast – signed, inscribed on the reverse – on panel – 15 x 20in.
(Sotheby's) **$1,319 £680**

WILLIAM MARSHALL CRAIG – A Gleaner – signed and inscribed – 10¼ x 6½in.
(Sotheby's) **$273 £140**

WILLIAM MARSHALL CRAIG – A Family On The Road Near A Cottage By A Stream – pencil and watercolour – 5½ x 8in.
(Sotheby's) **$349 £180**

W. F. CRAMPTON – Lake And Mountain Landscapes – signed – oil on board – 9 x 16in.
(Morphets of Harrogate) **$204 £105**

LUCAS CRANACH The Younger – Christ On The Cross – on panel – 16¼ x 11¼in.
(Sotheby's) **$27,160 £14,000**

WALTER CRANE – A Knight On A Grey Horse In A Valley – signed with monogram and dated 1870 – watercolour – 17¼ x 23¼in.
(Christie's) **$3,880 £2,000**

EDMUND T. CRAWFORD – Sailing Boats Offshore In A Calm – signed and indistinctly signed and inscribed on a label on the reverse – 9½ x 13½in.
(Christie's) **$1,455 £750**

E. T. CRAWFORD – Fisherfolk On The Beach – 13 x 22½in.
(Sotheby's) **$864** **£450**

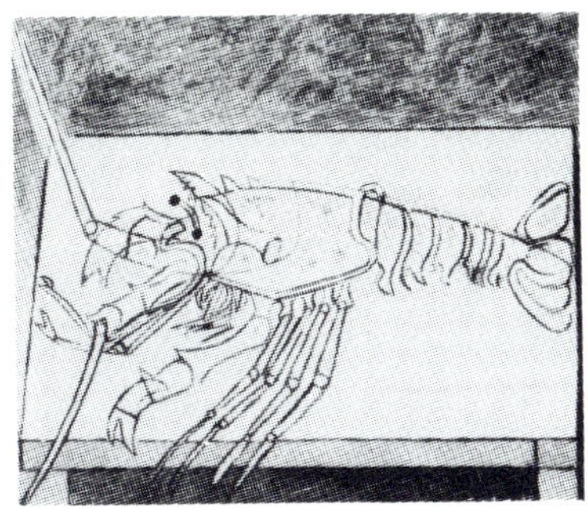

JOHN CRAXTON – Crayfish On A Table – signed and dated '58 – oil and gouache on board – 20 x 23½in.
(Sotheby's) **$713** **£360**

C. DE CRAYER – Saint Andrew – 40½ x 30½in.
(Christie's) **$1,552** **£800**

G. DE CRAYER – Abraham Entertaining The Three Angels, Who Are Seated At A Table Laden With Food And Wine – 51½ x 88in.
(Sotheby's) **$1,287** **£650**

CREDI – The Madonna And Child – on panel – 22½ x 17½in.
(Christie's) **$1,067** **£550**

LORENZO DI CREDI, Studio of – The Madonna And Child – on panel – 21¼ x 14¼in.
(Sotheby's) **$15,520** **£8,000**

GIUSEPPE CALETTI, Called Il Cremonese – Erminia And Vafrino Mourning Over Tancred; Tancred Baptizing Clorinda – 52¾ x 81in.
(Sotheby's) **$19,400** **£10,000 Pair**

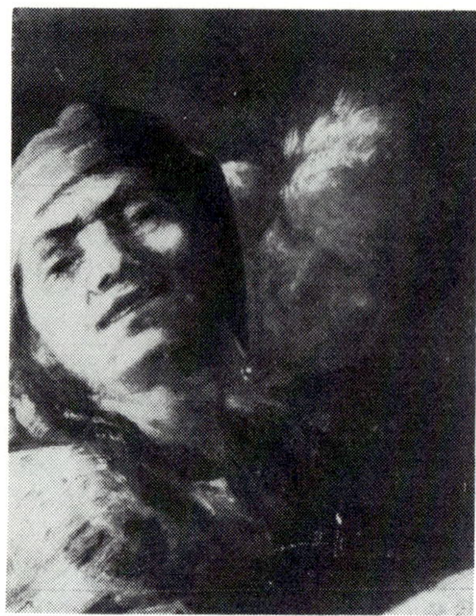

CRESPI – A Jester, Head And Shoulders, Wearing A Red Cap Trimmed With Bells, An Old Man Seated To The Right – 20¾ x 16½in.
(Sotheby's) **$1,228** **£620**

THOMAS CRESWICK – The Deserted Grange – on board – oval – 9½ x 7¾in.
(Sotheby's Belgravia) **$475** **£240**

T. CRESWICK, Attributed to – Two Men Fishing On River – oil on canvas – 14¾ x 7½in.
(Spear & Sons) **$302** **£150**

JOSHUA CRISTALL – In The Courtyard Of St. Donats Castle, Glamorgan – 11¼ x 16½in.
(Sotheby's) **$1,358** **£700**

DE CRITZ – A Group Portrait Of A Lady And Gentleman, Half Lengths, She Wearing A Dark Coat And Embroidered Collat, He Wearing A Green Coat – 30½ x 38¾in.
(Christie's) **$1,164** **£600**

VITTORIO CRIVELLI *(Active 1481-1501)* – The Madonna And Child Enthroned – signed and dated – panel transferred to canvas – 45½ x 29¼in.
(Sotheby's) **$47,520** **£24,000**

E. CROFTS – A Roundhead Standing Guard Outside A Castle, Winter Scene – signed – oil on canvas – 11 x 7½in.
(Morphets of Harrogate) **$543** **£280**

E. CROFTS – A Troop Of Mounted Roundheads Crossing A Bridge With A Castle In The Background – signed and dated 1885 – oil on canvas – 18 x 12½in.
(Morphets of Harrogate)
$1,358 £700

THOMAS HARTLEY CROMEK – Screen Of The Propylaea, Athens – 13¾ x 15in.
(Sotheby's) **$1,746 £900**

MURIEL ELISE CROOKE – Horses Grazing – all signed with studio stamps on the reverse – on panel – two 7 x 9¾in. and one 8¾ x 8¼in.
(Sotheby's Belgravia)
$96 £50 Three

RAY CROOKE – Summer Afternoon – signed – oil on canvas – 39 x 49cm.
(Australian Art Auctions)
$980 £500

RAY CROOKE – Figures in a Landscape – signed – oil on board – 46 x 59cm.
(Australian Art Auctions)
$445 £232

RAY CROOKE – Natives in Village Scene – signed – oil on board – 46 x 60cm.
(Australian Art Auctions)
$1,170 £610

ANTHONY JANSZ. VAN DER CROOS – An Extensive Dutch Landscape With Resting Travellers – on panel – 13½ x 18½in.
(Sotheby's) **$3,168 £1,600**

JACOB VAN DER CROOS – A Stormy Sea, With Several Galleons – signed with monogram and dated – 19¼ x 25¼in.
(Sotheby's) **$5,238 £2,700**

ENOCH CROSLAND – A River Scene – signed and dated '96 – 15½ x 23½in.
(Sotheby's Belgravia)
$760 £400

ENOCH CROSLAND – Country Scenes – signed – 11 x 9in. and 10 x 12in.
(Sotheby's Belgravia)
$178 £90 Pair

NICHOLAS JOSEPH CROWLEY – Portrait Of A Lady, Probably Mrs Shaw With Her Two Children, She Standing Full Length In The Centre Wearing A Brown Dress – 90 x 56in.
(Sotheby's) **$931 £480**

WILLIAM CRUIKSHANK – A Pheasant, Lapwing And Pigeon By A Jug And Vase On A Table; and A Mallard And Partridge Beside Apples, A Bottle And Bowl On A Table – signed and one dated '92 – watercolour and bodycolour – 15¾ x 22¾in. and smaller.
(Christie's) **$126 £65 Two**

WILLIAM CRUICKSHANK – Still Life Of Honeysuckle And A Chaffinch – signed – 9½ x 13½in.
(Sotheby's Belgravia) **$384 £200**

H. HADFIELD CUBLEY – Collecting The Herd, Glencoe; In The Isle Of Arran – signed, inscribed on the reverse – 19 x 29¼in.
(Sotheby's Belgravia)
$346 £180 Pair

GEORGE CUITT, JNR. – Gwydr Chapel Near Llanrwst, North Wales – signed, inscribed and dated 1831 on the reverse – oil on panel – 13¾ x 17½in.
(Neales of Nottingham)
$257 £130

R. H. NEVILLE CUMMINGS – The U.S. 'St. Louis' – signed and dated 1908 – heightened with bodycolour – 10 x 15in.
(Sotheby's Belgravia) $27 £14

WILLIAM CURRY – 'Where Newark's Stately Tower Looks Out From Yarrow's Birchen Bower' – signed and dated 1867, inscribed – 13¾ x 19½in.
(Sotheby's Belgravia) $376 £190

CUYP – A Wooded River Landscape With Cattle By A Cottage – bears signature – 22 x 29¾in.
(Christie's) $369 £190

CUYP – Portrait Of A Gentleman, Small Half Length, Wearing A Black Doublet And Hat – on panel – 12 x 10in.
(Christie's) $310 £160

AELBERT CUYP – The Maas At Doordrecht With The Groothoofdspoort On The Right And Fishing Boats In The Foreground – signed – 34 x 48¼in.
(Christie's) $67,200 £35,000

BENJAMIN GERRITZ. CUYP – Christ Disputing With The Elders In The Temple – on panel – 16 x 11½in.
(Sotheby's) $3,492 £1,800

J. G. CUYP – Portrait Of A Boy And A Dog – inscribed and dated 1650 – 40½ x 30¼in.
(Sotheby's) $7,920 £4,000

JACOB GERRITSZ. CUYP – Portrait Of A Young Girl, Standing Full Length – dated 1648 – on panel – 36 x 27¼in.
(Sotheby's) $7,760 £4,000

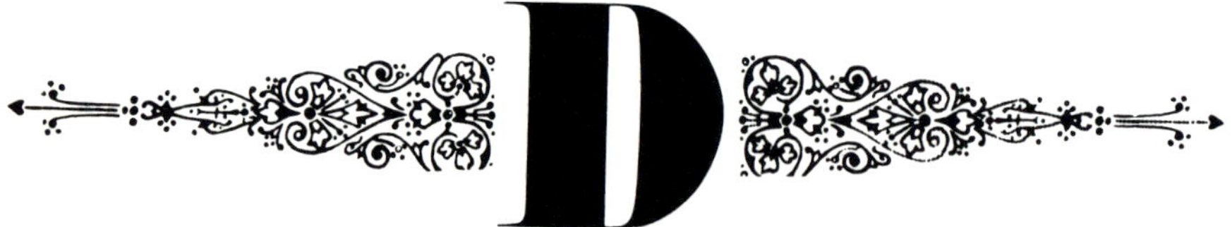

ERNEST DADE – A Tug Towing A Merchantman; Cottages By A Hayfield; and Figures On A Road By Houses – signed and dated '92 – watercolour, one heightened with white – 13¼ x 9½in. and smaller.
(Christie's) $310 £160 Three

ERNEST DADE – A Fishing Boat Approaching A Lobster Pot At Sea – watercolour heightened with white – 19¼ x 29in.
(Christie's) $291 £150

ERNEST DADE – Figures On A Beach By The Hull Of An Old Boat; and Sailing Boats At Sea – one signed and dated '89 – watercolour, one heightened with white – 13½ x 19¾in. and smaller.
(Christie's) $107 £55 Two

DALMATIAN SCHOOL, 17th century – Noli Me Tangere – canvas on panel – 12¼ x 8¼in.
(Sotheby's) $2,277 £1,150

DALZIEL – The Woods In Winter – 15½ x 19½in.
(Sotheby's Belgravia) **$29** **£15**

FRANCIS DANBY – Sunset Over A Bay, A Shrimper In The Foreground And A Castle On A Hill Beyond – 34 x 44in.
(Sotheby's) **$1,009** **£520**

FRANCIS DANBY, 19th century – A Shepherd Rests At The Foot Of A Tree At Leigh Woods With A View Across The Avon Gorge Towards Clifton – watercolour – 6¼ x 9½in.
(Osmond, Tricks & Son) **$3,762** **£1,900**

J. DANBY – Fetching Driftwood – indistinctly signed with initials and dated – 9½ x 18½in.
(Christie's) **$427** **£220**

J. F. DANBY – Winter Sunset On The Thames At Chelsea – inscribed – 11 x 20½in.
(Sotheby's Belgravia) **$266** **£140**

JAMES FRANCIS DANBY – A Mountainous Lake Landscape With A Fisherman By A Ruin – signed and dated 1854 – 30 x 47½in.
(Christie's) **$1,940** **£1,000**

SAMUEL DANIELL – A Female Koodoo – inscribed – pencil – 7 x 7¾in.
(Sotheby's) **$936** **£480**

WILLIAM DANIELL – The Lat Of Feroze Shah, Old Delhi – pencil and watercolour – 4 x 5¾in.
(Sotheby's) **$213** **£110**

H. DANKAERTS – The Arrival Of Aeneas In Carthage, Accompanied By Queen Dido, Venus And Cupid Appearing In A Celestial Cloud – 13 x 8¼in.
(Sotheby's) **$1,386** **£700**

DANUBE SCHOOL, 16th century – The Adoration Of The Kings – on panel – 37¾ x 25¼in.
(Sotheby's) **$10,780** **£5,500**

CHARLES-FRANCOIS DAUBIGNY – Paysage Au Soleil Couchant – signed and indistinctly dated 1866 – pen and indian ink – 4½ x 6in.
(Sotheby's) **$1,805** **£950**

ADRIEN DAUZATS – Patibulo De Alicante A Villena – signed and dated 1846 – watercolour – 8 x 10½in.
(Sotheby's) **$627** **£330**

DAVID – The Deposition, Saints Joseph Of Arimathaea And Nicodemus Lowering The Body Of Christ From The Cross – on panel – 38¾ x 32in.
(Sotheby's) **$16,660** **£8,500**

JACQUES LOUIS DAVID – A Pyramid – pencil and brown wash – 9.2 x 15.2cm.
(Christie's) **$576** **£300**

ALAN DAVIE – Discovery Of The White Mountain – signed and dated '57 – resin-oil on paper – 16½ x 21in.
(Sotheby's) **$1,188** **£600**

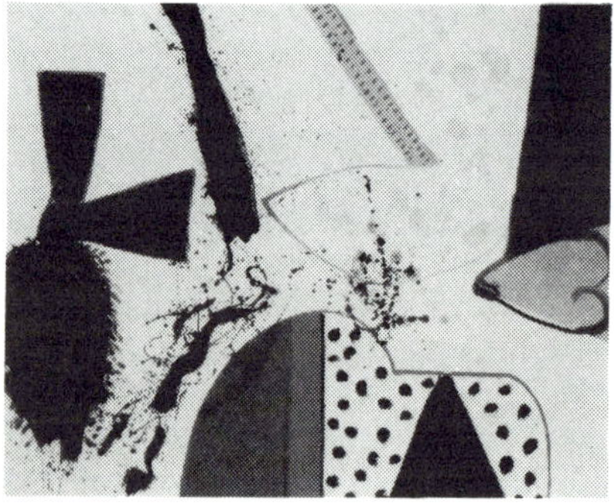

ALAN DAVIE – Sweet Scents For The Teddy-Bear – signed and dated '64 on the reverse – oil on canvas – 48 x 60in.
(Sotheby's) **$3,762** **£1,900**

ARTHUR E. DAVIES – A View Of Caernarvon Castle, Wales – signed – watercolour – 12 x 16in.
(G. A. Key) **$396** **£200**

LOUIS B. DAVIES – A Procession – black chalk – 51 x 25in.
(Sotheby's Belgravia) **$304** **£160**

B. DAVIS – The Mill Burn – signed, inscribed on the stretcher – 14½ x 10in.
(Sotheby's Belgravia) **$61** **£32**

H. B. DAVIS – A Highland Loch - signed – 19½ x 29½in.
(Sotheby's Belgravia) **$163** **£85**

WILLIAM DAVIS – Spring – signed with initials and dated 1861 – on panel – 7½ x 10in.
(Sotheby's) **$970** **£500**

WILLIAM DAVIS – On The Menai Straits – on panel – 8¾ x 12½in.
(Sotheby's) **$388** **£200**

HORACE DAWES – On A Loch; Evening – one signed – 19½ x 29½in.
(Sotheby's Belgravia) **$422** **£220 Pair**

ALFRED DAWSON – Boston Stump – signed and dated April 1880, inscribed on the reverse – on panel – 11¾ x 9¾in.
(Sotheby's Belgravia) **$1,536** **£800**

HENRY DAWSON, JNR. – Fishing Vessels Off A Port – signed and dated 1871 – on panel – 6½ x 8½in.
(Sotheby's Belgravia)
$2,012 **£1,000**

HENRY DAWSON – Windsor Castle From The Brocas – signed – watercolour – 13 x 19¼in.
(Christie's) **$873** **£450**

HENRY DAWSON – Sunset On A Highland Loch – signed and dated 1852 – on panel – 11¾ x 16in.
(Sotheby's Belgravia) **$730** **£380**

MONTAGUE DAWSON – Pressing On – The Clipper 'Outlook' – signed – 19½ x 29¾in.
(Sotheby's) **$23,364** **£11,800**

MONTAGUE DAWSON – The Golden Hind – signed – 23¼ x 35in.
(Sotheby's) **$9,504** **£4,800**

WILLIAM DAY – View Looking From The Head Of Mona Mine Into The Head Of Parys Mine, As They Appeared In July 1794, Angelsea – inscribed on the reverse – pencil and watercolour – 9½ x 15½in.
(Sotheby's) **$293** **£150**

JOHN DEARMAN – Cattle By A Loch – signed and dated 1846 – 15 x 25½in.
(Sotheby's Belgravia) **$211** **£110**

ALEXANDRE GABRIEL DECAMPS – Etude D'Arabe Assis – watercolour – 7¼ x 6¼in.
(Sotheby's) **$1,148** **£580**

ALEXANDRE GABRIEL DECAMPS – La Defaite Des Cimbres – pencil, heightened with white gouache – 12½ x 16½in.
(Sotheby's) **$3,040** **£1,600**

A. DEHODENCQ – Paysans Marocains Se Rendant Au Marche – pen and ink and brown wash – 8¾ x 6¾in.
(Sotheby's) **$380** **£200**

EUGENE DELACROIX – Cheval Pur Sang A L'Ecurie – varnished watercolour – 5¼ x 8½in.
(Sotheby's) **$5,148** **£2,600**

PAUL DELAROCHE – Portrait De Jeune Femme – signed, dated and inscribed 1843 – watercolour – 9½ x 8¼in.
(Sotheby's) **$3,960** **£2,000**

VALENTINE DELAWARR – A Waterfall In New South Wales – signed – oil on board – 51¼ x 13¼in.
(Sotheby's) **$177** **£90**

ALBERT DELERIVE – A Dentist At Work In An Extensive Landscape – signed – on panel – 10¼ x 8in.
(Christie's) **$2,522** **£1,300**

SCHOOL OF DELFT, 17th century – Portrait Of A Lady, Standing, Half Length, In A Black Dress With White Apron, Holding A Small Book – 36¼ x 28in.
(Sotheby's) **$5,148** **£2,600**

DELFT SCHOOL, mid 17th century – A Painter In His Studio – on panel – 16 x 12½in.
(Sotheby's) **$3,528** **£1,800**

JOHN H. DELL – A Rustic Nursery; A Farmyard Corner – signed with monogram and dated '54 – on panel – 6 x 9½in.
(Sotheby's Belgravia) **$1,811** **£900 Pair**

W. N. DENBY – 'Prospect Of Whitby'; and 'Seascape' – one signed – watercolour – 6¾ x 9¾in.
(Dacre, Son & Hartley) **$68** **£34 Two**

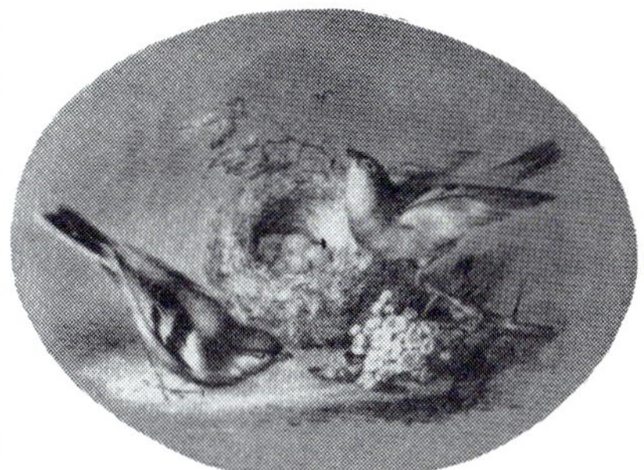

W. DENTER – Still Lives Of Birds And Nests – signed – heightened with bodycolour – oval – 8½ x 12in.
(Sotheby's Belgravia)
$1,358 **£700 Pair**

REMI-FURCY DESCARSIN – Portrait Of A Lady Said To Be Madame D'Alencou, Seated Half Length, Wearing A Blue And White Dress – signed and dated 1785 – 28¼ x 23in.
(Christie's) **$679** **£350**

CHARLES MAURICE DETMOLD – Studies Of The Head Of A Lynx – one signed with initials, the other in full and dated 1899 – pencil and watercolour heightened with white, one on grey paper – 8¾ x 7¼in.
(Christie's) **$155** **£80 Pair**

EDWARD JULIUS DETMOLD – Irises In A Chinese Jar – watercolour – 15¾ x 15in.
(Christie's) **$126** **£65**

EDWARD JULIUS DETMOLD – Poppies, Escholtzia And Blue Butterflies; and Clematis, Wild Roses And Laburnum – watercolour – oval – 13¾ x 10¼in.
(Christie's) **$252** **£130 Pair**

EDWARD JULIUS DETMOLD – A Christmas Party: A Robin, A Wren And Bluetits In The Snow – watercolour heightened with white – 14¼ x 11in.
(Christie's) **$272** **£140**

EDWARD JULIUS DETMOLD – Bluetits On Apple Blossom – watercolour – 10 x 8in. and smaller.
(Christie's) **$272** **£140 Pair**

EDWARD JULIUS DETMOLD – Tete A Tete – signed with monogram – watercolour – 24½ x 18½in.
(Christie's) **$1,261** **£650**

EDWARD JULIUS DETMOLD – Monkeys On A Tree Stump – watercolour – 23¾ x 19½in.
(Christie's) **$504** **£260**

W. H. DEVERELL – Musicians Making Music On A Balcony – 10½ x 15¼in.
(Christie's) **$776** **£400**

ANTHONY DEVIS – A Rustic Family By A Lake, A Ruined Abbey On A Promontory – signed with initials – black crayon, pen and grey ink, watercolour – 10¼ x 13½in.
(Sotheby's) **$683** **£350**

GIUSEPPE DIAMANTINI – The Triumph Of Galatea – inscribed – red chalk – 22.2 x 15.8cm.
(Christie's) **$345** **£180**

THOMAS COLMAN DIBDIN – The Transept Of Orleans Cathedral Seen From The Street – signed and dated 1883 – watercolour heightened with bodycolour – 21¾ x 15in.
(Sotheby's) **$429** **£220**

THOMAS COLEMAN DIBDIN – An Old Gateway In A French Cathedral Town – signed and dated 1870 – heightened with white – 29½ x 20½in.
(Sotheby's) **$718** **£370**

DICKINSONS – Portrait Of A Politician – signed – on panel – 12 x 10in.
(Sotheby's Belgravia) **$26** **£14**

HERBERT DICKSEE – 'The Grandfather At The Grave Of Little Nell' – signed and dated 1887 – watercolour – 75 x 107cm.
(King & Chasemore) **$394** **£200**

MARGARET J. DICKSEE – As Shepherds Watched – signed and dated 1883 – heightened with bodycolour – 12¾ x 23¾in.
(Sotheby's Belgravia) **$67** **£35**

THOMAS FRANCIS DICKSEE – Evening – 14¼ x 11¾in.
(Sotheby's Belgravia) **$1,006** **£500**

THOMAS FRANCIS DICKSEE – Portrait Study Of Miranda, Small Bust Length – 8 x 10in.
(Christie's) **$737** **£380**

DIEPENBECK – The Raising Of The Cross – on copper – 22½ x 17in.
(Christie's) **$1,164** **£600**

ABRAHAM VAN DIEPENBECK, Attributed to – Five Children With A Kite – black chalk, pen and brown ink, grey wash – 12 x 15.2cm.
(Christie's) **$173** **£90**

WILLEM VAN DIEST – The Battle Of The Sound, 29 October 1658 – 27½ x 52in.
(Sotheby's) **$8,148** **£4,200**

WILLEM VAN DIEST – The Battle Of The Sound, 29 October 1658 – 27½ x 52in.
(Sotheby's) **$8,148** **£4,299**

WILLEM VAN DIEST – Dutch Shipping In A Choppy Sea – signed with initials and dated 1677 – on panel – 18½ x 24¼in.
(Christie's) **$14,400** **£7,500**

C. W. E. DIETRICH – A Hermit Monk In Prayer – on panel – 17½ x 13¾in.
(Christie's) **$1,843** **£950**

W. DILLON – Off Hawth – heightened with bodycolour – 11½ x 18in.
(Sotheby's Belgravia) **$69** **£35**

JIM DINE – Ties – signed and dated 1961 – charcoal and gouache on paper – 18 x 24in.
(Sotheby's) **$2,772** **£1,400**

C. DINGWALL – Fort Denison, Sydney Harbour – signed indistinctly, inscribed and dated 1853 – watercolour – 10½ x 7½in.
(Sotheby's) **$55** **£28**

ALFRED DIXON – Don Quixote In His Study – signed with monogram and dated 1870, and signed, inscribed and dated on the reverse – 19½ x 15½in.
(Christie's) **$388** **£200**

ANNA DIXON – A Carthorse – signed – on panel – 10 x 13in.
(Sotheby's Belgravia)
$19 **£10**

CHARLES DIXON – Blackwall Reach – signed, inscribed and dated '01 – heightened with bodycolour – 10¼ x 30½in.
(Sotheby's Belgravia)
$768 **£400**

CHARLES DIXON – Men-O'-War – signed and dated 1928 – watercolour drawing – 14½ x 20½in.
(Andrew Sharpe & Partners)
$384 **£195**

HENRY DIXON – On The Beach – signed – on board – 15½ x 19½in.
(Sotheby's Belgravia)
$288 **£150**

JOHN DOBBIN – Palace Of The Escorial, Spain – signed – watercolour – 26½ x 39in.
(Morphets of Harrogate)
$792 **£400**

HENRY JOHN DOBSON – First Footsteps – signed with initials and dated '98, inscribed on the reverse – 13½ x 17½in.
(Sotheby's Belgravia)
$832 **£420**

H. J. DOBSON – The Last Bawbee – 44 x 59cm.
(Edmiston's) **$814** **£420**

HENRY RAEBURN DOBSON – Part Of The Town And Conway Castle – signed, inscribed and dated May, 1929 on the reverse – heightened with white – 21½ x 29½in.
(Sotheby's Belgravia)
$230 **£120**

W. C. T. DOBSON – A Buttercup Girl – 10½ x 8¼in.
(Sotheby's Belgravia)
$134 **£70**

ALEXANDER BROWNLEE DOCHARTY – Half-Way House, Kilmarnock And Ayr Road – signed – 13½ x 19½in.
(Sotheby's) **$594** **£300**

ALEXANDER BROWNLIE DOCHARTY – On The Beach – signed – 5¾ x 9¾in.
(Sotheby's) **$422** **£220**

ALEXANDER BROWNLEE DOCHARTY – In A Vale – signed – 27½ x 35in.
(Sotheby's) **$729** **£380**

ALEXANDER BROWNLIE DOCHARTY – Sunshine And Shadow – signed, inscribed on a label – 36 x 48in.
(Sotheby's) **$832** **£420**

CHARLES TATTERSHALL DODD – An Overshot Mill – signed and dated 1863 – 16 x 23½in.
(Sotheby's Belgravia) **$266** **£140**

J. VAN DER DOES – An Italianate Wooded Landscape With Cattle And Peasants – bears signature – 20¼ x 24in.
(Christie's) **$1,455** **£750**

DOLCI – The Madonna – 24½ x 19¼in.
(Christie's) **$136** **£70**

DOLCI – Female Head – on metal panel – oval – 21 x 16.2cm.
(Edmiston's) **$369** **£190**

DOLCI – The Virgin And Child – watercolour – 292 x 380mm.
(Christie's) **$190** **£100**

C. DOLCI – Ecce Homo – 11½ x 9in.
(Christie's) **$384** **£200**

CARLO DOLCI, and Studio – Hagar And Ishmael In The Wilderness – 36 x 48¾in.
(Sotheby's) **$25,220** **£13,000**

W. ANSTEY DOLLAND – Garlanding Neptune – signed – 17½ x 10½in.
(Sotheby's Belgravia) **$665** **£350**

DOMENICHINO – The Persian Sibyl – 47½ x 34½in.
(Christie's) **$349** **£180**

DOMENICHINO – A Woman, Small Half Length, Wearing Classical Style Costume – bears signature – on copper – oval – 6¾ x 5in.
(Christie's) **$384** **£200**

DOMENICO ZAMPIERI, IL DOMENICHINO, Attributed to – Two Figures On The Ramparts Of A Castle, With Trees And A Landscape Beyond – inscribed – pen and brown ink, brown wash – 36.7 x 28.2cm.
(Christie's) **$576** **£300**

DOMENICHINO, Circle of – The Assumption Of Saint Dominic, Supported By Angels – on metal – 19 x 14in.
(Sotheby's) **$1,901** **£980**

PIETER CHRISTIAN DOMMERSEN – Extensive Mountainous Lakeland Landscape – signed and dated 1889 – 29.5 x 44.5cm.
(Henry Spencer & Sons) **$1,029** **£520**

WILLIAM DOMMERSEN – 'Maastrecht On The Mass, Holland' – signed, inscribed and signed on verso – oil – 12 x 16in.
(Woolley & Wallis) **$878** **£420**

ELIZABETH DONALD – A New Zealand Lake With The Remarkables In The Distance – oil on canvas – 11½ x 18in.
(Sotheby's) **$433** **£220**

H. M. DONCKER – A Family Portrait In A Landscape – 37½ x 30in.
(Sotheby's) **$2,716** **£1,400**

DIONYS VAN DONGEN – An Italianate Wooded River Landscape With Peasants, Cattle And Sheep – signed and indistinctly dated – on panel – 17½ x 21½in.
(Christie's) **$2,910 £1,500**

GIROLAMO DONINI – The Madonna And Child – 45 x 30¼in.
(Christie's) **$2,716 £1,400**

L. E. DONNELLY – Deer In The Highlands – signed – 16 x 30in.
(Sotheby's) **$345 £180**

DOU – Saint Jerome In The Wilderness – on panel – 10 x 8in.
(Christie's) **$168 £85**

G. DOU – A Young Woman Playing A Virginal, In A Green Jacket Trimmed With Ermine – on panel – 13¾ x 11¼in.
(Sotheby's) **$4,158 £2,100**

G. DOU – A Woman With A Bunch Of Grapes At A Window – on panel – 8½ x 6¼in.
(Christie's) **$1,940 £1,000**

JAMES DOUBTING – Cattle Resting In A Sunny Pasture – signed and dated 1877 – 13½ x 26in.
(Sotheby's Belgravia) **$436 £220**

WILLEM DOUDIJNS – St. John Baptizing, In A Landscape – signed – 35 x 44in.
(Sotheby's) **$1,980 £1,000**

ANDREW DOUGLAS – Cattle Watering In A Highland Loch – signed – on board – 14½ x 21½in.
(Sotheby's Belgravia) **$384 £200**

JAMES DOUGLAS – Nearly Bunkered – signed – heightened with white – 16 x 22in.
(Sotheby's) **$614 £320**

CHARLES R. DOWELL – At Home – signed – 23½ x 29in.
(Sotheby's) **$356** **£180**

JOHN PATRICK DOWNIE – Evening Off Ailsa Craig – signed – heightened with white – 14 x 20¾in.
(Sotheby's) **$614** **£320**

JOHN PATRICK DOWNIE – The Mirror Of The Sunset, Firth Of Clyde – signed and dated 1933, inscribed on the reverse – 27 x 35in.
(Sotheby's) **$921** **£480**

PATRICK DOWNIE – Dippers, Galway Bay, Ireland – signed, inscribed and dated 1903 on the reverse – 10½ x 14¾in.
(Sotheby's Belgravia) **$154** **£80**

PATRICK DOWNIE – Mid Quay, Greenock, 1887 – signed – heightened with bodycolour – 13¾ x 9¼in.
(Sotheby's Belgravia) **$105** **£55**

PATRICK DOWNIE – A Fine Morning, Ayrshire Coast – signed – on board – 9 x 13in.
(Sotheby's) **$499** **£260**

BROWNIE DOWNING – Ballerina – signed – gouache – 66 x 53cm.
(Australian Art Auctions) **$57** **£29**

DESMOND DOWNING – Scene From Ned Kelly, by Douglas Stewart – signed – gouache – 30 x 47cm.
(Australian Art Auctions) **$161** **£82**

DESMOND DOWNING – Scene From Vintage For Heros, by Warwick Fairfax – signed and dated '52 – watercolour – 33 x 52cm.
(Australian Art Auctions) **$80** **£41**

JOHN DOWNMAN – Brothers, One In Napoleonic Volunteer Uniform, The Other In Light Grey Coat – watercolour and charcoal heightened with white – oval – 11¼ x 9¼in.
(Sotheby's) **$1,014** **£520**

GABRIEL FRANCOIS DOYEN – Portrait Of A Gentleman, Bust Length, Wearing A Brown Coat And White Cravat – 25 x 20¾in.
(Christie's) **$1,940** **£1,000**

CHARLES ALTIMONT DOYLE – Figures Dancing; A Peacock Train; and Figures On The Tail Of A Peacock – one signed or inscribed with initials – pen and grey ink and watercolour or blue wash – 6¼ x 13¼in. and smaller.
(Christie's) **$310** **£160 Three**

JOHN DOYLE – A Chestnut Hunter, Standing Outside A Stable With Its Groom, A Terrier To The Left – signed and dated 1825 – 20 x 26in.
(Sotheby's) **$4,752** **£2,400**

JOHN DOYLE – A Chestnut Hunter With Its Groom And Owner, A Whippet In The Foreground – 19 x 25¾in.
(Sotheby's) **$2,178** **£1,100**

W. VAN DRIELENBURGH – A View Beside A Canal, Figures On A Bridge, Others Fishing – bears a monogram and dated 166' – on panel – 18¼ x 25¼in.
(Sotheby's) **$3,880** **£2,000**

MILTON DRINKWATER – On The Wharfe, Yorkshire; Near Bettws-y-Coed, North Wales – signed – heightened with white – 18 x 11½in.
(Sotheby's Belgravia) **$211** **£110 Pair**

DROOCHSLOOT – A Village Scene With Peasants Making Merry – 36 x 36in.
(Sotheby's) **$1,940** **£1,000**

CORNELIS DROOCHSLOOT The Younger – A River Landscape With Figures – signed with initials and dated 166' – on panel – 13½ x 18¼in.
(Sotheby's) **$4,268** **£2,200**

CORNELIS DROOCHSLOOT – A View In A Dutch Village, Numerous Figures Gathered Outside Cottages – on panel – 13¼ x 17½in.
(Sotheby's) **$7,920** **£4,100**

JOOST CORNELISZ. DROOCHSLOOT – A Raiding Party In A Village – indistinctly signed and dated 1627 – 26½ x 44½in.
(Christie's) **$86,400** **£45,000**

JAMES DRUMMOND – Meditation – 11¾ x 9½in.
(Sotheby's) **$345** **£180**

JAMES DRUMMOND – Daft Sandy – on panel – 9 x 7½in.
(Sotheby's) **$634** **£320**

MALCOLM DRUMMOND – Girl Sitting At A Window – 23½ x 19½in.
(Sotheby's) **$1,683** **£850**

A. J. DRYSDALE – Live Oaks In City Park – signed – watercolour – 19 x 29in.
(Morton's Auction Exchange, Inc.) **$1,200** **£609**

GUILLAUME DUBOIS, Attributed to – A Village Seen Among Trees – black chalk and grey wash – 7.8 x 14.6cm.
(Christie's) **$384** **£200**

JACOB DUCK – Interior With Soldiers – on panel – 14 x 19¼in.
(Sotheby's) **$5,820** **£3,000**

J. DUCKER – Lakeland Scenes – signed – oil – 20 x 30in.
(Andrew Sharpe & Partners) **$729** **£370 Pair**

JOHAN LE DUCQ – Greyhounds With A Dead Hare In A Landscape – signed – 20½ x 26½in.
(Christie's) **$5,044** **£2,600**

THOMAS DUDGEON – Dunoon Castle, Argyllshire – mixed media – on board – 16 x 25in.
(Sotheby's) **$384** **£200**

THOMAS DUDGEON – Kilchurn Castle, Argyllshire – signed and dated 1870 – mixed media – on board – 17 x 27½in.
(Sotheby's Belgravia) **$144** **£75**

ARTHUR DUDLEY – Still Lives Of Fruit, Baskets And Bottles – signed – one heightened with bodycolour – 15 x 21½in.
(Sotheby's Belgravia) $99 £50 Pair

MARY ELIZABETH DUFFIELD – Still Life Of Roses – signed – arched top – 7 x 9¼in.
(Sotheby's Belgravia) $250 £130

WILLIAM DUFFIELD – Still Life Of Fruit And Game – signed – 29 x 39in.
(Sotheby's Belgravia) $11,066 £5,500

GASPARD DUGHET – An Extensive Landscape With A Hill Town – black chalk, grey wash heightened with white on grey paper – 29.7 x 43.2cm.
(Christie's) $1,344 £700

G. DUGHET – An Italianate River Landscape – 66½ x 96½in.
(Christie's) $1,552 £800

JEAN DEMOSTHENE DUGOURC – Leonard De Vinci, Meurt Dans Les Bras De Francois I; and Soupe D'Henry IV A Coutras – both signed with initials and dated 1776 and 1775 – pencil and grey wash – 19.1 x 14.8cm.
(Christie's) $537 £280 Pair

HENRY E. DUGUID – Edinburgh From The Braid Hills – signed and inscribed on a label on the reverse – 19½ x 29½in.
(Sotheby's) $499 £260

PIETER JACOBSZ. DUIFHUIZEN – Peasants Preparing A Meal And Merry-making In An Interior – signed – on panel – 15 x 20¼in.
(Christie's) $1,746 £900

K. DUJARDIN – Horsemen Resting Outside An Inn – bears signature – 16¼ x 20in.
(Christie's) $4,268 £2,200

HIPPOLYTE FRANCOIS LEON DULUARD – 'The Expert Nobleman' – signed – oil on canvas – 36 x 25in.
(Morton's Auction Exchange, Inc.) $1,025 £517

JOHN DUN – Arch Of Tilus, Rome – dated 1891 – watercolour – 33 x 24cm.
(Edmiston's) $33 £17

JOHN DUN – Family In The Forest – 60 x 76cm.
(Edmiston's) $262 £135

RONALD OSSORY DUNLOP – Cagnes – 20¾ x 25¼in.
(Sotheby's) **$475** **240**

D. R. DUNN – A Dutch Town – signed – on board – 10½ x 13in.
(Sotheby's Belgravia)
$67 **£35**

A. DUNNINGTON – Dunluce Castle, Portrush, N. Ireland – signed – oil – 15½ x 24in.
(Warner Sheppard & Wade)
$94 **£45**

BERNARD DUNSTAN – Amadeus Quartet, II – signed with initials – on board – 8 x 11¼in.
(Sotheby's) **$515** **£260**

JULES DUPRE – Paysage Boise – charcoal – 26 x 42in.
(Sotheby's) **$1,045** **£550**

F. DURANTI – An Angel And A Putto In The Clouds – black chalk, pen and brown ink, brown wash – 120 x 174mm.
(Christie's) **$53** **£28**

FORTUNATO DURANTI – A Military Commander Taking Monastic Vows – indistinctly inscribed, and signed on the reverse – 24 x 16½in.
(Christie's) **$1,056** **£550**

DURER – The Last Supper – pen and brown ink on brown paper – 36.7 x 23.8cm.
(Christie's) **$1,344** **£700**

DUSART – An Interior, A Peasant Smoking At A Table; and An Interior, A Peasant Seated On A Bench Before A Barrel – on panel – circular – diameter 8½in.
(Sotheby's) **$815** **£420 Pair**

DUTCH SCHOOL – Peasants Smoking And Drinking, In An Interior; and A Peasant Family Spinning In An Interior – on panel – 11 x 9in.
(Sotheby's) **$330** **£170 Pair**

DUTCH SCHOOL, 17th century – Ruth And Boaz – pen and brown ink – 15.8 x 22.6cm.
(Christie's) **$211** **£110**

DUTCH SCHOOL, 17th century -- A Still Life Of Kitchen Utensils, Including Terracotta Bowls And Ewers On The Floor Of A Kitchen, In Which Fires Are Burning In Two Stoves – 13¼ x 17½in.
(Sotheby's) **$2,970** **£1,500**

DUTCH SCHOOL, 18th century, In 17th century Style – Still Life With Peonies, Tulips And Other Flowers In A Blue And White Bottle Vase With A Brass Candlestick, A Sea-Shell, Pocket Watch, Scroll, Clay Pipe And Other Items On A Stone Ledge – indistinctly signed – oil on canvas – 53 x 43cm.
(Henry Spencer & Sons)
$3,564 **£1,800**

DUTCH SCHOOL, 19th century – An Estuary Scene With Fishing Barges, Figures And A Windmill In The Distance – oil on canvas – 51 x 79cm.
(King & Chasemore)
$1,000 **£520**

DUTCH SCHOOL, 19th century – Inn Interiors, With Many Figures Drinking And Making Merry – one signed and dated 1673 – the other signed and dated 1646 – oil on panel – 55 x 72.5cm.
(Henry Spencer & Sons)
$776 **£400 Pair**

JOHN DUVAL, Attributed to – 'The Fly Fisherman' – oil on board – 8¾ x 5¾in.
(J. W. Hilham) **$523** **£260**

JOHN DUVALL – Cattle And Sheep On Country Roads – signed – 7½ x 15½in.
(Sotheby's Belgravia) **$570 £300 Pair**

THEOPHILE EMMANUEL DUVERGER – 'A Stitch In Time', A Study Of A Mother And Her Two Children – signed – on panel – 11¾ x 9½in.
(Sotheby Bearne) **$7,760 £4,000**

SIR A. VAN DYCK – Portrait Of Queen Henrietta Maria As Saint Catherine, Half Length, Wearing A Red Dress – 28¾ x 24in.
(Christie's) **$2,328 £1,200**

SIR A. VAN DYCK – Portrait Of John, Count Of Nassau, Full Length, Standing, Wearing Armour – 83 x 46in.
(Christie's) **$7,372 £3,800**

SIR A. VAN DYCK – Portrait Of Lady Albemarle, Bust Length, Wearing A Blue Dress And A Yellow Shawl – 27½ x 23in.
(Christie's) **$1,940 £1,000**

SIR ANTHONY VAN DYCK – The Adoration Of The Kings – pen and brown ink, with touches of grey wash – 19.2 x 20.7cm.
(Christie's) **$11,520 £6,000**

P. VAN DYCK – A Lady Wearing Classical Costume Seated In A Landscape With A Boy Nearby – on panel – 9¼ x 7¼in.
(Christie's) **$1,940 £1,000**

MARCEL DYF – 'Le Passage, Bretagne', Estuary In Brittany With Two Sailing Boats Moored Before A Low Promontary – signed – oil on canvas – 17½ x 21¼in.
(Osmond, Tricks & Son)
$1,980 £1,000

ROBERT EADIE – Dinan – signed, inscribed on the reverse – heightened with white – 18 x 13in.
(Sotheby's) **$218 £110**

ROBERT EADIE – Wellington Church – drawing – 21 x 28cm.
(Edmiston's) **$124 £64**

ROBERT EADIE – Glasgow Cathedral – drawing – 22 x 27cm.
(Edmiston's) **$85 £44**

T. EARL – 'View On The Ex Near Topsham Quay' – signed and dated 1827 – oil on canvas – 22 x 31in.
(Lalonde Bros. & Parham)
$1,960 £1,000

CHARLES EARLE – Figures On A Hill Above A Cornfield – signed – watercolour and bodycolour – 10¼ x 16½in.
(Christie's) **$252 £130**

RALPH E. W. EARLE – President Andrew Jackson – oil on canvas – 29 x 25in.
(Morton's Auction Exchange, Inc.)
$5,500 £2,791

HENRY EARP, SNR. – Pastoral Scene With Cattle, A Valley With Windmill Beyond – signed – watercolour – 9 x 20½in.
(Neales of Nottingham)
$158 £80

HENRY EARP, SNR. – The Arun, Arundel – signed – on board – 11 x 8½in.
(Sotheby's Belgravia) **$403 £210**

EAST – Sheep Grazing – on board – 12¾ x 9½in.
(Sotheby's Belgravia) **$89 £45**

SIR ALFRED EAST – Gathering Brushwood – signed – 60 x 39½in.
(Sotheby's Belgravia) **$960 £500**

SIR ALFRED EAST – Summertime In Norfolk – signed – 20 x 30in.
(Sotheby's Belgravia) **$3,018 £1,500**

W. EASTALL – Loading The Haycart – watercolour – 10 x 15in.
(G. A. Key) **$208** **£105**

JOSEPH EASTER – The Exterior Of An Exhibition Hall; and A View Of An Oriental Town, Perhaps Jerusalem – one signed with monogram – 10 x 12in. and 6¼ x 8½in.
(Christie's) **$125** **£65 Two**

EASTLAKE – Christ And Mary Magdalen – canvas on panel – 8 x 12in.
(Sotheby's Belgravia)
$89 **£45**

FRANCIS H. EASTWOOD – A Fine Step – signed – 34 x 51in.
(Sotheby's Belgravia)
$2,817 **£1,400**

G. EDEMA – An Extensive Wooded Landscape With Peasants And Animals, A Castle Beyond – 68¾ x 52¾in.
(Christie's) **$1,455** **£750**

GERARD VAN EDEMA – A View Of Florence From The South, The Apennine Hills In The Distance – 48½ x 63½in.
(Sotheby's) **$4,950** **£2,500**

JAMES H. EDGAR – Off To Market – signed, inscribed on the reverse – 23¼ x 19¼in.
(Sotheby's Belgravia)
$364 **£190**

AGNES EDMINSTON – Evening – signed, inscribed on a label on the reverse – 7 x 10in.
(Sotheby's Belgravia)
$86 **£45**

SAMUEL EDMONSTON – Rainbows On The Coast – signed – on panel – 11½ x 15in.
(Sotheby's Belgravia)
$247 **£130**

SAMUEL EDMONSTON – The Old Mill – signed – 21½ x 29½in.
(Sotheby's Belgravia)
$361 **£190**

HENRY EDRIDGE – A Busy Street In Northern France – pencil on buff paper – 15½ x 11in.
(Sotheby's) **$195** **£100**

HENRY EDRIDGE – Hampton Court, Herefordshire – pencil and brown and blue washes – signed below and dated 1802 – inscribed on the reverse – 8 x 11in.
(Sotheby's) **$257** **£130**

G. EDWARDS – An Emu; and An Ostrich – inscribed – watercolour – 10½ x 8¾in.
(Christie's) **$310** **£160 Pair**

LIONEL DALHOUSIE ROBERTSON EDWARDS – 'We're In For A Run' – signed – on millboard – 9½ x 6½in.
(Sotheby Bearne)
$931 **£480**

W. C. EDWARDS – Dutch Fishing Boats On A Beach – signed – 25¼ x 27½in.
(Sotheby's Belgravia) **$633** **£320**

G. VAN DEN EECKHOUT – Portrait Of A Bearded Old Man, Small Bust Length, Wearing Dark Robes And Cap – on panel – 15½ x 12¼in.
(Christie's) **$1,940** **£1,000**

AUGUSTUS LEOPOLD EGG – A Teasing Riddle, A Sketch – on board – 8¼ x 6in.
(Sotheby's Belgravia)
$228 **£120**

FRANK J. EGGINTON – The Kenmare River, Co. Kerry – signed – 10 x 14in.
(Sotheby's) **$388** **£200**

W. M. EGLEY – The Garden Wall – 28 x 18in.
(Sotheby's Belgravia) **$1,308 £650**

WILLIAM MAW EGLEY – Forget-Me-Not – signed and dated 1872 – 11½ x 9½in.
(Sotheby's Belgravia) **$634 £320**

SYMON EIKELENBERG – A Wooded River Landscape With Figures In The Foreground And Cottages Beyond – signed – on panel – 14½ x 19in.
(Christie's) **$7,600 £4,000**

GEO. S. ELGOOD – A Continental Backwater With A Cathedral – signed and dated 1886 – 13 x 11in.
(Warner Sheppard & Wade) **$94 £45**

FRED ELLIOT – Entering Sydney Harbour – signed – watercolour – 23 x 30cm.
(Australian Art Auctions) **$63 £32**

ALFRED J. ELLIS – A Moonlit Harbour – signed and dated 1901 – on panel – 15½ x 7½in.
(Sotheby's Belgravia) **$57 £30**

EDWIN ELLIS – St. Ives – signed and inscribed on the reverse – on board – oval – 11¼ x 9in.
(Sotheby's Belgravia) **$67 £35**

TRISTRAM J. ELLIS – Hammerfest – signed, inscribed and dated 1902 – 7 x 14½in.
(Sotheby's Belgravia) **$119 £60**

STEPHEN ELMER – Studies Of Partridges – 18¾ x 24in.
(Sotheby's) **$576 £300**

ELSHEIMER – Saint John The Evangelist – on copper – 8¾ x 6¾in.
(Christie's) **$621** **£320**

JOHN EMMS – A Quiet Pipe – signed – 19½ x 17in.
(Sotheby's Belgravia)
$1,509 **£750**

JOHN EMMS – Time For Bed – signed – 15¼ x 12¼in.
(Sotheby's Belgravia)
$532 **£280**

JOHN EMMS – Friends – 7 x 5½in.
(Sotheby's Belgravia)
$345 **£180**

JOHN EMMS – 'Grouse' And 'Sybil', Two Spaniels – signed, inscribed and dated 1876 – 13½ x 11½in.
(Sotheby's Belgravia) **$990** **£500 Pair**

JOHN EMMS – Ponies By A Stream – signed – 15 x 25in.
(Sotheby's Belgravia) **$673** **£340**

THOMAS ENDER – A Swimming Bath In The Neo-Classical Taste – signed – pencil and watercolour – 108 x 160mm.
(Christie's) **$34** **£18**

C. ENGELBRECHTSZ. – The Lamentation – on panel – 11¾ x 8¾in.
(Sotheby's) **$9,312** **£4,800**

W. ENGLES – 'Sleighs Racing' – signed – oil on canvas – 27½ x 33½in.
(Morton's Auction Exchange, Inc.) **$950** **£480**

ENGLISH PROVINCIAL SCHOOL, 20th century – Blowing Bubbles – on board – 23½ x 19in.
(Sotheby's Belgravia) **$304** **£160**

ENGLISH SCHOOL – Nottingham Castle From The South-West – watercolour – 11½ x 21in.
(Neales of Nottingham) **$59** **£30**

ENGLISH SCHOOL, early 19th century – Early Prospectors Panning Gold In A River; and An Australian Encampment With Men Felling Trees And Digging Pits In The Search For Gold – oil on canvas – 15 x 21¼in.
(Sotheby's) **$5,516** **£2,800 Pair**

ENGLISH SCHOOL – Portrait Of A Lancer Officer, Half Length, Wearing Full Dress Uniform – oil on ivory – 3½ x 4in.
(Wallis & Wallis) **$198** **£100**

ENGLISH SCHOOL, early 19th century – View Of The Indian Hut Below The Camp Looking Northward – inscribed – pencil, pen and grey ink, grey wash – 5 x 8in.
(Sotheby's) **$59** **£30**

ENGLISH SCHOOL, circa 1720 – Portrait Study Of A Gentleman – black and white chalks – recto; and Portrait Of A Cleric – black, red and white chalks on blue paper – verso – 10¾ x 7¾in.
(Sotheby's) **$291** **£150**

ENGLISH SCHOOL, circa 1790 – Mount Thomas Near Madras; A British Fort In Southern India – one inscribed – pencil and watercolour – 9½ x 14½in. and 12¾ x 16¼in.
(Sotheby's) **$177** **£90 Two**

ENGLISH SCHOOL, 18th century – Man In Armour.
(Dee & Atkinson)
$485 **£240**

ENGLISH SCHOOL, circa 1800 – Fort George, The Old Military Barracks In Upper Titchfield, Port Antonio, Jamaica – oil on canvas – 25 x 40½in.
(Sotheby's) **$887** **£450**

ENGLISH SCHOOL, 18th century – Half Length Portrait Inscribed 'Sir Butler Cavendish Wentworth, Bt.', In Red Velvet Buttoned Jacket – oil – 30 x 25in.
(James Harrison)
$1,045 **£500**

ENGLISH SCHOOL, circa 1850 – Hobart From Across The Harbour; The Quay, Hobart Town; and Longford, Tasmania – inscribed – watercolour – 9½ x 13½in., 9½ x 12in. and 10 x 13in.
(Sotheby's) **$591** **£300 Three**

ENGLISH SCHOOL, circa 1850 – Port Arthur; Port Darwin; Perth; and Mount Laura – inscribed – watercolour – 9¾ x 13¼in., 8¼ x 10¼in., 9¾ x 12¾in. and 9½ x 12¾in.
(Sotheby's) **$512** **£260 Four**

ENGLISH SCHOOL, circa 1850 – Panoramic View Of Kingston House, Knightsbridge, With Princes Gate, Looking South – heightened with white – 15½ x 36in.
(Sotheby's) **$1,940** **£1,000**

ENGLISH SCHOOL, 19th century, In The Manner Of Henry Bone – The Sailor's Farewell: A Young Man Stands Beside A Young Woman, With Trees And A Boat Beyond; And A Young Man With A Young Lady By A Large Tree – enamels – 12 x 9cm.
(Henry Spencer & Sons)
$368 £190 Pair

ENGLISH SCHOOL, 19th century – A Portrait Of A White Hussar – oil on ivory – 7 x 5cm.
(King & Chasemore)
$424 £215

ENGLISH SCHOOL, 19th century – A Portrait Of An Elderly Lady Wearing A Bonnet – oil on ivory – 9 x 6cm.
(King & Chasemore)
$217 £110

ENGLISH SCHOOL, 19th century – Scene On A Deck Of A Galleon, With Figures – oil on canvas – 79 x 107cm.
(King & Chasemore)
$2,475 £1,250

ENGLISH SCHOOL, circa 1850 – A View Of Kowloon – watercolour – 11½ x 11¼in.
(Sotheby's (Hong Kong) Ltd.)
$1,189 £601

ENGLISH SCHOOL, 19th century – A Portrait Of The British Ambassador To Russia – oil on ivory – 6 x 5cm.
(King & Chasemore)
$433 £220

ENGLISH SCHOOL, 19th century – Wooded Landscapes With Figures And Boats At Lake Side – oil on canvas – 19 x 23in.
(Morphets of Harrogate)
$446 £225 Pair

ENGLISH SCHOOL, mid 19th century – Thomas Miller – A Miner At Mount Vernon Copper Mines, Port Royal Mountains, Jamaica; and Native Thatched Huts In A Clearing – one inscribed and dated 1844 – watercolour – and the other pencil and watercolour – 9¼ x 6½in. and 8½ x 11in.
(Sotheby's) **$69 £35 Two**

ENGLISH SCHOOL, 19th century – Cottage Interior, With A Young Lady Conversing With Two Elderly Ladies, Seated By A Table, A Gentleman Stands In The Doorway, Hills And Trees Beyond – monogrammed – 34 x 28.5cm.
(Henry Spencer & Sons) **$407** **£210**

ENGLISH SCHOOL – Norfolk Woodland Scene With Cottage And Figures On Path – oil – 18 x 24in.
(G. A. Key) **$150** **£76**

ENGLISH SCHOOL, circa 1850 – Melbourne Seen From The South; and Melbourne Seen From The River – inscribed – watercolour – 10 x 13in. and 9½ x 12¾in.
(Sotheby's) **$433** **£220 Two**

ARTHUR HENRY ENOCK – A Three-Masted Barque In An Estuary – signed – 20 x 30in.
(Sotheby's Belgravia) **$640** **£320**

SIR JACOB EPSTEIN – Hollyhocks – signed – watercolour, heightened with bodycolour – 22½ x 17¼in.
(Sotheby's) **$792** **£400**

SIR JACOB EPSTEIN – Reclining Nude – pencil on buff paper – 13¼ x 16¾in.
(Sotheby's) **$198** **£100**

ANDRIES VAN ERTVELT – Men-O'-War In A Storm – 40½ x 63¾in.
(Christie's) **$3,648** **£1,900**

ANDRIES VAN ERTVELT – A Battle Between Spanish And Dutch Ships – on panel – 18 x 24in.
(Sotheby's) **$7,920** **£4,000**

JACOB VAN ES – Oysters On A Plate With A Roemer And A Lemon On A Table – on panel – 9¾ x 13½in.
(Christie's) **$6,208** **£3,200**

ARTHUR ESAM – A Wounded Comrade In The Outback – signed and dated '94 – watercolour – 7¼ x 11¾in.
(Sotheby's) **$493** **£250**

ARTHUR ESAM – Settlers Working In The Fields, New South Wales – watercolour – 8 x 15in.
(Sotheby's) **$414** **£210**

JACOB ESSELENS – A River Landscape With Boats Near A Lock – black chalk, pen and brown ink – 7.2 x 20cm.
(Christie's) **$537** **£280**

WILLIAM ETTY – A Nude Study – on board – 19½ x 23½in.
(Sotheby's Belgravia) **$1,006** **£500**

WILLIAM ETTY – A Nude Woman, Seated, With A Landscape Beyond – on board – 15 x 12½in.
(Christie's) **$873** **£450**

RICHARD EURICH – Silver Morning On The Solent – signed and dated '72 – on board – 20 x 30in.
(Sotheby's) **$495** **£250**

BERNARD EVANS – Near Barmouth – signed – 13¾ x 20¼in.
(Sotheby's) **$110** **£55**

MERLYN EVANS – Desert Scene, North Africa – 12 x 16in.
(Sotheby's) **$198** **£100**

POWYS ARTHUR LENTHALL EVANS – Nathaniel, Marquess Curzon Of Kedleston – signed 'Quiz' and inscribed – heightened with white – 13½ x 9in.
(Sotheby's Belgravia) **$9** **£5**

WILLIAM EVANS OF ETON – Windsor Castle From The River, With Figures In A Punt In The Foreground – watercolour heightened with white – 11¾ x 15½in.
(Christie's) **$291** **£150**

WILLIAM EVANS OF ETON – A Tinker's Encampment By A Ruined Abbey – watercolour heightened with white – 10½ x 15in.
(Christie's) **$184** **£95**

WILLIAM EVANS OF ETON – A Village In The Highlands – watercolour heightened with white – 26 x 36¼in.
(Christie's) **$873** **£450**

JOHN WILSON EWBANK – A Classical Landscape – 24½ x 29½in.
(Sotheby's) **$576** **£300**

KASPAR VAN EYCK – A Galley Docking In A Southern Port, A Towing Vessel And Several Sailing Ships Offshore – 33½ x 53½in.
(Sotheby's) **$3,298** **£1,700**

JO. VAN EYKEN – The Figures And Donkeys With Sheep On Pathway – signed – wood panel – 9½ x 12in.
(Morphets of Harrogate) **$772** **£390**

E. EYRE – Broadstairs, Kent, 'Neptune' At Low Tide – 8¾ x 12½in.
(Sotheby's) **$320** **£160**

JAMES FAED, JNR. – At Cramond, Early Spring – signed and dated 1885 – 9¾ x 13½in.
(Sotheby's) **$2,304** **£1,200**

JAMES FAED – A River Landscape – signed and dated 1877 – 12¾ x 18¾in.
(Sotheby's Belgravia) **$67** **£35**

JOHN FAED – A Lancashire Wench – inscribed and dated 1884 – 24 x 29in.
(Sotheby's) **$693** **£350**

THOMAS FAED – The First Break In The Family – signed, inscribed and dated 1857 – heightened with bodycolour – 31 x 43in.
(Sotheby's) **$4,800** **£2,500**

THOMAS FAIRBAIRN – Tarbert, Loch Fyne – watercolour – 11 x 26cm.
(Edmiston's) **$113** **£58**

THOMAS FAIRBAIRN – The Bull Inn – signed – heightened with bodycolour – 8½ x 21in.
(Sotheby's Belgravia) **$288** **£150**

VAN FALENS – A Hawking Party Resting Outside A Country House – on copper engraving plate – oval – 4½ x 5¾in.
(Christie's) **$1,067** **£550**

CAREL VAN FALENS – A Stag Hunt In A Wooded River Landscape, A Party Crossing A Ford, Mountains Beyond – on panel – 12 x 15¾in.
(Sotheby's) **$3,168** **£1,600**

LUIS RICARDO FALERO – The Lily Fairy – signed with monogram and dated '88 – 39 x 21in.
(Sotheby's Belgravia) **$4,829** **£2,400**

PIETRO FANCELLI – A Male Nude Lying On The Ground – inscribed – black and white chalk on buff paper – 430 x 575mm.
(Christie's) **$91** **£48**

JO. FANT – Native Women Preparing Food In Their Hut, Two Men In A Canoe On The River, Another On The Bank, The South American Jungle Beyond – indistinctly signed and dated 1830 – oil on canvas – 17½ x 25½in.
(Sotheby's) **$1,182** **£600**

JOSEPH FARINGTON – A Cottage And Barn On A Stream – pen and brown ink and grey wash – 12½ x 10¾in.
(Christie's) **$87** **£45**

CORRALL FARMER – A Woodland Path; A Country Stream – one signed and dated 1905 – 16 x 22in.
(Sotheby's Belgravia)
$806 **£420 Pair**

DAVID FARQUHARSON – A Ruined Castle On A Rocky Coast – signed and dated '83-5 – 30 x 21in.
(Sotheby's) **$752** **£380**

DAVID FARQUHARSON – "Hedgerows In May", Children Gathering Blossom On A Cliff Top – signed and dated 1906 – oil on canvas – 16 x 22in.
(Morphets of Harrogate)
$1,261 **£650**

DAVID FARQUHARSON – In Lamlash, Arran – signed and dated 1880 – 19½ x 35½in.
(Sotheby's) **$2,976** **£1,550**

DAVID FARQUHARSON – Early Snow On Ben Wyvis – signed and dated 1906 – 29 x 49in.
(Sotheby's) **$1,632** **£850**

DAVID FARQUHARSON – Glenfalloch Wood, Loch Lomond – signed and dated 1905 – 15½ x 23½in.
(Sotheby's) **$960** **£500**

DAVID FARQUHARSON – Salmon Fishing, Balmoral – signed and dated '92/3 – 59½ x 89½in.
(Sotheby's) **$2,880** **£1,500**

DAVID FARQUHARSON – Home From The Moors – signed and dated 1881 – 21½ x 25½in.
(Sotheby's) **$1,536** **£800**

JOSEPH FARQUHARSON – Over Snowfields – signed – 23¼ x 19¼in.
(Sotheby's) **$2,970** **£1,500**

JOSEPH FARQUHARSON – Deeside – signed – 19 x 29in.
(Sotheby's) **$1,980** **£1,000**

JOSEPH FARQUHARSON – 'Sheep In Snow Covered Pine Copse' – signed – oil – 45 x 33in.
(Husseys) **$2,765** **£1,425**

JOSEPH FARQUHARSON – Sunset – signed – 25½ x 39½in.
(Sotheby's) **$4,224** **£2,200**

JOSEPH FARQUHARSON – When Snow The Pasture Sheets – signed, inscribed on a label on the reverse – 36 x 59in.
(Sotheby's) **$7,920** **£4,000**

JOSEPH FARQUHARSON – Sheep On A Wooded Path, Autumn – signed – 31 x 41in.
(Sotheby's) **$6,336** **£3,200**

FARRIER – A Quiet Moment – on board – 12½ x 10in.
(Sotheby's Belgravia) **$67** **£35**

R. FARRIER – The Old Curiosity Shop – 19 x 16in.
(Sotheby's Belgravia) **$554** **£280**

JAMES G. FAULDS – On The Shore – signed, inscribed on a label on the reverse – 10 x 14in.
(Sotheby's Belgravia)
$268 **£140**

C. FAULKNER – The London to Brighton Coach – signed – on board – 16 x 34cm.
(King & Chasemore)
$614 **£320 Pair**

C. FAULKNER – Coaching Scenes – both signed, one dated 1897 – on board – 7 x 12¼in.
(Sotheby's Belgravia)
$365 **£190 Pair**

JOHN FAULKNER – A Warwickshire Farm – signed and inscribed – heightened with bodycolour – 17 x 27¾in.
(Sotheby's Belgravia)
$792 **£400**

J. FAULKNER – 'Near Wicklow' – watercolour – 12 x 20½in.
(W. H. Lane & Son)
$614 **£320**

J. FAUREL – Young Woman Feeding Hens – on oak panel – 38 x 27cm.
(Edmiston's) **$179** **£92**

THE MASTER OF THE FEMALE HALF-LENGTHS, Circle of – Saint Catherine; and Saint Mary Magdalen – 27 x 8¾in.
(Christie's) **$15,360 £8,000**

THE MASTER OF THE FEMALE HALF-LENGTHS – The Madonna And Child – on panel – 15 x 11in.
(Christie's) **$4,268 £2,200**

W. W. FENN – Painting Under The Cliff At Low Water – signed, inscribed on the stretcher – 13 x 30in.
(Sotheby's Belgravia) **$268 £140**

FENWICK – Ravenscraig Castle – 30 x 49cm.
(Edmiston's) **$58 £30**

FERG – A Harbour Scene – on panel – 7½ x 8¾in.
(Christie's) **$679 £350**

FRANS DE PAULA FERG – A Landscape With Peasants Dancing; A Fair Outside A Southern Town – on copper – 10¼ x 14in.
(Sotheby's) **$19,600 £10,000** Two

F. DE PAULA FERG – A Wooded Landscape With A Traveller Conversing With Peasants – 13½ x 16¾in.
(Sotheby's) **$2,178 £1,100**

J. T. FERGUSON – The Beach At Scarborough – signed – 4¾ x 11½in.
(Sotheby's Belgravia) $27 £14

JAMES W. FERGUSON – On A Venetian Canal – signed and dated 1921 – canvas on panel – 30 x 71in.
(Sotheby's Belgravia) $342 £180

JOHN DUNCAN FERGUSSON – An Evening Sky, Peebles – signed and inscribed on the reverse – on panel – 7 x 9in.
(Sotheby's) $729 £380

JOHN FERNELEY, JNR. – A Mounted Cavalry Officer, In A Landscape – 12¼ x 10¼in.
(Christie's) $582 £300

JOHN FERNELEY, JNR. – A Mounted Officer Of The 2nd Dragoon Guards – inscribed and dated 1857 – 11 x 13½in.
(Christie's) $776 £400

FERRARESE SCHOOL, circa 1600 – The Madonna And Child With Saints Augustine And Nicholas Of Tolentino – 29½ x 25¼in.
(Sotheby's) $1,261 £650

FERRARI – The Madonna And Child – 35 x 31in.
(Christie's) $1,552 £800

CIRO FERRI – Design For The Front Panel Of A Stage Coach – signed or inscribed – black chalk – 24 x 17.5cm.
(Christie's) $537 £280

FIAMMINGO – Mercury And Paris – canvas on board – 15¾ x 15½in.
(Christie's) $252 £130

HARRY FIDLER – Sheep Grazing – signed – 14 x 12in.
(Sotheby's Belgravia) $211 £110

HARRY FIDLER – Cattle In The Shade – signed with monogram – 10¾ x 13½in.
(Sotheby's Belgravia) $192 £100

C. FIELDHOUSE – On The Wymon, Dolgelly – signed and inscribed on the reverse – on board – 12 x 19in.
(Sotheby's Belgravia) $67 £35

FIELDING – An Oyster Girl – inscribed on the reverse – oval – 11 x 9in.
(Sotheby's Belgravia) $209 £110

ANTHONY VANDYCK COPLEY FIELDING – Cattle By A Lake; and Boats On A Lake – 6¼ x 9½in. and 6¾ x 10in.
(Sotheby's) $873 £450 Pair

ANTONY VANDYKE COPLEY FIELDING – Skiddaw From Derwentwater, Cumberland – signed and dated 1839 – 6¾ x 9¾in.
(Sotheby's) $1,067 £550

ANTHONY VANDYKE COPLEY FIELDING – Cattle In A Landscape With A Lone Tower – signed – 5¾ x 7¾in.
(Sotheby's) $349 £180

ANTHONY VANDYKE COPLEY FIELDING – An East Indiaman Wrecked On A Headland – signed and dated 1831 watercolour – 27¾ x 45in.
(Christie's) $1,843 £950

COPLEY FIELDING – Landscape – watercolour – 7 x 10¼in.
(Outhwaite & Litherland) $141 £70

T. FIELDING – Mountainous Lakeland Landscape, With Figures And Buildings On The Shore, Trees And A Castle Ruins On The Hilltop – signed and dated 1831 – watercolour – 37 x 57cm.
(Henry Spencer & Sons) $194 £100

FIERAVINO – A Still Life Of Fruit, On A Wooden Table Covered By A Multi-Coloured Tapestry – 30 x 55in.
(Sotheby's) $3,564 £1,800

F. FIERAVINO – Still Life With Fruit And A Parrot – 30½ x 56¼in.
(Sotheby's) **$10,780 £5,500**

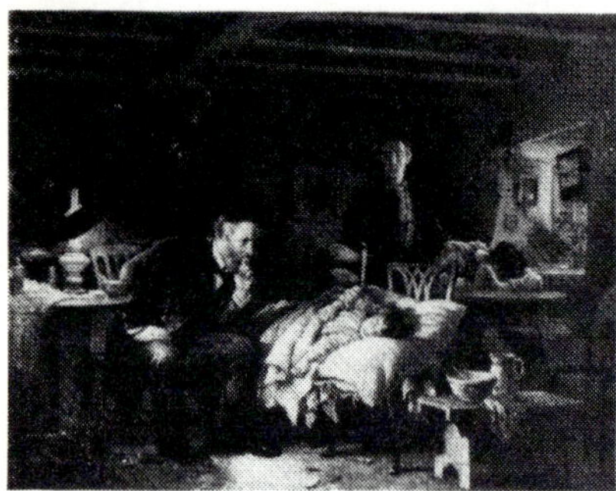

L. FILDES, After – The Sick Child – 15 x 19in.
(Sotheby's Belgravia) **$228 £120**

ALEXANDRE WILLE LE FILS – A Portrait Of A Young Woman, Head And Shoulders – oval – 21 x 17¼in.
(Sotheby's) **$1,358 £700**

HENEAGE FINCH – At Packington, Warwickshire, Trees By A Gate – inscribed – pen and brown ink and brown and grey washes – 8½ x 11in.
(Sotheby's) **$585 £300**

W. FINCHER – 'May Acre', A Bay Hunter, Outside His Stable – signed, inscribed and dated 1869 – 20 x 24in.
(Sotheby's Belgravia) **$266 £140**

JACOBELLO DEL FIORE *(Active 1401; ca 1439)* – The Madonna Of Humility – gold ground – on panel – 11¼ x 18½in.
(Sotheby's) **$75,240 £38,000**

MARIO NUZZI, Called Mario Dei Fiori – Danae In A Surround Of Flowers Supported By Putti – 49¾ x 65½in.
(Christie's) **$9,600 £5,000**

LUDWIG HANS FISCHER – Venice: The Bacino With Fishermen From The Riva Dei Schiavoni – signed and dated 1895 – watercolour heightened with white – 300 x 465mm.
(Christie's) **$722 £380**

ISAAC FISCHES – David And Goliath – signed and dated 1689 – pencil and brown wash heightened with white on light brown paper – 25.3 x 31.3cm.
(Christie's) **$576 £300**

G. R. FISHER – Ed. Anderson Defending Himself From Grizzly Bears – signed, inscribed and dated '26 – oil on board – 9 x 12½in.
(Sotheby's) **$20 £10**

CAPT. G. DRUMMOND FISH – The Last Hole, Prestwick – signed – 12 x 18in.
(Sotheby's) **$288** **£150**

WILLIAM MARK FISHER – A Summer's Day – on panel – 21¼ x 17¼in.
(Sotheby's Belgravia) **$845** **£420**

MARK FISHER – Shepherd With His Sheep – signed and indistinctly dated – 17½ x 25in.
(Sotheby's) **$891** **£450**

MARK FISHER – Watermill And Weir – 21½ x 30in.
(Sotheby's) **$693** **£350**

WILLIAM MARK FISHER – Hatfield Heath, Sussex – signed, inscribed on a label on the reverse – 20½ x 23¾in.
(Sotheby's Belgravia) **$2,213** **£1,100**

WILLIAM MARK FISHER – Cattle In A Meadow – signed – 18 x 21in.
(Sotheby's Belgravia) **$1,811** **£900**

EDWARD H. FITCHEW – Peasant Girl Wearing A Green-Striped Dress With Brown Shawl And Petticoat, A Small Pup Seated Before Her, A Landscape Beyond – monogramed and dated 1877 – 31.5 x 21.5cm.
(Henry Spencer & Sons) **$673** **£340**

JOHN ANSTER FITZGERALD – The Release Of Ariel – The Tempest – signed with monogram, signed and inscribed on a label on the reverse – watercolour, heightened with white – 19 x 11½in.
(Sotheby's Belgravia) **$7,042 £3,500**

JOHN ANSTER FITZGERALD – The Waitress – signed – 24 x 20in.
(Sotheby's Belgravia) **$905 £450**

DAN FLAVIN – Composition – 'From August 5th 1964' – signed and dated '66 – white gouache on black paper – 11¾ x 11¾in.
(Sotheby's) **$1,683 £850**

JOHN FLAXMAN – Portrait Of The Rev. John Clowes, Head And Shoulders – pencil – 6¼ x 5¾in.
(Sotheby's) **$507 £260**

GEORG FLEGEL – A Still Life With A Crayfish – on panel – 14 x 17in.
(Sotheby's) **$54,320 £28,000**

FLEMISH SCHOOL, 16th century – Christ On The Cross, A Wooded Landscape, With Magdalen Kneeling At The Foot Of The Cross, The Virgin With Hands Clasped, St. John Weeping – on panel – 12¾ x 9½in.
(Sotheby's) **$3,880 £2,000**

FLEMISH SCHOOL, 17th century – Christ On The Cross, The Three Marys Below – on metal – 8¾ x 6½in.
(Sotheby's) **$107 £55**

FLEMISH SCHOOL, 17th century – Portrait Of A Lady, Bust Length, In Black With A White Ruff And Cap, Adorned With A Red Coral Necklace – on panel – 22½ x 17¾in.
(Sotheby's) **$1,683 £850**

FLEMISH SCHOOL, early 17th century, After Correggio – The Rest On The Flight Into Egypt – canvas on board – 56 x 44¼in.
(Sotheby's) **$3,104 £1,600**

FLEMISH SCHOOL, 17th century – The Adoration Of The Shepherds – black chalk, pen and brown ink, brown wash – 42 x 27.7cm.
(Christie's) **$537 £280**

FLEMISH SCHOOL, circa 1700 – A Sacrifice – red chalk, brown wash, squared in black chalk – 25.2 x 47.2cm.
(Christie's) **$729 £380**

FLEMISH SCHOOL, 17th century – A Pagan Sacrifice – on panel – 30¼ x 26¾in.
(Sotheby's) **$4,950 £2,500**

FLEMISH SCHOOL, early 18th century – A Mountainous River Landscape With Travellers – 10½ x 15¼in.
(Sotheby's) **$1,591 £820**

C. FLETCHER – Coaching In The Country – both signed – on panel – 9¾ x 11¾in.
(Sotheby's Belgravia) **$748 £390 Pair**

FLINCK – Portrait Of Saskia Van Uylenburgh, Standing Half Length, In A Gold Brocade Dress – on panel – 26 x 19½in.
(Sotheby's) **$2,079 £1,050**

GOVAERT FLINCK – Portrait Of A Gentleman, In Black With A Broad-Brimmed Black Hat, A Grey Curtain Behind – signed and dated 1641 – on panel – oval – 29¾ x 23½in.
(Sotheby's) **$13,580 £7,000**

RUSSELL FLINT – Reclining Nude – signed – colour wash drawing – 14 x 19in.
(G. A. Key) **$75 £38**

SIR WILLIAM RUSSELL FLINT – Alpine Landscape With A Sunlit Road Before A Distant Village – signed, inscribed on the reverse – watercolour – 10¾ x 15in.
(Osmond, Tricks & Son) **$1,505 £760**

SIR WILLIAM RUSSELL FLINT – Blazing Weather, Uzes, June, 1936 – signed – watercolour – 19½ x 26¾in.
(Sotheby's) **$10,296 £5,200**

SIR WILLIAM RUSSELL FLINT – Three Girls By A Wall – signed – watercolour – 13½ x 15¼in.
(Sotheby's) **$2,178 £1,100**

SIR WILLIAM RUSSELL FLINT – Dwellers On The Ground Floor – signed – watercolour, heightened with bodycolour – 21½ x 30in.
(Sotheby's) **$15,048 £7,600**

SIR WILLIAM RUSSELL FLINT – Lydia – signed – watercolour – 19 x 26in.
(Sotheby's) **$8,316 £4,200**

SIR WILLIAM RUSSELL FLINT – Venturers – signed – watercolour – 13¾ x 10¾in.
(Sotheby's) **$6,336 £3,200**

SIR WILLIAM RUSSELL FLINT – The Toilet Of Venus – signed with initials – 24¼ x 31¼in.
(Sotheby's) **$4,158 £2,100**

SIR WILLIAM RUSSELL FLINT – Morning – signed – watercolour – 13¼ x 20in.
(Sotheby's) **$3,960 £2,000**

SIR WILLIAM RUSSELL FLINT – Romantic River, Languedoc – signed – watercolour – 13 x 24¾in.
(Sotheby's) **$3,762 £1,900**

SIR WILLIAM RUSSELL FLINT – The Piazzetta, Venice – signed – watercolour – 19½ x 26½in.
(Sotheby's) **$6,930 £3,500**

SIR WILLIAM RUSSELL FLINT – Loch Morar Side – signed – watercolour – 12½ x 19¼in.
(Sotheby's) **$2,574 £1,300**

SIR WILLIAM RUSSELL FLINT – The Gareloch And The Cobbler – watercolour – 37 x 54cm.
(Edmiston's) **$1,746 £900**

FLORENTINE SCHOOL, circa 1465 – A Knight In Armour With Drawn Sword, On A Black Leaping Horse, With A Soldier On Foot, In An Open Rocky Landscape With A Winding River And Mountains In The Distance – on panel – 19 x 17in.
(Christie's) **$16,320 £8,500**

FLORENTINE SCHOOL, circa 1500 – Study Of The Head Of An Angel – pen and brown ink – 4.4 x 3.5cm.
(Christie's) **$153 £80**

FLORENTINE SCHOOL, circa 1570 – Cosimo De' Medici, Head And Shoulders – grisaille – on paper on canvas – 15¼ x 9¾in.
(Christie's) **$460 £240**

FLORENTINE SCHOOL, circa 1600 – A Standing Nude – inscribed on the reverse – red chalk – 430 x 280mm.
(Christie's) **$143 £75**

FLORENTINE SCHOOL, late 16th century – Studies Of Nudes And Heads – red chalk on two attached sheets – 18.6 x 19.7cm.
(Christie's) **$288 £150**

FLORIS – The Death Of Lucretia – on panel – 41 x 29in.
(Sotheby's) **$776 £400**

FRANS FLORIS – The Infancy Of Bacchus – on panel – 45 x 66in.
(Christie's) **$6,208** **£3,200**

F. FLORIS – Diana, Head And Shoulders, In Yellow, Adorned With Pearls And Holding An Arrow – on panel – 17¾ x 14¾in.
(Sotheby's) **$990** **£500**

DAVID FOGGIE – Bostonstump, Lincolnshire – signed and dated '32 – 15¼ x 10¾in.
(Sotheby's) **$168** **£85**

LUCIO FONTANA – Concetto Spaziale – signed on the reverse – lacquered wood and perforated canvas – 39¼ x 43¼in.
(Sotheby's) **$7,920** **£4,000**

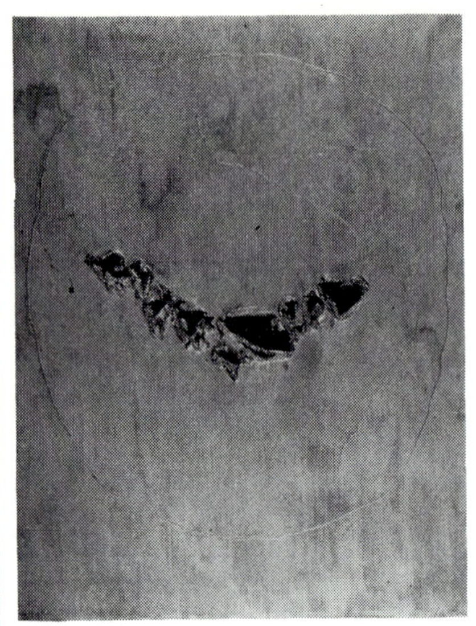

LUCIO FONTANA – Concetto Spaziale – signed – gold paint and oil on canvas – 57½ x 45in.
(Sotheby's) **$12,870** **£6,500**

FRANCESCO FONTEBASSO – The Presentation In The Temple, The High Priest, In A Cape Lined With Red, Standing On The Steps Of An Altar With The Infant Christ In His Arms – 21¾ x 24in.
(Sotheby's) **$4,268** **£2,200**

STANHOPE ALEXANDER FORBES – Marazion Beach – signed and dated 1927 – oil on canvas – 24 x 30in.
(Geering & Colyer) **$1,116** **£575**

WILLIAM FORBES – Westminster And The Thames – signed and dated 1905 – 19 x 29½in.
(Sotheby's Belgravia) **$139** **£70**

E. FORNARI – Interior Scene With A Girl In A Blue Dress Taking A Yellow Garment From A Kist – signed – oil on wood panel – 11 x 7in.
(Morphets of Harrogate) **$1,901 £980**

CHARLES FORSTER, JNR. – Rustic Figures – oil on board – 9½ x 7½in.
(Outhwaite & Litherland) **$586 £290**

RICHARD FORSYTH – Farm Near Largo, Winter Morning – 29 x 40cm.
(Edmiston's) **$47 £24**

BIRKET FOSTER – Wooded Landscape And Stream – watercolour – 16.2 x 22cm.
(Edmiston's) **$54 £28**

MILES BIRKET FOSTER – English Country Scene – signed – watercolour – 17 x 25cm.
(Australian Art Auctions) **$819 £427**

M. BIRKET FOSTER – "The Stepping Stones", Depicting Two Children Crossing A Stream – monogram signed – watercolour – 21 x 15¼in.
(Richard Baker & Baker) **$1,261 £650**

W. FOSTER – The S.S. 'City of Grafton' – signed and dated 1885, inscribed on a label on the reverse – heightened with body-colour – 13 x 25½in.
(Sotheby's Belgravia) **$173 £90**

EMANUEL PHILLIPS FOX – Sydney Harbour – signed – oil on panel – 17 x 21.5cm.
(Australian Art Auctions) **$490 £705**

H. C. FOX – 'Cattle Watering' – watercolour – 14½ x 21in.
(W. H. Lane & Son) **$250 £130**

ROBERT FOX – After The Masque – signed – 23½ x 19in.
(Sotheby's Belgravia) **$158 £80**

JEAN-HONORE FRAGONARD *(1732-1806)* – 'Le Pont De Bois' – 24½ x 33in.
(Sotheby's) **$297,000 £150,000**

J. H. FRAGONARD – The Return From The Fields – 17½ x 14¼in.
(Christie's) **$19,200 £10,000**

FRAGONARD – Figures In A Park – 20 x 25½in.
(Christie's) **$136 £70**

FRAMPTON – By A Window – 17 x 13in.
(Sotheby's Belgravia) **$192 £100**

CHARLES FRANCE – Cattle By A River – signed – 15¼ x 23¼in.
(Sotheby's Belgravia) **$604 £300**

FRANCESCHINI – Hagar And Ishmael In The Wilderness – 14½ x 18¼in.
(Sotheby's) **$1,513 £780**

FRANCIA – A Church By A River At Sunset – watercolour – 6¾ x 3¾in.
(Christie's) **£68 £35**

FRANCOIS LOUIS THOMAS FRANCIA – A Lake In The Mountains, Possibly Bala – pencil and grey wash – 5¾ x 9¼in.
(Christie's) **$87 £45**

FRANCOIS LOUIS THOMAS FRANCIA – Fishing Boats Moored In A Harbour – signed and dated 1829 – heightened with white – 19¾ x 26in.
(Sotheby's) **$388** **£200**

SAM FRANCIS – Untitled Composition – signed with initials and dated '56 – gouache on paper – 24½ x 35½in.
(Sotheby's) **$15,444** **£7,800**

H. FRANCK – Rural Landscape With A Girl And Geese By A Pond, And Cottage Among Trees – signed – oil on canvas – 58.5 x 85.5cm.
(Henry Spencer & Sons) **$792** **£400**

FRANCKEN – The Adoration Of The Shepherds – on metal – 6½ x 8¾in.
(Sotheby's) **$184** **£95**

FRANCKEN – The Marriage At Cana – on metal – 6¼ x 8¼in.
(Sotheby's) **$554** **£280**

FRANCKEN, After Marinus – Saint Jerome In His Study – inscribed – on panel – 22 x 17in.
(Christie's) **$1,746** **£900**

F. FRANCKEN – The Crucifixion, Christ On The Cross Flanked By The Two Thieves, Soldiers Bartering For The Robe Of Christ In The Foreground, Other Passion Scenes Depicted Beyond – on panel – 19 x 14½in.
(Sotheby's) **$1,980** **£1,000**

F. FRANCKEN The Younger – The Adoration Of The Shepherds – on copper panel – 14 x 11¼in.
(Lawrence) **$1,683** **£850**

F. FRANCKEN The Younger – Peasants Merrymaking In An Interior – on panel – 21½ x 27in.
(Christie's) **$8,148** **£4,200**

FRANS FRANCKEN, Manner of – The Apparition Of The Figure Of Death To A Young Dandy; and The Apparition Of The Figure Of Death To An Old Man – on panel – 14 x 10in.
(Sotheby's) **$6,930** **£3,500 Pair**

FRANS FRANCKEN The Younger – An Artist's Studio – signed and inscribed – on panel – 19½ x 27½in.
(Christie's) **$13,580** **£7,000**

S. FRANGIAMORE-ROME – 'The Rebuff', A Wife Scolding Her Courtier Husband In The Salon With Three Bemused Onlookers – signed – oil – 24 x 19in.
(Husseys) **$3,996** **£2,060**

FRANKENTHAL SCHOOL – The Angel Appearing To Balaam – on copper – 5¼ x 7¾in.
(Christie's) **$4,656** **£2,400**

ALEXANDER FRASER – Dancing To The Pipes – 16 x 20in.
(Sotheby's) **$960** **£500**

ALEXANDER FRASER – Awakening Vapours – on panel – 16 x 14in.
(Sotheby's) **$460** **£240**

ALEXANDER FRASER – Love's Face At The Window – signed – 9¼ x 11½in.
(Sotheby's) **$729** **£380**

MALCOLM FRASER – A Maiden Playing A Lute – signed – oil on canvas – 22¾ x 15¾in.
(Sotheby's) **$217** **£110**

WILLIAM MILLER FRAZER – Whitekirk, East Linton – signed, inscribed – 17½ x 23in.
(Sotheby's) **$576** **£300**

WILLIAM MILLER FRAZER – A Woodland Pool – signed – 23½ x 35½in.
(Sotheby's) **$576** **£300**

WILLIAM MILLER FRAZER – An Atholl Moorland – signed and dated 1918 – 33 x 43in.
(Sotheby's) **$960** **£500**

WILLIAM MILLER FRAZER – On The Nene, Islip – signed, inscribed on a label – 13 x 17in.
(Sotheby's) **$652** **£340**

WILLIAM MILLER FRAZER – Summertime – signed – 24½ x 29½in.
(Sotheby's) **$960** **£500**

WILLIAM MILLER FRAZER – A Glimpse In The Woods – signed and dated '96 – 23½ x 15½in.
(Sotheby's) **$691** **£360**

WILLIAM MILLER FRAZER – The Mill Pond, Autumn – 22 x 16in.
(Sotheby's) **$614** **£320**

W. P. B. FREEMAN – Cromer Beach With Shipping – oil on panel – 5½ x 9in.
(W. H. Lane & Son) **$307** **£160**

W. P. BARNES FREEMAN – 'Great Yarmouth By Moonlight' watercolour – 12 x 22½in.
(J. W. Hilham) **$201** **£100**

ANNIE FRENCH – 'The Bryde Heedes Not Hyr Garments But Hyr Deere Brydegroomes Face' – signed and dated 1905 on the reverse – heightened with bodycolour, gold and silver paint – 5¼ x 5¼in.
(Sotheby's) **$576** **£300**

ANNIE FRENCH – 'Toss A Ball, Toss A Ball, Tell Me True, How Many More Years Shall I Go Through?' – signed and dated 1902 – heightened with bodycolour and gold – on buff paper – 9½ x 6in.
(Sotheby's) **$1,056** **£550**

ANNIE FRENCH – The Three Graces – watercolour – 15 x 24.5cm.
(Edmiston's) **$660** **£340**

PERCY FRENCH – A Bog Scene With Rain Clouds Over Distant Hills – signed and dated 1904 – 4¾ x 7in.
(Sotheby's) **$543** **£280**

FRENCH SCHOOL, circa 1680 – An Italian Town – red chalk, pen and brown ink – 187 x 273mm.
(Christie's) **$76** **£40**

FRENCH SCHOOL – A View Of Subiaco; and A View Of The Colosseum – on panel – 7 x 8¾in. and 4½ x 8¼in.
(Christie's) **$614** **£320 Two**

FRENCH SCHOOL, circa 1700 – Arrangements Of Flowers On Ledges Covered With Carpets – one inscribed – bodycolour on vellum – 22.2 x 18.9cm.
(Christie's) **$2,496** **£1,300 Pair**

FRENCH SCHOOL, 18th century – A Still Life Of Flowers In A Gilt Bowl, On A Table Covered With A Cloth Trimmed With Gold Brocade – 29 x 44½in.
(Sotheby's) **$4,356** **£2,200**

FRENCH SCHOOL, 19th century – Enfant Epluchant Un Fruit – inscribed and dated 1863 – oil, pen and ink – 9½ x 7in.
(Sotheby's) **$475** **£250**

FRENCH SCHOOL, early 19th century – Indian Woman And Child; Jhon Canacadia – Indian Of Canacadia Village; and Marry, Femme D'Un Chef Sauvage, Washington – all inscribed, one dated 1821 and one dated 1808 – pencil and watercolour – 6½ x 4¾in., 7½ x 6in. and 7½ x 5in.
(Sotheby's) **$1,182** **£600 Three**

FRENCH SCHOOL, 19th century – Homme Nu Courant – pastel – 10¼ x 14¼in.
(Sotheby's) **$124** **£65**

FRENCH SCHOOL, 19th century – Peasants In National Costume Resting In A Harvest Field – oil on canvas – 23 x 33in.
(Morton's Auction Exchange, Inc.)
$850 £429

FRENCH SCHOOL, circa 1800 – A Decorative Panel With Putti Holding A Swag Of Flowers – 24¾ x 66¾in.
(Sotheby's) **$2,970 £1,500**

FRENCH SCHOOL, 19th century – A Portrait Study Of An Officer Of The Guard – oil on ivory – 7 x 5cm.
(King & Chasemore)
$512 £260

FRENCH SCHOOL, 18th century – An Allegorical Group With Musicians – 30 x 40in.
(Woolley & Wallis)
$13,376 £6,400

FRENCH SCHOOL, 19th century – Portrait Presume De Peintre Henri Fantinlatour – pencil – 8¾ x 4¼in.
(Sotheby's) **$297 £150**

FRENCH SCHOOL, circa 1800 – A Still Life Of Flowers In A Classical Urn, On A Wooden Ledge – 32 x 40¼in.
(Sotheby's) **$3,564 £1,800**

FRENCH SCHOOL, early 18th century – The Aftermath Of A Battle, An Army Tending The Wounded – on metal – on panel – 13¼ x 17¼in.
(Sotheby's) **$1,584** **£800**

FRENCH SCHOOL, early 18th century – A Capriccio Of Classical Ruins – red chalk, pen and brown ink, grey wash – 147 x 185mm.
(Christie's) **$209** **£110**

JOSEPH FRICERO – A View Of Nice – signed, dated 1845 and inscribed – watercolour – 178 x 263mm.
(Christie's) **$266** **£140**

DONALD FRIEND – A Tropical Beach Scene – signed and dated '39 – pen and ink and watercolour – 8¼ x 12¾in.
(Sotheby's) **$317** **£160**

WASHINGTON F. FRIEND – A Sailing Boat On Lake Megantic, Quebec – signed – watercolour, heightened with white – 9½ x 13¼in.
(Sotheby's) **$433** **£220**

ELISABETH FRINK – Head – signed and dated '63 – black chalk – 29¾ x 21½in.
(Sotheby's) **$218** **£110**

ELISABETH FRINK – Figure Composition – signed and dated '61 – black chalk – 30 x 22¼in.
(Sotheby's) **$158** **£80**

GEORGE ARTHUR FRIPP – Deer By A Burn – signed and dated 1863 – 13 x 20in.
(Sotheby's) **$729** **£380**

GEORGE ARTHUR FRIPP – By A Loch – 11 x 19in.
(Sotheby's) **$576** **£300**

G. A. FRIPP – Corn Stooks In A Field Near Windmills – watercolour heightened with white – 8¾ x 13½in.
(Christie's) **$116** **£60**

GEORGE ARTHUR FRIPP – The Dorset Coast: Dancing Ledge – signed and inscribed – pencil and watercolour – 9½ x 13½in.
(Christie's) **$136** **£70**

W. P. FRITH – The Canary – bears signature and date – oval – 13 x 11½in.
(Sotheby's Belgravia) **$307** **£160**

W. P. FRITH – Cavalrymen Outside An Inn – on panel – 7½ x 10½in.
(Christie's) **$388** **£200**

WILLIAM POWELL FRITH – Lord Foppinton Describes His Daily Life – signed and dated 1871 – 37 x 53in.
(Sotheby's Belgravia) **$7,646** **£3,800**

W. P. FRITH – William Penn In Prison With His Children – 32¼ x 26in.
(Sotheby's Belgravia) **$422** **£220**

WILLIAM POWELL FRITH – The Introduction – signed and dated 1886 – 17½ x 25¾in.
(Christie's) **$2,328** **£1,200**

EUGENE FROMENTIN – Paysage Du Maroc – signed – pen and watercolour – 11¾ x 15¼in.
(Sotheby's) **$760** **£400**

WILLIAM EDWARD FROST – A Woman Bathing – signed and dated 1855 – on board – 9¼ x 6½in.
(Christie's) **$1,261** **£650**

ROGER FRY – The Cove – 24¾ x 20¼in.
(Sotheby's) **$437** **£220**

ROGER FRY – House At Vence – signed, inscribed and dated 1920 – 11 x 14¼in.
(Sotheby's) **$594** **£300**

G. G. FRYER – Coastal Landscape With Fishing Barges In A Calm Sea At Dawn; and Estuary Scene With Windmills And Cattle In Extensive Landscape At Sunset – signed – oil on canvas – 24 x 59cm.
(Henry Spencer & Sons) **$1,188** **£600 Pair**

LEONARD FULLER – 'Childhood – My Son John' – oil on canvas – 36 x 28in.
(W. H. Lane & Son) **$192** **£100**

JOHN FULLEYLOVE – The Tower Of London – signed – heightened with white – 10½ x 13in.
(Sotheby's Belgravia) **$192** **£100**

JOHN FULLEYLOVE – View Of The Basilica, San Marco, Venice; With Many Figures In The Piazza – signed – watercolour – 27 x 38cm.
(Henry Spencer & Sons) **$407** **£210**

ALBERT HENRY FULLWOOD – Batlow, N.S.W. – signed and dated 1924 – watercolour – 27 x 37cm.
(Australian Art Auctions) **$176** **£91**

DAVID FULTON – On A Rocky Shore – signed – 15½ x 19½in.
(Sotheby's) **$211** **£110**

DAVID FULTON – Waiting For A Bite – signed – 9½ x 13½in.
(Sotheby's) **$960** **£500**

G. T. FURELY – Lady Wearing Cream Dress, Blue Jacket, And Holding A Whip, As She Talks To A Young Gentleman Wearing Black Coat And Red Breeches – signed and inscribed – 75 x 50cm.
(Henry Spencer & Sons)
$673 **£340**

FRANCESCO FURINI – Portrait Of A Nude Woman, Half Length, Covered By A Drape, Holding A Medallion – 28 x 22½in.
(Sotheby's) **$5,940** **£3,000**

FRANCESCO FURINI – Sofonisba And The Poisoned Cup – 27½ x 22½in.
(Christie's) **$8,064** **£4,200**

JOHANN HEINRICH FUSELI – Miss Mary Hoare Wearing An Elaborate Toque, Looking Over Her Shoulder – signed and inscribed – pencil, pen and black ink, grey wash – 7¼ x 5½in.
(Sotheby's) **$3,686** **£1,900**

J. FYT – Dead Game And Implements Of The Chase, With Two Spaniels, In A Landscape – bears signature – 24½ x 32½in.
(Christie's) **$16,490** **£8,500**

JOANNES FYT – Roses, Tulips And Other Flowers With An Upturned Vase – signed – 22 x 31¾in.
(Christie's) **$42,240** **£22,000**

GABBIANI – A Standing Classical Woman – red and white chalk on blue paper – 260 x 167mm.
(Christie's) **$67** **£35**

GASPARE GABRIELLI – A Stormy Coastal Scene, Possibly The Hellespont With The Dead Body Of Leander In The Foreground – signed and inscribed – 39 x 52in.
(Sotheby's) **$3,201** **£1,650**

AGNOLO GADDI, Close Follower of – The Madonna And Child – on gold ground panel – 15¾ x 11in.
(Christie's) **$36,480** **£19,000**

WILLIAM H. GADSBY – Two Girls Arranging Flowers – signed with monogram and signed on the reverse – 35 x 27¼in.
(Christie's) **$2,328** **£1,200**

BARENT GAEL – Horsemen And Figures Outside A Farrier's Shop – on panel – 7½ x 9¾in.
(Christie's) **$2,522** **£1,000**

SCIPIONE PULZONE, IL GAETANO, Circle of – The Crucifixion – inscribed – black chalk, pen and brown ink, brown wash heightened with white on blue paper – 36.9 x 28.2cm.
(Christie's) **$422** **£220**

THOMAS GAINSBOROUGH – Wooded Landscape With Buildings, Figures And Animals – grey wash, heightened with white – 10¾ x 14½in.
(Sotheby's) **$1,940** **£1,000**

ALPHONSE GALBRUND – La Robe Rose – signed and dated 1876 – pastel – 21½ x 13¾in.
(Sotheby's) **$798** **£420**

EUGENE GALIEN-LALOUE – Le Theatre Du Chatelet En Hiver – signed – watercolour and gouache – 7½ x 12in.
(Sotheby's) **$1,980** **£1,000**

ROBERT GALLON – Walking Up Grouse – signed and dated 1879 on the reverse – 11 x 17in.
(Sotheby's) **$832** **£420**

ROBERT GALLON – Fryers Crag, Derwentwater – signed and inscribed – oil on canvas – 6¼ x 10¼in.
(Geering & Colyer)
$698 **£360**

ROBERT GALLON – Glimpses Of Loch Katrine – signed – oil – 18 x 14in.
(Andrew Sharpe & Partners)
$1,281 **£650**

ROBERT GALLON – On The Llugwy Near Capel Curig – signed – 16½ x 12½in.
(Sotheby's Belgravia)
$1,308 **£650**

ROBERT GALLON – Going For Water – signed – 19¼ x 29½in.
(Sotheby's Belgravia)
$4,628 **£2,300**

J. GANTZ – An Indian House – one signed and dated 1847 – watercolour, heightened with bodycolour – 14 x 21½in.
(Sotheby's) **$827** **£420 Pair**

HENRY GARLAND – Droving Homewards – signed and dated 1877 – 19½ x 29½in.
(Sotheby's) **$1,089** **£550**

GARNERAY – Whaling Off The Cape, Table Mountain And Cape Town In The Distance; The Uncas In The Southern Seas Surrounded By Whales – oil on canvas – 19¼ x 23½in.
(Sotheby's) **$1,024** **£520 Two**

THOMAS BALFOUR GARRETT – The Artist Camp, Sirus Cove – signed – 22 x 78cm.
(Australian Art Auctions) **$527** **£274**

HENRY GASTINEAU – Castle And Town On Hillside In Germany With A Waggon On A Road And Distant Landscape – pencil and watercolour – 11 x 15¼in.
(Sotheby's) **$737** **£380**

HENRY GASTINEAU – Morning: Keswick, Cumberland – signed and inscribed – watercolour – 30 x 51½in.
(Christie's) **$1,746** **£900**

HENRI GAUDIER-BRZESKA – Seated Nude – pen and ink – 9½ x 15in.
(Sotheby's) **$495** **£250**

LOUIS GAUFFIER – Wooded Landscapes With Travellers – signed – on board – 7½ x 6in.
(Christie's) **$2,328** **£1,200 Pair**

DAVID GAULD – Calves Outside A Byre – signed – 24 x 36in.
(Sotheby's) **$2,976** **£1,550**

G. B. GAULLI – The Resurrection – sketch for a lunette – 18 x 26½in.
(Christie's) **$3,648** **£1,900**

JOHN GAUT – Reupahana Te Awa Tawha, Ngapuhi Chief – signed and dated 1886, signed, inscribed and dated on reverse – oil on canvas – 21½ x 15½in.
(Sotheby's) **$1,773** **£900**

RENE GEAN – Ballet Dancer – on board – 18 x 24cm.
(Edmiston's) **$66** **£34**

WILLIAM GEDDES – A Quiet Lake – signed with monogram – 15 x 23in.
(Sotheby's Belgravia) **$173** **£90**

GEIKE – The Miseries Of War – 12½ x 15½in.
(Sotheby's Belgravia) **$218** **£110**

JOHN GENDALL – On The River Exe – heightened with bodycolour – 11 x 15½in.
(Sotheby's) **$546** **£280**

B. GENNARI – Saint John The Baptist In The Wilderness – 62½ x 49¾in.
(Christie's) **$1,261** **£650**

A. GENOELS – Diana And Callisto – 23¾ x 28¾in.
(Christie's) **$582** **£300**

GENOESE SCHOOL, second half of the 17th century – David And Bathsheba, She Bathing At A Fountain, The King On The Roof Of A Palace – 44 x 59½in.
(Sotheby's) **$1,940** **£1,000**

GENTILESCHI – Joseph And Potiphar's Wife – 15½ x 19¼in.
(Christie's) **$582** **£300**

MARGUERITE GERARD – Three Ladies Decorating A Statue Of Cupid In An Interior – 23¾ x 19¼in.
(Christie's) **$12,480** **£6,500**

GERMAN SCHOOL – Portrait Of Augustus The Third, King Of Poland, Elector Of Saxony, Half Length, Wearing A Red Coat – bodycolour – 88 x 69mm.
(Christie's) **$57** **£30**

GERMAN SCHOOL, circa 1700 – A Kitchen Still Life With The Spoils Of The Hunt Attracting The Interest Of A Cat And Hound, On A Table Covered By A Linen Cloth – on metal – 9½ x 7in.
(Sotheby's) **$3,960** **£2,000**

GERMAN SCHOOL, early 18th century – Portrait Of Countess Aurora Von Konigsmark, Small Half Length, Wearing Green And Red Costume – canvas on board – oval – 15¾ x 12¼in.
(Christie's) **$537** **£280**

GERMAN SCHOOL, 17th century – The Virgin And Child – inscribed on the reverse – on panel – 8 x 5½in.
(Sotheby's) **$330** **£170**

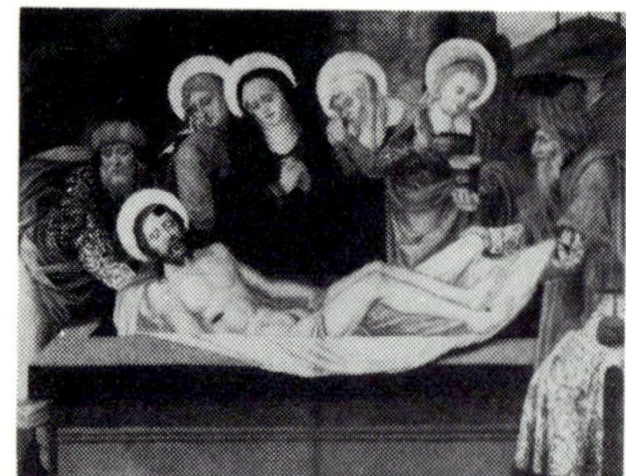

GERMAN SCHOOL, circa 1500 – The Entombment Of Christ – on panel – 21 x 20¾in.
(Sotheby's) **$2,178 £1,100**

G. E. TAYLOR GHEE – Government House, Melbourne, From The Botanic Gardens – signed – oil on board – 15½ x 13½in.
(Sotheby's) **$946 £480**

GEORGE TAYLOR GHEE – Near Healesville, Victoria – signed – oil on board – 19 x 29cm.
(Australian Art Auctions) **$234 £122**

M. GHEERAERTS – Portrait Of A Lady Standing Full Length, Wearing A Grey Embroidered Dress – 74 x 43¼in.
(Christie's) **$776 £400**

J. DE GHEYN – Saint John And Saint Luke – on panel – 14¾ x 31½in.
(Sotheby's) **$1,980 £1,000**

G. GHEZZI – Saint Francis Of Assisi Meditating In An Extensive Landscape, Brother Leo Beside A Stream To The Right – 28½ x 53in.
(Sotheby's) **$1,030 £520**

G. GHEZZI – The Trinity – on copper – 8½ x 6¼in.
(Christie's) **$537 £280**

PIETRO LEONE GHEZZI – Paolo De Matteis In His Studio – a caricature – signed, inscribed and dated 1726 – 15¼ x 11¼in.
(Christie's) **$3,840 £2,000**

PIETRO LEONE GHEZZI – Saint Philip Neri At Prayer – bears signature on the reverse – 11¾ x 8¾in.
(Christie's) **$537 £280**

PIETRO LEONE GHEZZI – Portrait Of Carlo Albani, 1st Prince Of Soriano, Wearing The Badge And Costume Of The Order Of Santo Stefano – 38 x 28½in.
(Christie's) **$7,296** **£3,800**

GIAMPIETRINO *(Active first half of XVI century)* – The Madonna And Child – 24 x 19½in.
(Sotheby's) **$23,760** **£12,000**

GIAQUINTO – Saint Francis Receiving The Stigmata – on copper – oval – 4¼ x 3¼in.
(Christie's) **$139** **£70**

CORRADO GIAQUINTO – Ulysses And Diomedes In The Camp Of The Trojans – 50 x 38½in.
(Christie's) **$17,280** **£9,000**

CORRADO GIAQUINTO – Portrait Of A Nobleman, Standing Three-Quarter Length, Wearing Armour, His Hand Resting On A Plumed Helmet – 38 x 28½in.
(Christie's) **$6,720** **£3,500**

CORRADO GIAQUINTO – Hercules With The Stymphalian Birds – 22 x 11in.
(Christie's) **$921** **£480**

CORRADO GIAQUINTO – A Shepherdess In A Landscape – 14¾ x 18¾in.
(Sotheby's) **$5,820** **£3,000**

C. GIAQUINTO – Ceres – 14½ x 18½in.
(Christie's) **$815** **£420**

ROBERT GIBB – 'Dargai', October 20th, 1897 – signed and dated 1909 – 61 x 91in.
(Sotheby's) **$3,762** **£1,900**

J. GIBBS – Mountainous River Landscapes With A Gentleman Fishing And A Waterfall – signed, inscribed and dated 1896 on verso – 60 x 50cm.
(Henry Spencer & Sons)
$218 **£110 Pair**

ALEX R. GIBSON – The Waterloo Inn – signed – 13½ x 17½in.
(Sotheby's) **$297** **£150**

GILBERT – A Mountainous River Landscape With A Figure By A Hut In The Foreground – 14¾ x 23½in.
(Christie's) **$621** **£320**

ARTHUR GILBERT – Noon, Near Wokingham; Night, Near Nutfield, Surrey – signed and dated 1888, inscribed on labels on the reverse – 6½ x 9½in.
(Sotheby's Belgravia)
$855 **£450 Pair**

ARTHUR GILBERT – Sunset – signed – 6¼ x 9½in.
(Sotheby's Belgravia)
$139 **£70**

HORACE W. GILBERT – Snowdon From Glaslyn – signed and dated 1891, inscribed on a label on the stretcher – 17 x 23½in.
(Sotheby's Belgravia)
$864 **£450**

JAMES GILES – Family Affection – signed and dated 1869 – 44¼ x 37in.
(Sotheby's) **$832** **£420**

JOHN GILES – In The Borghese Gardens, Rome, With Statue And Ruins In The Trees – inscribed, signed and dated 1824 – pen and black ink with pink washes – recto; Italian Hill Town – pencil – verso – 18 x 12¼in.
(Sotheby's) **$156** **£80**

EDMUND GILL – A Wooded Landscape With Anglers By A Cascade – signed – 11 x 15¼in.
(Christie's) **$427** **£220**

SAMUEL THOMAS GILL – Forest Creek Mount Alexander – Diggings From The Base Of Red Hill Near Argus Office – coloured lithograph – 14½ x 24¼in.
(Sotheby's) **$493** **£250**

MARGARET GILLIES – Rosalind And Celia: 'But is all this for your father?' – watercolour heightened with white – 17 x 12¾in.
(Christie's) **$233** **£120**

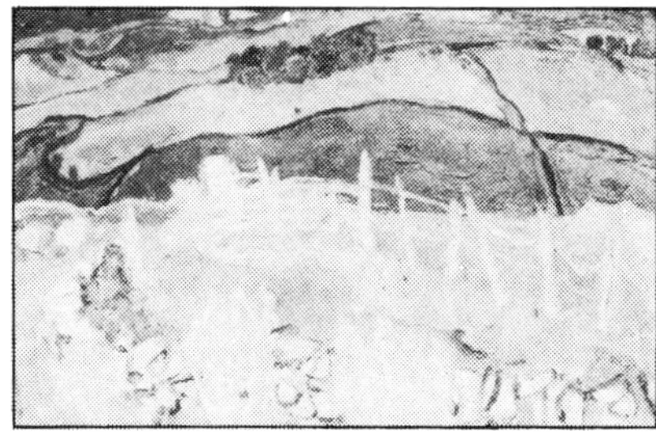

SIR W. G. GILLIES – The Hill Road Through The Meldons – 28 x 40cm.
(Edmiston's) **$1,145** **£590**

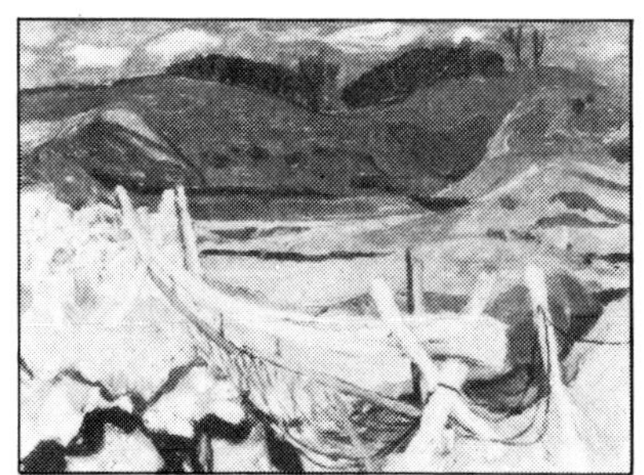

SIR WILLIAM GEORGE GILLIES – The Cattle Fence – signed – 17½ x 23½in.
(Sotheby's) **$115** **£600**

SIR W. G. GILLIES – Landscape Near Wooplaw – 23 x 49cm.
(Edmiston's) **$698** **£360**

WILLIAM GILPIN – Figures Below A Castle In The Mountains – pen and black ink, grey wash on tinted paper – 9¾ x 13½in.
(Christie's) **$97** **£50**

LUCA GIORDANO – A Blind Man With The Bust Of A Philosopher – 50½ x 40¼in.
(Sotheby's) **$25,480** **£13,000**

LUCA GIORDANO – The Miraculous Appearance Of Santiago At The Battle Of Clavijo – grisaille – 42 x 35in.
(Sotheby's) **$11,760** **£6,000**

LUCA GIORDANO – The Madonna And Child Enthroned With Saints – 36¼ x 20¾in.
(Sotheby's) **$14,700** **£7,500**

L. GIORDANO – Roman Charity – 40 x 32¾in.
(Christie's) **$3,104** **£1,600**

JACOPO NEGRETTI, IL PALMA GIOVANE – The Conversion Of Saint Paul – black chalk, pen and brown ink, brown wash – 22.3 x 19.7cm.
(Christie's) **$1,152** **£600**

JACOPO NEGRETTI, IL PALMA GIOVANE – An Allegory Of Venice – inscribed 'Palma' – black chalk, pen and brown ink, brown wash – 9.8 x 8.2cm.
(Christie's) **$288** **£150**

BENVENUTO DI GIOVANNI *(1436–ca. 1581(?))* – The Madonna And Child Enthroned With Angels – gold ground – on panel – 48 x 29¾in.
(Sotheby's) **$69,300** **£35,000**

ERNEST JOSEPH ANGELON GIRARD – Jeune Homme De Palazuenos, Province De Segovia, Espagna – signed and inscribed – watercolour – 9½ x 6½in.
(Sotheby's) **$218** **£110**

THOMAS GIRTIN – A Ruined Abbey By A River, A High Hill Beyond, With A Sportsman On A Bank In The Foreground – 15½ x 12½in.
(Sotheby's) **$2,910** **£1,500**

THOMAS GIRTIN – The Palace And Bridge Of Choisi – hand coloured soft-ground etching – 5¾ x 17¾in.
(Sotheby's) **$1,746** **£900**

THOMAS GIRTIN – A Volcano Erupting, A Town On The Coast In Foreground – inscribed on reverse – in pencil – 12¼ x 17½in.
(Sotheby's) **$970** **£500**

GLASGOW SCHOOL, circa 1890 – The Studio Door – 18 x 14in.
(Sotheby's) **$109** **£55**

HAMILTON GLASS – East Coast Fishing Village – watercolour – 34 x 49cm.
(Edmiston's) **$182** **£94**

HAMILTON GLASS – Loch Katrine – watercolour – 24 x 34cm.
(Edmiston's) **$135** **£70**

J. GLAUBER – A Rocky River Landscape – 14 x 19in.
(Sotheby's) **$1,584** **£800**

A. A. GLENDENING – By A River – 36 x 53in.
(Sotheby's Belgravia) **$5,231** **£2,600**

ALLERLEY GLOSSOP – The Close Of Day, In The Karroo – signed with monogram – oil on board – 8¼ x 11¼in.
(Sotheby's) **$168** **£85**

JOHN GLOVER – In The Sychnant Pass, Caernarvonshire – 7¼ x 11in.
(Sotheby's) **$659** **£340**

W. GLOVER – A Calm Evening In The Highlands – signed and dated 1915 – 15½ x 23½in.
(Sotheby's Belgravia) **$69** **£35**

GODFREY – The Clipper 'Quilpue' In Full Sail Off Newcastle, New South Wales – signed and inscribed – watercolour, heightened with bodycolour – 16½ x 23in.
(Sotheby's) **$552** **£280**

JOHN WILLIAM GODWARD – Contemplation – signed and dated 1903 – circular – diameter 20in.
(Sotheby's Belgravia) **$8,048** **£4,000**

NORBERT GOENEUTTE – Sens – signed with initials, inscribed and dated 1890 – watercolour – 7 x 5in.
(Sotheby's) **$361** **£190**

PETER GOETKINT – Justice, Standing On A Block In The Foreground Inscribed, Blindfold And Holding A Sword – 33 x 50in.
(Sotheby's) **$20,580** **£10,500**

FREDERICK CHARLES GOLDIE – Portrait Of A Maori Woman – signed – pencil drawing – 18 x 15cm.
(Australian Art Auctions)
$517 £264

HAROLD GOLDTHWAITE – Rural Landscape With Shepherd And Flock In Foreground – signed – oil on canvas – 20 x 30in.
(Morphets of Harrogate)
$518 £270

GOLLINGS – Buckin' Bronco – signed – pencil and watercolour – 13¼ x 9½in.
(Sotheby's) **$1,182 £600**

HENDRICK GOLTZIUS – A Youth Holding A Fish – signed with monogram and dated 1607 – black chalk heightened with white on blue paper – 29.5 x 13.7cm.
(Christie's) **$5,376 £2,800**

PIETRO DI GOTTARDO GONZAGA – Escalier Des Ambassadeurs Au Palais D'Hiver A St. Petersbourg – signed – pen and brown ink, brown and grey wash – 156 x 193mm.
(Christie's) **$209 £110**

A. M. GOODALL – Johannesburg From Hospital Hill – signed and dated 1905, inscribed on the reverse – watercolour – 6¼ x 15½in.
(Sotheby's) **$118 £60**

EDWARD ANGELO GOODALL – Procida, Bay Of Naples – signed – watercolour – 6¼ x 11¾in.
(Christie's) **$427 £220**

FREDERICK GOODALL – Trespassers – signed with monogram and dated 1886 – oil on canvas – 44 x 39in.
(Bonham's) **$13,720 £7,000**

FREDERICK GOODALL – Water For The Camp – signed with monogram and dated 1878 – 14 x 23¼in.
(Christie's) **$873 £450**

F. GOODALL – An Opium Den; At The Bazaar – inscribed with monogram and dated 1896 – 14½ x 10in.
(Sotheby's Belgravia)
$144 £75 Pair

FREDERICK GOODALL – Gypsy Encampment In A Dune Landscape – signed and dated 1858 – 14 x 21in.
(Christie's) **$1,067 £550**

WALTER GOODALL – Crossing The Ford – signed and dated 1859 – heightened with bodycolour – 13½ x 20in.
(Sotheby's Belgravia) **$307 £160**

J. C. GOODMAN – On A River Bank – signed – 8½ x 14in.
(Sotheby's Belgravia) **$83 £42**

MAUDE GOODMAN – Summer Flowers – signed and dated '94 – 22¾ x 35¼in.
(Sotheby's Belgravia) **$7,042 £3,500**

ROBERT GWELO GOODMAN – A Farmhouse Near Stellenbosch – A Summer Garden – oil on canvas – 15 x 19in.
(Sotheby's) **$1,200 £650**

ROBERT GWELO GOODMAN – Table Mountain From The Landward Side – signed – watercolour – 12¾ x 14½in.
(Sotheby's) **$177 £90**

ROBERT GWELO GOODMAN – The Drakensburg Mountains – signed with initials – oil on board – 11¾ x 14in.
(Sotheby's) **$394 £200**

ALBERT GOODWIN – Morte Point, North Devon – signed, inscribed and dated 1918 – heightened with white – 9¾ x 13½in.
(Sotheby's Belgravia) **$369 £190**

ALBERT GOODWIN – 'Sunset In Quiet Waters' – signed and dated 1907 – 10¾ x 15¼in.
(Messenger May Baverstock) **$926 £460**

W. S. GOODWIN – On Salisbury Plain; The Mouth Of The Dart – paper – on board – 7¼ x 10in.
(Sotheby's Belgravia) **$384 £200 Pair**

FREDERICK W. GOOLDEN – The Serenade, Venice; Sunset On The Coast – signed and dated 1913 – 10 x 14in.
(Sotheby's Belgravia) **$106 £55 Pair**

ARTHUR GORDON – Battersea; Mortlake – signed and dated 1903 – 19½ x 29½in.
(Sotheby's Belgravia) **$1,152 £600 Pair**

ARTHUR GORDON – Seascape. 1905 – watercolour – 8½ x 14½in.
(Outhwaite & Litherland) **$45 £22.50**

WILLIAM HENRY GORE – By The River – signed – 11½ x 17½in.
(Sotheby's Belgravia) **$537 £280**

SYLVIA GOSSE – Le Chateau, Dieppe – signed – 29½ x 24½in.
(Sotheby's) **$990 £500**

THOMAS COOPER GOTCH – Asleep – signed – 16½ x 13in.
(Sotheby's Belgravia) **$192 £100**

ADOLF GOTTLIEB – Pink Ground – signed and dated 1959 on the reverse – oil on canvas – 60 x 36in.
(Sotheby's) **$24,750 £12,500**

ALEXANDER GOUDIE – Head Studies – signed – red chalk – 10 x 8½in.
(Sotheby's) **$96** **£50**

ALEXANDER GOUDIE – Blustery Day, Pluzevet – signed – 31½ x 33½in.
(Sotheby's) **$356** **£180**

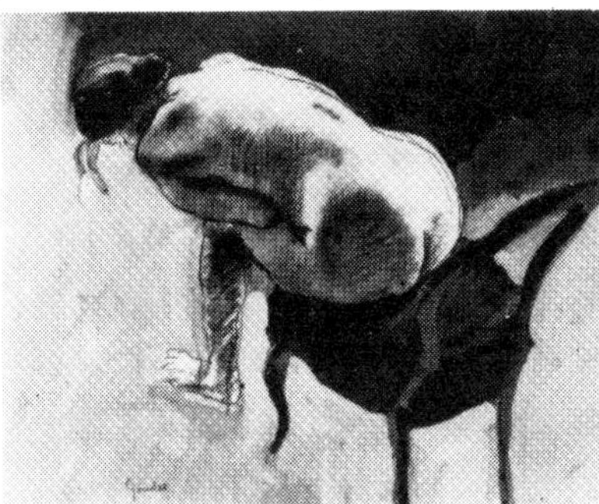

ALEXANDER GOUDIE – Study Of A Nude Bending Forward – signed – black chalk, wash and gouache – 7½ x 21in.
(Sotheby's) **$317** **£160**

T. GOUGELET – 'Promenade' – signed oil on canvas – 14 x 17in.
(Morton's Auction Exchange, Inc.) **$2,350** **£1,192**

MARY L. GOW – Ladies And Children With Bunches Of Pink Roses – signed and dated 1900 – watercolour – 26½ x 47¾in.
(Christie's) **$815** **£420**

J. VAN GOYEN – An Estuary Scene With Fishermen Drawing In Their Nets – inscribed '1654 VG' – black chalk and grey wash – 160 x 265mm.
(Christie's) **$361** **£190**

JAN JOSEFSZ. VAN GOYEN – Peasants And Wagons Outside An Inn, In An Extensive Wooded Landscape – signed with initials and dated 1629 – on panel – 11½ x 20½in.
(Christie's) **$61,440** **£32,000**

JAN JOSEFSZ. VAN GOYEN – A Village Fair With Numerous Figures, Riders And Carts – signed and dated 1644 – 41 x 58¼in.
(Christie's) **$67,200** **£35,000**

JAN JOSEFSZ. VAN GOYEN – A View Of Dordrecht With The Grote Kerk And A Windmill, With Figures And Boats In The Foreground – signed with initials and dated 1647 – on panel – 15 x 25½in.
(Christie's) **$80,640** **£42,000**

VAN GOYEN – A River Landscape With Fishing Vessels And A Windmill Beyond – 11¾ x 16¼in.
(Christie's) **$1,683** **£850**

VAN GOYEN – A Coastal Landscape, A Rowing Vessel With A Figure Unloading Cargo – bears initials and dated 1640 – on panel – 15 x 23½in.
(Sotheby's) **$9,312** **£4,800**

J. W. GOZZARD – The Farm Pond; In The Village – signed, inscribed on the stretchers – 29 x 19in.
(Sotheby's Belgravia)
$499 **£260 Pair**

GOZZOLI – The Madonna And Child With Saints, Peter, John The Baptist, Anthony Of Padua And Paul Kneeling In Adoration – on gold ground panel – 16½ x 32in.
(Christie's) **$5,044** **£2,600**

B. GRAAT – A Young Girl Holding A Fan Standing, Three-Quarter Length – 14¾ x 11¾in.
(Sotheby's) **$1,552** **£800**

COLIN GRAEME – Retrievers And Pointers – signed – 9½ x 13½in.
(Sotheby's) **$691** **£360 Pair**

COLIN GRAEME – A Setter In The Highlands – signed and dated '91 – 24 x 36in.
(Sotheby's) **$475** **£240**

ANTON GRAF – Prince Heinrich Of Prussia In A Blue Velvet Coat And A Yellow Silk Waistcoat – 53 x 38½in.
(Sotheby's) **$15,680** **£8,000**

PETER GRAHAM – Highland Cattle By A Burn – signed and dated 1918 – 21½ x 29in.
(Sotheby's) **$1,344** **£700**

FRANCOIS MARIUS GRANET – L'Heure De La Messe Au Couvent – signed and dated 1877 – grey wash – 27 x 37in.
(Sotheby's) **$836** **£440**

JOSEPH GRANIE – Portrait De Jeune Femme Aux Yeux Fonces; and Portrait De Jeune Fille De Trois-Quart – signed and inscribed – one pencil, coloured crayons, heightened with white and the other pencil – 12 x 9½in. and 8 x 6in.
(Sotheby's) **$342** **£180 Pair**

DUNCAN GRANT – St. Paul's From The River – 9¼ x 17½in.
(Sotheby's) **$436** **£220**

DUNCAN GRANT – Still Life With A Lamp – 25 x 31½in.
(Sotheby's) **$495** **£250**

DUNCAN GRANT – An Open Landscape With A Gate – signed and dated 1921 – 13¾ x 21½in.
(Sotheby's) **$554** **£280**

HUBERT FRANCOIS B. D'A. GRAVELOT – Design For A Monument – signed – pen and brown ink and wash – 7 x 9in.
(Sotheby's) **$156** **£80**

A. C. GRAY – A Wagon On A Country Road – signed – 9½ x 13½in.
(Sotheby's Belgravia)
$134 **£70**

GEORGE GRAY – A Highland Loch At Sunset – signed – 13½ x 16½in.
(Sotheby's Belgravia)
$57 **£30**

J. C. GRAY – On The Shore – signed and dated 1914 – 9½ x 13½in.
(Sotheby's Belgravia)
$115 **£60**

NORAH NEILSON GRAY – Toast To Bacchus – watercolour – 35 x 26cm.
(Edmiston's) **$213** **£110**

WALTER GREAVES – Chelsea In The Old Days, Early Morning – signed, inscribed on the reverse – pencil and coloured wash – 8¼ x 12¾in.
(Sotheby's) **$297** **£150**

WALTER GREAVES – The Tower Of London From The Thames – signed – 14¾ x 22¾in.
(Sotheby's) **$792** **£400**

P. DE GREBBER – The Deposition – on panel – 19½ x 14½in.
(Sotheby's) **$594** **£300**

PIETER DE GREBBER – Saints Dominic, Francis And The Magdalene Interceding With Christ To Save A Burning Town – 23½ x 17¼in.
(Sotheby's) **$815** **£420**

GIOVANNI BENEDETTO CASTIGLIONE, IL GRECHETTO – The Migration Of Jacob – 55¼ x 80¾in.
(Christie's) **$57,600** **£30,000**

EL GRECO – The Crucifixion – on panel – 23¼ x 14¾in.
(Christie's) **$194** **£100**

GRECO-BQZANTINE SCHOOL, 16th century – The Head Of Saint John The Baptist, On A Gilt Tazza, With A Sword, On A Ledge – inscribed in Greek and inscribed on the reverse – on panel – 5 x 5in.
(Sotheby's) **$543** **£280**

GREEK SCHOOL – Saint George As Bishop – inscribed – on gold ground – recto; Saint George – inscribed – on gold ground – verso – on panel – 13¼ x 4in.
(Christie's) **$345** **£180**

ALFRED H. GREEN – Feeding The Calf – signed and dated '74 – 29 x 24in.
(Sotheby's Belgravia) **$570** **£300**

ROLAND GREEN – A Study Of A Group Of British Birds – signed – watercolour – 18 x 11in.
(G. A. Key) **$257** **£130**

WILLIAM GREEN – Langdale Pikes And Blea Tarn – 12½ x 16½in.
(Sotheby's) **$136** **£70**

J. GREENHALGH – Venice – signed – 17 x 11in.
(Sotheby's Belgravia) **$76** **£40**

THOMAS GREENHALGH – Richmond, Yorkshire – signed – 19½ x 27½in.
(Sotheby's Belgravia) **$238** **£120**

THOMAS GREENHALGH – The Tropical House, Kew Gardens – signed and dated 1884 – 49 x 23in.
(Sotheby's Belgravia) **$9,054** **£4,500**

JAMES GREENLEES – Dunblane Cathedral – signed with monogram and dated 1884 – on panel – 9 x 14in.
(Sotheby's Belgravia) **$188** **£95**

J. R. GREIG – A Woodland Pool – canvas on panel – 10 x 13in.
(Sotheby's Belgravia) **$44** **£22**

HAROLD GRESLEY – Haymaking – signed – heightened with white – 9½ x 17½in.
(Sotheby's Belgravia) **$107** **£55**

JEAN-BAPTISTE GREUZE *(1725-1805)* – A Girl With A Dog – 17½ x 14½in.
(Sotheby's) **$59,400 £30,000**

JEAN-BAPTISTE GREUZE *(1725-1805)* – A Girl With A Dove – on panel – 25½ x 21¾in.
(Sotheby's) **$51,480 £26,000**

GRIFFIER – A Wooded River Landscape With Traveller On A Path And A Town Beyond – on panel – 9¾ x 14½in.
(Christie's) **$1,649 £850**

JAN GRIFFIER – Wooded River Landscapes, With Peasants And Shipping – on panel – 10¼ x 15in.
(Christie's) **$9,600 £5,000 Pair**

J. GRIFFIER – A Mountainous River Landscape With Shipwrights And A Village Beyond – bears indistinct signature – on panel – 11¼ x 15in.
(Christie's) **$4,268 £2,200**

JAN GRIFFIER The Elder – An Extensive Wooded River Landscape With Figures On A Path And A Town Beyond – on panel – 12¼ x 18¾in.
(Christie's) **$3,492 £1,800**

R. GRIFFIER – Skaters On A Frozen Lake, An Inn And Various Figures To The Right, Peasants Carrying Wood On A Path To The Left – 16¼ x 22in.
(Sotheby's) **$4,742 £2,400**

MOSES GRIFFITH – Davenport House, Near Bridgnorth, Shropshire, The Seat Of William Yelverton Davenport Esqr. – inscribed and dated 1793 – 8 x 15in.
(Sotheby's) **$776** **£400 Pair**

MOSES GRIFFITH – Holyhead – signed and dated 1776; and Caernarvon Castle – pen and black ink and watercolour – 9 x 13¼in. and 9¼ x 11¾in.
(Sotheby's) **$585** **£300 Pair**

GIOVANNI FRANCESCO GRIMALDI, Attributed to – A Classical Landscape With A Peasant Fishing – pen and brown ink – 17.3 x 24.2cm.
(Christie's) **$365** **£190**

GRIMALDI – The Flight Into Egypt – 17¾ x 24¼in.
(Christie's) **$1,649** **£850**

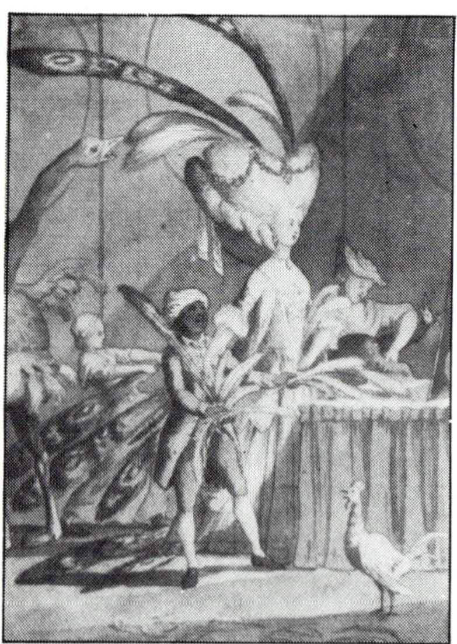

SAMUEL HIERONYMUS GRIMM – Plucking The Birds – pen and black ink and watercolour – 7¾ x 5¾in.
(Sotheby's) **$679** **£350**

ABEL GRIMMER – The Interior Of A Church – signed indistinctly – on panel – 28½ x 39¼in.
(Sotheby's) **$18,430** **£9,500**

GRIMOUX – A Lady Feeding A Bird In A Cage – 34¼ x 26¾in.
(Christie's) **$3,104** **£1,600**

JOHN ATKINSON GRIMSHAW – Elaine – Idylls Of The King, Tennyson – signed and dated 1877 – 32 x 47¼in.
(Sotheby's Belgravia) **$15,090** **£7,500**

JOHN ATKINSON GRIMSHAW – In Autumn's Golden Glow – signed – 29½ x 24½in.
(Sotheby's Belgravia) **$11,669** **£5,800**

JOHN ATKINSON GRIMSHAW – A Wet Winter's Evening – on panel – 17½ x 13¼in.
(Sotheby's Belgravia) **$8,450** **£4,200**

JOHN ATKINSON GRIMSHAW – Autumn Gold – signed and dated 1880, inscribed on the reverse – on board – 17¾ x 14¼in.
(Sotheby's Belgravia) **$4,426** **£2,200**

JOHN ATKINSON GRIMSHAW – On Guard – signed, inscribed and dated 1877 – on board – 12 x 24in.
(Sotheby's Belgravia) **$6,036** **£3,000**

ATKINSON GRIMSHAW – 'The Waning Glory Of The Year' – signed and dated 1882 and signed, inscribed and dated on the reverse – 18¾ x 28¾in.
(Christie's) **$12,610** **£6,500**

ATKINSON GRIMSHAW – Chilworth Common, Oxfordshire – signed and dated 1868 – mixed media on paper – 14 x 19¾in.
(Christie's) **$3,492 £1,800**

ATKINSON GRIMSHAW – Yew Court, Scalby, On A November Night – signed and dated 1874 and signed, inscribed and dated 1874 on the reverse – paper on panel – 7¾ x 17in.
(Christie's) **$3,880 £2,000**

ATKINSON GRIMSHAW – The Old Gates, Yew Court, Scalby Near Scarborough – signed and dated 1874 and signed, inscribed and dated 1874 on the reverse – paper on panel – 7¾ x 17in.
(Christie's) **$2,910 £1,500**

A. DE GROOTE – Dutch Coastal View With Figures On The Shore – signed – oil on panel – 11½ x 17in.
(Morton's Auction Exchange, Inc.) **$900 £454**

MARY GROVES – A South Of England Landscape, With Three Horses In The Foreground, A House And Huntsmen In The Distance – signed and dated 1846 – watercolour – 14½ x 9½in.
(Geering & Colyer) **$231 £120**

T. GRUTZNER – 'Monks Feast' – signed – oil on panel – 8½ x 10in.
(Morton's Auction Exchange, Inc.) **$875 £441**

DE GRYEFF – Ducks And Ducklings On A Pond – 5½ x 7½in.
(Christie's) **$543 £280**

DE GRYEFF – A Sportsman Resting In A Rocky Landscape – on panel – 12 x 14in.
(Christie's) **$427 £220**

PEDRO GUALDI – The Grand Square, Cathedral And Palace Of Mexico City – signed – oil on canvas – 27 x 37¼in.
(Lawrence) **$4,750 £2,500**

GUARDI – A Capriccio River Landscape With A Bridge And Ruins – 6¼ x 11½in.
(Christie's) **$485 £250**

ANTONIO GUARDI – The Sultan Receiving A Delegation Of Merchants; and Turks At Prayer In A Mosque – 17½ x 24¼in.
(Christie's) **$28,800 £15,000 Pair**

FRANCESCO GUARDI *(1712-1793)* – An Architectural Caprice With A Ruined Building – 7½ x 9¾in.
(Sotheby's) **$55,440 £28,000**

FRANCESCO GUARDI *(1712-1793)* – A Caprice Landscape With A Ruined Arch And A Villa; A Caprice Landscape With A Villa By The Sea – 12 x 21¼in.
(Sotheby's) **$118,800 £60,000 Pair**

FRANCESCO GUARDI *(1712-1793)* – Venice: The Piazza San Marco – 14 x 17in.
(Sotheby's) **$63,360 £32,000**

FRANCESCO GUARDI – A Capriccio Landscape With Figures And A Ruined Tower – on board – 3¾ x 5¾in.
(Christie's) **$13,440 £7,000**

FRANCESCO GUARDI *(1712-1793)* – An Architectural Caprice With A Lady And Gentleman; An Architectural Caprice With Two Men Digging – on panel – 7¼ x 5½in.
(Sotheby's) **$71,280 £36,000 Pair**

FRANCESCO GUARDI *(1712-1793)* – An Architectural Caprice With A Ruined Temple; An Architectural Caprice With A Ruined Arch – on panel - 5½ x 4¼in.
(Sotheby's) **$35,640 £18,000 Pair**

RALSTON GUDGEON – Plovers – signed – heightened with bodycolour – 19½ x 23½in.
(Sotheby's Belgravia)
$154 £80

DAVID JOHN GUE – Seascape – oil – 19½ x 29½in.
(Outhwaite & Litherland)
$1,050 £520

GUERCINO – A Landscape – pen and brown ink – 180 x 256mm.
(Christie's) **$42 £22**

G. F. BARBIERI, IL GUERCINO – Youth In Conversation With A Turbanned Man – pen and brown ink – 23.3 x 17.2cm.
(Christie's) **$806 £420**

GIOVANNI FRANCESCO BARBIERI, IL GUERCINO – Diana – 28½ x 25¾in.
(Christie's) **$6,528 £3,400**

GIOVANNI FRANCESCO BARBIERI, IL GUERCINO – The Assumption Of The Virgin – 46 x 58in.
(Christie's) **$32,640 £17,000**

G. F. BARBIERI, IL GUERCINO – An Extensive Upland Landscape – inscribed – pen and brown ink on brown paper – 168 x 256mm.
(Christie's) **$380 £200**

GUERCINO – The Raising Of Tabitha – 38½ x 52in.
(Sotheby's) **$388 £200**

GIOVANNI FRANCESCO BARBIERI, IL GUERCINO, Circle of – Study Of A Gentleman Holding A Stick In His Outstretched Hand – red chalk – 15.7 x 19.8cm.
(Christie's)
$288 £150

GIOVANNI FRANCESCO BARBIERI, IL GUERCINO – Study Of The Head Of A Bearded Man In Profile To The Right – pen and brown ink on the reverse of a letter – 18.8 x 15cm.
(Christie's) **$864 £450**

GIOVANNI FRANCESCO BARBIERI, IL GUERCINO, Workshop of – A Romantic Landscape With Peasants On A Track Between Two Outcrops – pen and brown ink, brown wash – 20.2 x 28.7cm.
(Christie's) **$480 £250**

G. GUGLIELMI – Interior Scene With Six Boy Figures, Caught At Cards – signed – oil – 18 x 24½in.
(Richard Baker & Baker)
$6,014 £3,100

F. S. GURNEY – Grey And Chestnut Horses In A Woodland Glade – signed and dated 1838 – watercolour – 35 x 46cm.
(Henry Spencer & Sons)
$213 £110

JOHANN GEORG GUTWEIN – Christ On The Cross, With God The Father And The Holy Spirit, Attendant Angels, Cherubim And Seraphim – signed and inscribed – on metal – 8¾ x 6in.
(Sotheby's) **$1,188 £600**

NICOLAAS DE GYSELAER – Hannah And Eli In The Temple – on panel – 20½ x 28½in.
(Christie's) **$873 £450**

P. GYSELS – Landscape With Travellers Outside An Inn – on panel – 5¾ x 8½in.
(Sotheby's) **$19,600 £10,000**

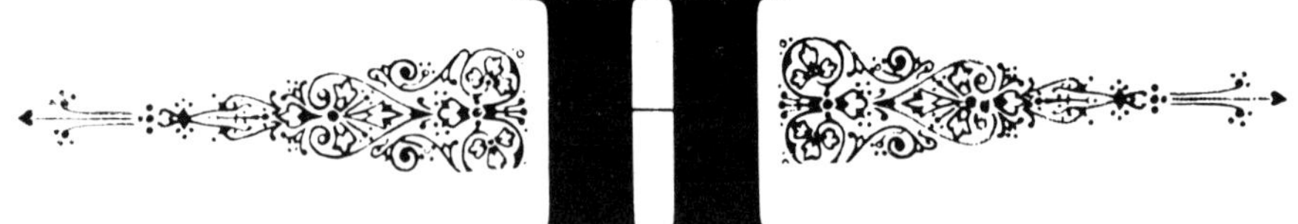

CARL HAAG – Portrait Of An Italian Lady – signed and dated 1857 – 19 x 13½in.
(Sotheby's Belgravia) **$152** **£80**

CARL HAAG – 'A Bedairee From The Sinai' – signed and inscribed – watercolour – 36 x 25cm.
(King & Chasemore) **$706** **£360**

CARL HAAG – Temple Ruins, Near Baalbec – signed and dated 1860 – 11½ x 23½in.
(Sotheby's) **$776** **£400**

CARL HAAG – A Greek Girl – signed and dated 1855 – 18 x 12in.
(Sotheby's Belgravia) **$460** **£240**

VAN HAARLEM – Saints Catherine, Sebastian And Roch With A Putto – on panel – 17½ x 13½in.
(Sotheby's) **$582** **£300**

VAN HAARLEM – The Judgement Of Paris – on panel – 12¼ x 17¾in.
(Sotheby's) **$388** **£200**

C. VAN HAARLEM – The Baptism Of Christ – bears initials – 24¼ x 34in.
(Christie's) **$1,358** **£700**

J. HACKAERT – A Southern Landscape With A Stag Hunt, In A Wooded Clearing In The Foreground – 27 x 35in.
(Sotheby's) **$5,544** **£2,800**

J. P. HACKAERT – An Extensive Classical Landscape With Diana And Her Nymphs Returning From The Hunt – 41¼ x 54¼in.
(Sotheby's) **$10,088** **£5,200**

HADDON – A Flower Girl – bears another signature and date – 15 x 10in.
(Sotheby's Belgravia) **$61** **£32**

ARTHUR TREVOR HADDON – Market Day, Gerona, Spain – watercolour – 13 x 17in.
(Outhwaite & Litherland) **$404** **£200**

JOHAN VAN HAENSBERGEN – Figures In A Landscape With Ruins – signed with initials – on panel – 6¼ x 8¼in.
(Sotheby's) **$6,790** **£3,500**

PARKER HAGARTY – The Grandchild; Eventide – signed, inscribed on labels on the reverse – 6½ x 9½in.
(Sotheby's Belgravia)
$163 **£85 Pair**

PARKER HAGARTY – The Call Of The Sea Maiden – signed, inscribed on label on the reverse – heightened with white – 13 x 9½in.
(Sotheby's Belgravia)
$209 **£110**

J. VAN DER HAGEN – A Wooded River Landscape, With A Horse-Drawn Cart And A Ferry – on panel – 21 x 32¼in.
(Christie's) **$18,430** **£9,500**

LOUIS HAGHE – The Council Of War At Coutrai – signed – 40¼ x 54¼in.
(Christie's) **$4,268** **£2,200**

AXEL HERMAN HAIG – Roman Ruins In The Eastern Mediterranean – signed and dated 1876 – watercolour heightened with white – 26 x 18¼in.
(Christie's) **$194** **£100**

J. HERMISTON HAIG – A Hill On The Black Adder, Berwickshire – signed and dated 1901 – 20 x 30in.
(Sotheby's) **$158** **£80**

J. HAITE – Wooded Lake Scene With Fishing Boats And Figures Outside A Cottage – signed – watercolour – 14 x 23in.
(Morphets of Harrogate)
$149 **£75**

J. HAITE – Lake And Mountain Landscape With Blossom – watercolour – 12½ x 28½in.
(Morphets of Harrogate) **$59** **£30**

HAKES – The 'Emperor' In A Gale – inscribed and dated 1864 – 27½ x 35in.
(Sotheby's Belgravia) **$211** **£110**

ERNEST HALL – A Busy Port – signed and dated '18 – heightened with white – 15½ x 23½in.
(Sotheby's Belgravia) **$250** **£130**

HARRY HALL – 'Iroquois', A Dark Bay Racehorse – 16¾ x 20½in.
(Christie's) **$287** **£148**

HARRY HALL – Portrait Of Colonel Townley's Gamekeeper – on board – 16¼ x 8½in.
(Christie's) **$760** **£400**

HARRY HALL – Portrait Of Julius, A Bay Racehorse, With Jockey Up, A Gentleman Holding A Black Pony Stands Nearby, Four Riders Beyond, In An Extensive Landscape – signed and dated 1865 – oil on canvas – 70 x 98cm.
(Henry Spencer & Sons) **$6,790** **£3,500**

HARRY HALL – A study of 'Ellington' winner of the Derby 1856 – signed and dated 1856 – on canvas – 76 x 60cm.
(King & Chasemore) **$4,224** **£2,200**

H. R. HALL – Denizens Of The Hills; Highland Rovers – both signed, inscribed on the reverse – 15½ x 23½in.
(Sotheby's Belgravia) **$537** **£280 Pair**

H. R. HALL – Highland Cattle, Loch Lomond – signed, inscribed and dated 1897 on the reverse – 20 x 30in.
(Sotheby's Belgravia) **$250** **£130**

H. R. HALL – Denizens Of The Highlands; Highland Cattle, Loch Lomond – signed, inscribed on the reverse – 15½ x 23½in.
(Sotheby's Belgravia) **$154** **£80 Pair**

PATRICK HALL – The Harbour, St. Jean de Luz – watercolour drawing – 30 x 41cm.
(Edmiston's) **$105** **£54**

S. E. HALL – 'Upper Lake Killarney' – signed – watercolour – 9¼ x 23½in.
(Dacre, Son & Hartley) **$48** **£24**

THOMAS P. HALL – Tea Time – signed with monogram and dated 1868 – 23 x 17½in.
(Sotheby's Belgravia) **$2,817** **£1,400**

G. HALLER – Woodland Paths – signed – 20 x 11in.
(Sotheby's Belgravia) **$418** **£220 Pair**

DIRK HALS – Elegant Figures Merrymaking In An Interior – on panel – 17½ x 23in.
(Christie's) **$10,560 £5,500**

F. HALS – Head Of A Laughing Boy Holding A Flute – bears monogram – on panel – diameter 112in.
(Christie's) **$5,044 £2,600**

FRANS HALS, Attributed to – Two Singing Youths – signed with monogram – 28 x 24in.
(Christie's) **$57,600 £30,000**

FRANS HALS, Circle of – Portrait Of A Boy, Head And Shoulders, Wearing A Black Cap And A Brown Coat – on panel – 16 x 14¾in.
(Christie's) **$10,560 £5,500**

FRANS HALS, Follower of – Portrait Of A Gentleman, Standing, Three Quarter Length, In A Gold Brocade Jacket With White Collar And Cuffs And A Black Hat – 45 x 31in.
(Sotheby's) **$1,980 £1,000**

KEELEY HALSWELLE – 'Roba di Roma' – signed, inscribed and dated 1868 – oil on canvas – 45 x 72in.
(Bonham's) **$6,272 £3,200**

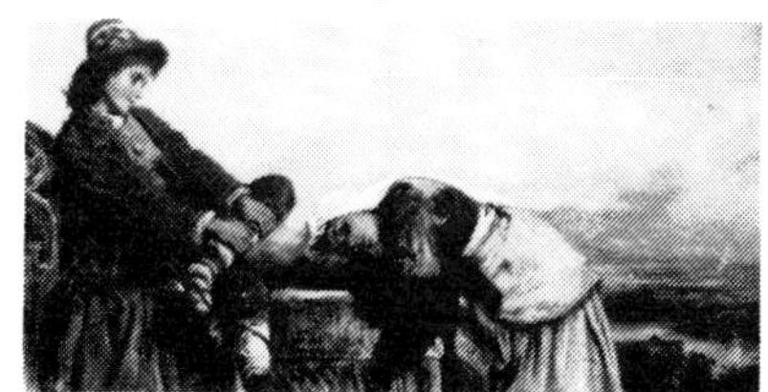

KEELEY HALSWELLE – At The Well – signed, inscribed and dated 1869 – 24 x 39¼in.
(Christie's) **$5,044 £2,600**

KEELEY HALSWELLE – Venice – signed with initials, inscribed and dated 1873 – 15 x 21in.
(Sotheby's) **$499** **£260**

JUAN VAN DER HAMEN – A Still Life Of Fruit And Cakes; A Still Life Of Fruit, With Birds – signed, one dated 1621 and the other dated 1622 – 22½ x 39½in.
(Sotheby's) **$62,720** **£32,000 Pair**

EVA H. HAMILTON – The Village Street, Roundstone – signed with initials – 20 x 15¾in.
(Sotheby's) **$466** **£240**

HUGH DOUGLAS HAMILTON – Hugh, 2nd Duke Of Northumberland, Head And Shoulders, Seated, Wearing A Red Surcoat And Blue Striped Waistcoat – signed and dated 1777 – pastel – oval – 9¼ x 7½in.
(Sotheby's) **$737** **£380**

LETITIA HAMILTON – Chiesa Della Salute, The Grand Canal Venice – signed with initials – 19½ x 23½in.
(Sotheby's) **$1,009** **£520**

LETITIA HAMILTON – A Country Road In Summer, The West Of Ireland – canvas on board – 11¾ x 15¾in.
(Sotheby's) **$698** **£360**

RICHARD HAMILTON – Pin-Up Sketch V – dated '60 – gouache, pen, Indian ink and pencil on paper – 14½ x 9in.
(Sotheby's) **$6,930** **£3,500**

GERTRUDE E. DEMAIN HAMMOND – Romeo And Juliet – signed and dated '10 – 14½ x 9¾in.
(Sotheby's Belgravia) **$288** **£150**

HANBIDGE – A Tower By The Sea – signed – 17 x 26in.
(Sotheby's Belgravia) **$153** **£80**

T. H. H. HAND – A Man-O'-War At Sea – signed – 10¾ x 15¾in.
(Sotheby's Belgravia) **$157** **£80**

W. L. HANKEY – Fair Maid's House, Perth; Marshal Place, Perth – inscribed on the reverse – canvas on board – 14 x 24in.
(Sotheby's) **$434** **£220 Two**

WILLIAM LEE HANKEY – A Village Street – signed – 14 x 10in.
(Sotheby's Belgravia) **$644** **£320**

ANDREW G. HANNAH – The Rising Moon – signed and dated '28 – 9 x 13½in.
(Sotheby's Belgravia)
$173 **£90**

HANNEMAN – Portrait Of A Gentleman, Standing Three-Quarter Length, Wearing Black Costume – 37 x 26½in.
(Christie's) **$970** **£500**

J. HARCOURT – Cornish Shore Scenes – signed – 15½ x 19½in.
(Sotheby's Belgravia)
$143 **£75 Pair**

CHARLES MARTIN HARDIE – Near Rosyth On The Banks Of The Forth – signed with monogram – on panel – 8½ x 10½in.
(Sotheby's) **$384** **£200**

C. M. HARDIE – A Lowland Farm – 9½ x 17½in.
(Sotheby's Belgravia) **$19** **£10**

CHARLES MARTIN HARDIE – Alluvial Panning, Scotland – signed and dated '81 – 15¾ x 9in.
(Sotheby's) **$752** **£380**

CHARLES MARTIN HARDIE – Dutch Deliveries – signed with initials and dated '94 – on panel – 11 x 14in.
(Sotheby's) **$614** **£320**

PIETER HARDIME – Flowers In An Elaborately Sculpted Urn With Two Putti, One Seated And One Kneeling, Against An Architectural Background – signed and dated 1719 – 76½ x 46in.
(Christie's) **$14,400** **£7,500**

PIETER HARDIME – Flowers In An Urn On A Plinth With Two Standing Putti Against An Architectural Background – signed and dated 1719 – 76½ x 46in.
(Christie's) **$8,064** **£4,200**

P. HARDIME – A Still Life Of Flowers In A Silver Urn – 24½ x 29½in.
(Sotheby's) **$4,752** **£2,400**

JAMES DUFFIELD HARDING – A Mountain Range – signed with initials, indistinctly inscribed and dated 1843 – pencil, watercolour, heightened with bodycolour – 13¼ x 19¼in.
(Sotheby's) **$312** **£160**

JAMES DUFFIELD HARDING – Rome From The Borghese Gardens – pencil, watercolour, heightened with white on buff paper – 9¾ x 16½in.
(Sotheby's) **$349** **£180**

L. HARDT – Spring; and Winter – 28 x 51cm.
(Edmiston's) **$563** **£290 Pair**

CYRIL HARDY – Bootham Bar, York – signed – watercolour heightened with white – 7¾ x 14¾in.
(Christie's) **$116** **£60**

D. HARDY – Peeling Potatoes – 14 x 12in.
(Sotheby's Belgravia) **$345** **£180**

FREDERICK DANIEL HARDY – The Sweep; and The Pedlar – signed and dated 1869 – on board – 6½ x 8¾in.
(Christie's) **$9,312** **£4,800 Pair**

FREDERICK DANIEL HARDY – The Doctor – signed and dated 1863 – on panel – 22 x 30in.
(Sotheby's Belgravia) **$44,264** **£22,000**

HEYWOOD HARDY – A Ride On The Beach – signed – 17¼ x 26in.
(Sotheby's Belgravia) **$7,243** **£3,600**

HEYWOOD HARDY – 'The Lost Scent' – signed – oil on canvas – 20 x 30in.
(Bonham's) **$6,336** **£3,200**

HEYWARD HARDY – In The Lap Of Luxury – signed and dated 1880 – on panel – 13½ x 9½in.
(Christie's) **$10,670** **£5,500**

JAMES HARDY, JNR. – Stalking In The Highlands – signed and dated '77 – on panel – 10½ x 15½in.
(Sotheby's) **$3,465** **£1,750**

HARDY, JNR. – The Gamekeeper's Son – on board – 22½ x 16in.
(Sotheby's Belgravia) **$228** **£120**

JAMES HARDY, JNR. – A Wee Dram – signed and dated '73 – heightened with white – 25 x 35in.
(Sotheby's) **$6,528** **£3,400**

THOMAS BUSH HARDY – Ships Off Calais Harbour On A Breezy Day – signed – 9 x 28in.
(Messenger May Baverstock) **$463** **£230**

THOMAS BUSH HARDY – Shipping Off Calais Pier – signed with initials – heightened with bodycolour – 10¼ x 30in.
(Sotheby's Belgravia) **$614** **£320**

THOMAS BUSH HARDY – Venice: Bragozzi Moored Near A Jetty With San Marco And The Riva Degli Schiavone In The Distance – signed and inscribed – watercolour – 17½ x 27½in.
(Christie's) **$1,455** **£750**

THOMAS BUSH HARDY – Bragozzi In The Bacino Near San Giorgio Maggiore – signed and inscribed – watercolour heightened with white – 17½ x 27½in.
(Christie's) **$1,164** **£600**

THOMAS BUSH HARDY – A Busy Harbour – signed and dated 1868 – heightened with bodycolour – 10½ x 20in.
(Sotheby's Belgravia) **$768** **£400**

THOMAS BUSH HARDY – 'The Flying Dutchman' – watercolour – 29 x 21in.
(W. H. Lane & Son) **$290** **£150**

ST. GEORGE HARE – The Welcome – signed – 28 x 20in.
(Sotheby's) **$698** **£360**

EDWARD HARGITT – Fisherfolk On A Pier – signed and dated 1866/7 – heightened with bodycolour – 19 x 28½in.
(Sotheby's Belgravia) **$345 £180**

GUDGE HARKE – A Chestnut Hunter In A Stable – signed and dated '02 – 21½ x 25½in.
(Sotheby's Belgravia) **$182 £95**

HENRY ANDREW HARPER – Cairo – signed, inscribed and dated 1872 – watercolour – 17 x 24in.
(Christie's) **$87 £45**

HENRI-JOSEPH HARPIGNIES – Paysage Meridional – signed and dated 1864 – pencil and watercolour – 6¾ x 9½in.
(Sotheby's) **$1,558 £820**

R. B. HARRADEN – Eton College From Windsor Castle Terrace – signed and dated 1823 – oil on canvas – 14½ x 20½in.
(Bonham's) **$8,514 £4,300**

RICHARD BANKES HARRADEN – A Country House With Figures In The Garden; and Figures In A Garden, With Ships In An Estuary Beyond – on panel – 9 x 12¼in.
(Christie's) **$2,522 £1,300 Pair**

GEO. HARRIS – 'Stapleton Bridge With Herdsman And Four Cows In Foreground'; and 'Wooded River Landscape With Three Figures Bathing At Snuff Mills' – both signed and dated 1904 and 1907 – oil on canvas – 22 x 34in.
(Lalonde Bros. & Parham)
$314 £160 Pair

EDWIN HARRIS – A Quiet Read – signed – 19½ x 15½in.
(Sotheby's Belgravia) **$1,408 £700**

HENRY HARRIS – Chepstow Castle; Tintern Abbey – signed and inscribed – 11 x 24in.
(Sotheby's Belgravia) **$456 £240 Pair**

HENRY HARRIS, late 19th century – 'Snuff Mills Bridge, Stapleton' – oil on canvas – 14½ x 29in.
(Lalonde Bros. & Parham)
$196 £100

CHARLES HARMONY HARRISON – Yarmouth Herring Fishing Fleet Off The Coast – signed and dated 1881 – 10 x 16in.
(G. A. Key) **$495 £250**

JOHN CYRIL HARRISON – A Peregrine Falcon Perched On A Rock – indistinctly signed – 13 x 18in.
(Sotheby's) **$134 £70**

JOHN CYRIL HARRISON – Pintails – signed – heightened with white – 18 x 13in.
(Sotheby's) **$495 £250**

JOHN CYRIL HARRISON – An Eagle With A Salmon – signed and dated 1899 – heightened with white – 5½ x 8½in.
(Sotheby's) **$480** **£250**

JOHN CYRIL HARRISON – Pheasants And Grouse Curling – both signed – 13 x 9in.
(Sotheby's) **$537** **£280 Pair**

JOHN CYRIL HARRISON – Grouse In Flight – signed – heightened with bodycolour – 12¾ x 18¼in.
(Sotheby's) **$691** **£360**

JOHN CYRIL HARRISON – Morning Flight – signed – 22 x 30½in.
(Sotheby's) **$1,056** **£550**

JOHN CYRIL HARRISON – October Partridges – signed – heightened with bodycolour – 22 x 30in.
(Sotheby's) **$1,056** **£550**

JOHN CYRIL HARRISON – Seven Grouse Over Slopes – signed – heightened with white – 22 x 30in.
(Sotheby's) **$1,440** **£750**

W. HARROWING – A Shire Horse – bears monogram and dated 1892 – 24½ x 29½in.
(Sotheby's Belgravia) **$307** **£160**

HART – A Tavern Girl – 21 x 17½in.
(Sotheby's Belgravia) **$109** **£55**

PRO HART – Desert Landscape – signed – oil on board – 31 x 60cm.
(Australian Art Auctions) **$351 £183**

S. HART – Cottages Near Chobham; Village Near Oxshott, Surrey – signed – heightened with white – 9½ x 14in.
(Sotheby's Belgravia) **$96 £50 Pair**

THOMAS HART – A View Of Falmouth Harbour, Cornwall, And Pendennis Castle From Above St. Mawes – signed – pencil and watercolour heightened with white – 6¾ x 12¾in.
(Christie's) **$116 £60**

ALBERT HARTLAND – Pont-y-Carth, Capel Curig, North Wales – signed – 12 x 21in.
(Sotheby's Belgravia) **$149 £75**

H. A. HARTLAND – Carriganass Castle, County Cork, Eire – 25 x 38¼in.
(Sotheby's Belgravia) **$230 £120**

SIR G. HARVEY – Highlanders Crossing A Burn – heightened with bodycolour – 23¼ x 36¼in.
(Sotheby's Belgravia) **$257 £130**

HAROLD HARVEY – 'The Kite Flyers' – oil on canvas – 30 x 25in.
(W. H. Lane & Son) **$528 £275**

DUBOIS FENELON HASBROUCK – Winter Landscape In Upper New York – signed, inscribed and dated '95 – watercolour, heightened with white – 9¾ x 19¾in.
(Sotheby's) **$138 £70**

JOHN HASSALL – 'Rosemary, That's For Remembrance' – signed and inscribed – heightened with bodycolour – 19 x 11½in.
(Sotheby's Belgravia) **$209 £110**

JOHN HASSELL – The Golden Ball – signed – 23½ x 17in.
(Sotheby's Belgravia) **$499 £260**

ALICE MARY HAVERS – La Modele S'Amuse – 33 x 45½in.
(Sotheby's Belgravia)
$7,243 £3,600

J. HAY, 19th century – 'Scarborough, South Bay' – signed – oil on canvas – 18½ x 25in.
(Morphets of Harrogate)
$359 £185

ARTHUR HAYES – A Moorland Road, Perthshire – signed – heightened with bodycolour – 10½ x 14½in.
(Sotheby's Belgravia)
$48 £25

CLAUDE HAYES – In The Meadows – signed – heightened with white – 5 x 8½in.
(Sotheby's Belgravia)
$36 £18

EDWIN HAYES – Dutch Fishing Boats Coming Into Harbour – signed, inscribed and dated 1888 – 6½ x 10in.
(Sotheby's Belgravia)
$713 £360

EDWIN HAYES – On The Irish Coast – on board – 6¼ x 10¾in.
(Sotheby's) **$543 £280**

EDWIN HAYES – Unloading The Catch, Sunset – signed – 15½ x 21½in.
(Sotheby's) **$2,910 £1,500**

EDWIN HAYES – A Seascape With Fishing Boats Sailing In Rough Weather, Figures In A Rowing Boat, And A Distant Windmill – signed and dated 1872 – 16 x 24in.
(Russell, Baldwin & Bright) **$2,940 £1,500**

EDWIN HAYES – Shipping On The Scheldt – signed and dated 1877 and signed, indistinctly inscribed and dated on the reverse – 14¾ x 24in.
(Sotheby's) **$3,104 £1,600**

EDWIN HAYES – Shipping Off The Coast, A Castle On A Headland To The Right – signed – 11½ x 19½in.
(Sotheby's) **$3,880 £2,000**

FREDERICK WILLIAM HAYES – Ponty-y-Pair, Bettws-y-Coed; and Roman Bridge, Bettws-y-Coed – oil on board – 10½ x 6¾in.
(Geering & Colyer) **$504 £260 Pair**

FREDERICK WILLIAM HAYES – Llyn Cranfinant, Trefriw; and Lledr Valley, Bettws-y-Coed – oil on board – 6¾ x 10½in.
(Geering & Colyer) **$504 £260 Pair**

EDITH HAYLLAR – More Hindrance Than Help – signed and dated 1893 – 26½ x 19½in.
(Sotheby's Belgravia) **$1,207 £600**

JAMES HAYLLAR – The Picture Gallery At The Hall, Corporation Of Southport – signed and inscribed on a label – 40 x 59in.
(Sotheby's Belgravia) **$14,084 £7,000**

JAMES HAYLLAR – A Lochside View – signed and dated 1870 – 17½ x 35½in.
(Sotheby's Belgravia) **$269 £140**

JESSICA HAYLLAR – Portrait Of An Old Man, Shoulder Length, Wearing A Red Hat – signed and dated 1874 – vignette – oil on board – 9½ x 7in.
(Christie's) **$111 £55**

W. C. HEDA – A Still Life On A Table Covered By A Turkey Carpet – on panel – 26½ x 21¼in.
(Sotheby's) **$3,168 £1,600**

WILLEM CLAESZ. HEDA – A Vanitas Still Life With A Broken Roemer, A Roemer, An Upturned Tazza And A Peeled Lemon On A Plate, On A Ledge – signed and dated 1648 – on panel 18¾ x 24½in.
(Christie's) **$76,800 £40,000**

JOHNSON HEDLEY – A Highland Loch – signed – 12½ x 18¼in.
(Sotheby's Belgravia) **$67 £35**

C. DE HEEM – Peaches, Grapes And Plums In A Porcelain Bowl And Cherries, Oysters And A Melon On A Pewter Plate On A Draped Table – on panel – 10¼ x 12¾in.
(Christie's) **$5,044 £2,600**

C. DE HEEM – A Still Life Of Fruit And Oysters On A Wooden Ledge – bears signature – 24¼ x 30¾in.
(Sotheby's) **$8,730 £4,500**

CORNELIS DE HEEM – A Banquet Still Life With Oysters, Fruit, A Silver-Gilt Cup, An Ewer And A Sugar Castor On A Draped Table – signed and dated 1655 – 38 x 47½in.
(Christie's) **$86,400 £45,000**

CORNELIS DE HEEM – A Still Life Of Fruit – on panel – 14 x 21¼in.
(Sotheby's) **$43,120 £22,000**

CORNELIS DE HEEM – A Garland Of Flowers And Fruit – signed and dated 1656 – on panel – 22¼ x 16¾in.
(Sotheby's) **$31,040 £16,000**

CORNELIS DE HEEM – Peaches, Oysters, Grapes And A Half-Peeled Lemon, With A Tazza On A Draped Ledge – signed – 11 x 14¾in.
(Christie's) **$49,920 £26,000**

HEEMSKERK – A Woman Counting Money – on panel – 8½ x 6½in.
(Christie's) **$252 £130**

E. VAN HEEMSKERK – Peasants Smoking In An Interior – bears monogram – on panel – 5¼ x 4¼in.
(Christie's) **$873 £450**

E. VAN HEEMSKERK – A Confessional – bears signature – on panel – 6½ x 5½in.
(Sotheby's) **$1,591 £820**

EGBERT VAN HEEMSKERK – Peasants Smoking And Drinking In A Barn With Vegetables And Earthenware Vessels Nearby – on panel – 18½ x 25½in.
(Christie's) **$3,298 £1,700**

EGBERT VAN HEEMSKERK – Peasants Playing Cards – on copper – 6 x 5in.
(Christie's) **$1,008 £520**

EGBERT VAN HEEMSKERK – The Interior Of A Schoolroom, A Teacher Punishing A Small Boy Who Stands Before A Desk – 17¼ x 20¾in.
(Sotheby's) **$4,356 £2,200**

THOMAS HEEREMANS – A Winter Landscape With Figures On The Ice Outside A Town – signed and dated 1686 – on panel – 11½ x 14½in.
(Christie's) **$14,400** **£7,500**

THOMAS HEEREMANS – A Riverside Village, To The Left A Ferry-Boat And Figures Outside An Inn And A Village With A Church Beyond – signed – on panel – 24½ x 31in.
(Sotheby's) **$17,640** **£9,000**

THOMAS HEEREMANS – A Winter Scene With Skaters – signed and dated 1685 – 33½ x 42½in.
(Sotheby's) **$29,400** **£15,000**

THOMAS HEEREMANS – A Wooded Landscape With Peasants By A Path And Cottages Beyond – signed with monogram – on panel – 11 x 14in.
(Christie's) **$3,492** **£1,800**

GEORG HEINTZ – A Still Life Of Fruit, Including Pears On A Silver Platter, Pears And White Grapes In A Blue And White Bowl, All On A Marble Table – signed – 46½ x 36¼in.
(Sotheby's) **$6,930** **£3,500**

PAUL-CESAR HELLEU – Portrait De Mademoiselle Helleu – signed – charcoal and red chalk – 18¼ x 13¼in.
(Sotheby's) **$1,425** **£750**

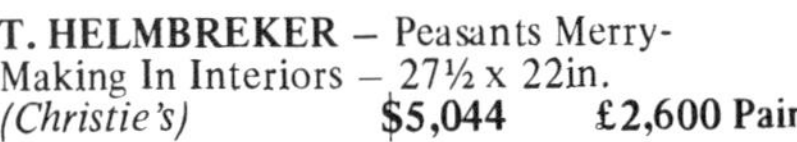

T. HELMBREKER – Peasants Merry-Making In Interiors – 27½ x 22in.
(Christie's) **$5,044** **£2,600 Pair**

M. VON HELMONT – A Family Making Music In An Interior – on panel – 12½ x 10½in.
(Sotheby's) **$3,366** **£1,700**

B. VAN DER HELST – Portrait Of A Lady, Half Length, Wearing A Black Dress With A White Collar – inscribed – on panel – 26½ x 22in.
(Christie's) **$931** **£480**

NICOLAES VAN HELT-STOCADE – The Queen Of Sheba Visiting Solomon – signed – 34¾ x 47in.
(Sotheby's) **$1,940** **£1,000**

VAN HEMESSEN – St. Jerome – on panel – 16 x 11¼in.
(Christie's) **$126** **£65**

WILLIAM HEMSLEY – 'Open Your Mouth And Close Your Eyes' – 16½ x 13½in.
(Sotheby's Belgravia)
$1,308 **£650**

WILLIAM HEMSLEY – 'Setting A Rabbit's Snare' – signed, signed and inscribed on the reverse – on panel – 9¾ x 7¾in.
(Sotheby Bearne)
$2,425 **£1,250**

WILLIAM HEMSLEY – Granny's Charge – signed and inscribed on a label on the reverse – on panel – 8½ x 6½in.
(Sotheby's Belgravia)
$1,107 **£550**

C. N. HEMY – Moored Fishing Boats – inscribed on the reverse – on panel – 11¾ x 15¼in.
(Sotheby's Belgravia) **$326** **£170**

CHARLES NAPIER HEMY – Clovelly – signed and dated 1866/7 – 20 x 30in.
(Sotheby's Belgravia)
$1,609 **£800**

C. NAPIER HEMY – Triple-Masted Schooner Riding A Storm – initialled and dated 1913 – oil on canvas – 20 x 30in.
(Morphets of Harrogate)
$737 **£380**

C. NAPIER HEMY – Three Figures In A Yacht – signed – watercolour – 14 x 27in.
(Morphets of Harrogate)
$620 **£320**

CHARLES COOPER HENDERSON – A Carriage With Coachman And Four Passengers Drawn By A Pair Of Greys – oil on canvas – 12½ x 23½in.
(Osmond, Tricks & Son) **$2,376** **£1,200**

CHARLES COOPER HENDERSON – French Diligence On A Sandy Road – pencil and watercolour heightened with white – 6¼ x 10in.
(Sotheby's) **$388** **£200**

CHARLES COOPER HENDERSON – A Royal Mail Coach Travelling At Night – 12½ x 23½in.
(Christie's) **$737** **£380**

C. C. HENDERSON – Home From The Shoot – inscribed with monogram – 12½ x 23½in.
(Sotheby's Belgravia)
$665 **£350**

J. HENDERSON – Off To Market – signed with monogram – 18 x 13in.
(Sotheby's) **$495** **£250**

JOHN HENDERSON – Summertime – signed – 17½ x 29½in.
(Sotheby's) **$1,152** **£600**

JOHN HENDERSON – By The Burn – 38 x 49cm.
(Edmiston's) **$640** **£330**

JOSEPH HENDERSON – Elm Trees – signed with monogram – on board – 11½ x 15in.
(Sotheby's Belgravia) **$96** **£50**

JOSEPH MORRIS HENDERSON – Ballantrae; Glen Moriston – signed – on board – 5¼ x 6¾in.
(Sotheby's Belgravia)
$152 **£80 Pair**

JOSEPH MORRIS HENDERSON – Harvest Time – signed – 7½ x 11½in.
(Sotheby's) **$297** **£150**

JOSEPH MORRIS HENDERSON – By A Winding River Bank – signed – 12 x 19in.
(Sotheby's) **$268** **£140**

G. HENDRIKS – Cattle, Sheep And Goats In A Continental Landscape With Ducks On A Pond – signed and dated 1868 – oil – 27 x 45½in.
(Heathcote Ball & Co.) **$3,636** **£1,800**

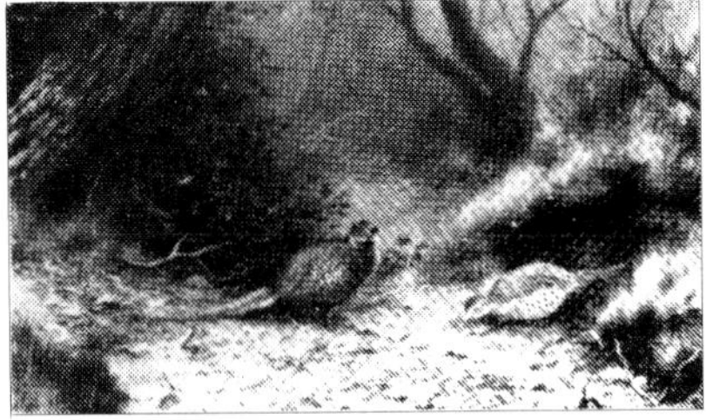

DAVID M. REID HENRY – Old English Pheasants – signed – heightened with body-colour – 12 x 19½in.
(Sotheby's) **$537** **£280**

DAVID M. REID HENRY – Red Grouse On A Moor – signed – gouache – 15 x 11in.
(Sotheby's) **$729** **£380**

DAVID M. REID HENRY – Covey Gathering At Evening – signed – gouache – 6½ x 9½in.
(Sotheby's) **$499** **£260**

DAVID M. REID HENRY – Grouse In Spring – signed – heightened with bodycolour – 7 x 10¼in.
(Sotheby's) **$364** **£190**

DAVID M. REID HENRY – Woodcock In Undergrowth – signed – heightened with bodycolour – 7¾ x 10¾in.
(Sotheby's) **$384** **£200**

GEORGE HENRY – A Japanese Girl – coloured chalks – 19½ x 14¾in.
(Sotheby's) **$1,188** **£600**

GEORGE HENRY – A Promenade – signed – 44½ x 22in.
(Sotheby's) **$19,200** **£10,000**

GEORGE HENRY – A Geisha Girl – signed, inscribed and dated '94 – 21½ x 12½in.
(Sotheby's) **$10,560** **£5,500**

PAUL HENRY – Morning In Donegal – signed, inscribed on a label on the reverse – 19 x 23in.
(Sotheby's) **$6,984** **£3,600**

FREDERICK HENRY HENSHAW – A View Of Windsor Great Park – 19 x 29½in.
(Christie's) **$1,649** **£850**

GEORGE MOORE HENTON – Groby Pool, Leicestershire – signed, inscribed and dated 1886 – 20 x 29in.
(Sotheby's Belgravia)
$297 **£150**

I. HENZELL – Playing At Doctors – inscribed – 35¾ x 27½in.
(Sotheby's Belgravia)
$1,408 **£700**

HAROLD B. HERBERT – Valley Landscape – signed – watercolour – 24 x 25.5cm.
(Australian Art Auctions)
$280 **£146**

ROBERT HERD – A View In North Wales – signed and dated 1889 and inscribed – 20 x 27in.
(Sotheby's Belgravia)
$178 **£90**

ROBERT HERDMAN – The Posie – signed with monogram and dated '71 – on board – 11½ x 8¼in.
(Sotheby's) **$998** **£520**

HERIBERG – View Of Cape Town And Its Environs – signed and inscribed – watercolour – 16 x 24½in.
(Sotheby's) **$138** **£70**

JOSEF HERMAN – Mother And Child, 1963-64 – 47½ x 35¼in.
(Sotheby's) **$990** **£500**

JOSEF HERMAN – Man With Goat – signed – gouache – 19¾ x 24½in.
(Sotheby's) **$437** **£220**

L. HERMANN – River Scene With Buildings – oil on canvas – 12 x 19in.
(Bracketts) **$2,508** **£1,200**

LEON L'HERMITTE – Les Vendanges – signed – charcoal – 19½ x 16in.
(Sotheby's) **$3,610** **£1,900**

LEON L'HERMITTE – Rue De Village – signed – charcoal – 14 x 18in.
(Sotheby's) **$950** **£500**

LEON L'HERMITTE – Six Women Washing Clothes At The Edge Of A River, With Cattle Grazing And Trees On The Far Bank – signed – pastel – 36 x 53cm.
(Henry Spencer & Sons) **$3,069** **£1,550**

WILLEM VAN HERP, After Rubens – Otanes On The Chair Of The Judge – on panel – 18½ x 24¼in.
(Christie's) **$1,261** **£650**

WILLEM VAN HERP – Moses And The Israelites Rejoicing On The Banks Of The Red Sea – 15 x 22½in.
(Sotheby's) **$2,079** **£1,050**

BEN HERRING – The Tandem; and The Drag – signed and dated 1869 – on panel – 11½ x 9½in.
(Christie's) **$2,910** **£1,500 Pair**

BENJAMIN HERRING – On The London Road – signed – 15½ x 15½in.
(Sotheby's Belgravia) **$3,018** **£1,500**

J. F. HERRING – A Farmyard Scene – bears signature – 19½ x 29in.
(Christie's) **$2,522** **£1,300**

J. F. HERRING – Cattle And Goats In A Stable – 17½ x 23½in.
(Sotheby's Belgravia) **$537** **£280**

J. F. HERRING – Many Horses Drinking From A Stream; And Horses And Pigs In A Paddock – bears signature – watercolour – 20 x 30cm.
(Henry Spencer & Sons) **$427** **£220 Pair**

J. F. HERRING, JNR. – A Farmyard Scene With Horses And Ducks – oil on canvas – 28 x 45cm.
(King & Chasemore) **$3,168** **£1,600**

J. F. HERRING, JNR. – By A Farm Pond – inscribed – 9½ x 13½in.
(Sotheby's Belgravia) **$634** **£320**

JOHN FREDERICK HERRING, JNR. – A Troop Of Roundhead Cavalry At A Ford – signed – 24 x 36in.
(Sotheby's Belgravia)
$2,414 **£1,200**

JOHN FREDERICK HERRING, JNR. – Down At The Farm – signed – 22¼ x 32¼in.
(Sotheby's Belgravia)
$5,030 **£2,500**

J. F. HERRING, SNR. – Farmyard Scene With Horses And Other Farmyard Birds And Animals – signed – oil – 21 x 35in.
(Richard Baker & Baker)
$10,032 **£4,800**

JOHN FREDERICK HERRING, SNR. – Andover And Mincemeat: Two Bay Racehorses With Jockeys Up, A Racehorse Beyond, With Many Figures, A Marquee And Buildings – signed – oil on canvas – 45 x 70cm.
(Henry Spencer & Sons)
$3,201 **£1,650**

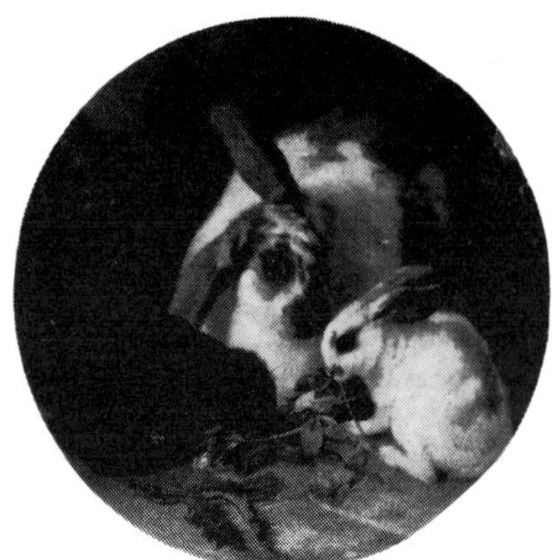

JOHN FREDERICK HERRING, SNR. – Bunnies – signed and dated 1851 – diameter 17in.
(Sotheby's Belgravia) **$9,054** **£4,500**

JOHN FREDERICK HERRING, SNR. – Companions – signed and dated 1848 – on panel – diameter 14in.
(Sotheby's Belgravia) **$12,072** **£6,000**

JACOB DE HEUSCH – A Southern Landscape With Roman Ruins, In The Foreground Peasants With Mules By A Roman Ruin, And Beyond, A Broad Flight Of Steps Leading To Building – signed indistinctly – 25¼ x 35in.
(Sotheby's) **$5,044** **£2,600**

T. P. HEWITT – Classical Grace – signed – sepia – 6½ x 22in.
(Sotheby's Belgravia) **$61** **£32**

JAN JANSZ. VAN DER HEYDEN – A Capriccio Of A Town Square With A Shoemaker's Shop And Numerous Figures – signed and dated 1676 – on panel – 18 x 23½in.
(Christie's) **$364,800** **£190,000**

G. HICKIN – Rural Scene With Family By Camp Fire With Windmill Behind – signed – oil on canvas – 15½ x 11½in.
(Manchester Auction Mart)
$1,161 **£575**

HICKS – Portraits Of Fashionable Ladies – heightened with white – oval – 18 x 14½in.
(Sotheby's Belgravia) **$115** **£60 Pair**

GEORGE ELGAR HICKS – The Reaper; and The Croquet Player – signed with initials – pencil and red chalk heightened with white on grey paper – 10½ x 7¾in. and 10½ x 7in.
(Sotheby's Belgravia) **$382** **£190 Pair**

FRANK HIDER – A Rocky Cove – signed and dated 1916 – 17 x 14in.
(Sotheby's Belgravia) **$96** **£50**

JOHN HILDER – Wooded River Landscapes With Figures, Cattle And Sheep By Cottages – signed – on panel – 11½ x 15in.
(Christie's) **$1,746** **£900 Pair**

J. J. HILDER – Landscape – signed – watercolour – 14 x 23cm.
(Australian Art Auctions)
$819 **£427**

RICHARD HILDER – Cattle Watering – 11½ x 15¾in.
(Christie's) **$2,328** **£1,200**

A. STUART HILL – Toledo – 44 x 57cm.
(Edmiston's) **$101** **£52**

D. O. HILL – Edinburgh From The East – 16 x 23¾in.
(Sotheby's) **$576** **£300**

DAVID HILL – Autumn Evening On The Common; Near Petersfield, Hants – both signed – 19½ x 14½in.
(Sotheby's Belgravia)
$345 **£180 Pair**

ROLAND HENRY HILL – Fairhead, Balleycastle, County Antrim; and On The Irish Coast – signed, one inscribed and dated 1941 – heightened with white – 8 x 14in.
(Sotheby's) **$194** **£100 Two**

P. VAN HILLEGAERT – Elegant Figures At A Booth In A Military Camp – 17 x 21¾in.
(Christie's) **$6,790** **£3,500**

WILLIAM HENRI HILLIARD – Tropical Landscapes – signed – oil on canvas – 15½ x 11½in.
(Sotheby's) **$355** **£180 Two**

TRISTRAM HILLIER – L'Abbaye Du Chalard – signed and dated 1964 – 13½ x 19½in.
(Sotheby's) **$594** **£300**

THOMAS HILLS – In The Rockies, An Encampment In The Foreground – signed with monogram, and dated 1885 – oil on canvas – 23¾ x 35½in.
(Sotheby's) **$2,955** **£1,500**

HENRY HILTON – A View Down A Vale – signed – 10½ x 28½in.
(Sotheby's Belgravia) **$68** **£35**

WILLIAM HILTON – Love Taught By The Graces – inscribed on a label on the reverse – 69 x 90½in.
(Christie's) **$2,328** **£1,200**

GODFREY C. HINDLEY – Perseverance – signed – on board – 12 x 16½in.
(Sotheby's) **$729** **£380**

FREDERICK HINES – Beside Some Waters' Rushy Brink, Autumn – signed and dated 1893, inscribed on the reverse – 39½ x 29½in.
(Sotheby's Belgravia) **$396** **£200**

FREDERICK HINES – A Surrey Landscape – signed and dated '83, inscribed on the reverse – 19½ x 29½in.
(Sotheby's Belgravia) **$346** **£180**

FREDERICK HINES – Winter Time – signed – 14 x 10in.
(Sotheby's Belgravia) **$79** **£40**

F. HINKLEY – A Nude Study – signed – 9 x 17½in.
(Sotheby's Belgravia) **$49** **£25**

GEORGE DUNKERTON HISCOX – Extensive Autumn Landscape With A Gypsy Preparing A Meal Over An Open Fire In A Cornfield – signed and dated '90 – oil on canvas – 19½ x 29½in.
(Osmond, Tricks & Son) **$713** **£360**

M. HOBBEMA – A Wooded Landscape With A Village Beyond – on panel – 10 x 13½in.
(Christie's) **$1,552** **£800**

MEINDERT HOBBEMA – Landscape With A Cottage Among Trees – signed and dated 1659 – on panel – 13½ x 17¼in.
(Sotheby's) **$58,800** **£30,000**

DAVID HOCKNEY – Reclining Figure – signed with initials and dated '64 – pencil and pink crayon on paper – 17¾ x 22¾in.
(Sotheby's) **$178** **£90**

DAVID HOCKNEY – Concert At The Royal Albert Hall – signed – pencil on paper – 15¼ x 13¼in.
(Sotheby's) **$1,624** **£820**

JOHN MULCAHY HODGES – An Extensive Classical Landscape With Laeda And The Swan – signed and dated 1823 – 47 x 56in.
(Sotheby's) **$5,544** **£2,800**

W. S. HODGES – South American Indian Spearing Fish At Dusk, Native Women Resting In A Hut – signed and dated 1835 – oil on canvas – 15½ x 28½in.
(Sotheby's) **$1,084** **£550**

FRANCES HODGKINS – Farmer's Boy – signed – black chalk – 21½ x 16in.
(Sotheby's) **$990** **£500**

FRANCES HODGKINS – Northern Barn – signed and dated 1939 – pencil and watercolour, heightened with bodycolour – 21 x 16in.
(Sotheby's) **$792** **£400**

WILLIAM MATHEW HODGKINS – Changing Pastures, New Zealand – signed, inscribed and dated 1888 – watercolour – 9¼ x 19¼in
(Sotheby's) **$473** **£240**

JAN VAN DER HOECKE – Cupid Triumphant – 68 x 97½in.
(Sotheby's) **$7,920** **£4,000**

G. HOET – Christ Healing The Blind Man – 12½ x 15¼in.
(Christie's) **$1,358** **£700**

WILLIAM HOGGATT – The Silverburn Above Grenaby – signed – 6¾ x 7¾in.
(Warner Sheppard & Wade) **$79** **£38**

HOLBEIN – Erasmus In A Black Robe And A Black Cap, Seated At A Table – on panel – 14½ x 11in.
(Sotheby's) **$11,760** **£6,000**

ABEL HOLD – Grouse On The Moor – signed and dated 1898 – 19 x 29in.
(Sotheby's) **$614** **£320**

TOM HOLD – Pheasants And Partridges – signed, one dated 1886 – 9½ x 11½in.
(Sotheby's) **$921** **£480 Pair**

EDWARD HENRY HOLDER – Dovedale – signed, inscribed – 19¼ x 29¼in.
(Sotheby's Belgravia) **$1,610** **£800**

EDWARD HENRY HOLDER – Going For A Boat Trip – signed and dated '90 – 19¼ x 29¼in.
(Sotheby's Belgravia) **$874** **£460**

EDWARD HENRY HOLDER – The Llugwy From Miners Bridge – signed and dated '85 – on board – 11¾ x 17¾in.
(Christie's) **$582** **£300**

THOMAS W. HOLGATE – Summer Songs – signed – 25½ x 17in.
(Sotheby's Belgravia) **$2,414** **£1,200 Pair**

THOMAS W. HOLGATE – Lost In Thought – signed – 19½ x 10in.
(Sotheby's Belgravia) **$653** **£340**

JAMES HOLLAND – An Arrangement Of Roses, Anemones, Speedwell And Other Flowers On A Stone Ledge – signed with monogram and indistinctly signed and dated 1863 – watercolour heightened with white – 13 x 9¼in.
(Christie's) **$388** **£200**

JAMES HOLLAND – Dover Harbour – signed with monogram, inscribed and dated '46 – pencil, grey and pale green wash heightened with white on grey-green paper – 10¼ x 15in.
(Christie's) **$116** **£60**

JAMES HOLLAND – The Coast At Lynmouth, North Devon – signed and inscribed – 23½ x 35½in.
(Christie's) **$1,067** **£550**

F. MABEL HOLLANS – 'Follow Through', A Hunter – signed and inscribed – on panel – 13 x 17½in.
(Sotheby's) **$815** **£420**

JOHN HOLLINS – 'Charles I At Reckling Hall, Ditchling' – oil on canvas – 97 x 126cm.
(King & Chasemore) **$673** **£340**

EDWARD HOLMES – Sweet Nothings – 17½ x 14½in.
(Sotheby's Belgravia) **$2,414** **£1,200**

B. HOLT – A Boy Fishing On A River – signed – 15½ x 11½in.
(Sotheby's Belgravia) **$134** **£70**

E. F. HOLT – 'The Busy Blacksmith' – signed – oil – 15½ x 22½in.
(Andrew, Hilditch & Son) **$397** **£190**

E. F. HOLT – An Unexpected Visitor – signed, inscribed and dated 1889 – 19½ x 23½in.
(Sotheby's Belgravia) **$1,006** **£500**

WILLIAM HOLYOAKE – Scene From Shakespeare's "Midsummer Night's Dream" – signed – oil on canvas – 56 x 42in.
(Morphets of Harrogate) **$1,202** **£620**

HONDECOETER – A Concert Of Birds – red chalk, pen and brown ink brown wash – 314 x 406mm.
(Christie's) **$86** **£45**

ABRAHAM HONDIUS – Hounds Putting Up Storks, In Wooded Landscapes – signed – on panel – 13 x 15¼in.
(Sotheby's) **$6,208** **£3,200 Pair**

ABRAHAM HONDIUS – A Commemorative Portrait Of Infant Twins, Lying On A Bed Covered With A Red Velvet Cloth – inscribed indistinctly, signed and dated 1654 – on panel – 20½ x 34in.
(Sotheby's) **$2,772** **£1,400**

ABRAHAM HONDIUS – A Boar Hunt – 37¾ x 49¾in.
(Christie's) **$1,164** **£600**

G. DE HONDT – A Merry Party In A Dutch Village, Peasants Dancing In The Foreground – 16 x 29in.
(Sotheby's) **$2,134 £1,100**

EVIE HONE – The Wood, A Scene At Rockview Killucan, Co. Westmeath, September 1945 – indistinctly inscribed – black chalk and bodycolour – 10 x 14in.
(Sotheby's) **$310 £160**

HONTHORST – Christ Before Caiaphas – 28 x 22in.
(Christie's) **$126 £65**

HONTHORST – Christ Before Caiaphas – 59 x 82½in.
(Christie's) **$15,520 £8,000**

W. VAN HONTHORST – A Portrait Of A Gentleman, Half Length, In Black – on panel – 28¼ x 23¼in.
(Sotheby's) **$1,590 £820**

DE HOOCH – A Musical Party In An Interior, Elegant Figures Around A Table – 18¾ x 16in.
(Sotheby's) **$1,358 £700**

KENNETH HOOD – Still Life With Flowers – signed and indistinctly dated – on board – 24 x 20in.
(Sotheby's) **$79 £40**

THE MASTER OF HOOGSTRAATEN – Triptych: The Holy Family And Saints Catherine And Barbara – on panel – centre panel 25¼ x 22½in. and each wing 35 x 9¼in.
(Sotheby's) **$46,560 £24,000**

JAMES CLARKE HOOK – The Bauble Boat – 23¾ x 39in.
(Christie's) **$1,552 £800**

C. LANCASTER HOOPER – Country Scenes – signed – 19¾ x 29¾in.
(Sotheby's Belgravia)
$285 £150 Pair

HOOPER & Co., Designed by – Design For Queen Victoria's Semi-State Dress Landau – inscribed and dated 1885; and Postillion Landau – pen and black ink, watercolour – 6 x 10¼in. and 5½ x 9in.
(Sotheby's) **$819 £420 Pair**

E. LANCASTER HOOPER – Sunset On The Avon – signed, inscribed on the reverse – 9½ x 13½in.
(Sotheby's Belgravia)
$99 £50

JOHN HORACE HOOPER – Twilight – signed, and signed, indistinctly inscribed and dated '96 on the reverse – 35½ x 27½in.
(Christie's) **$970 £500**

JOHN HORACE HOOPER – Mapledurham, Evening – signed, inscribed on the reverse – 29 x 49in.
(Sotheby's Belgravia) **$1,308** **£650**

WILLIAM G. HOOPER – A Pumpkin, Grapes, Peaches, A Basket Of Fruit And A Jug On A Ledge – signed and dated 1886 – 19¼ x 23¼in.
(Christie's) **$543** **£280**

WILLIAM HOPE – A Trapper Seated Holding His Gun – signed and inscribed – oil on panel – 13¾ x 9¾in.
(Sotheby's) **$96** **£50**

JAN JOSEF HOREMANS – The Interior Of A Peasant Cottage – 16 x 20in.
(Sotheby's) **$2,772** **£1,400**

JAN JOSEF HOREMANS – Musical Parties Beneath The Classical Portico Of A Palace – signed, one dated 1716 – 25½ x 32¼in.
(Sotheby's) **$11,880** **£6,000 Pair**

JAN JOSEF HOREMANS – Hunters Outside A Cottage, Conversing With A Peasant Woman – 12¼ x 15¼in.
(Sotheby's) **$3,201** **£1,650**

JAN JOSEF HOREMANS – An Artist In His Studio – 21¾ x 18in.
(Christie's) **$5,432** **£2,800**

HORLOR – Farm At Rho's, Colwyn Bay, North Wales – indistinctly signed, inscribed on the reverse – 11½ x 19½in.
(Sotheby's Belgravia) **$285** **£150**

G. W. HORLOR – A Hilly Landscape With Figures And A Cart On A Path – 19½ x 30in.
(Christie's) **$1,261** **£650**

GEORGE W. HORLOR – Sportsmen Resting In A Highland Landscape – signed – 13½ x 17in.
(Christie's) **$3,686** **£1,900**

JOSEPH HORLOR – Extensive Coastal Landscape With Peasant Woman And Two Cows About To Cross A Stream – signed – oil on canvas – 36 x 24in.
(Lalonde Bros. & Parham) **$634** **£320**

JOSEPH HORLOR – Wooded Landscapes With Cattle Watering – one signed and dated 1855 – on board – 9½ x 13¼in.
(Christie's) **$1,940** **£1,000 Pair**

JOSEPH HORLOR – A View Of Middleham Castle, Wensleydale, Yorkshire – signed and dated 1878 – 15¾ x 23½in.
(Christie's) **$970** **£500**

JOSEPH HORLOR – A Waterfall – signed – 14¼ x 11¼in.
(Sotheby's Belgravia) **$105** **£55**

HORNEL – Portrait Of A Girl Holding A Flower – on board – 14½ x 11½in.
(Sotheby's Belgravia) **$118** **£60**

EDWARD ATKINSON HORNEL – Woodland Scene With Four Girls – dated 1900 – 38 x 29cm.
(Edmiston's) **$6,984** **$3,600**

EDWARD ATKINSON HORNEL – 'Hark! Hark! The Lark' – signed and dated 1918, inscribed on a label on the reverse – canvas on panel – 21¼ x 8¼in.
(Sotheby's) **$4,800** **£2,500**

EDWARD ATKINSON HORNEL – Pick-A-Back – signed and dated 1911 – 35½ x 39½in.
(Sotheby's) **$10,296** **£5,200**

EDWARD ATKINSON HORNEL – In The Orchard, Buckland, Kirkcudbright – signed and dated '98, inscribed on a label on the reverse – 8¾ x 10in.
(Sotheby's) **$1,920** **£1,000**

WILLIAM SAMUEL HORTON – A Summers Day With A Village By A River – inscribed on the reverse – oil on board – 15 x 18in.
(Sotheby's) **$887** **£450**

WILLIAM SAMUEL HORTON – A Pony And Trap On A Tree Lined Road – signed – oil on board – 12¾ x 16in.
(Sotheby's) **$887** **£450**

ARNOLD HOUBRAKEN – Bathsheba And Uriah Watched By King David – signed – on panel – 13 x 10¼in.
(Christie's) **$2,522** **£1,300**

GEORGE HOUSTON – Neidpath Castle – 70 x 90cm.
(Edmiston's) **$1,183** **£610**

GEORGE HOUSTON – Moonlight On The Beach – signed and dated '96 – 24 x 29½in.
(Sotheby's) **$297** **£150**

GEORGE HOUSTON – A Scottish Estuary – signed – on board – 16 x 24in.
(Sotheby's) **$288** **£150**

GEORGE HOUSTON – Arran From The Ayrshire Coast – 40 x 63cm.
(Edmiston's) **$504** **£260**

GEORGE HOUSTON – Autumn Snow – signed – 29 x 39½in.
(Sotheby's) **$1,152** **£600**

GEORGE HOUSTON – Iona – signed, inscribed and dated 1901 – 17 x 25½in.
(Sotheby's) **$768** **£400**

JOHN ADAM P. HOUSTON – The Vedette, Who Goes There?; The Black Mount, Twixt Day And Night – signed and dated '79, one inscribed on the reverse – 11 x 17½in.
(Sotheby's) **$2,880** **£1,500 Pair**

JOHN ADAM P. HOUSTON – On The Orwell – 6¼ x 9¾in.
(Sotheby's) **$55** **£28**

JOHN R. HOUSTON – Youth And Age – 50 x 59cm.
(Edmiston's) **$621** **£320**

ROBERT HOUSTON – Inverglass – signed – 39 x 49in.
(Sotheby's) **$990** **£500**

ROBERT HOUSTON – Ardlui, Loch Lomond – signed – 20 x 23½in.
(Sotheby's) **$1,190** **£620**

ROBERT HOUSTON – Mountains Of Skye – signed – 27¼ x 35¼in.
(Sotheby's) **$499** **£260**

EMILY G. HOWARD – Self-Portraits: Repose; and The Artist At Work – one signed and inscribed on the reverse and the other dated '80 – watercolour or pencil and watercolour – 6¾ x 9¼in. and 8½ x 5¾in.
(Christie's) **$213 £110 Pair**

GEORGE JAMES HOWARD, 9th Earl Of Carlisle – A View Of Pompei – on panel – 7¼ x 14¾in.
(Christie's) **$776 £400**

B. A. HOWE – Waiting To Go For A Walk – signed and dated 1869 – 19½ x 23in.
(Sotheby's Belgravia) **$57 £30**

E. M. J. HOWELL – Ready For Bed – signed – 30½ x 19½in.
(Sotheby's Belgravia) **$228 £120**

W. HOWGATE – East Coast Scene With Fishermen And Cart With Horse – signed and dated 1895 – oil on canvas.
(Alfred Mossop & Co.) **$396 £200**

SAMUEL HOWITT – 'Calypso', A Greyhound Stands In Open Landscape – signed – 10¼ x 12½in.
(Sotheby's) **$621 £320**

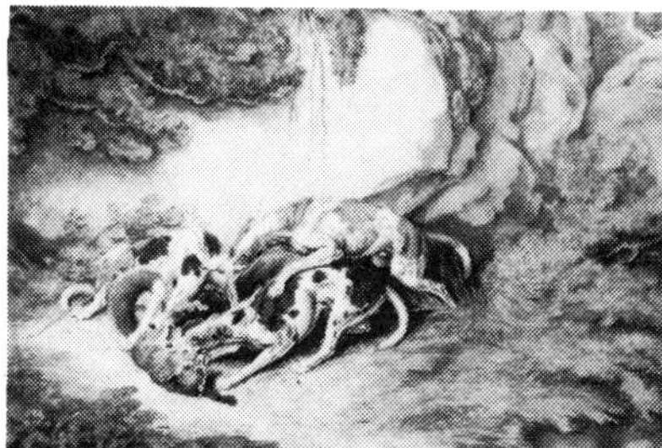

SAMUEL HOWITT – Death Of The Fox – pen and sepia ink and watercolour – 12¼ x 18in.
(Sotheby's) **$485 £250**

JAN VAN HUCHTENBURG – The Ottoman Army Sacking A Town – 34½ x 39¾in.
(Christie's) **$7,372 £3,800**

JAN VAN HUCHTENBURG – A Cavalry Skirmish In A Rocky Landscape – signed and dated 1671 – 26½ x 34¼in.
(Christie's) **$4,850 £2,500**

JAN VAN HUCHTENBURG – Cavalry Attacking A Baggage Train – 31 x 38½in.
(Christie's) **$5,376 £2,800**

J. B. HUET – A Classical Landscape, With A Shepherd And His Family Resting Beneath A Monument – 75½ x 34¼in.
(Christie's) **$6,144 £3,200**

J. B. HUET – A Classical Landscape, With Figures Resting Near Classical Ruins, A Boat In The Background – 75½ x 34¼in.
(Christie's) **$4,992** **£2,600**

J. B. HUET – A Wooded Lake Landscape, With Women And Children In The Foreground – 76 x 43½in.
(Christie's) **$5,760** **£3,000**

J. B. HUET – A Classical Landscape, With Figures By A Monument – 76 x 43½in.
(Christie's) **$7,296** **£3,800**

WILLIAM HUGGINS – Cattle In A Mountainous Landscape – signed and dated 1873 – 27¼ x 35½in.
(Christie's) **$2,328** **£1,200**

ARTHUR HUGHES – St. Cecilia – signed on panel – 12 x 10½in.
(Sotheby's Belgravia) **$1,610** **£800**

ARTHUR HUGHES – A Birthday Picnic: Portraits Of The Children Of William And Anne Pattinson Of Felling, Near Gateshead – signed – 39 x 50in.
(Sotheby's Belgravia) **$44,264** **£22,000**

ARTHUR FOORD HUGHES – Sharpening A Scythe – signed – 15 x 12½in.
(Sotheby's Belgravia) **$326** **£170**

EDWARD HUGHES – At The Well – signed and dated 1875 twice – 25¾ x 19½in.
(Christie's) **$1,649** **£850**

EDWARD ROBERT HUGHES – Faust And Helen – signed – 22 x 16in.
(Sotheby's Belgravia) **$456** **£240**

VICTOR HUGO – Chateau Montorgueil a Jersey – inscribed 1855 – charcoal, indian ink and coloured chalks – 10 x 8in.
(Sotheby's) **$9,880** **£5,200**

C. HUILLIOT – A Still Life Of Flowers And Fruit, On A Marble Ledge – 35 x 54in.
(Sotheby's) **$3,762** **£1,900**

HULK – Mid-Winter – 11½ x 8¾in.
(Sotheby's Belgravia)
$152 **£80**

HULK – Fishing Boats On A Beach – inscribed – 11½ x 15in.
(Sotheby's Belgravia)
$182 **£95**

ABRAHAM HULK – A Storm Off Ilfracombe, Devon – signed – heightened with white – 7 x 11¼in.
(Sotheby's Belgravia) **$35** **£18**

JOHN F. HULK – Shooting Duck – signed – 23½ x 34¾in.
(Sotheby's) **$422** **£220**

WILLIAM FREDERICK HULK – Cattle At Pasture – both signed – 20 x 16in.
(Sotheby's Belgravia)
$787 **£410 Pair**

EDWARD HULL – Royalist Cavalry Crossing A Stream – watercolour – 6¼ x 9¼in.
(Christie's) **$107** **£55**

WILLIAM HULL – Farm Buildings In A Ruined Priory – signed and dated 1865 – 9¾ x 14¼in.
(Sotheby's) **$543** **£280**

WILLIAM HULL – Figures By A Stream In A Wooded Landscape – signed and dated 1849 – watercolour – 17 x 11¼in.
(Christie's) **$184** **£95**

F. W. HULME – Resting By A River – 29½ x 46½in.
(Sotheby's Belgravia) **$1,509** **£750**

FREDERICK WILLIAM HULME – A Summer Afternoon In The Country – signed and dated 1870 – 19 x 29in.
(Sotheby's Belgravia) **$2,817 £1,400**

FRANS DE HULST – A View Of Nijmegen – inscribed and dated 1648 – on panel – 17¼ x 27¾in.
(Sotheby's) **$15,680 £8,000**

OZIAS HUMPHREY – Portrait Of A Gentleman, Half Length, Wearing A Grey Jacket And Waistcoat – signed with initials and dated 1782 on the reverse – coloured chalks – on paper – 8 x 6¾in.
(Sotheby's) **$429 £220**

C. HUNT – Her Favourite Pet – 17½ x 12½in.
(Sotheby's Belgravia) **$356 £180**

EDGAR HUNT – A Farmyard Repast – signed and dated 1913 – on panel – 6½ x 8½in.
(Sotheby's Belgravia) **$5,634 £2,800**

EDGAR HUNT – Farmyard Scenes – signed and dated '09 – 7½ x 10in.
(Sotheby's Belgravia) **$17,102 £8,500 Two**

EDGAR HUNT – The Dovecote – signed and dated 1914 – 9½ x 7½in.
(Sotheby's Belgravia) **$5,634 £2,800**

EDGAR HUNT – A Strange Visitor; Manger Companions – signed, one dated 1936 – 10 x 15½in.
(Sotheby's Belgravia)
$18,108 £9,000 Two

EDGAR HUNT – Poultry In A Yard; Farmyard Friends – signed and dated 1912 – 6½ x 9½in.
(Sotheby's Belgravia)
$18,108 £9,000 Two

EDGAR HUNT – Still Life: A Glass Comport Containing Two Oranges And Orange Peel On A Table; With Cherries On A Leaf, Strawberries In A Torn Open Paper Bag, Half Of An Orange And Three Apples – signed – oil on board – 24 x 34.5cm.
(Henry Spencer & Sons)
$776 £400

THOMAS HUNT – Moving The Herd – signed and dated '79 – 23 x 35in.
(Sotheby's) **$634 £320**

W. H. HUNT – White Hawthorn; and Red Hawthorn – bears signature – watercolour heightened with white – diameter 8¾in.
(Christie's) **$349 £180 Pair**

WILLIAM HENRY HUNT – Portia, The Casket – signed – 14 x 9½in.
(Sotheby's Belgravia)
$250 £130

WILLIAM HENRY HUNT – Portrait Of A Lady – signed – oval – 10½ x 8in.
(Sotheby's Belgravia)
$86 £45

WILLIAM HENRY HUNT – Fisher Boy With His Girl Holding A Pitcher – 15 x 11¼in.
(Sotheby's) **$485** **£250**

WILLIAM HOLMAN HUNT – Study Of A Head Of A Woman, Wearing An Ornate Hairband – 21½ x 13¾in.
(Christie's) **$3,040** **£1,600**

WILLIAM HOLMAN HUNT – Study Of Firelight – on panel – 7½ x 7½in.
(Sotheby's Belgravia) **$9,255** **£4,600**

COLIN HUNTER – Evening On The Coast – signed and dated '81 – 12 x 20½in.
(Sotheby's Belgravia) **$173** **£90**

COLIN HUNTER – Fern Gatherers Returning Home – signed and dated 1869 – 17 x 27in.
(Sotheby's) **$1,056** **£550**

COLIN HUNTER – A Fishing Village On The East Coast – signed and dated 1880 – 15½ x 30in.
(Sotheby's) **$480** **£250**

GEORGE LESLIE HUNTER – Nude Female Studies – signed – heightened with coloured chalks – 14½ x 11in. and 12 x 8¾in.
(Sotheby's) **$230** **£120 Two**

GEORGE LESLIE HUNTER – A Mediterranean View – signed – 17½ x 21in.
(Sotheby's) **$4,554** **£2,300**

GEORGE LESLIE HUNTER – Continental Street Scene – signed – coloured chalks – 15 x 17in.
(Sotheby's) **$614** **£310**

LESLIE HUNTER – Fishing Boats Off The Fife Coast – 29 x 44cm.
(Edmiston's) **$388** **£200**

WILLIAM HUNTER – Chrysanthemums – signed – 23¼ x 19¼in.
(Sotheby's) **$178** **£90**

LOUIS BOSWORTH HURT – Cattle Grazing In The Highlands – signed – 12½ x 18½in.
(Sotheby's) **$3,072** **£1,600**

LOUIS BOSWORTH HURT – A Highland Glen – signed, inscribed – canvas on panel – 15½ x 19½in.
(Sotheby's) **$356** **£180**

LOUIS B. HURT – Scottish Mountainous Landscape, With Highland Cattle, A Herdsman And His Dog – signed and dated (18)92 – oil on canvas – 90 x 75cm.
(Henry Spencer & Sons) **$5,044** **£2,600**

L. B. HURT – Taking A Rest Underneath Some Pines – bears signature and date – 18¼ x 12½in.
(Sotheby's Belgravia) **$153** **£80**

ROBERT GEMMEL HUTCHISON – Fetching Water – signed – 17½ x 11½in.
(Sotheby's) **$1,029** **£520**

ROBERT GEMMEL HUTCHISON – Portrait Of A Dutch Boy – signed – on board – 9 x 6in.
(Sotheby's) **$537 £280**

ROBERT GEMMEL HUTCHISON – The Little Shrimper – signed – on board – 4¾ x 4in.
(Sotheby's) **$998 £520**

ROBERT GEMMEL HUTCHISON – 'Shadows Amid The Sunshine' – signed, inscribed on a label on reverse – 44 x 64½in.
(Sotheby's Belgravia) **$15,090 £7,500**

ROBERT GEMMEL HUTCHISON – A Sunny Afternoon – signed – 19 x 23in.
(Sotheby's) **$7,920 £4,000**

ROBERT GEMMEL HUTCHISON – Washing The Creel – signed – on board - 9¼ x 11in.
(Sotheby's) **$6,336 £3,300**

ROBERT GEMMEL HUTCHISON – Reading The Will – signed – 13 x 17½in.
(Sotheby's) **$3,366 £1,700**

VAN HUYSUM – Tulips And Other Flowers In A Vase On A Stone Ledge – 18¼ x 14½in.
(Christie's) **$2,522 £1,300**

J. VAN HUYSUM – Tulips, Roses And Other Flowers In A Vase, And Grapes, Peaches And Nuts On A Stone Ledge – 37¼ x 30¾in.
(Christie's) **$34,560 £18,000**

J. VAN HUYSUM – An Italianate Wooded Landscape With Shepherds, Cattle And Sheep By Classical Ruins – 15¼ x 19½in.
(Christie's) **$970 £500**

JAN VAN HUYSUM – Tulips, Hollyhocks, Daisies, Convolvulus And Other Flowers In A Glass Vase On A Ledge With A Snail – signed – 24¾ x 21in.
(Christie's) **$30,720 £16,000**

JAN VAN HUYSUM – Roses, Tulips, Carnations And Other Flowers In A Sculptured Urn On A Stone Ledge With A Bird's Nest – signed – on panel – 31 x 23¾in.
(Christie's) **$288,000 £150,000**

JUSTUS VAN HUYSUM – Flowers In A Vase – 31 x 24¾in.
(Sotheby's) **$25,480 £13,000** Two

GEORGE HYDE – Windsor Castle, From The Thames – inscribed – on board – 8 x 11½in.
(Sotheby's Belgravia) **$480 £250**

BERTRAM HYLES – Returning From Market – signed – 9 x 20¼in.
(Sotheby's Belgravia) **$38 £20**

S. HYLES – Butterflies In The Woods – indistinctly signed – 23½ x 19½in.
(Sotheby's Belgravia) **$380 £200**

I

RUDOLPH IHLEE – The Gutter, A Landscape – signed and dated 1926 – 24¾ x 29¾in.
(Sotheby's) **$396** **£200**

FRANCESCO FERNANDI, Called Imperiali – Alexander Rewarding His Captains – a modello – 21½ x 30¼in.
(Christie's) **$4,224** **£2,200**

GIROLAMO INDUNO – Lago Maggiore e Isola Bella – signed and inscribed – pen and black ink, watercolour heightened with white – 10¾ x 16¼in.
(Sotheby's) **$2,565** **£1,350**

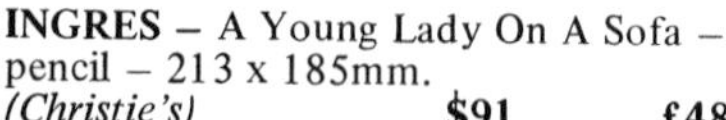

INGRES – A Young Lady On A Sofa – pencil – 213 x 185mm.
(Christie's) **$91** **£48**

IRISH PRIMITIVE SCHOOL, circa 1825 – Pembroke House, Dublin, Seen From Across The Railway Line – inscribed on the reverse – on panel – 12 x 16in.
(Sotheby's) **$7,128** **£3,600**

IRISH SCHOOL, circa 1740 – A View Of Woodbrook House, Near Bray, Co. Wicklow – on panel – 10¾ x 15¼in.
(Sotheby's) **$2,277** **£1,150**

IRISH SCHOOL, circa 1820 – A Riverside Town, Possibly Limerick, At Evening, With Figures In The Foreground; and A View Of A Village, A Small Lake To The Right, Hills Beyond – on panel – 10 x 13in.
(Sotheby's) **$2,037** **£1,050 Two**

EUGENE ISABEY – Le Vieux Moulin – watercolour – 6¼ x 8½in.
(Sotheby's) **$3,990** **£2,100**

EUGENE ISABEY – Port De Normandie – watercolour – 6½ x 8½in.
(Sotheby's) **$5,130** **£2,700**

ISENBRANDT, After – The Madonna And Child – on panel – 23¼ x 18½in.
(Sotheby's) **$990** **£500**

ITALIAN SCHOOL, 18th century – Classical Figure Subject – oil on canvas – 101 x 135cm.
(King & Chasemore) **$792** **£400**

ITALIAN SCHOOL – The Madonna Of Humility – on panel – 26 x 15in.
(Sotheby's) **$3,960** **£2,000**

ITALIAN SCHOOL – The Madonna And Child, Saint Antony Of Padua And Saint John The Baptist Kneeling Below – on panel – 20¾ x 15in.
(Sotheby's) **$2,079** **£1,050**

ITALIAN SCHOOL, 18th century – Study Of A Wreathed Woman: Poetry – black chalk and pastel on grey paper – 46.8 x 36.8cm.
(Christie's) **$3,072** **£1,600**

P. JACKMAN – Girl Feeding A Horse Outside A Cottage – signed – oil on canvas – 30 x 41in.
(Morphets of Harrogate) **$480** **£250**

SAMUEL JACKSON, 19th century – River Landscape With A View Of Sailing Vessels In The Avon Gorge – watercolour – 8 x 11¼in.
(Osmond, Tricks & Son) **$1,901** **£960**

SAMUEL JACKSON – St. Michael's Hill, Bristol, The Academy On The Right – pencil and watercolour – 8½ x 12in.
(Sotheby's) **$1,164** **£600**

SAMUEL PHILIPS JACKSON – Seascape With A Sailing Vessel At Anchor In A Choppy Sea – signed and dated 1852 – watercolour heightened with bodycolour – 13¾ x 20in.
(Osmond, Tricks & Son) **$832** **£420**

DAVID JAMES – A Coastal Landscape With Fishing Vessels Offshore – signed and dated '81 - 24¼ x 49in.
(Christie's) **$1,746** **£900**

RICHARD S. JAMES – 'The Minister's Rebuke' – signed with monogram and dated 1866 – oil on canvas – 34 x 41cm.
(King & Chasemore)
$725 **£366**

JOHN JAMESON – 'The Fishing Hole' – signed and dated '68, and inscribed – 15 x 17½in.
(Morton's Auction Exchange, Inc.)
$900 **£454**

F. E. JAMIESON – The Old Mill, Brora, Sutherland – bears another signature – 19½ x 29½in.
(Sotheby's Belgravia)
$114 **£60**

F. E. JAMIESON – A Country Cottage – signed – on board – 9½ x 13½in.
(Sotheby's Belgravia) **$67** **£35**

H. J. JANSEN – M.S. 'Katherine-Piree' – signed and inscribed – 14 x 22in.
(Sotheby's Belgravia) **$129** **£65**

DU JARDIN – The Adoration Of The Shepherds – bears signature – 19¼ x 13½in.
(Christie's) **$659** **£340**

JENNENS AND BETTRIDGE – The Coronation Of Queen Victoria – on board – 33 x 45½in.
(Sotheby's Belgravia) **$845** **£420**

JENNENS AND BETTRIDGE – Edinburgh From The Castle – signed and inscribed – on panel – 29 x 33in.
(Sotheby's) **$2,304** **£1,200**

REGINALD G. JENNINGS – A Spring Song – signed and dated 1912 – 42 x 27½in.
(Sotheby's Belgravia) **$119** **£60**

WILLIAM JENNINGS – Tarbet Loch – signed – 24¼ x 29¼in.
(Sotheby's) **$515** **£260**

PIETER DE JODE, Attributed to – A Saint On His Deathbed, With Angels Elevating His Spirit – black chalk, pen and brown ink, brown wash heightened with white – 19.7 x 26cm.
(Christie's) **$422** **£220**

JOEL – Highland Views – both bear monogram and dated – 13½ x 9½in.
(Sotheby's Belgravia) **$61** **£32 Pair**

H. B. JOEL – The Fringe Of The Forest – indistinctly signed – 20 x 15in.
(Sotheby's Belgravia) **$173** **£90**

AUGUSTUS JOHN – Seated Female Nude – signed – pencil – 16 x 12¾in.
(Sotheby's) **$832** **£420**

AUGUSTUS JOHN – Portrait Of The Hon. Alvan T. Fuller, Governor Of Massachusetts – dated 1928 – 44 x 35½in.
(Sotheby's) **$990** **£500**

CHARLES EDWARD JOHNSON – Harvest Time – signed and dated 1879 – 25½ x 35½in.
(Sotheby's Belgravia) **$2,012** **£1,000**

CORNELIS JOHNSON – Portrait Of A Lady, Probably Elizabeth Petre, Head And Shoulders – signed with initials and dated 1620 – on panel – 27 x 20½in.
(Sotheby's) **$7,524** **£3,800**

EDWARD KILLINGWORTH JOHNSON – Teasing Kitty – heightened with bodycolour – 18¾ x 10in.
(Sotheby's Belgravia) **$1,308** **£650**

LOUISA JOHNSON – Setters And A Pony In The Highlands – signed and dated 1890 – 43 x 33½in.
(Sotheby's) **$1,227** **£620**

JOHNSTON – A Hawking Party – on board – 13¾ x 17¾in.
(Sotheby's Belgravia)
$118 **£60**

GEORGE WHITTON JOHNSTONE – Hammerin, Fife – signed, inscribed on the reverse – 9 x 13in.
(Sotheby's) **$129** **£65**

GEORGE WHITTON JOHNSTONE – An Afternoon On The River – signed and dated 1878 – 18½ x 39¼in.
(Sotheby's) **$384** **£200**

GEORGE WHITTON JOHNSTONE – A Sunny River Bank – signed – 11 x 17½in.
(Sotheby's) **$307** **£160**

GEORGE WHITTON JOHNSTONE – On The Lunan Burn, Near Blairgowrie – signed and dated 1879, and signed and inscribed on the reverse – 24½ x 39½in.
(Christie's) **$1,649** **£850**

A. JOLI – A Capriccio Of Roman Ruins With A Church By A River Beyond – 50½ x 37¾in.
(Christie's) **$3,880 £2,000**

A. JOLI – A View Of The Campo Vaccino, Rome, With Various Travellers And Herdsmen – 29½ x 46½in.
(Sotheby's) **$5,432 £2,800**

ANTONIO JOLI – A Distant View Of Venice – 23¼ x 40in.
(Sotheby's) **$11,252 £5,800**

ANTONIO JOLI – A View Of Naples From Santa Lucia – 34¼ x 60in.
(Sotheby's) **$23,280 £12,000**

JONES – Sportsmen Shooting Pheasants In A Wooded Landscape – 15¾ x 20in.
(Christie's) **$931 £480**

CHARLES JONES – Landscape With A Flock Of Sheep Beside A Farm – signed and dated 1871 – oil – 22 x 44in.
(Phillips) **$1,960 £990**

P. JONES – Interior Of A Barn With Two Terriers Frightening A Cat; and Scrubby Landscape With Two Terriers With A Fox At Bay – signed and dated 1876 – oil on canvas – 20 x 30cm.
(Henry Spencer & Sons) **$1,188 £600 Pair**

PAUL JONES – Pheasant Shooting – on board – 8¾ x 12½in.
(Sotheby's) **$345 £180**

PAUL JONES – Deer Stalking; Patience Rewarded – signed and dated 1871 – 7¼ x 11¼in.
(Sotheby's) **$2,976 £1,550 Pair**

PAUL JONES – Two Terriers Watching A Rat Caught In A Cage In The Entrance Of A Barn – signed and dated 1857 – oil on canvas – 18.5 x 24cm.
(Henry Spencer & Sons) **$1,125 £580**

JAN MARTSEN DE JONGE – A Cavalry Action – signed and dated 16(32?) – on panel – 17¼ x 30¾in.
(Sotheby's) **$7,840 £4,000**

GABRIEL DE JONGH – In The Drakensbergs – signed – oil on canvas – 23½ x 35½in.
(Sotheby's) **$236 £120**

TINUS DE JONGH – A View In The Cape At Sunset – signed – 9 x 11¼in.
(Sotheby's) **$356** **£180**

JOSEPH MIDDLETON JOPLING – Joan Of Arc – signed with monogram and dated 1869 – watercolour and bodycolour – 27¾ x 20½in.
(Christie's) **$621** **£320**

JACOB JORDAENS – The Holy Family With St. Anne – 46 x 44½in.
(Sotheby's) **$32,980** **£17,000**

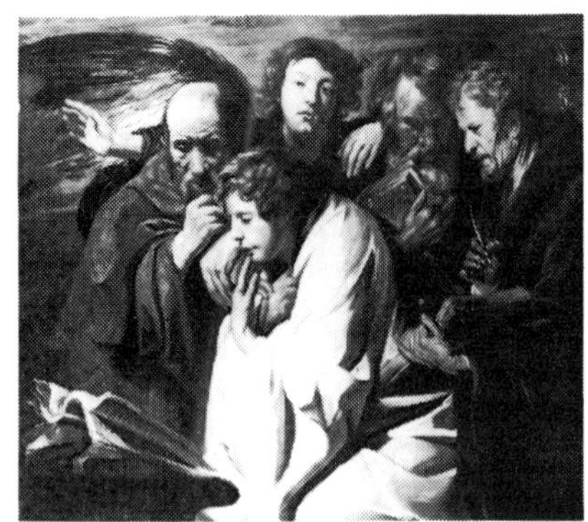

J. JORDAENS – The Four Evangelists With An Angel – 50 x 57in.
(Christie's) **$13,580** **£7,000**

PIO JORIS – Nettuno – signed and inscribed – watercolour heightened with white – 375 x 530mm.
(Christie's) **$532** **£280**

ASGER JORN – Ballet Immobile – signed, signed and dated '57 on the reverse – oil on canvas – 63¾ x 51¼in.
(Sotheby's) **$26,730** **£13,500**

ASGER JORN – Head – signed, signed and dated '61 on the reverse – oil on canvas – 15¼ x 12¼in.
(Sotheby's) **$6,732** **£3,400**

ISAAC DE JOUDERVILLE – Portrait Of Rembrandt, Bust Length, Dressing In Armour And Wearing A Plumed Helmet – on panel – 24¾ x 19¼in.
(Sotheby's) **$4,158 £2,100**

WILLIAM JOY – Stormy Weather – A Three-Master And A Cutter – signed and dated 1856 – 12¾ x 19in.
(Sotheby's) **$1,358 £700**

WILLIAM AND JOHN CANTILOE JOY – Rowing Out To A Departing Ship – 7½ x 10½in.
(Sotheby's) **$1,067 £550**

WILLIAM AND JOHN CANTILOE JOY – Two-Master At Anchor With Other Shipping And Fishermen With Net – 11¼ x 15¾in.
(Sotheby's) **$3,201 £1,650**

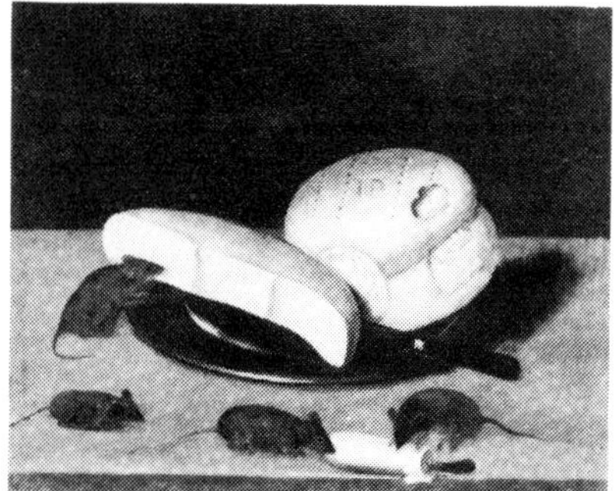

J. JUNCKER – A Still Life With A Wedge Of Cheese And A Bread Roll, On A Pewter Plate, Providing A Meal For Mice – on panel – 10¼ x 12½in.
(Sotheby's) **$9,900 £5,000**

NILO W. JUNGMAN – A Dutch Woman – heightened with bodycolour – 15 x 11½in.
(Sotheby's Belgravia) **$173 £90**

HENRY JUTSUM – Trout Fishing In Berwickshire – signed and inscribed on the reverse – 14 x 20in.
(Sotheby's) **$1,584 £800**

HENRY JUTSUM – Near Godalming, Surrey – signed – watercolour heightened with white – 21 x 16½in.
(Christie's) **$1,358 £700**

K

FRANZ KAISERMANN – The Cascades At Tivoli – pencil and watercolour – 255 x 358mm.
(Christie's) **$1,900** **£1,000**

HERMAN TEN KATE – An Interior With A Girl Tending A Poacher – signed – watercolour and bodycolour – 242 x 352mm.
(Christie's) **$1,330** **£700**

K. KAUFFMAN – A View On The Grand Canal, Venice, With Santa Maria Della Salute – bears signature – on panel – 9¼ x 11¼in.
(Christie's) **$233** **£120**

ARCHIBALD KAY – A Winter River – signed – on board – 7 x 10in.
(Sotheby's) **$396** **£200**

ARCHIBALD KAY – The Old Mill, Broadford, Skye – signed – 13¾ x 17¾in.
(Sotheby's) **$672** **£350**

ARCHIBALD KAY – Avery Mill, Dorchester – signed, inscribed on a label on the reverse – on board – 15 x 10in.
(Sotheby's) **$178** **£90**

ARCHIBALD KAY – Autumn Waters – signed – 29 x 39in.
(Sotheby's) **$883** **£460**

ARCHIBALD KAY – Cattle By A Highland Loch – signed – canvas on panel – 13½ x 17½in.
(Sotheby's) **$422** **£220**

JAMES KAY – Summer Shower, Alloway – signed and dated '96 – 12½ x 16½in.
(Sotheby's) **$768** **£400**

JAMES KAY – Cottages By A River – signed – on panel – 19½ x 24in.
(Sotheby's) **$844** **£440**

C. J. KEATS – Cairo – signed – heightened with white – 19½ x 12in.
(Sotheby's Belgravia)
$92 **£48**

HARRY KEIR – Personality Kaleidoscope – pen and ink – 63 x 50cm.
(Edmiston's) **$23** **£12**

R. G. KELLY – The Gleaners With Two Female Figures – monogram signed and dated 1867 – watercolour – oval – 19 x 15in.
(Richard Baker & Baker)
$330 **£170**

R. KEMM – A Lady At Prayer – oval – 10 x 8¼in.
(Sotheby's Belgravia) **$194** **£100**

ROBERT KEMM – A Senorita – signed – on panel – 10 x 8in.
(Sotheby's Belgravia) **$380** **£200**

JEKA KEMP – Still Life Of Flowers And Fruit – signed – 24 x 19¾in.
(Sotheby's) **$384** **£200**

JEKA KEMP – Canal Scene, France – on board – 18 x 15in.
(Sotheby's) **$172** **£90**

C. KENSINGTON – The S.S. 'City of Calcutta' – signed, inscribed and dated 1897 – gouache – 16½ x 23½in.
(Sotheby's Belgravia) **$163** **£85**

DORIAN KER – Yew Tree By An Open Gate – signed and dated '77 – canvas on board – 36 x 48in.
(Sotheby's) **$693** **£350**

JAMES KERR-LAWSON – Studies Of Peasants And Animals; and Studies Of Arabs And Animals – grisaille – 19½ x 115¼in.
(Christie's) **$679** **£350 Pair**

JAMES KERR-LAWSON – Shoeing A Cow; and Going To Market – grisaille – 19½ x 41¼in.
(Christie's) **$369** **£190 Pair**

JAMES KERR-LAWSON – The Baptistry, Florence; and A Collage Of A Villa – oval – 66 x 49¾in. and 17 x 25½in.
(Christie's) **$2,328** **£1,200**

JAMES KERR-LAWSON – A View Of The Piazza Del Popolo, Rome; and A Collage Of A Capriccio Of Classical Ruins – oval – 66½ x 48¼in. and 17 x 25½in.
(Christie's) **$2,134** **£1,100**

JAMES KERR-LAWSON – A Canal Scene, Venice – 55 x 46in.
(Christie's) **$970** **£500**

JAMES KERR-LAWSON – View Of San Geremia At The Entrance To The Cannaregio Venice; and A Grisaille Of A Girl With A Pitcher And Old Man – oval – 66½ x 41in. and 17 x 25½in.
(Christie's) **$737** **£380**

JAMES KERR-LAWSON – Wheelwrights; and Peasants With A Donkey – grisaille – 19½ x 41¼in.
(Christie's) **$310** **£160 Pair**

JAMES KERR-LAWSON – The Piazza Signioria, Florence; and A Collage Of A Town, With A Ruined Church – oval – 66¼ x 41¼in. and 17 x 25½in.
(Christie's) **$1,552** **£800**

JAMES KERR-LAWSON – The Piazzetta Looking South Towards San Giorgio Maggiore; and A View Of The Dogana – oval – 66¼ x 41¼in. and 17 x 25½in.
(Christie's) **$1,164** **£600**

JAMES KERR-LAWSON – A View Of The Piazzo San Lorenzo, Florence – 66½ x 46½in.
(Christie's) **$2,910** **£1,500**

FERDINAND VAN KESSEL – An Iris, An Ant, A Beetle, A Woodlouse, With Moths And Other Insects – signed with initials – on copper – 3¾ x 5in.
(Christie's) **$57,600 £30,000**

J. VAN KESSEL – A Bowl Of Grapes And Apples, With A Glass Of Wine And Other Fruit On A Table – 5¼ x 8in.
(Christie's) **$4,656 £2,400**

JAN VAN KESSEL – A Rose, Butterflies And Insects – on panel – 5½ x 6¾in.
(Sotheby's) **$10,088 £5,200**

JAN VAN KESSEL – Ceres Receiving Offerings In A Landscape (The Element Of Earth) – 24½ x 37½in.
(Christie's) **$13,824 £7,200**

JAN VAN KESSEL – Vulcan's Forge (The Element Of Fire) – 24½ x 37½in.
(Christie's) **$13,440 £7,000**

JOHAN VAN KESSEL – A Landscape With A Cornfield, Peasants Reaping A Cornfield Surrounding A Farmhouse – 16¼ x 21¼in.
(Sotheby's) **$3,880 £2,000**

CORNELIS KETEL – Portraits Of A Gentleman And His Wife, Bust Length – dated 1585 – on panel – 4¼ x 4¼in.
(Sotheby's) **$2,716 £1,400 Pair**

FRIEDRICH WILHELM KEYL – Stags And Hinds At Sunset – 29½ x 47in.
(Sotheby's) **$2,304** **£1,200**

W. KIDD – Courtship; Parting Admonition – on board – oval – 12¼ x 9¼in.
(Sotheby's Belgravia)
$342 **£180 Pair**

ARTHUR KIETH – 'The Fairy Tale Tellers' – signed – watercolour – 15 x 11in.
(Andrew, Hilditch & Son)
$96 **£46**

G. G. KILBURNE – Interior Scene With Figures Conversing – signed – watercolour – 8 x 11in.
(Morphets of Harrogate) **$368** **£190**

G. G. KILBURNE – 'Victorian Street Scene With Figures' – signed – watercolour drawing – 25 x 18in.
(J. Entwistle & Co.)
$259 **£135**

GEORGE GOODWIN KILBURNE – A Full Length Portrait Of A Young Girl In A Red Coat With A Muff – signed with initials – oil on board – 29¼ x 18½in.
(Geering & Colyer)
$376 **£190**

GEORGE GOODWIN KILBURNE – The Morning Call – signed and dated 1902 – on panel – 5¾ x 9in.
(Christie's) **$970** **£500**

GEORGE GOODWIN KILBURNE – Learning The Steps – signed and dated 1869 – gouache – 17½ x 13¾in.
(Sotheby's Belgravia) **$768** **£400**

GEORGE GOODWIN KILBURNE – Asleep – signed and dated 1864 – heightened with bodycolour – 9½ x 12½in.
(Sotheby's Belgravia)
$806 **£420**

GEORGE GOODWIN KILBURNE – Memories – signed – heightened with bodycolour – 21½ x 35½in.
(Sotheby's Belgravia)
$1,056 **£550**

HAYNES KING – Minding The Baby – signed and dated '69 – heightened with bodycolour – 8½ x 11½in.
(Sotheby's Belgravia)
$595 **£310**

HENRY JOHN YEEND KING – A Cottage In A Meadow – signed – on panel – 7 x 11in.
(Sotheby's Belgravia)
$384 **£200**

HENRY JOHN YEEND KING – Seaward – signed – watercolour and bodycolour – 9¾ x 6¾in.
(Christie's) **$213** **£110**

HENRY JOHN YEEND KING – Bidford; and Pebworth – signed – heightened with white – 12 x 15in.
(Sotheby's Belgravia)
$396 **£200 Two**

JOHN YEEND KING – Sheep Grazing In A Lush Meadow Beside A Stream – signed – oil – 19 x 29in.
(Phillips) **$1,328** **£671**

KING – By The Well – bears signature – on panel – 14 x 10in.
(Sotheby's Belgravia) **$475** **£240**

JESSIE M. KING – Pipe In The Spring – watercolour – 27 x 45cm.
(Edmiston's) **$1,067** **£550**

JESSIE MARION KING – Three Full-Scale Working Drawings For Stained Glass Windows – watercolour – on paper – 69½ x 51in., 54 x 30½in. and 70 x 27½in.
(Sotheby's) **$134** **£70 Three**

JESSIE MARION KING – A Fairy Glade – pen and ink and wash – heightened with white – on vellum – 13 x 17in.
(Sotheby's) **$921** **£480**

JOHN W. KING – The Wheat Stack – signed – 9½ x 13½in.
(Sotheby's Belgravia)
$194 **£100**

YEEND KING – 'Woman In Peasant Costume Seated Against Pillar' – signed – oil on panel – 11½ x 7¼in.
(Dacre, Son & Hartley)
$1,509 **£750**

YEEND KING – 'Waiting For The Ferry' – signed – oil on canvas – 18 x 24in.
(Bonham's) **$2,352 £1,200**

GARRETT KINGSLEY – Bush Gums At The Vineyard – signed – oil on board – 60 x 70cm.
(Australian Art Auctions) **$208 £106**

F. G. KINNAIRD – A New Toy – signed – 27 x 35½in.
(Sotheby's Belgravia) **$2,617 £1,300**

HENRY J. KINNAIRD – On The Thames Above Henley; A View Near Henfield, Sussex – signed and inscribed – heightened with white – 19½ x 14½in.
(Sotheby's Belgravia) **$594 £300 Pair**

HENRY KINNAIRD – 'Haymaking In Surrey' – signed – watercolour – 13 x 9in.
(Husseys) **$140 £72**

F. KIRCHNER – A Continental Lake Scene With Fishing Boats, Town And Mountains Beyond – signed and dated – 22 x 29in
(Russell, Baldwin & Bright) **$3,136 £1,600**

ALBERT JANSZ. KLOMP – A Wooded Landscape With Cattle – signed – 21 x 27in.
(Christie's) **$2,716 £1,400**

KNELL – Fishing Boats Off The Coast – 29 x 52in.
(Sotheby's Belgravia) **$346 £180**

SIR G. KNELLER – Half Length Portrait Of John Churchill, 1st Duke Of Marlborough, In Ramillies Wig And Scarlet Military Uniform With Gold Braided Lapels – oil – 30 x 25in.
(James Harrison) **$1,149 £550**

FRANS VAN KNIBBERGEN – Amelroy Castle In Gelderland, Figures Conversing Beneath Trees, A Lady And Several Hounds On A Path Alongside The Moat – 30¼ x 24¾in.
(Sotheby's) **$6,930 £3,500**

DAME LAURA KNIGHT – Morning Walk, Pay-Up Having Morning Exercise – signed – 29½ x 33¼in.
(Sotheby's) **$1,584 £800**

GEORGE KNIGHT – Shipping Off The Coast – signed – 15 x 23½in.
(Sotheby's Belgravia) **$672 £350**

WILLIAM HENRY KNIGHT – The See-Saw – signed with initials and dated '58 – on panel – 8 x 16in.
(Christie's) **$4,656 £2,400**

W. KNIJFF – A Dutch Canal Landscape, Figures In Conversation, Others Fishing With A Net – 50¼ x 63in.
(Sotheby's) **$3,492 £1,800**

GEORGE SHERIDAN KNOWLES – Summer Bounty – signed and dated 1904 – 10 x 15in.
(Sotheby's Belgravia) **$168 £85**

W. KNOX – Gondolas – signed – heightened with bodycolour – 10 x 5¾in.
(Sotheby's Belgravia) **$317 £160 Pair**

NICHOLAS KNUPFER – David And Saul – on panel – 13½ x 20¼in.
(Christie's) **$4,656 £2,400**

KOBELL – A Cow In A Landscape – paper on panel – 8 x 10¼in.
(Christie's) **$291 £150**

H. P. KOEKKOEK – 'Deer In A Snowy Landscape' – signed – oil on canvas – 44 x 31in.
(Gribble Booth & Taylor) **$1,207 £600**

JOAHNNES KOEKKOEK – Shipping Off A Coast – signed – grey wash – 137 x 212mm.
(Christie's) **$532 £280**

JOHANN KOENIG – Diana And A Nymph In A Wooded Landscape With Actaeon And His Hounds In The Distance – on copper – 10½ x 8¼in.
(Christie's) **$3,072 £1,600**

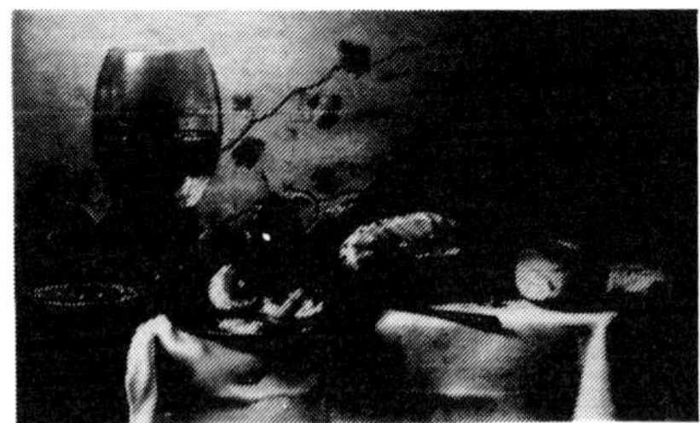

ROELOF KOETS – A Still Life With Roemer On A Wooden Ledge Covered By A White Linen Cloth – on panel – 20 x 32½in.
(Sotheby's) **$30,070 £15,500**

GUSTAV KOLLER – Faust And Marguerite – signed – watercolour – 338 x 258mm.
(Christie's) **$247 £130**

PHILIPS AERTSZ. KONINCK – An Extensive Wooded River Landscape, With Peasants And Sheep – 32 x 43¾in.
(Christie's) **$384,000 £200,000**

DE KONINCK – A Landscape, In The Foreground A Sunken Road With A Gipsy Family To The Left, Beyond A Landscape With Hedgerows And Cottages Among Trees – canvas on hardboard – 24½ x 33¾in.
(Sotheby's) **$3,564 £1,800**

S. KONINCK – The Adoration Of The Magi – 66 x 55in.
(Sotheby's) **$3,960 £2,000**

SALOMON KONINCK – A Bearded Man, Half Length, Wearing A Black Cloak – 38 x 29in.
(Christie's) **$3,686 £1,900**

SALOMON KONINCK – A Debtor's Tribunal, A Judge Presiding Over A Trial, Seated Between An Accusing Moneylender And A Crouching Debtor – 30½ x 36¼in.
(Sotheby's) **$5,148 £2,600**

JACOB KRAMER – Woman Knitting – signed – on board – 30¾ x 25½in.
(Sotheby's) **$238 £120**

KREIGHOFF – A Red Indian Family By Their Tepee And Canoe – bears signature watercolour – circular – diameter 8¼in.
(Sotheby's) **$4,039 £2,050**

CORNELIUS KREIGHOFF – An Indian Trapper Crossing The Snow – signed – oil on canvas – 11 x 8½in.
(Sotheby's) **$11,820 £6,000**

T. KUNZE – Christ On The Cross – on panel – 15 x 8¼in.
(Christie's) **$730 £380**

KUPETZKY – Cupid Painting At An Easel – 21 x 16in.
(Christie's) **$233 £120**

CHARLES EUPHRASIE KUWASSEG – Tempete En Mer – signed with initials and dated 1881 – pencil – 7½ x 10in.
(Sotheby's) **$86 £45**

LABRADOR – Still Lives Of Flowers And Birds – oval – 32 x 26¼in.
(Christie's) **$1,125** **£580**

CARLO LABRUZZI – The Appian Way: Ruins Near Lago Di Fondi – pencil and watercolour – 388 x 547mm.
(Christie's) **$285** **£150**

JOHN BERNEY LADBROOKE – A Wooded River Landscape With A Shepherdess And Sheep, And A Cottage Beyond – 28 x 35¾in.
(Christie's) **$3,104** **£1,600**

EDWARD LADELL – Still Life Of Fruit – signed with monogram – 16½ x 13in.
(Sotheby's Belgravia) **$26,156** **£13,000**

JAN LAGOOR – A Wooded Landscape With A Figure On A Path – on panel – 10 x 12in.
(Christie's) **$7,372** **£3,800**

WILLIAM JAMES LAIDLAW – A Yacht Off The Coast – signed – 17 x 24in.
(Sotheby's) **$230** **£120**

JAMES G. LAING – Rowan Sprigs – watercolour – 34 x 24cm.
(Edmiston's) **$32** **£17**

JAMES G. LAING – Amiens – signed and inscribed – 17½ x 13½in.
(Sotheby's Belgravia) **$105** **£55**

TOMSON LAING – Collecting Wrack – signed – 20 x 40in.
(Sotheby's) **$297** **£150**

LAIRESSE – A Scene From Roman History – 27½ x 35½in.
(Christie's) **$515** **£260**

GERARD DE LAIRESSE – Portrait Group Of Four Children Playing In An Ornamental Garden – indistinctly signed – 40¾ x 67½in.
(Christie's) **$13,580** **£7,000**

CHARLES LAMB – An Extensive Mountain Lake Scene – signed – 13 x 15¾in.
(Sotheby's) **$582** **£300**

HENRY LAMB – Breton Peasant Woman – pencil and grey wash – 10 x 7¼in.
(Sotheby's) **$317** **£160**

B. LAMBERT – Birch Trees With Figure Gathering Wood – signed – oil on panel – 19 x 10in.
(Husseys) **$101** **£52**

G. LAMBERT – An Extensive Wooded River Landscape – oil on canvas – 36 x 53in.
(Bonham's) **$4,312** **£2,200**

GEORGE WASHINGTON LAMBERT – The Impression – signed – pen drawing – 26.5 x 21cm.
(Australian Art Auctions)
$304 **£158**

W. H. LAMBERT – A Dutch Cottage, Interior With Figures – signed and dated 1895 – oil on board – 11 x 16½in.
(Morphets of Harrogate)
$75 **£38**

GEORGE LAMBERT And FRANCESCO ZUCCARELLI – 'Veduta D'Un Paese Chiamato Stifone Sotto Narni' – inscribed on the reverse – pen and brown ink, blue and grey washes – 11¼ x 18¼in.
(Sotheby's) **$1,365** **£700**

GEORGE LAMBERT And FRANCESCO ZUCCARELLI – A Pastoral – signed and inscribed on the reverse – pencil and grey washes – 6¾ x 9¾in.
(Sotheby's) **$488** **£250**

J. M. LAMBRECHTS – A Music Party On The Steps Of A Country House – 25¼ x 31in.
(Christie's) **$1,261** **£650**

WILLIAM B. LAMOND – Driving The Flock Home On A Windy Day – signed – 13 x 17in.
(Sotheby's) **$768** **£400**

WILLIAM B. LAMOND – Returning From Pasture – signed – 9½ x 13½in.
(Sotheby's) **$537** **£280**

WILLIAM B. LAMOND – The Plough Team; A Cottage By The Coast – signed – heightened with bodycolour – 14 x 17½in.
(Sotheby's) **$499** **£260 Pair**

AUGUSTUS OSBORNE LAMPLOUGH – 'Philoe'; By The Nile – signed, one dated 1905 and one inscribed – 8¼ x 23½in.
(Sotheby's Belgravia)
$136 **£70 Pair**

AUGUSTUS OSBORNE LAMPLOUGH – On The Banks Of The Nile – signed – 13½ x 9¼in.
(Sotheby's Belgravia)
$192 **£100**

AUGUSTUS OSBORNE LAMPLOUGH – A View Of The Pyramids – signed – 6¼ x 11in.
(Sotheby's Belgravia)
$96 **£50**

AUGUSTUS OSBORNE LAMPLOUGH – Travellers By The Nile – signed – 4 x 13½in.
(Sotheby's Belgravia)
$86 **£45**

LAMQUA, Style of – Portrait Of A Mow Qua, Half Length, Seated In An Interior – 11 x 9¼in.
(Sotheby's (Hong Kong) Ltd.)
$909 **£459**

LAMQUA, Style of – Portrait Of Hou Qua, Seated In An Interior, With A Red Curtain And A Window Behind – 11 x 9¼in.
(Sotheby's (Hong Kong) Ltd.)
$1,407 **£710**

LAMQUA, Style of – A Woman In An Interior – 11½ x 9in.
(Sotheby's (Hong Kong) Ltd.)
$1,116 **£564**

OSBERT LANCASTER – Isola Bella – watercolour, heightened with bodycolour – 13¾ x 19¾in.
(Sotheby's) **$178** **£90**

GEORGE LANCE – Study Of A Hawk – signed and dated 1833 – 11½ x 9¼in.
(Sotheby's Belgravia)
$347 **£120**

GEORGE LANCE – An Ornate Glass Decanter, Caskets, A String Of Pearls And Other Jewellery And Fruit On A Draped Table – signed and dated '850 – on board – oval – 17½ x 15¼in.
(Christie's) **$5,432 £2,800**

N. LANCRET – A Maiden Waking A Sleeping Shepherd – oval – 23½ x 19½in.
(Christie's) **$1,455 £750**

NICOLAS LANCRET *(1690-1743)* – Fete Champetre With A Dancing Couple – 45 x 39in.
(Sotheby's) **$178,200 £90,000**

NICOLAS LANCRET – Young Lovers In A Wooded Landscape – 14¾ x 18½in.
(Christie's) **$53,760 £28,000**

NICOLAS LANCRET – A Fete Champetre – 18½ x 25¾in.
(Christie's) **$28,800 £15,000**

LANDSEER, After – A St. Bernard – 19 x 23in.
(Sotheby's Belgravia) **$38 £20**

LANDSEER, After – Stag Roaring – on board – 9½ x 14½in.
(Sotheby's Belgravia) **$230 £120**

CHARLES LANDSEER – A Sketch For 'Scots Children Feeding An Eagle' – pencil – 10¾ x 13¾in.
(Sotheby's Belgravia) **$79 £40**

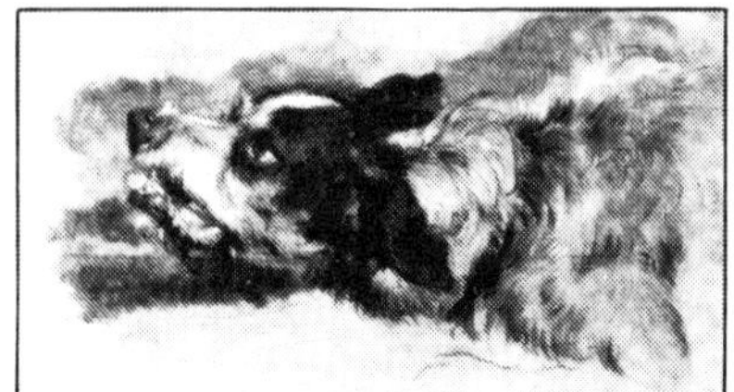

SIR EDWIN HENRY LANDSEER – Study Of A Hound's Head – 16 x 26½in.
(Sotheby's) **$1,440 £750**

SIR EDWIN LANDSEER – Portrait Of Lady Dyke, Seated, Small Half Length Wearing A Grey Dress And Holding A Book – signed with initials and inscribed and dated 1831 – on board – 13¾ x 9¾in.
(Christie's) **$15,520 £8,000**

SIR EDWIN LANDSEER – Portrait Of Lady Dyke, Small Bust Length, Seated – on board – 11¾ x 8in.
(Christie's) **$5,044 £2,600**

SIR EDWIN HENRY LANDSEER – The Head Of A Zebra – pencil – 4¼ x 6½in.
(Sotheby's Belgravia)
$99 £50

SIR EDWIN HENRY LANDSEER – The Keeper John Crerar With His Pony – inscribed on a label on the reverse – on board – a sketch – 23 x 17in.
(Sotheby's) **$4,992 £2,600**

SIR EDWIN HENRY LANDSEER – A Love Letter – 17 x 12½in.
(Sotheby's) **$5,346 £2,700**

SIR EDWIN HENRY LANDSEER – Portrait Of Lord Charles Russell's Charger Pretender – signed with initials and dated 1834 – on board – 8 x 10in.
(Sotheby's) **$4,554** **£2,300**

SIR EDWIN LANDSEER – A Pair Of Doves – 10 x 12¼in.
(Christie's) **$737** **£380**

SCHOOL OF MAIR VON LANDSHUT – Two Saints, A Sainted King Holding An Orb And Sceptre, And A Sainted Bishop Holding A Pastoral Staff And Manacles – on panel – 28½ x 21in.
(Sotheby's) **$2,475** **£1,250**

F. LANE – Spring – signed and inscribed on a label on the reverse – 29¼ x 24¼in.
(Sotheby's Belgravia)
$163 **£85**

DIRCK LANGENDYK – The Battle Of The Pyramids – pencil and watercolour – 158 x 232mm.
(Christie's) **$798** **£420**

LANGETTI – The Denial Of Saint Peter – 45¼ x 37in.
(Christie's) **$1,164** **£600**

W. LANGHAM – Three Children In A Cottage Interior Playing With A Wooden Horse – signed – oil on canvas – 52 x 42cm.
(Henry Spencer & Sons)
$812 **£410**

WALTER LANGLEY – 'Fishergirl With Cawl' – watercolour – 18 x 15in.
(W. H. Lane & Son)
$230 **£120**

WALTER LANGLEY – 'I'll Be A Sailor' – watercolour – 10 x 14in.
(W. H. Lane & Son)
$960 **£500**

WILLIAM LANGLEY – In The Highlands; The Old Mill – signed – 19 x 29in.
(Sotheby's Belgravia)
$1,710 **£850 Pair**

WILLIAM LANGLEY – On The Beach – signed – 15 x 23½in.
(Sotheby's Belgravia) **$99** **£50**

LANGLEY – Fishing A Highland River – 24 x 36in.
(Sotheby's Belgravia) **$124** **£65**

J. LANGLOIS – Terriers Ratting – signed – on board – oval – 25 x 20½in.
(Sotheby's Belgravia) **$194** **£100**

MARK W. LANGLOIS – Teasing The Puppy – signed – 21 x 16¾in.
(Sotheby's Belgravia) **$532** **£280**

M. W. LANGLOIS – The Pet Rabbits – 51 x 41cm.
(Edmiston's) **$601** **£310**

ANDRE LANSKOY – Les Degres Des Operations – signed – oil on canvas – 33½ x 26in.
(Sotheby's) **$3,366** **£1,700**

N. LAPICCOLA – Saint Monica Receiving A Stock From The Madonna And Child – bears signature and the date 1719 on the reverse – 17¼ x 10¾in.
(Christie's) **$921** **£480**

GEORGE HENRY LAPORTE – Horses Of The 10th Hussars In Landscapes – signed and dated 1870 – 13¾ x 17½in.
(Christie's) **$2,522** **£1,300**

G. LARA – Farmyard Scenes – indistinctly signed and dated – 9½ x 17¾in.
(Christie's) **$1,358** **£700**

GEORGE LARA – Village Scenes With Figures – one signed and dated 1868 – oil on canvas – 8 x 15in.
(Bonham's) **$3,136** **£1,600 Pair**

LARGILLIERRE – La Marquise De Vandenesse, In A Blue Dress With Gold Embroidery And A Red Cloak – 31 x 24½in.
(Sotheby's) **$1,764** **£900**

LARGILLIERRE – Portrait Of A Gentleman, Half Length, Wearing A Red Cloak – 31¼ x 25in.
(Christie's) **$621** **£320**

NICOLAS DE LARGILLIERRE – Portrait Of Marie Madeleine Jassaud, Three-Quarter Length With Two Children In An Interior – 54¼ x 41in.
(Christie's) **$26,880 £14,000**

N. M. LARGILLIERRE – Portrait Of A Lady, Standing Three-Quarter Length By An Urn, Wearing A Mauve Dress – 45¼ x 34¼in.
(Christie's) **$970 £500**

JAMES ECKFORD LAUDER – Preparations Before The Wedding – inscribed on a label on the reverse – 49½ x 39in.
(Sotheby's) **$288 £150**

R. S. LAUDER – Launcelot And Guinevere – on board – 11¾ x 23in.
(Sotheby's Belgravia) **$192 £100**

ROBERT SCOTT LAUDER – Ferdinand Reunited With His Father, The Duke Of Naples, from The Tempest – 43 x 56in.
(Sotheby's Belgravia) **$653 £340**

LAURI – Venus And Adonis – 11½ x 19in.
(Christie's) **$582 £300**

LAURI – Hagar And The Angel – 25 x 30in.
(Sotheby's) **$427 £220**

F. LAURI – A Wooded Landscape With Saint Francis Meditating In A Clearing – 18½ x 14in.
(Sotheby's) **$3,465 £1,750**

FILIPPO LAURI, Circle of – The Crucifixion – on panel – 17¼ x 18¾in.
(Sotheby's) **$4,158 £2,100**

SIR JOHN LAVERY – Lady On Horseback – signed – 18 x 20in.
(Sotheby's) **$1,782 £900**

SIR JOHN LAVERY – Moonrise – signed, signed, inscribed and dated '09 on the reverse – 24½ x 29½in.
(Sotheby's) **$4,554 £2,300**

SIR JOHN LAVERY – A Day In Mid-Summer – signed, inscribed and dated 1884 – on panel – 31¼ x 20½in.
(Sotheby's) **$9,216** **£4,800**

SIR JOHN LAVERY – The Green Sofa – indistinctly signed – 12¼ x 9in.
(Sotheby's) **$2,178** **£1,100**

SIR JOHN LAVERY – The Turquoise Sea, Mimizan, 1917 – signed – 24½ x 29¼in.
(Sotheby's) **$1,148** **£580**

SIR JOHN LAVERY – The Market Place, Tetuan – signed – on panel – 5 x 8¼in.
(Sotheby's) **$1,782** **£900**

J. LAVERY – Small Boy Playing With A Puppy, Seated By A Table In A Cottage Interior – signed – oil on canvas – 20 x 15cm.
(Henry Spencer & Sons) **$388** **£200**

ANDREW LAW – St. Monance, Fife – on panel – 9¼ x 11in.
(Sotheby's) **$198** **£100**

ANDREW LAW – Still Life Of Writing Materials And A Stone Bust – signed and dated 1891 – 29 x 19½in.
(Sotheby's Belgravia) **$211** **£110**

ERNEST PEEL LAW – A Venetian Lagoon, Evening; Venice – one signed, the other inscribed on the reverse – 39 x 59in.
(Sotheby's Belgravia) **$672** **£350 Pair**

GEORGE FEATHER LAWRENCE – 'La Rue Saint Rustique' Sacre Coeur, Paris – signed – oil on board – 54.5 x 45cm.
(Australian Art Auctions)
$806 **£411**

GEORGE FEATHER LAWRENCE – Landscape – signed – 60 x 75cm.
(Australian Art Auctions)
$1,522 **£793**

GREGORIO LAZZARINI – A Bishop Saint Writing At A Desk – signed on the reverse – 37¾ x 32¼in.
(Christie's) **$730** **£380**

BENJAMIN WILLIAMS LEADER – A Surrey Farmhouse – signed – 12 x 24in.
(Sotheby's Belgravia)
$1,408 **£700**

BENJAMIN WILLIAMS LEADER – Colwyn Bay; On The Llugwy, Below Capel Curig, North Wales – both signed and dated 1899, inscribed on the reverse – on board – 7½ x 11½in.
(Sotheby's Belgravia)
$1,920 **£1,000 Pair**

BENJAMIN WILLIAMS LEADER – The Incoming Tide On The Cornish Coast – signed and dated 1905 – 43¾ x 71¾in.
(Christie's) **$2,280** **£1,200**

BENJAMIN WILLIAMS LEADER – Kempsey Common – signed and dated 1894 – 11½ x 19½in.
(Christie's) **$970** **£500**

BENJAMIN WILLIAMS LEADER – Evening, Worcestershire – signed and dated 1895 – on board – 13¼ x 10in.
(Sotheby's Belgravia) **$4,426** **£2,200**

BENJAMIN WILLIAMS LEADER – Sunset In North Wales – signed and dated 1866, and inscribed on the reverse – 21¼ x 35½in.
(Christie's) **$2,134 £1,100**

BENJAMIN WILLIAMS LEADER – Summertime – 24 x 36in.
(Sotheby's Belgravia)
$480 £250

JUAN DE NISA VALDES LEAL – Christ In The House Of Martha And Mary – panel – signed – 9½ x 13½in.
(Bonham's) **$49,500 £25,000**

EDWARD LEAR – Nice – signed, inscribed and dated 1864 – pen and brown ink – 6¼ x 9¼in.
(Sotheby's) **$3,104 £1,600**

EDWARD LEAR – Lago Di Garda – extensively inscribed and dated 1867 – pen and brown ink, brown and pale blue wash – 5½ x 8¾in.
(Christie's) **$349 £180**

EDWARD LEAR – A View Of The Lake At Cattaro With A Sailing Vessel Before Distant Mountains – inscribed and dated 1866 – watercolour heightened with white bodycolour – 8½ x 13¼in.
(Osmond, Tricks & Son)
$990 £500

EDWARD LEAR – Mount Tomohrit, Albania – signed with monogram – 48 x 73in.
(Sotheby's Belgravia)
$90,540 £45,000

EDWARD LEAR – Fort Of Isle Sante Marguerite, Cannes – inscribed and dated 1865 – pencil, pen and brown ink, watercolour, heightened with white – 10¾ x 19¼in.
(Sotheby's) **$1,940 £1,000**

EDWARD LEAR – Cannes – inscribed and dated 1865 – pencil, pen and brown ink and watercolour – recto; A Bay Near Cannes – pencil, pen and brown ink – verso – 13¼ x 21in.
(Sotheby's) **$2,328 £1,200**

EDWARD LEAR – Lake Of Sils In The Upper Engadine, Looking Towards St. Moritz, Switzerland – pencil, pen and grey ink, watercolour, heightened with white on blue grey paper – 10¾ x 19½in.
(Sotheby's) **$4,656 £2,400**

EDWARD LEAR – Mahatta, Egypt – inscribed and dated 1854 – pen and brown ink, with brown and green washes, heightened with white – 7¼ x 12¼in.
(Sotheby's) **$233 £120**

EDWARD LEAR, 19th century – Extensive Landscape With A View Of The Bay And The Town At Zante – inscribed – watercolour – 13½ x 20¾in.
(Osmond, Tricks & Son) **$7,128 £3,600**

CHARLES LEAVER – Winter Landscape; and Winter Landscape With Figure And Dog – signed and dated 1855 – oil on canvas – 35 x 35cm.
(King & Chasemore)
$1,666 £850 Pair

ELIZABETH-LOUISE VIGEE LEBRUN *(1755-1842)* – The Artist And Her Daughter – 42 x 33½in.
(Sotheby's) **$59,400 £30,000**

FREDERICK RICHARD LEE – In The Highlands, Extensive Mountainous Landscape At The Head Of A Loch – signed and dated 1862 – oil on canvas – 93 x 143cm.
(Henry Spencer & Sons)
$3,069 £1,550

DERWENT LEES – Near Collioure – signed and dated 1913 – pencil, pen and ink and watercolour – 9¾ x 13¾in.
(Sotheby's) **$752 £380**

C. LEFEBRE – Portrait Of A Gentleman, Half Length, Wearing Brown Dress – oval – 33 x 25½in.
(Christie's) **$776 £400**

ALEXANDER LEGGETT – The Day's Catch At Musselburgh – 11½ x 16in.
(Sotheby's) **$307 £160**

CHARLES LEICKERT – A Sunlit Dutch River Landscape – signed and dated 1866 – oil – 37¼ x 75in.
(Bonham's) **$27,720 £14,000**

LEIGH – The Hay Cart; and The Timber Cart – signed – 20 x 30in.
(Sotheby's Belgravia)
$285 £150 Pair

FREDERIC, LORD LEIGHTON – Fishing Boats Beached – paper on board – 4½ x 11¼in.
(Sotheby's Belgravia) **$644 £320**

FREDERIC, LORD LEIGHTON – A River Landscape – 8½ x 13¼in.
(Sotheby's Belgravia)
$1,006 £500

RICHARD PRINCIPAL LEITCH – Views In Northern Italy – signed, one with monogram, one inscribed and dated 1870 – heightened with bodycolour – 12¼ x 9½in.
(Sotheby's Belgravia) **$238 £120 Pair**

WILLIAM LEIGHTON LEITCH – Figures On A Road Near A Scottish Castle At Dusk – signed and dated 1872 – watercolour – 5 x 8½in.
(Christie's) **$155 £80**

HARRY LEITH-ROSS – Zena Road; Golden Autumn – signed, inscribed on the reverse – oil on board – 8 x 10in.
(Sotheby's) **$394 £200 Two**

HARRY LEITH-ROSS – A Village Street; Cow Pasture In Spring – signed, inscribed on the reverse – oil on board – 8 x 10in.
(Sotheby's) **$335 £170 Two**

HENRY LEJEUNE – Barefooted Peasant Girl With Water Pitcher, Seated On Rocky Ledge Near Pool – monogram signed and dated 1872 – oil on board – 16 x 12in.
(Richard Baker & Baker)
$4,947 £2,550

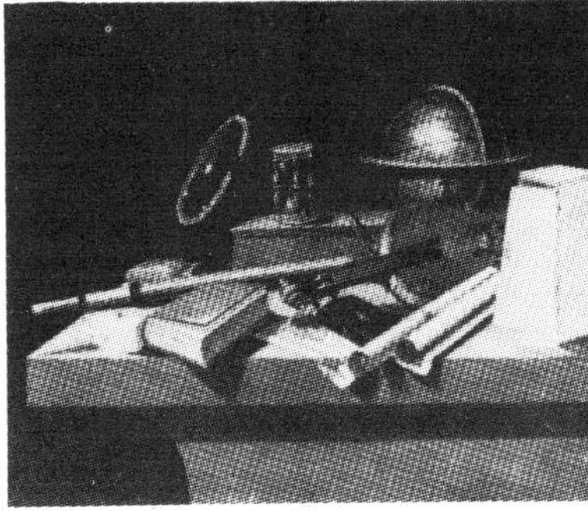

LELONG – Musical Instruments, A Metronome, And A Globe On A Ledge. and Musical Instruments And Flowers On A Ledge – bodycolour – 156 x 208mm.
(Christie's) **$2,375 £1,250 Pair**

LELONG – Nature Morte Au Grand Bouquet Et Aux Cerises – gouache – 6¼ x 8½in.
(Sotheby's) **$722 £380**

LELONG – Nature Morte Au Petit Temple D'Amour – gouache – 6 x 8in.
(Sotheby's) **$760** **£400**

PIERRE LELU – The Birth Of The Virgin – black chalk, pen and brown ink, brown wash – 25.8 x 15.3cm.
(Christie's) **$460** **£240**

SIR PETER LELY, After – Portrait Of Oliver Cromwell – indistinctly signed – oil on canvas – 29½ x 25in.
(Morton's Auction Exchange, Inc.) **$1,000** **£505**

SIR PETER LELY – Portrait Of King Charles II.
(Dee & Atkinson) **$606** **£300**

LELY – Portrait Of Nell Gwyn, Half Length, Holding An Amethyst Choker – watercolour heightened with white – 15¼ x 19in.
(Christie's) **$543** **£280**

ROBERT LEMAN – Norfolk Wooded Landscapes With Figures Sketching – watercolour – 11 x 8in.
(G. A. Key) **$455** **£230 Pair**

LEMOYNE – The Judgment Of Paris – 29 x 39¼in.
(Christie's) **$873** **£450**

LENS – An Angel Holding The Cross With The Symbol Of The Trinity Above His head – semi-circular – 64½ x 129in.
(Christie's) **$388** **£200**

ANDREW BENJAMIN LENS – Hampton Court Ferry, The Mitre And Toy And The Entrance Into The Court – inscribed and dated 1731 – pen and brown ink, grey wash – 7¾ x 12¼in.
(Christie's) **$233** **£120**

BERNARD LENS III – Bridgnorth Castle In Shropshire – pen and grey ink and washes – 8 x 12½in.
(Sotheby's) **$351** **£180**

LEONARDO – The Madonna And Child With Saint Anne – paper on panel – 15 x 10½in.
(Christie's) **$1,261** **£650**

LEPICIE – A Woman Feeding Chickens In A Barn – on panel – 8½ x 7½in.
(Christie's) **$504** **£260**

CHARLES LESLIE – Evening In The Highlands – signed and dated '84 – 11½ x 23½in.
(Sotheby's Belgravia) **$326** **£170**

CHARLES LESLIE – Sunset In The Highlands – signed and dated 1878 – 29½ x 49in.
(Sotheby's Belgravia) **$1,811** **£900**

J. LESLIE – A Highland Loch – signed – 11½ x 23½in.
(Sotheby's Belgravia) **$153** **£80**

ADOLPHE ALEXANDRE LESREL – The Card Players, Two Musicians Dressed As Cavaliers, One With A Trumpet Slung Over His Back, Playing Cards On A Drum – signed and dated 1918 - oil – on panel – 80 x 62cm.
(Henry Spencer & Sons) **$4,950** **£2,500**

THERESE LESSORE – Box At The Theatre – signed and dated 1913 – 21½ x 23¾in.
(Sotheby's) **$495** **£250**

JOHN FREDERICK LEWIS – The Ponte Vecchio, Florence – pencil, watercolour heightened with white on buff paper – 8 x 13¾in.
(Sotheby's) **$1,658** **£850**

JOHN FREDERICK LEWIS – An Old Moor Wearing A Gold And Red Headdress – pencil, watercolour, heightened with white on buff paper – 13 x 10¼in.
(Sotheby's) **$776** **£400**

LENNARD LEWIS – Old Admiralty Pier, Dover; On The Beach – signed and dated '95 – heightened with white – 9½ x 21in.
(Sotheby's Belgravia) **$213** **£100 Pair**

LENNARD LEWIS – Dove Dale; Miller's Dale, Derbyshire – signed and dated '82 – one heightened with white – 9½ x 18in.
(Sotheby's Belgravia) **$55** **£28 Pair**

PERCY WYNDHAM LEWIS – Study For 'To Wipe Out' – signed and dated 1918 – black chalk, pen and ink and watercolour – 13¼ x 19¾in.
(Sotheby's) **$3,960** **£2,000**

LEWIS – Study Of A Dead Woodpigeon – watercolour and bodycolour – 16¼ x 12¾in.
(Christie's) **$49** **£25**

GYSBRECHT LEYTENS, The Master Of The Winter Landscapes – A Winter Landscape With A Monastery – inscribed and dated – on copper – 9¼ x 12in.
(Sotheby's) **$67,900** **£35,000**

GIROLAMO DAI LIBRI – Saint Onuphrius In The Desert – on panel – 7 x 7½in.
(Christie's) **$6,144 £3,200**

CHARLES SILLEM LIDDERDALE – The Vicar's Daughter – signed with monogram and dated '78 – on panel – 17 x 11in.
(Christie's) **$1,067 £550**

CHARLES SILLEM LIDDERDALE – A Gypsy Girl – signed with monogram and dated '82 – 23 x 19in.
(Sotheby's Belgravia) **$576 £300**

CHARLES SILLEM LIDDERDALE – A Country Girl – signed with monogram – 23½ x 19½in.
(Sotheby's Belgravia) **$864 £450**

HENRI LIERON – Extensive River Landscapes With Small Boats, Cattle Drinking and Buildings On The Far Banks – signed and dated 1884, inscribed on verso – oil on canvas – 46 x 69cm.
(Henry Spencer & Sons) **$990 £500 Pair**

J. LIEVENS – Portrait Of A Bearded Elderly Man, Bust Length, In A Brown Cloak – 24 x 21in.
(Sotheby's) **$2,376 £1,200**

J. LIEVENS – Adoration Of The Magi – on panel – 18 x 31¾in.
(Christie's) **$970 £500**

LIGOZZI – The Magdalene In Penitence – inscribed on the reverse – pen and brown ink, brown wash heightened with white – 242 x 199mm.
(Christie's) **$285 £150**

SIR LIONEL LINDSAY – Spanish Still Life – signed – woodcut – 33 x 21in.
(Australian Art Auctions) **$110 £56**

SIR LIONEL LINDSAY – Gypsy Dance – signed – etching – 20 x 17cm.
(Australian Art Auctions) **$187 £97**

SIR LIONEL LINDSAY – Ibis – signed – woodcut – 15 x 15cm.
(Australian Art Auctions) **$108 £55**

NORMAN LINDSAY – Damsel In Distress – signed – pen drawing – 28.5 x 22cm.
(Australian Art Auctions)
$692 £353

LINGELBACH – Beggars By Classical Ruins – on panel – 17¼ x 14¼in.
(Christie's) **$776 £400**

LINGELBACH – A Street Scene, With Elegantly Dressed Figures – 7 x 12¼in.
(Sotheby's) **$213 £110**

EDWARD J. LINGWOOD – On A Heath – signed and dated 1889 – canvas on board – 11½ x 15½in.
(Sotheby's Belgravia)
$39 £20

LINNELL – Herding Homewards – bears signature – 8½ x 10½in.
(Sotheby's Belgravia)
$192 £100

JOHN LINNELL – A Hilly Landscape – signed – pencil and watercolour – 3½ x 4¾in.
(Christie's) **$175 £90**

JOHN LINNELL – A View Of Windsor Great Park With A Shepherd And Sheep – signed and dated 1863 – 19½ x 27¼in.
(Christie's) **$2,716 £1,400**

JOHN LINNELL – The Harvester's Noon-Day Rest – signed and dated 1859 – 26 x 38in.
(Christie's) **$1,552 £800**

JOHN LINNELL, SNR. – Fisherfolk On A Beach – signed – on panel – 23 x 30½in.
(Sotheby's Belgravia)
$1,610 £800

JOHN LINNELL, SNR. – Harvest Dinner – signed and dated 1864, inscribed on a label on the reverse – on panel – 11 x 15in.
(Sotheby's Belgravia)
$6,036 £3,000

THOMAS GEORGE LINNELL – Harvest Time – signed and dated 1865 – on panel – 9 x 11¾in.
(Christie's) **$369 £190**

CHARLES LINSELL – A Little Girl By A Couch – signed and dated 1830 – pencil and watercolour – 10 x 8in.
(Lawrence) **$68 £36**

H. VAN LINT – The Colosseum, Rome – 38½ x 61½in.
(Christie's) **$11,640 £6,000**

HENDRICK VAN LINT – Italianate Wooded River Landscapes With Peasants – both signed and dated 1751 – oval – 14½ x 18½in.
(Christie's) **$21,120 £11,000 Pair**

PIETER VAN LINT – The Madonna In Glory, With Saint John The Baptist And Saint Catherine – on panel – 60 x 38in.
(Christie's) **$2,328 £1,200**

ALBERT LINTON – A Chinese River Scene – signed – 19½ x 29½in.
(Sotheby's Belgravia) **$48 £25**

SIR JAMES DROGMOLE LINTON – The Snuff Taker – signed with initials – 17¾ x 10¾in.
(Sotheby's Belgravia) **$230 £120**

SIR W. LINTON – 'Ullswater From Lyulphs Tower', Rural Scene Of The Lake District – oil on panel – 13½ x 10in.
(Manchester Auction Mart) **$586 £290**

WILLIAM LINTON – A View In Sicily – on board – 10½ x 14½in.
(Christie's) **$291 £150**

JEAN ETIENNE LIOTARD – Portrait Of Lady Charles Spencer, Half Length, In Green Dress With A White Bodice, White Sleeves Tied With Red Ribbons And A White Shawl About Her Hair – pastel – 62.4 x 52.5cm.
(Christie's) **$69,120 £36,000**

LIPPI, Circle of – The Holy Family And Two Angels – oil on panel – diameter 34¼in.
(Bonham's) **$4,752 £2,400**

L. LIPPI – A Winged Youth, Cupid, Holding A Laurel Wreath And Scroll – indistinctly inscribed – 28¾ x 22¾in.
(Christie's) **$2,496 £1,300**

R. LITTLE – Richmond, Yorkshire – watercolour – 20 x 25cm.
(Edmiston's) **$21 £11**

W. H. LITTLEWOOD – An Aesthetic Garden – signed and dated 1905 – 33¾ x 24in.
(Sotheby's Belgravia)
$455 £230

E. LLOYD – A Terrier With A Hare – signed and indistinctly dated – oval – 19½ x 16½in.
(Sotheby's Belgravia)
$172 £90

G. LLOYD – Near Camberley, Surrey – signed, inscribed on the stretcher – 19 x 29½in.
(Sotheby's Belgravia)
$422 £220

W. STUART LLOYD – The River Crossing – signed – heightened with bodycolour – 11 x 17¼in.
(Sotheby's Belgravia)
$115 £60

LOCATELLI – A View Of Tivoli With Shepherds In The Foreground – 49¾ x 37½in.
(Christie's) **$2,328 £1,200**

LOCATELLI – A Wooded River Landscape With Fisherfolk – 8 x 16in.
(Christie's) **$436 £220**

LOCATELLI – An Italianate Landscape With Brigands Camping By A Cave – 12¼ x 17½in.
(Christie's) **$582 £300**

A. LOCATELLI – Italianate Wooded River Landscapes, With Peasants – 20 x 15in.
(Christie's) **$4,656 £2,400 Pair**

ANDREA LOCATELLI – Peasants Outside A Country Inn – 14¾ x 24½in.
(Sotheby's) **$8,624 £4,400**

WILLIAM EWART LOCKHART – Paris, Morning – signed, inscribed and dated 1871 – 8½ x 14½in.
(Sotheby's Belgravia) **$125 £65**

WILLIAM EWART LOCKHART – Auld Robin Gray – signed with symbol – 27¼ x 35½in.
(Sotheby's) **$806 £420**

MONTAGUE LODER – An Aquaduct Over A River – signed – 20 x 24in.
(Sotheby's Belgravia) **$23 £12**

GEORGE EDWARD LODGE – Ptarmigan In Flight – signed – watercolour and bodycolour – 11 x 17¼in.
(Christie's) **$1,843 £950**

GEORGE EDWARD LODGE – An Osprey In Flight Over A Lake – signed – watercolour and bodycolour – 6½ x 9½in.
(Christie's) **$310 £160**

GEORGE EDWARD LODGE – Pheasants And Blackgame – signed – grisaille – 12½ x 19in.
(Sotheby's) **$729 £380 Pair**

GEORGE EDWARD LODGE – Pheasants In Flight – signed – watercolour and bodycolour – 11 x 17¼in.
(Christie's) **$1,067 £550**

GEORGE EDWARD LODGE – Grouse On A Moor – signed – watercolour and bodycolour – 11 x 17¼in.
(Christie's) **$1,843 £950**

GEORGE EDWARD LODGE – Partridges In A Stubble Field – signed – watercolour and bodycolour – 11 x 17¼in.
(Christie's) **$1,455** **£750**

GEORGE EDWARD LODGE – Fledglings – signed – heightened with bodycolour – 8½ x 10½in.
(Sotheby's) **$1,190** **£620 Pair**

GEORGE EDWARD LODGE – A White-Tailed Or Sea Eagle On A Rock – signed – watercolour and bodycolour – 11 x 17¼in.
(Christie's) **$679** **£350**

GEORGE EDWARD LODGE – Mallard At The Edge Of A Lake – signed – watercolour and bodycolour – 11 x 17¼in.
(Christie's) **$1,067** **£550**

GEORGE EDWARD LODGE – Ptarmigan In A Highland Landscape – signed – watercolour and bodycolour – 11 x 17¼in.
(Christie's) **$1,455** **£750**

HEINRICH LOENSTAM – Young Girl Standing By A Stone Pillar In The Snow Selling Oranges From A Basket At Her Feet – initialled – oil on canvas – 30 x 22.5cm.
(Henry Spencer & Sons)
$950 **£480**

WILLIAM LOGSDAIL – Maria, from 'The Sentimental Journey' – signed – 62¼ x 46½in.
(Christie's) **$2,910** **£1,500**

WILLIAM LOGSDAIL – Pigeons Feeding By A Well – on board – 15 x 12in.
(Christie's) **$543** **£280**

LUIGI LOIR – Paris – La Maison Rouge – signed – pencil and watercolour, heightened with white gouache – on board – 9¼ x 13in.
(Sotheby's) **$3,420 £1,800**

JOHN ARTHUR LOMAX – Connoisseurs – signed – on panel – 11½ x 9½in.
(Sotheby's Belgravia)
$1,683 £850

JOHN ARTHUR LOMAX – The Accusation – signed – on panel – 12 x 18¼in.
(Sotheby's Belgravia)
$1,509 £750

L. LOMBARD – The Baptism Of Christ, With Two Donors – on panel – 13 x 10½in.
(Christie's) **$1,940 £1,000**

LOMBARD SCHOOL, 17th century – A Ceiling Design With The Apotheosis And Scenes From The Life Of San Carlo Borromeo – a bozzetto – 36¾ x 27½in.
(Sotheby's) **$2,134 £1,100**

AURELIO LOMI, Attributed to –A Female Saint Receiving Her Crown And Martyr's Palm – inscribed on the reverse – black chalk, pen and brown ink, brown wash – 26.5 x 19.2cm.
(Christie's) **$268 £140**

EDWIN LONG – Ancient Cyprus – signed with a monogram and dated 1887 – 49½ x 33½in.
(Christie's) **$1,940 £1,000**

A. LONGHI – Portrait Of A Lady, Standing Three-Quarter Length, In A Landscape – 39½ x 30¼in.
(Sotheby's) **$2,079 £1,050**

P. LONGHI – A Reveller Buying Pastry – 17 x 13½in.
(Christie's) **$2,134 £1,100**

CARLE VAN LOO – A Seated Satyr, A Study – signed and indistinctly inscribed – on panel – 6 x 4½in.
(Christie's) **$1,344 £700**

CARLE VAN LOO – The Angel Appearing To Tobias – 57½ x 44½in.
(Christie's) **$42,680 £22,000**

VAN LOO – Venus And Cupid, Attended By Putti – 27 x 28¾in.
(Christie's) **$466 £240**

VAN LOO – The Madonna And Child, Adored By Seraphim – 29 x 21½in.
(Sotheby's) **$184 £95**

HENRY LOOS – 'The William' Off The Dutch Coast – signed, inscribed and dated 1904 – 23½ x 35½in.
(Sotheby's Belgravia) **$634 £320**

GASPARO LOPEZ – A Still Life Of Fruit And Flowers, In The Foreground Of A Landscape – 16½ x 28½in.
(Sotheby's) **$3,783 £1,950**

C. PORTELLI DA LORO – Judith Slaying Holofernes – on panel – 38½ x 30¼in.
(Sotheby's) **$1,067 £550**

BICCI DI LORENZO – The Madonna And Child Enthroned, With A Donor – on panel – 44½ x 23½in.
(Sotheby's) **$29,100 £15,000**

GABRIEL LORY II – Peasants On The Simplon Pass – signed, and signed and inscribed – watercolour – 222 x 292mm.
(Christie's) **$2,470 £1,300**

LOTH – Elijah – 38 x 46½in.
(Christie's) **$1,552 £800**

LORENZO LOTTO And Studio – The Holy Family With Saint Catherine, Saint Joseph In A Red Robe And Yellow Cloak – 33¼ x 43¾in.
(Sotheby's) **$10,980 £5,500**

J. LOWERANCE – Evening Near Lytham – signed and inscribed on the reverse – 11½ x 15¼in.
(Sotheby's Belgravia) **$59 £30**

LAURENCE STEPHEN LOWRY – Dock Scene With Children – signed and dated 1969 – indelible ink – 9¾ x 13¾in.
(Sotheby's) **$990 £500**

LAURENCE STEPHEN LOWRY – A Street Corner – signed and dated 1963 – on panel – 17 x 11½in.
(Sotheby's) **$4,950 £2,500**

LAURENCE STEPHEN LOWRY – 'Good Morning' – signed and dated 1975 – pencil – 6¼ x 4½in.
(Sotheby's) **$594 £300**

LAURENCE STEPHEN LOWRY – On The Quay, Maryport – signed and dated 1954 – 23¼ x 19¼in.
(Sotheby's) **$8,910** **£4,500**

LAURENCE STEPHEN LOWRY – The Steps – signed and dated 1940 – 20½ x 16½in.
(Sotheby's) **$23,760** **£12,000**

ALBERT DURER LUCAS – Still Life Study Of Heather, Gorse And Red Admiral Butterfly – signed and dated 1874 – oil – 10 x 8in.
(Husseys) **$1,377** **£710**

LAURENCE STEPHEN LOWRY – Rushburgh Manor House – signed and dated 1943 – pencil – 7 x 10½in.
(Sotheby's) **$594** **£300**

JOHN SEYMOUR LUCAS – Charles I Demands The Surrender Of Gloucester – signed and dated 1881 – 44½ x 72¾in.
(Christie's) **$6,790** **£3,500**

JOHN SEYMOUR LUCAS – A Toper – signed – 23½ x 17½in.
(Sotheby's Belgravia)
$576 **£300**

JOHN SEYMOUR LUCAS – You Don't Say So – signed and dated 1883 and signed, inscribed and dated on the reverse – 13½ x 17¼in.
(Christie's) **$1,552** **£800**

J. SEYMOUR LUCAS – 'Portrait Of The Late Mrs Graham Harris, Formerly Of Everton Grange, Near Lymington' – signed and dated 1906 – oil – 54 x 40in.
(Elliott & Green) **$322** **£160**

JOHN TEMPLETON LUCAS – 'The Beggars Mark' – signed – 10 x 8in.
(Sotheby Bearne) **$427** **£220**

SEYMOUR LUCAS – Castle Interior With A Musketeer Feeding A Raven Perched On A Drum – signed and dated 1885 – oil on canvas – 18 x 26½in.
(Morphets of Harrogate)
$1,164 **£600**

A. LUDOVICI – 'Guy Fawkes Day', Children Playing Around A Table – oil on canvas – 13½ x 17in.
(Manchester Auction Mart)
$909 **£450**

ALBERT LUDOVICI – 'Tete-a-Tete' – oil on canvas – 12 x 7in.
(W. H. Lane & Son) **$582** **£300**

ALBERT LUDOVICI, JNR. – Summer Morning In The Park – signed – 6¾ x 10¼in.
(Sotheby's Belgravia)
$115 **£60**

LUTI – The Madonna And Child, Adored By Saint Anthony Of Padua, Angels To The Right, A Putto With A Book Below – 17 x 12½in.
(Sotheby's) **$291** **£150**

ISAAC LUTTICHUYS – Portrait Of A Gentleman, Half Length; Portrait Of A Lady, Seated – on panel – 36½ x 28in.
(Sotheby's) **$2,970** **£1,500 Pair**

LUTTICHUYS – Portrait Of King Charles II, Half Length, Wearing Armour – 29½ x 24½in.
(Christie's) **$291** **£150**

LUTYEN – A Peasant Boy And Girl In 18th Century Costume, And Another Boy, With Sheep – indistinctly signed – oil on canvas – 12 x 18in.
(Geering & Colyer) **$455** **£230**

VICTOR LUTYENS – Putti – signed – 13½ x 17½in.
(Sotheby's Belgravia)
$475 **£240 Pair**

C. DE LYON – Portrait Of A Gentleman, Small Half Length, Wearing A Dark Coat And Cap – 8 x 5¾in.
(Christie's) **$4,656** **£2,400**

JOHN HOWARD LYON – A Highland Landscape – 13½ x 19½in.
(Sotheby's Belgravia)
$142 **£75**

JOHN HOWARD LYON – Walking Up; The End Of The Day – signed – 13 x 19in.
(Sotheby's) **$3,072** **£1,600 Pair**

JAN GOSSAERT, Called Mabuse – Ruben Perduyn, In A Fur-Lined Black Surcoat Over A Red Robe And A Black Cap – on panel – 25 x 18¼in.
(Sotheby's) **$31,360 £16,000**

WALTER McADAM – A Walk In The Snow – signed – 15½ x 21½in.
(Sotheby's) **$288 £150**

WALTER McADAM – Silver Birches By A Scottish River – signed – on panel – 12 x 8in.
(Sotheby's Belgravia) **$115 £60 Pair**

WALTER McADAM – North Italian Village – 19 x 33cm.
(Edmiston's) **$140 £72**

WALTER McADAM – Near Howwood – dated 1888 – watercolour – 24 x 16.5cm.
(Edmiston's) **$68 £35**

EVAN MACALLISTER – A Highland Battle – signed and dated 1865 – heightened with white – 11½ x 22½in.
(Sotheby's) **$172 £90**

HAMILTON MACALLUM – The Falls Of Idun – signed and dated 1852, inscribed on the reverse – 17 x 23in.
(Sotheby's) **$238 £120**

W. McALPINE – A View Of St. Michael's Mount, With Fishing Boats And Figures In The Foreground – oil on panel – 21 x 40cm.
(King & Chasemore) **$630 £329**

ROBERT WALKER MACBETH – The Smuggler's Wife – signed with initials and dated 1903 – 40½ x 31½in.
(Christie's) **$582 £300**

ROBERT WALKER MACBETH – The Nightingale's Song – signed with initials and dated 1904 – 55 x 45in.
(Christie's) **$737 £380**

JAMES McBEY – Mejdelyaba – signed and inscribed – heightened with coloured washes – 7½ x 21¾in.
(Sotheby's Belgravia) **$115 £60**

JAMES McBEY – Banff Harbour – watercolour drawing – 36 x 49cm.
(Edmiston's) **$660** **£340**

JAMES McBEY – At Sizewell – watercolour drawing – 24 x 37cm.
(Edmiston's) **$388** **£200**

ANDREW McCALLUM – A View Of Ash-Down Forest – 28½ x 40in.
(Christie's) **$1,940** **£1,000**

SAMUEL McCLOY – In The Heather – signed with monogram – 8½ x 10¼in.
(Sotheby's Belgravia) **$49** **£25**

JOHN McCOLVIN – A Dancing Maiden – signed – 24 x 11in.
(Sotheby's Belgravia) **$133** **£70**

JOHN McCOLVIN – Venetian Flower Girls – signed – 19½ x 29½in.
(Sotheby's Belgravia) **$515** **£260**

McCULLOCH – Loch Striven – inscribed on a label on the reverse – on board – 6 x 9in.
(Sotheby's Belgravia) **$96** **£50**

HORATIO McCULLOCH – On The Clyde – signed – 18½ x 27½in.
(Sotheby's) **$806** **£420**

H. McCULLOCH – After Culloden – 35 x 49in.
(Sotheby's) **$2,880** **£1,500**

H. McCULLOCH – A Mountainous Landscape; and A Fisherman By A River – on board – 16 x 12in. and 13 x 10in.
(Sotheby's Belgravia) **$396** **£200 Pair**

WILLIAM MacDUFF – The Auld Folks At Hame – signed and dated 1868 – on panel – 14 x 18in.
(Sotheby's) **$537** **£280**

AMBROSE McEVOY – The Black Beret, A Lady Seated – pencil and watercolour – 21¼ x 14½in.
(Sotheby's) **$1,287** **£650**

TOM McEWAN – Neighbours – signed and dated '85 – 8½ x 11½in.
(Sotheby's) **$768** **£400**

J. M. McGEEHAN – The Request – signed – 15½ x 23½in.
(Sotheby's) **$499** **£260**

WILLIAM STEWART MacGEORGE – Near Kirkcudbright – signed, inscribed on a label on the reverse – on board – 12½ x 16½in.
(Sotheby's) **$673** **£340**

WILLIAM STEWART MacGEORGE – Water Lilies – signed – 39½ x 33in.
(Sotheby's) **$12,480** **£6,500**

JOHN McGHIE – Breakers On The Beach – signed – 17½ x 23½in.
(Sotheby's) **$198** **£100**

J. McGHIE – The Fishergirl – signed – oil on canvas – 27 x 35½in.
(Andrew Sharpe & Partners)
$1,485 **£750**

HANNAH CLARKE PRESTON MacGOUN – 'Wind Up The Clock, The Day's Work Is Done' – signed and dated 1906 – heightened with bodycolour – 23¼ x 19in.
(Sotheby's) **$806** **£420**

HARRY McGREGOR – Golden Gleams – dated 1911 – 48 x 60cm.
(Edmiston's) **$85** **£44**

ROBERT McGREGOR – At The Garden Gate – signed – 13½ x 9½in.
(Sotheby's) **$288** **£150**

ROBERT McGREGOR – Running To Mummy – signed – on panel – 8½ x 5in.
(Sotheby's) **$422** **£220**

ROBERT McGREGOR – The Fishergirl – signed – 15 x 11½in.
(Sotheby's) **$326** **£170**

BINGHAM McGUINNESS – A Lake Scene – signed – 7 x 10¼in.
(Sotheby's) **$126** **£65**

JAMES McINTYRE – 'Touch Me If You Dare' – signed with monogram and dated 1877 – 21½ x 35½in.
(Sotheby's) **$1,536** **£800**

JAMES McINTYRE – The Return Of The Fisherman – signed with monogram – 19 x 29in.
(Sotheby's) **$672** **£350**

RAYMOND McINTYRE – A Lady At The Ball – signed – oil on canvas – 24 x 20in.
(Sotheby's) **$591** **£300**

D. P. MACKAY – The Stincher At Barr – dated 1894 – 35 x 25cm.
(Edmiston's) **$144** **£74**

JAMES M. MACKAY – A Fisherman On A River – signed and dated 1899 – 19 x 23½in.
(Sotheby's Belgravia) **$307** **£160**

WILLIAM DARLING MACKAY – Tired Out – signed with initials – 8¼ x 13¼in.
(Sotheby's) **$960** **£500**

DUNCAN MACKELLAR – Interior, Sunshine And Shadow – 44 x 59cm.
(Edmiston's) **$524** **£270**

FRANK McKELVEY – A River Landscape, Two Boys Fishing To The Right, Mountains In The Distance – signed – 17½ x 23½in.
(Sotheby's) **$2,522** **£1,300**

IVOR MACKENZIE – Still Life Of Roses – signed – coloured chalks – 13 x 17in.
(Sotheby's Belgravia) **$19** **£10**

DAVID HALL McKEWAN – Pagoda Island, N.E. Coast Of China – inscribed and dated 1858 on the reverse – 5 x 14¼in.
(Sotheby's Belgravia) **$30** **£16**

DAVID HALL McKEWAN – Brington, Huntingtonshire, The Village Green – signed with initials, inscribed and dated '56 – pencil and watercolour – 13¼ x 20in.
(Sotheby's) **$118** **£60**

CHARLES HODGE MACKIE – The Thames Embankment, Dusk – signed and dated 1905 – 22¼ x 17¼in.
(Sotheby's) **$297** **£150**

THOMAS HOPE McLACHLAN – Cattle In Marshy Ground – 15 x 23½in.
(Sotheby's) **$403** **£210**

DUNCAN McLAURIN – Highland Cattle On A Track – canvas – on board – 9½ x 15in.
(Sotheby's Belgravia) **$61** **£32**

McNEAL MACLEAY – In A Highland Glen – signed and dated 1868 – gouache – 8 x 13in.
(Sotheby's) **$499** **£260**

D. F. McLEA – Fishing In A Highland Loch – signed – 8 x 12in.
(Sotheby's Belgravia) **$285** **£150**

WILLIAM DOUGLAS MACLEOD – Arran From The Links, Western Gailes – signed – on board – 20 x 24in.
(Sotheby's) **$192** **£100**

W. DOUGLAS MACLEOD – Teruel, Spain – watercolour – 24 x 40cm.
(Edmiston's) **$113** **£58**

DANIEL MACLISE – Olivia And Sophia Fitting Out Moses For The Fair – signed and dated 1837 – on panel – 27½ x 35½in.
(Christie's) **$11,640** **£6,000**

PETER MACNAB – Carrying Peat In The Lews – signed, inscribed and dated 1880 on the reverse – 29½ x 49½in.
(Sotheby's) **$1,113** **£580**

ROBERT RUSSELL MACNEE – A Grey Day On An Estuary – signed – 11½ x 17½in.
(Sotheby's) **$109** **£55**

ROBERT RUSSELL MACNEE – Corpach Mull; Old Road, Loch Vennacher – both signed – 11½ x 15½in. and 13½ x 17½in.
(Sotheby's) **$672** **£350 Two**

ROBERT RUSSELL MACNEE – Summer In The Country – signed and dated '94 – 11 x 15in.
(Sotheby's) **$356** **£180**

ROBERT RUSSELL MACNEE – Helensburgh – signed and dated '34 – 19 x 27½in.
(Sotheby's) **$345** **£180**

SIR D. MACNEE – Portrait Of A Field-Marshal – on board – 17 x 10in.
(Sotheby's Belgravia)
$49 **£25**

ANN McPHERSON – A Crofter's Wife – signed and dated 1850 – pencil heightened with coloured washes – 12¾ x 9¼in.
(Sotheby's Belgravia)
$26 **£14**

MARY MACRAE – The Knife-Grinder – signed and dated '92 – 25 x 19in.
(Sotheby's Belgravia)
$268 **£140**

W. McTAGGART – Elevenses – 19 x 15in.
(Sotheby's) **$950** **£480**

SIR WILLIAM MacTAGGART – Bellevue – 59 x 67cm.
(Edmiston's) **$1,668** **£860**

SIR WILLIAM MacTAGGART – A Summer's Day On The Coast – signed – on panel – 18¾ x 23in.
(Sotheby's) **$499** **£260**

SIR WILLIAM McTAGGART – A Highland River – signed and dated '20 – 19 x 23½in.
(Sotheby's) **$554** **£280**

SIR WILLIAM McTAGGART – Adrift – 16 x 24in.
(Sotheby's) **$3,840** **£2,000**

JOHN MacWHIRTER – Spring In The Grampian Hills; Autumn In The Trossachs – signed – heightened with bodycolour – 14 x 10in.
(Sotheby's) **$337** **£170 Two**

JOHN MacWHIRTER – 'Iona' – signed with monogram – 34 x 55in.
(Sotheby's) **$1,152** **£600**

CHURCHILL MACE – Cape Town And Table Mountain From Blaauwberg – signed – oil on board – 12 x 20in.
(Sotheby's) **$59** **£30**

ADOLPHUS M. MADOT – Babes In The Wood – signed with monogram – on panel – 16 x 26¼in.
(Sotheby's Belgravia) **$704** **£350**

N. MAES – Portrait Of A Man, Half Length, Wearing Black Costume And A White Cravat – indistinctly dated 1670 – 33¼ x 26¾in.
(Christie's) **$931** **£480**

NICOLAES MAES, Circle of – Two Women Kneeling Near A Column – inscribed – pen and brown ink, brown wash – 114 x 115mm.
(Christie's) **$190** **£100**

NICOLAES MAES – Portrait Of A Gentleman, Standing Three-Quarter Length, Wearing A Brown Dress With Black Cloak And Hat – signed and dated 1657 – 48½ x 39½in.
(Christie's) **$7,760** **£4,000**

NICOLAES MAES – Portrait Of A Child, Seated Small Three-Quarter Length, Wearing A Brown And White Dress Holding A Lamb – oval – 16 x 12in.
(Christie's) **$2,328 £1,200**

NICOLAES MAES – A Portrait Of A Gentleman, Bust Length, Wearing A White Shirt And Brown Robe – 16¼ x 11½in.
(Sotheby's) **$621 £320**

NICOLAES MAES – A Portrait Of A Gentleman, Bust Length, In A Gold Doublet – 16 x 11½in.
(Sotheby's) **$679 £350**

DOMENICO MAGGIOTTO – A Young Boy With A Flute, In White With A Grey Cloak And A Red Hat, Seated – 27 x 21in.
(Sotheby's) **$4,950 £2,500**

JOHN CHARLES MAGGS – Coaching Scenes – The London To Bath Coach In Snow Ten Miles From Bath; and A Coach Drawing Up Outside The Bear Inn In Snow On A Winter's Afternoon – signed and dated 1873 – oil on canvas – 13¼ x 25½in.
(Osmond, Tricks & Son)
$4,554 £2,300 Pair

CARLO MAGINI – Still Life With A Bowl Of Figs And A Flask – 24¾ x 30½in.
(Sotheby's) **$7,760 £4,000**

MAGNASCO – The Martyrdom Of Saint Erasmus – 38½ x 29in.
(Sotheby's) **$970 £500**

ALESSANDRO MAGNASCO – Saint Anthony Preaching To The Fishes – 33½ x 24in.
(Christie's) **$14,400 £7,500**

ALESSANDRO MAGNASCO – The Temptation Of Saint Anthony – 28½ x 22½in.
(Christie's) **$7,296 £3,800**

ALESSANDRO MAGNASCO – Saint Jerome – 28½ x 22½in.
(Christie's) **$7,296** **£3,800**

JAMES MAHONEY – Shipping Off The Yorkshire Coast – signed with monogram – on board – 9¾ x 8in,
(Sotheby's Belgravia) **$304** **£160 Pair**

JAMES MAHONEY – On The Seas – signed with monogram – on board – 4¾ x 8¼in.
(Sotheby's Belgravia) **$285** **£150 Pair**

JAMES MAHONEY – Leaving Whitby Harbour – signed with monogram – on board – 9¾ x 7¾in.
(Sotheby's Belgravia) **$304** **£160**

HENRY MAIDMENT – Near Brentwood – signed with monogram and dated '94 – 20 x 16in.
(Sotheby's Belgravia) **$672** **£350**

GIOVANNI FRANCESCO MAINERI – The Flagellation, With A Kneeling Dominican, Christ Bound To A Column And Beaten By Four Men – on panel – 16¼ x 11¼in.
(Sotheby's) **$47,040** **£24,000**

PAUL MAITLAND – Hyde Park Corner – 13½ x 9½in.
(Sotheby's) **$1,881** **£950**

LOUIS FERDINAND MALESPINA – 'Coming Out Of The Turn' – signed – on millboard – 6 x 8in.
(Sotheby Bearne) **$737** **£380**

GIOVANNI BATTISTA TROTTI, IL MALOSSO – The Assumption Of The Virgin – inscribed on the reverse – pen and brown ink, brown wash, squared in black chalk – 54.3 x 36cm.
(Christie's) **$576** **£300**

J. MAN – The Road To Alton – signed – on panel – 9 x 7¼in.
(Sotheby's Belgravia)
$594 **£300**

EDOUARD MANDON – The Rock – signed – oil on canvas – 18 x 30½in.
(Neales of Nottingham)
$118 **£60**

FRANCESCO MANCINI – Christ The Redeemer – bears signature on the reverse – on paper on panel – oval – 4 x 3¼in.
(Christie's) **$288** **£150**

WILLIAM HENRY MANDER – In A Highland Glen – signed and dated '95 – canvas on board – 17½ x 23½in.
(Sotheby's Belgravia)
$3,823 **£1,900**

EDWARD MANDON – Morning Breakers – signed – 19 x 38½in.
(Sotheby's Belgravia)
$307 **£160**

A. MANGLARD – A Harbour Scene, Numerous Sailing And Rowing Vessels Off A Quay, A Fortress And A Lighthouse On The Mountainous Coast – 39 x 61¾in.
(Sotheby's) **$5,742 £2,900**

FLORENCE MANN – On The Fiddle – signed – 25½ x 18¼in.
(Sotheby's Belgravia) **$198 £100**

WILLIAM MANNERS – Silver Birches Beside A Lake In Winter – signed and dated 1885 – watercolour heightened with white – 5 x 7¾in.
(Christie's) **$126 £65**

MANNING – Portrait Of Harriet Mansell, Wife Of John Charles White – inscribed on the reverse – 16 x 12in.
(Sotheby's Belgravia) **$69 £35**

PIERO MANZONI – Achrome – signed on the reverse – kaolin on pleated canvas – 28¼ x 35½in.
(Sotheby's) **$5,742 $2,900**

CARLO MARATTA, Circle of – An Allegory Of The Arts – 29 x 38in.
(Sotheby's) **$1,584 £800**

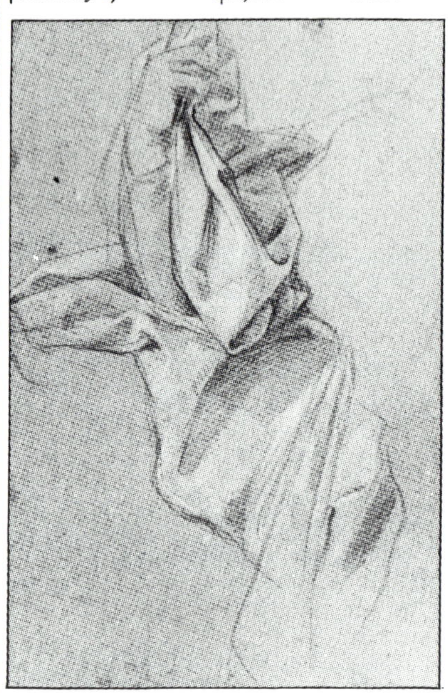

CARLO MARATTA – Study Of Drapery (recto); Figure Studies (verso) – black and white chalk on blue paper – 27.9 x 19cm.
(Christie's) **$268 £140**

CARLO MARATTA – Head Of A Young Woman Looking Down To The Left – red and white chalk on blue paper – 18.8 x 23cm.
(Christie's) **$384 £200**

CARLO MARATTA – Study Of The Drapery Of A Standing Saint – red and white chalk on blue paper – 40.7 x 22.8cm.
(Christie's) **$460** **£240**

CARLO MARATTA, Attributed to – Study Of Legs – red and white chalk on blue paper; and Study Of A Woman's Legs – black and white chalk on blue paper – 23.5 x 35.4cm. and smaller.
(Christie's) **$307** **£160 Pair**

C. MARATTA – Head Of A Boy – black chalk – circular – diameter 121mm.
(Christie's) **$72** **£38**

MARATTA, After – The Flight Into Egypt, The Holy Family Approached By Angels Bearing A Basket Of Fruit And Flowers, In A Landscape – 56 x 46½in.
(Sotheby's) **$2,522** **£1,300**

C. MARATTI – The Madonna And Child With The Infant Saint John The Baptist – 36¼ x 26in.
(Christie's) **$2,910** **£1,500**

MARATTI – The Infant Saint John The Baptist – on copper – oval – 3¼ x 3¾in.
(Christie's) **$136** **£70**

MARATTI – The Madonna And Child – 43½ x 34in.
(Christie's) **$291** **£150**

MARATTI – The Holy Family With The Infant Saint John The Baptist – oval – 26½ x 33¼in.
(Christie's) **$1,552** **£800**

LUDOVIC MARCHETTI – 'Showing The Way', a scene in a country lane with a girl directing a soldier on horseback – signed and dated 1883 – on panel – 61 x 43cm.
(King & Chasemore) **$2,976** **£1,550**

JEAN BAPTISTE MARECHAL – The Falls At Tivoli – pencil and brown wash – 20.5 x 14.9cm.
(Christie's) **$134** **£70**

JEAN BAPTISTE MARECHAL – The Falls Of Tivoli – pencil and brown wash – 14.7 x 20.5cm.
(Christie's) **$134** **£70**

G. MARECHAL – Dutch Cottage Scenes By Riverside – signed – oil on canvas – 18 x 24in.
(Morphets of Harrogate) **$220** **£115 Pair**

C. MARIANNECCI – Religious Scene, Visions Of A Cardinal And A Monk With Madonna And Child – signed and dated 1867 – watercolour – 29¾ x 20in.
(Lalonde Bros. & Parham) **$238** **£120**

MARIESCHI – The Rialto Bridge, Venice - 24 x 39½in.
(Christie's) **$1,746** **£900**

WILLIAM MARIS – 'Duck Family At Waters Edge' – signed – watercolour – 7¾ x 10in.
(Dacre, Son & Hartley) **$1,388** **£690**

ALBERT ERNEST MARKES – Launching The Lifeboat – signed – watercolour – 21 x 17½in.
(Geering & Colyer) **$466** **£240**

ALBERT ERNEST MARKES – A Windmill In A Landscape – signed and dated 1884 – watercolour – 7 x 10¼in.
(Geering & Colyer) **$158** **£80**

RICHMOND MARKES – Shipping Off The Coast – signed – 6¾ x 10¼in.
(Sotheby's Belgravia) **$57** **£30**

HENRY STACY MARKS – Oil Studies Of A Girl And A Jester – 18¾ x 24in. – verso.
(Sotheby's Belgravia) **$111** **£55**

HENRY STACY MARKS – Bearing A Boar's Head – 15¾ x 9½in.
(Sotheby's Belgravia) **$30** **£16**

MARLOW – A Wooded Landscape With Peasants By A Barn – paper on panel – 8½ x 15in.
(Christie's) **$297** **£150**

PAUL MARNY – A Corner Of Caen, Normandy – signed – heightened with white – 17½ x 11½in.
(Sotheby's) **$237** **£120**

ANTON VON MARON – Portrait Of Doge Michelangelo Cambiaso Of Genoa, Small Full Length Standing Before A Chair – a bozzetto – 14½ x 10¼in.
(Christie's) **$1,536** **£800**

MAROT – A Design For A Trompe L'Oeil Archway – oil on paper – 266 x 186mm.
(Christie's) **$95** **£50**

W. MARSDEN – In A Stable Yard – signed – 15½ x 18½in.
(Sotheby's Belgravia) **$337** **£170**

ARTHUR H. MARSH – Gathering Sticks – signed – heightened with bodycolour – 26¼ x 18in.
(Sotheby's Belgravia) **$194** **£100**

CHARLES F. MARSH – The Hover Ground, Ludham – signed – 12 x 19in.
(Sotheby's Belgravia) **$304** **£160**

HERBERT MENZIES MARSHALL – San Giorgio Maggiore From The Dogana, Venice – signed with initials, inscribed and dated '75 – pencil and watercolour heightened with white on light brown paper – 6¼ x 6½in.
(Christie's) **$116** **£60**

HERBERT M. MARSHALL – A Village Scene At Exmouth – signed and dated 1905 – 10 x 13in.
(G. A. Key) **$143** **£72**

JOHN MILLER MARSHALL – An Australian Home – signed – 17 x 11½in.
(Sotheby's Belgravia) **$38** **£20**

R. MARSHALL – Returning By A Loch – indistinctly signed – 13½ x 21½in.
(Sotheby's Belgravia) **$297** **£150**

R. MARSHALL – Waterfalls In North Wales – signed – 11½ x 10in.
(Sotheby's Belgravia) **$134** **£70**

ROBERT ANGELO KITTERMASTER MARSHALL – A Hillside Spring Near Llanfoist, Monmouthshire; and Near Windmill Hill – signed and inscribed – watercolour, one heightened with white – 13½ x 9¾in.
(Christie's) **$873** **£450 Pair**

THOMAS FALCON MARSHALL – Children With May Day Garlands – signed with initials and dated 1860 – oil – on board – 9¾ x 7¾in.
(Christie's) **$1,552** **£800**

ELLIOT H. MARTEN – Amberley Mount And The Arun; Old Shoreham Church And The River Adur – both signed – 10 x 14in.
(Sotheby's Belgravia) **$345** **£180 Pair**

ELLIOT H. MARTEN – A Highland River; On The Coast – signed – 10½ x 14in.
(Sotheby's Belgravia) **$139** **£70 Pair**

CICELY BRIDGET MARTIN – In A Poppy Field – signed and dated 1901 – 17½ x 9½in.
(Sotheby's Belgravia) **$576** **£300**

F. MARTIN – Saint Pierre De Rome; and Le Forum – signed and inscribed – watercolour – 14 x 20in.
(Sotheby's) **$560** **£280 Two**

FRANC P. MARTIN – Autumn Frolic – signed – 40 x 50¼in.
(Sotheby's Belgravia) **$864** **£450**

HENRI MARTIN – Femme Dans Un Paysage – signed – oil on canvas – 15 x 23in.
(Sotheby's) **$3,200** **£1,600**

HENRI MARTIN – Maisons Au Bord D'un Ruisseau – signed – oil on canvas – 35½ x 45¾in.
(Sotheby's) **$10,000** **£5,000**

J. E. MARTIN – A Frothy Pint Of Guinness; and A Tinker – signed – 13½ x 11½in.
(Sotheby's) **$1,089** **£550 Two**

GERTRUDE MARTINEAU – Spring In Inverness-shire – signed and dated 1883, inscribed on a label on the reverse – heightened with bodycolour – 12 x 10in.
(Sotheby's) **$230** **£120**

T. MARTINEAU – Washing Baby – 57 x 49cm.
(Edmiston's) **$892** **£460**

CHEVALIER EDUARDO DE MARTINO – H.R.H. The Prince Of Wales Landing At Quebec – signed – grey wash – 4¾ x 8in.
(Sotheby's) **$148** **£75**

JAN MARTSEN The Younger – The Interior Of A Stable – signed – 12 x 15½in.
(Sotheby's) **$7,920** **£4,000**

TOMMASO REALFONZO, Called Masillo - A Still Life With A Basket Of Apples And Game And A Straw-Covered Bottle On A Ledge – 28½ x 38¾in.
(Sotheby's) **$9,312** **£4,800**

MASOLINO – Two Evangelists – on gold ground panel – 5¾ x 14½in.
(Christie's) **$1,552** **£800**

FRANK HENRY MASON – Venice – signed, inscribed and dated 1901 – heightened with bodycolour – 15½ x 25in.
(Sotheby's Belgravia)
$345 **£180**

FRANK HENRY MASON – Shipping Off A Quay – signed – heightened with white – 10 x 30in.
(Sotheby's Belgravia)
$557 **£290**

FRANK H. MASON – The Aftermath Of The War At Sea – signed and inscribed – black chalk and grisaille – 14 x 19½in.
(Sotheby's Belgravia) **$38** **£20**

JOHN JAMES MASQUERIER – Portrait Of Miss Hamilton – signed and inscribed on the reverse – on panel – 24 x 20½in.
(Sotheby's) **$3,072** **£1,600**

Q. MASSYS – Part Of A Religious Scene – on panel – 14½ x 10½in.
(Sotheby's) **$10,192** **£5,200**

G. A. DONDUCCI, Called Il Mastelletta – The Offering Of Abigail – 84 x 67in.
(Sotheby's) **$7,372 £3,800**

AGOSTINO MASUCCI, Attributed to – The Immaculate Conception – black, red and white chalk on grey paper – 41.1 x 26.7cm.
(Christie's) **$250 £130**

AGOSTINO MASUCCI – The Expulsion Of Adam And Eve From The Earthly Paradise – 11 x 21¾in.
(Christie's) **$730 £380**

EDUARDO MATANIA – The Foothills Of The Carpathians – signed – heightened with white – 14 x 20¾in.
(Sotheby's Belgravia) **$326 £170**

JOHN G. MATHIESON – Highland Loch Scene – watercolour – 30 x 45cm.
(Edmiston's) **$56 £29**

MATSYS – Mercenary Love – on panel – 25½ x 35½in.
(Christie's) **$1,940 £1,000**

MATTA (Roberto Echaurren) – Untitled Composition – signed – oil on canvas – 51¼ x 51¼in.
(Sotheby's) **$8,514 £4,300**

MATTEIS – The Adoration Of The Shepherds – 16 x 20¼in.
(Sotheby's) **$466 £240**

DE MATTEIS – Moses Striking The Rock, Surrounded By A Group Of Israelites – 38 x 44½in.
(Sotheby's) **$1,513 £780**

ANTON MAUVE – Winter Landscape With A Peasant Loading Kindling Into A Horse Drawn Cart – signed – watercolour heightened with bodycolour – 10½ x 15¼in.
(Osmond, Tricks & Son)
$3,564 £1,800

PHILIP WILLIAM 'PHIL' MAY – Studies Of Dutch Girls And A Crouching Boy – signed and dated '99 – pencil – 9¼ x 16½in.
(Christie's) **$87** **£45**

C. S. MEACHAM – In The Keur Kloof, Montague – Early Morning – signed, inscribed on an old label – oil on canvas – 23¾ x 35½in.
(Sotheby's) **$108** **£55**

ARTHUR JOSEPH MEADOWS – Fishing Boats Off Dieppe – signed and dated 1880 – 13 x 23½in.
(Sotheby's Belgravia) **$1,609** **£800**

ARTHUR JOSEPH MEADOWS – Sailing Vessels Off Hastings – signed and dated '62 – 9½ x 18½in.
(Christie's) **$1,552** **£800**

EDWIN L. MEADOWS – Carters At A Ford – signed and dated 1875 – 29 x 49in.
(Sotheby's Belgravia) **$2,414** **£1,200**

JAMES MEADOWS – Unloading The Catch Offshore – signed – 23½ x 41½in.
(Sotheby's Belgravia) **$2,414** **£1,200**

JAMES MEADOWS – Coastal Scene, With Two Fishing Smacks In Rising Seas Rounding A Headland, Other Vessels Beyond – initialled and dated 1852 – oil on canvas – 69.5 x 98.5cm.
(Henry Spencer & Sons) **$485** **£250**

J. E. MEADOWS – Beaching The Coble – 25 x 41in.
(Sotheby's Belgravia) **$752** **£380**

J. E. MEADOWS – A Ketch And Other Shipping Off The South Coast – 32½ x 53½in.
(Sotheby's Belgravia) **$2,414** **£1,200**

G. MEARS – The Paddle-Steamer 'Iron' In The Channel – 17½ x 30½in.
(Sotheby's Belgravia) **$192** **£100**

HARRY HALSEY MEEGAN – The Gate Of London – signed, inscribed and dated 1915 on the reverse – 28 x 36in.
(Sotheby's Belgravia) **$86** **£45**

HAN VAN MEEGEREN – The Artist's Wife Seated, Whilst Another Woman Is Seen Reading A Book – signed – oil – 17¾ x 21¾in.
(Bonham's) **$832** **£420**

CHARLES VAN MEER – 'A Peaceful Moment' – signed and dated 1851 – on panel – 24 x 19in.
(Sotheby Bearne) **$22,892 $11,800**

MEIJVOGEL – An Allegory Of Fire – signed and dated 1633 – pen and brown ink, brown wash heightened with white – 83 x 114mm.
(Christie's) **$285 £150**

LUIS MELENDEZ – Still Life With Quinces, A Dozen Quinces On A Table, A Pile Of Wooden Boxes Of Various Shapes And A Red Jar – signed – 19 x 14½in.
(Sotheby's) **$66,640 £34,000**

W. MELLOR – A Mountain River – inscribed – on board – 8 x 13in.
(Sotheby's Belgravia)
$288 £150 Pair

WILLIAM MELLOR – On The Llugwy; On The Dee, North Wales – signed, inscribed on the reverse – 11½ x 17½in.
(Sotheby's Belgravia)
$4,426 £2,200 Pair

WILLIAM MELLOR – In The Glaslyn, North Wales – signed, and inscribed on the reverse – 19½ x 29½in.
(Christie's) **$1,649 £850**

WILLIAM MELLOR – Sweden Bridge, On The Scandale, Near Ambleside – signed – 29½ x 19½in.
(Christie's) **$1,164 £600**

WILLIAM MELLOR – On The Greta Near Barnard Castle – signed, inscribed on the reverse – 29½ x 49½in.
(Sotheby's Belgravia)
$1,408 £700

WILLIAM MELLOR – On The Llugwn, North Wales: Mountainous Well-wooded River Landscape, With Sheep On The Far Bank – signed – oil on canvas – 50 x 75cm.
(Henry Spencer & Sons) **$1,396 £720**

WILLIAM MELLOR – Helks Ghyll, Nidderdale; and Skelwith Force, Near Ambleside: Extensive Rocky Well-Wooded River Landscapes – signed – oil on canvas – 60 x 45cm.
(Henry Spencer & Sons) **$1,358 £700 Pair**

WILLIAM MELLOR – Fairy Glen, North Wales – signed – 29½ x 19½in.
(Christie's) **$1,261 £650**

WILLIAM MELLOR – 'Lake Windermere', An Extensive View Of The Lake, Sheep Grazing; and View Near Rydal Water, Mountainous landscape, With Sheep Grazing By A Beck – signed – 29 x 44cm.
(Henry Spencer & Sons) **$2,970 £1,500 Pair**

ALTOBELLO MELONE *(Active 1497-1517)* – Portrait Of A Young Man – on panel – 27¾ x 22¼in.
(Sotheby's) **$85,140 £43,000**

WILLIAM MELVILLE – Off Dungeness – signed and inscribed on a label on the reverse – 32 x 42in.
(Sotheby's Belgravia) **$384 £200**

MEMLINC, After – Portrait Of A Gentleman, Bust Length – on panel – 8 x 6¼in.
(Christie's) **$582 £300**

ANTON RAPHAEL MENGS – Portrait Of A Baby, Probably The Infanta Dona Carlota Joaquina De Borbon, Seated, Full Length, In A Cot – on panel – 30 x 24½in.
(Christie's) **$14,400 £7,500**

ANTON RAPHAEL MENGS – Portrait Of Gavin Hamilton, Half Length, Wearing A Brown Coat And His Hand Resting On A Sculptured Head Of Homer – 28¼ x 22in.
(Christie's) **$15,360 £8,000**

BERNARD MENINSKY – Seated Nude – signed – 29½ x 21¾in.
(Sotheby's) **$792** **£400**

ADOLF MENZEL – Bildnis Einer Frau Mit Einem Schwarzen Hut – signed and dated '01 – pencil, black crayon, grey wash – 8¼ x 5in.
(Sotheby's) **$8,740** **£4,600**

MERCIER – A Young Girl, Wearing A Blue And Yellow Dress, Kneeling, A Landscape Beyond – 12½ x 9½in.
(Sotheby's) **$4,346** **£2,240**

METEYARD – A Delphic Sibyl – indistinctly signed – brown chalk – 13 x 8½in.
(Sotheby's Belgravia) **$61** **£32**

SIDNEY HAROLD METEYARD – Study For Crucifixion – black chalk, on white paper – 24 x 9in.
(Sotheby's Belgravia) **$9** **£5**

METSU – Elegant Figures Gaming Outside An Inn – on panel – 19¼ x 25in.
(Christie's) **$2,522** **£1,300**

VAN DER MEULEN – Horsemen Outside A Country Mansion – 8¼ x 11½in.
(Christie's) **$1,843** **£950**

SCHOOL OF ADAM FRANS VAN DER MEULEN – The French Army, Before A Northern Town, Possibly Dordrecht – 28½ x 54in.
(Sotheby's) **$2,772** **£1,400**

PIETER MEULENAER – The Entry Of The Cardinal-Infante Ferdinand Into Antwerp, 1635 – inscribed with monogram – on panel – 24¾ x 44¼in.
(Sotheby's) **$17,640** **£9,000**

MEXICAN SCHOOL, circa 1650 – The Archangel Gabriel; and The Immaculate Conception – on panel inlaid with mother-of-pearl – 16 x 10½in. and 17 x 11½in.
(Christie's) **$1,164** **£600 Pair**

JOHANN JAKOB MEYER – Vallee De Maghen – signed and dated 1815 – pencil and watercolour – 195 x 274mm.
(Christie's) **$285** **£150**

H. DE MEYER – A Coastal Scene, With Fisherfolk And Fishing Vessels On A Beach, With A Village Beyond – 38 x 57¼in.
(Christie's) **$3,104** **£1,600**

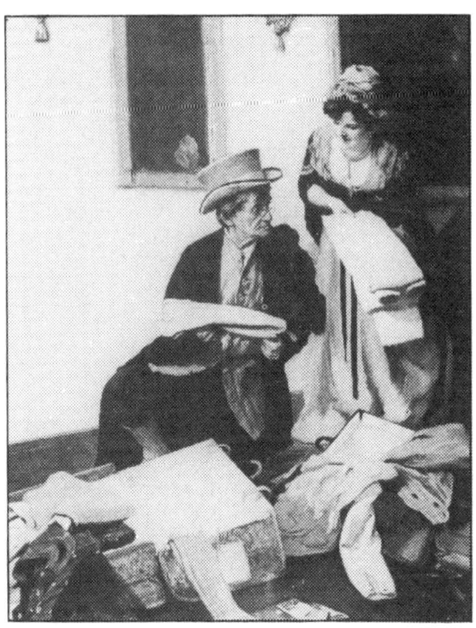

P. MEYER – 'Moving Day' – signed and inscribed – oil on panel – 21½ x 16in.
(Morton's Auction Exchange, Inc.)
$1,150 **£580**

MEYTENS – Portraits Of Ladies, Said To Be Members Of The De Salis Seewis Family, Half Lengths, Wearing Green And Red – oval – 29½ x 23¼in.
(Christie's) **$543** **£280 Two**

MICHAU – Wooded Landscapes With Peasants And Cattle – bears signature – canvas on panel – 7 x 9in.
(Christie's) **$1,358** **£700 Pair**

T. MICHAU – Fishing Vessels In A River Estuary – on panel – 9 x 12in.
(Christie's) **$3,686** **£1,900**

T. MICHAU – A Coastal Scene With Fishwives By A Cottage; and A Wooded River Landscape With A Hunting Party – on panel – 8 x 12in.
(Christie's) **$2,522** **£1,300 Pair**

T. MICHAU – A Wooded River Landscape With Figures In The Foreground – canvas on panel – 9 x 11¾in.
(Christie's) **$1,746** **£900**

T. MICHAU – A River Landscape With Figures On A Path – on metal – 9 x 13in.
(Sotheby's) **$4,950** **£2,500**

DOMENICO DI MICHELINO *(1417-1491)* – Four Figures Of The Liberal Arts, Arithmetic; Geometry; Music and Astrology – 16¾ x 17in.
(Sotheby's) **$83,160** **£42,000 Four**

DOMENICO DI MICHELINO *(1417-1491)* – The Madonna And Child With Four Saints – gold ground – on panel – 37 x 22½in.
(Sotheby's) **$148,500 £75,000**

MIERIS – Cleopatra – on metal – 6 x 5in.
(Sotheby's) **$194 £100**

MIERIS – A Sleeping Woman – on panel – 10¾ x 8½in.
(Sotheby's) **$1,067 £550**

JAN CHRISTIAENSZ. MICKER – The Tower Of Babel, Numerous Figures Engaged In Building The Tower – on panel – 9½ x 13in.
(Sotheby's) **$2,178 £1,100**

MIGNARD – La Celerrenin – black chalk and watercolour – 392 x 290mm.
(Christie's) **$38 £20**

MIGNARD – Portrait Of A Gentleman, Half Length, Wearing Armour And A White Jabot – 28 x 23in.
(Christie's) **$504 £260**

P. MIGNARD – A Portrait Of A Lady, Seated Three-Quarter Length, In A White Silk Dress, Holding A Jewelled Mirror – 35½ x 27½in.
(Sotheby's) **$2,772 £1,400**

AURELIANO MILANI – The Triumph Of Bacchus – 26¼ x 40in.
(Christie's) **$8,064 £4,200**

THOMAS ROSE MILES – Light Through The Storm – signed, inscribed on the reverse – 22¾ x 41¼in.
(Sotheby's Belgravia) **$384 £200**

THOMAS ROSE MILES – 'Signals Of Distress, Off Ventnor, Isle Of Wight' – signed and inscribed on the reverse – 20 x 30in.
(Messenger May Baverstock) **$885 £440**

JOHN EVERETT MILLAIS – The Girlhood Of St. Theresa – signed with monogram and dated 1893 – oil – 56 x 41in.
(Husseys) **$6,790 £3,500**

SIR JOHN EVERETT MILLAIS – Dew Drenched Furze – signed with a monogram and dated 1890 – 67½ x 48in.
(Christie's) **$2,134** **£1,100**

SIR JOHN EVERETT MILLAIS – Cinderella – signed with monogram and dated 1881 – 50 x 35in.
(Christie's) **$34,920** **£18,000**

FREDERICK MILLARD – 'He Loves Me; He Loves Me Not' – signed – 29½ x 19in.
(Sotheby's Belgravia) **$1,509** **£750**

A. E. HASWELL MILLER – Possillipo – watercolour – 36 x 25cm.
(Edmiston's) **$66** **£34**

CHARLES K. MILLER – Across The Western Ocean – signed, inscribed and dated 1891 on the reverse – on board – 16½ x 12½in.
(Sotheby's Belgravia) **$48** **£25**

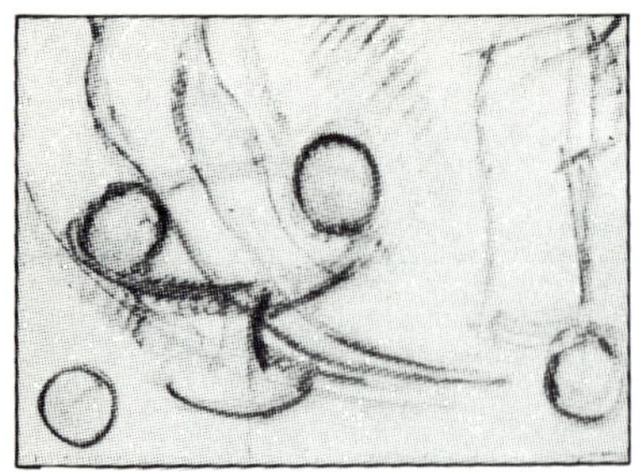

GODFREY MILLER – Still Life – 19¼ x 23¾in.
(Sotheby's) **$1,188** **£600**

JAMES H. C. MILLAR – The Final Glimpse Of Home, The Lizard, Cornwall – signed and inscribed – 23 x 35in.
(Sotheby's Belgravia) **$194** **£100**

JOHN MILLER – Still Life, Roses And Cherries – 50 x 65cm.
(Edmiston's) **$147** **£76**

E. H. MILLET – 'Birds In A Classical Landscape', Parrots, A Parakeet, A Cockatoo And Game-Cock In An Extensive Rural Landscape – monogrammed – oil – on panel – 25 x 33cm.
(Henry Spencer & Sons) **$871** **£440**

JEAN-FRANCOIS MILLET – Femme Assise – charcoal – 8 x 6½in.
(Sotheby's) **$2,850** **£1,500**

JEAN-FRANCOIS MILLET – Etude De Draperie – charcoal – 10 x 6¾in.
(Sotheby's) **$3,610** **£1,900**

JEAN-FRANCOIS MILLET – Paysanne S'Appuyant Sur Un Baton – charcoal on grey paper – 8¾ x 5½in.
(Sotheby's) **$2,660** **£1,400**

WILLIAM EDWARD MILLNER – A Gypsy Encampment – signed – 28 x 35in.
(Christie's) **$1,067** **£550**

MILNE – A Gamekeeper Taking His Rest – indistinctly signed – 15½ x 30in.
(Sotheby's) **$480** **£250**

JOHN MacLAUGHLAN MILNE – In Old St. Tropez – signed and dated '24 – canvas on panel – 13 x 16in.
(Sotheby's) **$1,029** **£520**

JOSEPH MILNE – At Tay Port – signed, inscribed on a label – 19½ x 23½in.
(Sotheby's) **$990** **£500**

JOSEPH MILNE – A Seaside Cottage – signed and dated 1883 – 19½ x 29½in.
(Sotheby's) **$345** **£180**

JOSEPH MILNE – On The River – signed – 16 x 19½in.
(Sotheby's) **$460** **£240**

J. M. MILNE – On A Quay – 9½ x 13in.
(Sotheby's Belgravia) **$48** **£25**

WILLIAM WATT MILNE – After A Shower – signed and dated 1910 – 25½ x 31½in.
(Sotheby's) **$990** **£500**

J. R. MILNER – Crofters By The Hearth – signed and dated 1852 on the reverse – 17½ x 23½in.
(Sotheby's) **$576** **£300**

HENDRIK VAN MINDERHOUT – A Capriccio Mediterranean Harbour Scene With A Frigate Setting Sail And Figures Embarking From A Quay – signed – 64¼ x 94¼in.
(Christie's) **$12,480** **£6,500**

FLAMINIO MINOZZI – Alternative Designs For A Ceiling – red chalk, pen and brown ink, brown wash – 147 x 205mm.
(Christie's) **$72** **£38**

FLAMINIO MINOZZI – Alternative Designs For A Trompe L'Oeil Ceiling – pen and brown ink and watercolour – 21.7 x 29.2cm.
(Christie's) **$729** **£380**

BENJAMIN EDWARD MINNS – A Fine Lady Being Helped Across A Wooden Bridge – signed and dated 1902 – watercolour – 10 x 14¼in.
(Sotheby's) **$709** **£360**

JOHN MINTON – Porthleven, Cornwall – signed and dated 1945 – 29¾ x 19¾in.
(Sotheby's) **$4,752** **£2,400**

JOHN MINTON – Cranes At Bankside – signed and dated 1947 – gouache – 14¾ x 9¾in.
(Sotheby's) **$1,188** **£600**

JOHN MINTON – St. Paul's From The River – signed and dated 1947 – watercolour heightened with bodycolour – 14½ x 10in.
(Sotheby's) **$832** **£420**

A. MIROU – A Wooded River Landscape With The Return Of A Falconing Party – on panel – 10 x 14¼in.
(Sotheby's) **$19,400** **£10,000**

ANTON MIROU – Landscape With Huntsmen In A Forest – on metal – 10 x 13½in.
(Sotheby's) **$47,040 £24,000**

C. K. MITCHELL – Sailing Ships In A Storm Off The Coast – 50 x 73cm.
(Edmiston's) **$243 £125**

JOHN CAMPBELL MITCHELL – The Hills Of Appin From Barcaldine Moss – signed – 11½ x 13½in.
(Sotheby's) **$594 £300**

JOHN CAMPBELL MITCHELL – On The West Coast – signed and dated 1904 – 20 x 23½in.
(Sotheby's) **$480 £250**

JOHN CAMPBELL MITCHELL – Breakers – signed and indistinctly dated – 17 x 29½in.
(Sotheby's) **$499 £260**

R. MITCHELL – Snow Scene With Winter Sun Showing Country Landscape With Cottages, Lane And Horse And Cart With Figures In Foreground – signed and dated 1809 – watercolour – 27 x 37in.
(Butler & Hatch Waterman) **$171 £85**

WILLIAM MITCHELL – Thirlemere Lake – 20 x 30in.
(Sotheby's Belgravia) **$192 £100**

WILLIAM MITCHELL – Coniston Lake – signed, inscribed and dated 1895 on the reverse – 17½ x 27½in.
(Sotheby's Belgravia) **$250 £130**

WILLIAM MITCHELL – Doe Castle, County Donegal, Ireland – signed with initials, inscribed and dated 1880 on the reverse – 23½ x 36in.
(Sotheby's Belgravia) **$194 £100**

AGOSTINO MITELLI – The Right Half Of A Design For A Door Frame With An Elaborate Entablature Supported By A Herm – black chalk, pen and brown ink, brown wash – 32.4 x 11.3cm.
(Christie's) **$288 £150**

AGOSTINO MITELLI – Alternative Designs For A Cartouche – red chalk, pen and brown ink, brown wash – 160 x 190mm.
(Christie's) **$76 £40**

BARNABA DA MODENA, Circle of *(Active 1361-1383)* – The Madonna And Child With Four Saints – on panel – 18 x 13¼in.
(Sotheby's) **$31,680 £16,000**

JOHN MOGFORD – 'Cowland Creek' – oil on canvas – 12 x 18½in.
(W. H. Lane & Son) **$922** **£475**

FREDERICO MOJA – A Street Scene In Venice – signed, inscribed and dated 1879 – oil on board – 25 x 34cm.
(King & Chasemore) **$2,688** **£1,400**

P. VAN MOL – Christ In The House Of Martha And Mary – 39½ x 99in.
(Christie's) **$5,626** **£2,900**

MOLA – An Extensive Southern Landscape With The Rest On The Flight Into Egypt – 29¾ x 39in.
(Sotheby's) **$1,746** **£900**

P. F. MOLA – The Angel Of The Flight Into Egypt – 24½ x 19½in.
(Christie's) **$815** **£420**

PIER FRANCESCO MOLA – The Magdalen In Penitence – red chalk, pen and brown ink – 16.7 x 28.5cm.
(Christie's) **$230** **£120**

JOHN HENRY MOLE – Tarbert Castle, Loch Fyne – signed and dated 1855 – watercolour heightened with white – 22¼ x 34¼in.
(Christie's) **$1,261** **£650**

J. H. MOLE – Fetching Waters From A Well – heightened with bodycolour – 14¾ x 20¾in.
(Sotheby's Belgravia) **$107** **£55**

J. H. MOLE – Mending Lobster Pots – heightened with bodycolour – 20¾ x 29½in.
(Sotheby's Belgravia) **$97** **£50**

JOHN HENRY MOLE – A Cottage And Barn Near A Lake – pencil and watercolour – 5¼ x 11¾in.
(Sotheby's) **$99** **£50**

KEES MOLEMA – Shipping In A Busy Port – signed – 15 x 30¾in.
(Lawrence) **$495** **£250**

BARTOLOMEUS MOLENAER – An Interior With A Slaughtered Pig, Surrounded By Peasants – signed in monogram – on panel – 15½ x 12¾in.
(Sotheby's) **$3,366** **£1,700**

MOLENAER – Portraits Of A Peasant Man And Woman – on panel – 6 x 4½in.
(Sotheby's) **$594** **£300**

CLAES MOLENAER – A Dutch Wooded River Landscape – signed – oil on panel – 15 x 20in.
(Bonham's) **$5,544** **£2,800**

KLAES MOLENAER – A Dune Landscape With A Group Of Peasants Conversing – on panel – 16½ x 22¾in.
(Lawrence) **$3,040** **£1,600**

R. MOLENTIN – Shipping In A Squall – signed and dated 1879 – 9½ x 16¾in.
(Sotheby's Belgravia)
$105 **£55**

MOLIJN – An Extensive Wooded Landscape With Figures On A Road By An Inn – on panel – 14¾ x 22½in.
(Christie's) **$1,881** **£950**

P. DE MOLIJN – A Sandy Landscape With Peasants Resting Beside A Path, A Cottage Built On A Dune To The Right Beyond – on panel – 10½ x 14in.
(Sotheby's) **$8,316** **£4,200**

PIETER DE MOLIJN – A Dune Landscape, Three Thatched Cottages Beside A Road Between Dunes Up One Of Which A Man Is Walking, Followed By A Dog – signed and dated 1650 – on panel – 13¾ x 21¼in.
(Sotheby's) **$6,790** **£3,500**

PIETER DE MOLIJN – A Dune Landscape With Figures In A Horse-Drawn Cart – on panel – 12½ x 17¼in.
(Sotheby's) **$4,850** **£2,500**

ROBERT MOLS – Spithead – signed, inscribed on a label on the reverse – on panel – 5½ x 13in.
(Sotheby's Belgravia)
$380 **£200**

ROBERT MOLS – Portsmouth – inscribed on a label on the reverse – on panel – 8½ x 13in.
(Sotheby's Belgravia)
$418 **£220**

F. DE MOMPER – A Moonlit Landscape With A Cleric Conversing With Travellers Outside A Church – on panel – 11¾ x 17½in.
(Sotheby's) **$1,782** **£900**

FRANS DE MOMPER – The Outskirts Of A Village On A Feast Day – signed – on panel – 33¼ x 44¾in.
(Sotheby's) **$36,860 £19,000**

JOOS DE MOMPER – A Mountain Landscape – on panel – 24¾ x 44¼in.
(Sotheby's) **$120,280 £62,000**

JOOS DE MOMPER – A Mountain Landscape – on panel – 18½ x 34½in.
(Sotheby's) **$19,400 £10,000**

JOOS DE MOMPER The Younger – A Valley Landscape With Travellers, A Horseman And Peasants On A Winding Road In A Valley Between Tall Wooded Cliffs – on panel – 19½ x 31¾in.
(Sotheby's) **$33,320 £17,000**

JOOS DE MOMPER The Younger – A Town Ablaze At Night – on panel – 19¼ x 26½in.
(Christie's) **$5,760 £3,000**

J. DE MOMPER – The Visit Of Saint Anthony Abbott To Saint Paul The Hermit – 44 x 62½in.
(Sotheby's) **$1,485 £750**

PIETRO MONALDI – Musicians Performing Outside A Farmhouse; and Peasants Feasting Outside A Farmhouse – both signed with initials – 14¼ x 17½in.
(Christie's) **$16,320 £8,500 Two**

DOMENICO MONDO – Saint Teresa – black chalk, grey wash – 214 x 148mm.
(Christie's) **$266** **£140**

MONNOYER – Still Lives Of Flowers In Sculptured Urns, On Wooden Ledges – 19½ x 14½in.
(Sotheby's) **$10,296** **£5,200 Pair**

MONNOYER – A Basket Of Roses, Tulips And Other Flowers On A Stone Ledge – 14 x 17in.
(Christie's) **$2,134** **£1,100**

J. B. MONNOYER – A Still Life Of Flowers In A Sculpted Gilt Urn, On A Stone Ledge – 29¼ x 24¼in.
(Sotheby's) **$8,316** **£4,200**

J. B. MONNOYER – Mixed Flowers In Vases On Ledges – 17½ x 13¼in.
(Christie's) **$9,312** **£4,800 Pair**

J. B. MONNOYER – Roses, Chrysanthemums, Daisies And Other Flowers In A Vase On A Stone Ledge – 28¾ x 24in.
(Christie's) **$13,580** **£7,000**

J. B. MONNOYER – A Still Life Of Chrysanthemums, Hyacinth, Narcissus, And Other Flowers In A Vase With Convolvulii On A Stone Ledge – 29½ x 24½in.
(Christie's) **$7,760** **£4,000**

J. B. MONNOYER – A Basket Of Roses, Chrysanthemums And Other Flowers On A Stone Ledge – bears signature – 14 x 18in.
(Christie's) **$9,312** **£4,800**

JEAN-BAPTISTE MONNOYER – Poppies, Roses, Lilac With Bunches Of Grapes And Other Fruit In A Landscape – signed – 42¾ x 58¼in.
(Christie's) **$46,080** **£24,000**

J. MONRO – Ruined Arches Near A House – pencil and grey wash – 7¾ x 7in. – and drawings by or attributed to H. Riballier and J. S. Cotman.
(Christie's) **$36** **£18**

ALFRED MONTAGUE – Streets In Delft – both signed – 13½ x 9½in.
(Sotheby's Belgravia) **$1,820** **£950 Pair**

CLARA MONTALBA – Thames Barge – signed and dated 1889, inscribed on a label on the reverse – heightened with white – 19 x 28in.
(Sotheby's Belgravia) **$192** **£100**

FRANCESCO MONTI – Saint Geminiano Exorcising The Emperor's Daughter – 21 x 13¾in.
(Christie's) **$6,144** **£3,200**

FANNIE MOODY – Caught – signed – coloured chalks, heightened with white on buff paper – 24½ x 20in.
(Sotheby's Belgravia)
$162 **£85**

FANNIE MOODY – Fox Hounds – signed – 12 x 16in.
(Sotheby's Belgravia) **$832** **£420**

FANNIE MOODY – The Rat Catcher – signed – coloured chalks, heightened with white on buff paper – 20 x 16in.
(Sotheby's Belgravia)
$194 **£100**

HENRY MOORE – Summer At Sea – signed and dated 1893 – 39 x 59in.
(Sotheby's Belgravia) **$2,817** **£1,400**

JOHN COLLINGHAM MOORE – Portrait Of A Child With A Hoop – signed and dated 1875 – 29 x 16in.
(Sotheby's Belgravia) $403 £210

ROBERT MOORE – Heading For Home, Calais – signed – 11½ x 15½in.
(Sotheby's Belgravia) $340 £170

MOR – Portrait Of A Don Juan Of Austria Standing, Three-Quarter Length, Wearing Armour – 54 x 40in.
(Christie's) $1,164 £600

MORANDI – Portrait Of A Cardinal, Bust Length, Wearing A Red Velvet Mantelletta And A Red Hat – 29½ x 24¼in.
(Sotheby's) $1,386 £700

JAN EVERT MOREL II – Extensive Dutch Landscape With Figures On A Country Road Leading To Town In Mid Distance – signed indistinctly – oil on panel – 9¾ x 13¾in.
(Lalonde Bros. & Parham) $871 £440

EVELYN DE MORGAN – Tobias And The Angel – signed and dated 1875 – canvas on board – 59 x 29in.
(Sotheby's Belgravia) $6,036 £3,000

J. MORGAN – A Foraging Party – inscribed on the reverse – on board – 10 x 8¼in.
(Sotheby's) $326 £170

JOHN MORGAN – Calming The Baby – indistinctly signed – 13½ x 10½in.
(Sotheby's Belgravia) $480 £250

FRIEDRICH WILHELM MORITZ – Les Cachines A Florence: Florence From The Gardens – signed and dated 1826 – water-colour – 307 x 409mm.
(Christie's) $1,615 £850

FRIEDRICH WILHELM MORITZ – A Couple By A Bollard – signed – water-colour; and A Study Of A Peasant Woman On Steps – 183 x 153mm.
(Christie's) $124 £65 Two

G. MORLAND – Coastal Scene, With A Fishing Smack Moored Off The Shore, Where Figures Load Fish Into Baskets, A Girl With A Donkey And A Dog Look On signed – 35 x 43cm.
(Henry Spencer & Sons) $203 £105

JAMES SMITH MORLAND – Springtime In The Woods – signed, inscribed on a label on the reverse – heightened with bodycolour – 8¼ x 12in.
(Sotheby's Belgravia) **$39** **£20**

HENRY CLAUDE MORNEWICK – Fishing Vessels Offshore In A Choppy Sea – signed and dated 1846 – on panel – 12 x 16in.
(Christie's) **$2,280** **£1,200**

GIOVANNI BATTISTA MORONI *(Active 1546; 1578)* – Portrait Of A Bearded Man – 22½ x 18in.
(Sotheby's) **$79,200** **£40,000**

ENA MORRIS – River Views – both signed – 11½ x 17in.
(Sotheby's Belgravia) **$288** **£150 Pair**

GARMAN MORRIS – Thames Barges – watercolour – 17 x 9.5cm.
(Edmiston's) **$25** **£13**

J. MORRIS – The Fans Of Clyde, The Artist Painting – signed, inscribed on the reverse – 14 x 17½in.
(Sotheby's Belgravia) **$79** **£40**

JOHN MORRIS – After Shooting – signed – 23 x 35in.
(Sotheby's) **$2,112** **£1,100 Pair**

JOHN MORRIS – From The Isle Of Arran – signed, inscribed on the stretcher – 20 x 30in.
(Sotheby's Belgravia) **$125** **£65**

J. T. MORRIS – 'Highland Cattle Watering - Morning and Evening' – oil on canvas – 36 x 28in.
(W. H. Lane & Son) **$388** **£200 Pair**

J. W. MORRIS – Sheep In The Highlands – signed and dated 1888 – 18 x 14in.
(Sotheby's Belgravia) **$109** **£55 Pair**

PHILIP RICHARD MORRIS – Fording The Stream – signed – 35¼ x 59¼in.
(Sotheby's Belgravia) **$2,616** **£1,300**

PHILIP RICHARD MORRIS – The Riven Shield – signed and dated '66 – 42 x 32in.
(Sotheby's Belgravia)
$4,024 £2,000

WILLIAM BRIGHT MORRIS – Gathering Chrysanthemums – signed – 10 x 15½in.
(Sotheby's Belgravia)
$288 £150

WILLIAM W. MORRIS – Young Boy Seated On A Rock, Holding A Fowling Piece, With Two Cairn Terriers And Game At His Feet – signed and dated '86 – 91 x 71.5cm.
(Henry Spencer & Sons)
$1,742 £880

W. WALKER MORRIS – After A Stalk – signed – 30 x 49½in.
(Sotheby's) **$806 £420**

MOSTAERT – The Betrayal Of Christ – on panel – 10½ x 15¾in.
(Christie's) **$504 £260**

G. MOSTAERT – Scenes From The Life Of Christ Depicted In Rosettes On The Tree Of Life – on panel – 27¾ x 20¾in.
(Christie's) **$1,261 £650**

TOM MOSTYN – Sanctuary – signed, inscribed on the stretcher – 30 x 40in.
(Sotheby's Belgravia) **$614 £320**

TOM MOSTYN – A Fisherman On A River – signed – 17½ x 23½in.
(Sotheby's Belgravia) **$307 £160**

GEORGE WILLIAM MOTE – The Vale Of Evesham – signed and dated 1887 – 29½ x 24¼in.
(Sotheby's Belgravia) **$1,509 £750**

F. DE MOUCHERON – An Italianate Wooded River Landscape With A Shepherd And Sheep In The Foreground – 31 x 27¼in.
(Christie's) **$2,910 £1,500**

FREDERIC DE MOUCHERON – A Wooded Landscape, A Herdsman On A Winding Path To The Left, An Extensive Valley Vista To The Right Beyond – 34 x 27½in.
(Sotheby's) **$1,386 £700**

FREDERICK DE'MOUCHERON, Attributed to – An Extensive Landscape Near Turin – inscribed on the reverse – black chalk, grey wash – 15.4 x 20.6cm.
(Christie's) **$537 £280**

ISAAC DE MOUCHERON – An Italianate Garden With Figures By A Pool, A Baroque Arcade And A Villa Behind – signed and dated 1743 – pen and brown ink and watercolour – 23.2 x 34.2cm.
(Christie's) **$8,064 £4,200**

E. MOULY – A Settlement In A Clearing In The Brazilian Jungle – signed, inscribed and indistinctly dated – oil on canvas – 10¼ x 28in.
(Sotheby's) **$552 £280**

T. LANGLEY MOURILYAN – Taking Fort Lin, Canton; Stockades Outside The Village Of Nia-Seang; Chuan-Pee Fort On The Canton River; The Pinnace Of HMS Nankin With A Flag Of Truce By The Walls Of Lambkin – watercolour – 6¼ x 9½in.
(Sotheby's (Hong Kong) Ltd.)
$434 £219 Four

RODRIGO MOYNIHAN – Tree In A Landscape – signed and dated '45 – 21¾ x 27¼in.
(Sotheby's) **$356 £180**

WILLIAM MUIR – Unloading The Catch – signed and dated 1900 – 11½ x 19in.
(Sotheby's) **$475 £240**

PIETER MULIER – A Coast Scene, Men Unloading A Vessel Beached On A Sandy Shore – signed in monogram – on panel – 20¼ x 25½in.
(Sotheby's) **$15,520 £8,000**

P. MULIER – A Capriccio Mediterranean Coastal Landscape With Ships In Distress And Numerous Figures On The Shore – 33¾ x 46½in.
(Christie's) **$1,358** **£700**

CHARLES LOUIS LUCIEN MULLER – Une Fete Galante – watercolour – 16¾ x 21¾in.
(Sotheby's) **$1,178** **£620**

WILLIAM JAMES MULLER – A Girl Fording A Stream – watercolour – 11¼ x 8¼in.
(Christie's) **$388** **£200**

WILLIAM JAMES MULLER – Sailing Barges In A River Estuary – signed – 14½ x 20½in.
(Christie's) **$3,686** **£1,900**

WILLIAM JAMES MULLER – A Fallen Tree Near Crags – watercolour heightened with white – 9¼ x 14¼in.
(Christie's) **$233** **£120**

WILLIAM JAMES MULLER – A Bridge Over A Waterfall Near A Castle In Italy – watercolour – 9 x 6½in.
(Christie's) **$310** **£160**

SIR ALFRED MUNNINGS – The Edge Of The Wood – indistinctly signed – canvas on board – 19¾ x 23½in.
(Sotheby's) **$8,316** **£4,200**

SIR ALFRED MUNNINGS – Herding The Sheep, Exmoor – signed – 19½ x 29½in.
(Sotheby's) **$12,870** **£6,500**

HENRY TURNER MUNNS – A Fisherman On A River – signed – heightened with bodycolour – 20 x 25in.
(Sotheby's Belgravia) **$116** **£60**

J. MUNRO – A Country Girl – signed and dated 1898 – 11 x 17½in.
(Sotheby's Belgravia) **$172** **£90**

F. DE MURA – Cupid And Psyche – a sketch – 16½ x 23in.
(Christie's) **$1,455** **£750**

F. DE MURA – The Finding Of Moses; and Christ And The Woman Of Samaria – 14½ x 30in.
(Christie's) **$1,843** **£950 Pair**

MURILLO – The Angel Delivering Saint Peter – 23 x 28in.
(Christie's) **$1,188** **£600**

MURILLO, After – The Madonna And Child – 64½ x 41¼in.
(Christie's) **$369** **£190**

MURILLO, After – The Immaculate Conception – on metal – 11¾ x 9in.
(Sotheby's) **$146** **£75**

SIR DAVID MURRAY – The River Avon Below Ringwood, Hampshire – signed and dated '92 – 9½ x 13in.
(Sotheby's) **$317** **£160**

SIR DAVID MURRAY – Cattle In A Meadow – signed and dated '97 – 17½ x 23½in.
(Sotheby's) **$1,728** **£900**

GRAHAM MURRAY – Red Flowers – 35 x 30cm.
(Edmiston's) **$38** **£20**

J. MURRAY – Autumn In The Highlands – signed – on board – 17¼ x 26½in.
(Sotheby's Belgravia)
$228 **£120 Pair**

ROBERT MURRAY – Portrait Of A Young Girl – signed and dated 1921 – 29½ x 21½in.
(Sotheby's Belgravia)
$49 **£25**

ROBERT MURRAY – The Dancer – signed and dated '15 – 49 x 29in.
(Sotheby's Belgravia)
$39 **£20**

ALICIA MUSPRATT – Dancer Tying Her Shoe – signed – 31½ x 25¼in.
(Sotheby's) **$713** **£360**

M. VAN MUSSCHER – Portrait Of A Gentleman, Standing, Small Three-Quarter Length Holding A Scroll – on copper – oval – 7 x 9in.
(Christie's) **$3,104** **£1,600**

H. VAN DER MY – A Woman And Child Holding Partridge – on metal – 11½ x 8¾in.
(Sotheby's) **$3,564** **£1,800**

W. S. MYLES – A Ruined Cathedral – signed – 18½ x 24½in.
(Sotheby's Belgravia)
$48 **£25**

VAN DER MYN – Portrait Of A Gentleman, Half Length, Wearing A Black Coat With Lace Cravat And Cuffs, Holding A Book – 29¼ x 24¼in.
(Christie's) **$291** **£150**

MYTENS – Portrait Of Lady Martha Cranfield As A Child, Standing Full Length – bears inscription – on panel – 44¼ x 27½in.
(Christie's) **$3,104** **£1,600**

M. VAN MYTENS The Younger – Portrait Of The Emperor Leopold II, As A Child, In Gold With A Blue And Gold Brocade Cloak Lined With Ermine, Holding The Order Of The Golden Fleece, On A Red Cushion Trimmed With Gold Brocade, Seated On A Rococo Chair Surmounted By A Coronet – 10½ x 8in.
(Sotheby's) **$1,782** **£900**

N

MATTHYS NAIVEU – A Man Reading In A Courtyard – signed and dated 1692 – on panel – 13 x 10in.
(Sotheby's) **$12,610 £6,500**

MATTHYS NAIVEU – A Couple Seated In A Garden – signed – on panel – 16½ x 20in.
(Sotheby's) **$2,178 £1,100**

MARIOTTO DI NARDO *(Active 1394; ca. 1424)* – The Madonna And Child Enthroned, With Saints – on panel – 37 x 25¼in.
(Sotheby's) **$79,200 £40,000**

FREDERICK NASH – Landscape At Windsor With Deer Grazing In Parkland – signed – watercolour – 10¼ x 14in.
(Osmond, Tricks & Son) **$455 £230**

JOHN NASH – Landscape Before A Storm – signed – black chalk, pen and ink and watercolour heightened with bodycolour – 15¼ x 17½in.
(Sotheby's) **$2,277 £1,150**

J. NASH – After A Hard Day – 11¼ x 16in.
(Sotheby's Belgravia) **$198** **£100 Pair**

JOSEPH NASH – On The Terrace, Haddon Hall, Derbyshire – 17 x 22¾in.
(Sotheby's) **$621** **£320**

JOSEPH NASH – On The Steps, Haddon Hall, Derbyshire – 19¾ x 13¾in.
(Sotheby's) **$466** **£240**

BARBARA NASMYTH – A Scottish River Scene – on panel – 18 x 24in.
(Sotheby's) **$3,648** **£1,900**

BARBARA NASMYTH – St. Bernard's Well, Waters Of Leith, Edinburgh – 18¼ x 25½in.
(Sotheby's) **$998** **£520**

CHARLOTTE NASMYTH – Possibly A View On The Moray Firth – on panel – 11 x 16in.
(Christie's) **$4,268** **£2,200**

CHARLOTTE NASMYTH – Old Trees By A Country Road – on panel – 11¼ x 16in.
(Sotheby's) **$1,344** **£700**

ELIZABETH WEMYSS NASMYTH – A Cottage By A Loch – signed with initials and dated 1848 – on panel – 8¾ x 6¾in.
(Sotheby's) **$2,688** **£1,400**

MARGARET NASMYTH – On The River Tay, Perthshire – signed and dated 1865 – 17 x 23in.
(Sotheby's) **$2,178** **£1,100**

NASMYTH – Morning And Evening – 19½ x 23in.
(Sotheby's) **$693** **£350 Pair**

CLAUDE JOSEPH NATOIRE – An Allegory Of The Arts – inscribed – black chalk and watercolour – 53.1 x 32.7cm.
(Christie's) **$1,728** **£900**

JEAN-MARC NATTIER – Portrait Of A Lady, Thought To Be Madame De Pompadour, As Diana, Seated Three-Quarter Length, In A Landscape – 39½ x 31¾in.
(Christie's) **$12,480** **£6,500**

JOHANNES NATUS – An Interior With Peasants Drinking – signed and dated 1661 – on panel – 20½ x 16in.
(Sotheby's) **$31,040** **£16,000**

JOHN PRESTON NEALE – Chirk Castle, Denbighshire – signed and dated 1815 – 6 x 8¾in.
(Sotheby's) **$351** **£180**

NEAPOLITAN SCHOOL

NEAPOLITAN SCHOOL, circa 1700 – The Martyrdom Of Saint Januarius, Depicted In A Landscape – 14½ x 18½in.
(Sotheby's) **$792** **£400**

NEAPOLITAN SCHOOL – 'Naples Bay' – gouache – 16½ x 25in.
(W. H. Lane & Son) **$349** **£180**

NEAPOLITAN SCHOOL, circa 1750 – A Mendicant – on copper – oval – 9¾ x 7¼in.
(Christie's) **$105** **£55**

NEAPOLITAN SCHOOL, early 19th century – Views Of Naples – bodycolour – 402 x 617mm.
(Christie's) **$1,140** **£600 Three**

NEAPOLITAN SCHOOL, early 18th century – A Kitchen Interior With A Woman Preparing Food – 55¾ x 85¼in.
(Christie's) **$4,656** **£2,400**

NEAPOLITAN SCHOOL, 17th century – The Adoration Of The Shepherds – on metal – 5 x 4in.
(Sotheby's) **$1,485** **£750**

NEAPOLITAN SCHOOL, early 18th century – An Alchemist In His Study – dated 1712 – 55¾ x 85¼in.
(Christie's) **$5,044** **£2,600**

NEAPOLITAN SCHOOL, 17th century – Saints John The Baptist And Francis Of Assisi; Saints Francis Of Paola And Blaise, Standing, Bust Length – 12½ x 18¼in.
(Sotheby's) **$3,880** **£2,000 Pair**

NEAPOLITAN SCHOOL, 18th century – The Visitation; The Annunciation; The Adoration Of The Shepherds; The Flight Into Egypt – 14 x 10in.
(Sotheby's) **$2,328** **£1,200 Four**

NEAPOLITAN SCHOOL, circa 1800 – Tempio Di Diana Antico E Deruccato Ne Luoghi Di Pozzuoli; and Sepolcro Per La Via Di Pozzuoolo – inscribed – bodycolour – 197 x 300mm.
(Christie's) **$494** **£260 Pair**

NEAPOLITAN SCHOOL, circa 1870 – 'The Glynn' Of St. Ives, J.B. Wallis, Master – inscribed – gouache – 16 x 22in.
(Sotheby's Belgravia) **$211** **£110**

NEAPOLITAN SCHOOL, 18th century – A Royal Palace, Naples; A Review Of Troops In The Port At Naples; Charles, King Of Naples Presenting His Son To The Court, October 1759; Charles IV Embarking At Naples To Assume The Throne Of Spain, October 1759 – 22½ x 40¼in.
(Sotheby's) **$34,920** **£18,000 Four**

BALTHASAR NEBOT – A Fishmonger, Beneath A Market Booth, Holding A Basket Of Fish; A Vegetable Vendor – one signed and dated 1730 – on metal – 10¼ x 8¼in.
(Sotheby's) **$6,732** **£3,400 Two**

PEETER NEEFFS I – The Interior Of A Gothic Cathedral With Numerous Figures – indistinctly dated – on panel – 13½ x 22¼in.
(Christie's) **$10,560** **£5,500**

PEETER NEEFFS The Elder And FRANS FRANCKEN The Younger – The Interior Of A Church With Services Taking Place – dated 1616 – on panel – 14 x 22¼in.
(Christie's) **$5,820** **£3,000**

PEETER NEEFFS The Elder And FRANS FRANCKEN II – Interior Of A Cathedral – signed and dated 1636 – on panel – 13 x 18¼in.
(Sotheby's) **$17,460** **£9,000**

PEETER NEEFFS, The Elder – The Interior Of A Gothic Church, With A View Of The North Transept – on panel – 9¾ x 7¾in.
(Sotheby's) **$4,158** **£2,100**

NEEFFS – The Interior Of A Cathedral With Figures – on panel – 15½ x 18½in.
(Christie's) **$873** **£450**

AERT VAN DER NEER – A Moonlit Estuary, A Man And Woman With A Girl On A Wooden Landing-Stage Awaiting A Ferry – signed in monogram – 13½ x 17¾in.
(Sotheby's) **$37,240** **£19,000**

EGLON HENDRICK VAN DER NEER – A Lady Swooning In An Interior – signed and dated 1680 – on panel – 20¼ x 16¾in.
(Christie's) **$48,000** **£25,000**

VAN DER NEER – A Moonlit River Landscape With An Angler – on panel – 16¾ x 21in.
(Christie's) **$1,188** **£600**

GEORGE NEIL – Carradale Bay – signed, inscribed on the reverse – on board – 14 x 21in.
(Sotheby's Belgravia) **$153** **£80**

MARTINUS NELLIUS – Still Life, A Bowl Of Nuts, An Orange And A Pipe On A Table, A Bird Suspended Above, And Butterflies – on panel – 11 x 9in.
(Sotheby's) **$5,096** **£2,600**

GIROLAMO PIERI NERLI – An Italian Town By The Sea – signed – oil on panel – 9¾ x 5½in.
(Sotheby's) **$1,537** **£780**

WILLIAM ANDREWS NESFIELD – Bamburgh Castle, Northumberland – watercolour – 20¼ x 27in.
(Christie's) **$504** **£260**

A. NETHERWOOD – Rural Landscape With Cottages – signed and dated 1896 – watercolour – 17 x 25in.
(Morphets of Harrogate) **$63** **£32**

NETSCHER – A Huntsman Beneath An Arched Window, In A Red Coat, Holding A Glass Of White Wine; A Small Boy Blowing Bubbles, Beneath An Arched Window – one bears signature – on panel – 9 x 7in.
(Sotheby's) **$2,970** **£1,500 Pair**

C. NETSCHER – Portrait Of A Boy, Standing Full Length In A Landscape. Wearing A Blue Coat With A Dog Nearby – 18¾ x 16½in.
(Christie's) **$1,940** **£1,000**

CASPAR NETSCHER – Portrait Of A Lady, In A Blue Dress, Seated In A Park By A Fountain – signed and dated 1684 – 19 x 15½in.
(Sotheby's) **$9,700** **£5,000**

C. NETSCHER – Portrait Of A Young Gentleman, Small Bust Length, Wearing A White Cravat And A Black Coat – bears signature – 12¾ x 10½in.
(Christie's) **$1,164** **£600**

JOHN TRIVETT NETTLESHIP – A Golden Eagle – signed and dated '96 – coloured chalks – 14½ x 11in.
(Sotheby's) **$79** **£40**

CHRISTOPHER RICHARD WYNNE NEVINSON – Seaford Bay – signed – on panel – 12¾ x 16in.
(Sotheby's) **$990** **£500**

CHRISTOPHER RICHARD WYNNE NEVINSON – The Temples Of New York – signed – 25½ x 15½in.
(Sotheby's) **$14,652** **£7,400**

J. C. NEWCOMB – Corrie, Isle Of Man, From Preacher's Rock, Evening In Summer – signed, inscribed and dated 1888 – heightened with white – 12½ x 19in.
(Sotheby's Belgravia) **$57** **£30**

BERTHA NEWCOMBE – At Verona – signed, inscribed and dated 1889 – on panel – 8¾ x 6¼in.
(Sotheby's Belgravia) **$86** **£45**

HENRY NEWTON – Ruins Of Monkstown Castle – inscribed on label – 20½ x 27½in.
(Sotheby's) **$1,455** **£750**

DE NEYN – A Wooded Landscape With Travellers On A Road – bears indistinct signature – on panel – circular – diameter 29in.
(Christie's) **$1,843** **£950**

RICHARD HENRY NIBBS – A Continental Seaport – signed – heightened with body-colour – 15 x 21¼in.
(Sotheby's Belgravia)
$310 **£160**

ERSKINE NICOL – The Donkey Race – 24 x 29in.
(Christie's) **$4,656** **£2,400**

ERSKINE NICOL – Study Of An Old Lady – signed and dated '55 – heightened with bodycolour – 8¼ x 6½in.
(Sotheby's) **$422** **£220**

ERSKINE NICOL – Balance On The Wrong Side – indistinctly inscribed – 13½ x 17½in.
(Sotheby's) **$1,056** **£550**

ERSKINE NICOL – An Ejected Family – signed and dated 1853, inscribed on a label on the reverse – 19½ x 32in.
(Sotheby's) **$25,220** **£13,000**

ANDREW NICHOLL – Wild Flowers – signed – heightened with white – 13 x 20in.
(Sotheby's) **$2,910** **£1,500**

C. W. NICHOLLS – Reading On The Shore – 13½ x 9½in.
(Sotheby's Belgravia) **$86** **£45**

BEN NICHOLSON – Hyacinth, 1923 – pencil – 12½ x 14¼in.
(Sotheby's) **$792** **£400**

FRANCIS NICHOLSON – A Mill On Rocks Above A River – watercolour – 12 x 17¾in.
(Christie's) **$97** **£50**

GEORGE WASHINGTON NICHOLSON – 'Winter Morning' – signed – oil on panel – 21 x 29in.
(Morton's Auction Exchange, Inc.) **$2,750** **£1,395**

SIR WILLIAM NICHOLSON – Sheep Grazing On Downland – signed and dated 1910 – on canvas board – 12¾ x 15¾in.
(Sotheby's) **$5,544** **£2,800**

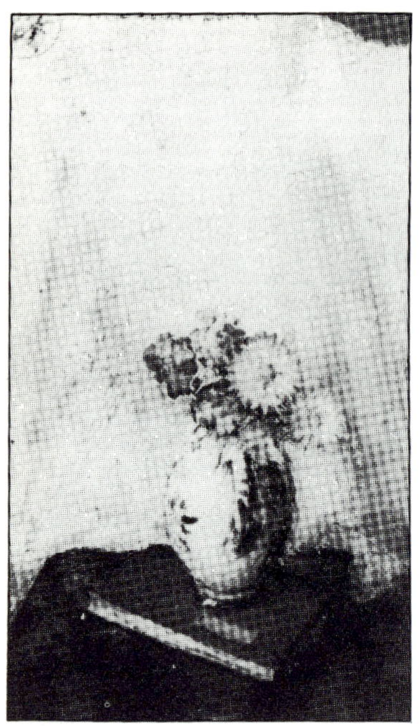

SIR WILLIAM NICHOLSON – Flowers In A Decorated Jug – signed and inscribed – canvas on board – 16 x 10½in.
(Sotheby's) **$1,188 £600**

ISAAK VAN NICKELEN – Interior Of The Groote Kerk, Haarlem – 13¼ x 11½in.
(Christie's) **$4,268 £2,200**

NIEMANN – 'View Of Windsor Castle' – signed – oil – 15½ x 25½in.
(J. Entwistle & Co.) **$537 £280**

EDMUND JOHN NIEMANN, JNR. – Windsor From Cooper's Hill; Windsor From Runnymede – signed, one inscribed, the other inscribed on the reverse, one dated 1870 – on board – 11¼ x 8¼in.
(Sotheby's Belgravia)
$594 £300 Pair

EDMUND JOHN NIEMANN, JNR. – Near Richmond – both signed and dated 1903, inscribed on the reverse – 19 x 29in.
(Sotheby's Belgravia)
$768 £400 Pair

EDMUND JOHN NIEMANN, JNR. – The Valley Of The Severn, Gloucester – 19 x 29½in.
(Sotheby's Belgravia)
$1,920 £1,000

EDMUND JOHN NIEMANN – Canterbury, A View From The River At Dusk With An Angler Seated On The Bank – signed and dated '62 – oil on canvas – 6½ x 19½in.
(Neales of Nottingham)
$1,346 £680

EDMUND JOHN NIEMANN – The Swale, Yorkshire With Richmond Castle – signed – 29¼ x 49¼in.
(Christie's) **$1,552 £800**

EDMUND JOHN NIEMANN – A Coastal Landscape With Fisherfolk And Beached Fishing Vessels – signed – on panel – 11½ x 8¼in.
(Christie's) **$970** **£500**

EDMUND JOHN NIEMANN – Dovedale – signed – 30 x 50in.
(Christie's) **$2,134** **£1,100**

NIEULANDT – A Ruined Castle In Italy – inscribed '1619' – pen and brown ink – 213 x 282mm.
(Christie's) **$228** **£120**

NIEULANDT – Virtutis Gloria – inscribed – on copper – 11¾ x 9¼in.
(Christie's) **$388** **£200**

BASIL NIGHTINGALE – His First Brush – signed, inscribed and dated 1905 – black chalk and coloured washes, heightened with white – 22½ x 34½in.
(Sotheby's Belgravia) **$436** **£220**

POLLOCK SINCLAIR NISBET – Gateway, Linlithgow Palace – signed, inscribed on the reverse – on board – 14 x 10in.
(Sotheby's) **$129** **£65**

POLLOCK SINCLAIR NISBET – San Remo; On A Swiss Lake – signed – on panel – 6 x 4½in.
(Sotheby's Belgravia) **$158** **£80 Pair**

POLLOCK SINCLAIR NISBET – The Queen's View – indistinctly signed and inscribed on the reverse – 24 x 36in.
(Sotheby's Belgravia) **$156** **£80**

POLLOCK S. NISBET – Loch Lomond – 42 x 71cm.
(Edmiston's) **$388** **£200**

ROBERT BUCHAN NISBET – Fishing Boats In Harbour – signed – 17½ x 22½in.
(Sotheby's) **$396** **£200**

ROBERT BUCHAN NISBET – Outside The Harbour – signed – 20½ x 19in.
(Sotheby's) **$277** **£140**

NOBLE – On The Dee, Balmoral – signed and dated 1878 – 19½ x 27½in.
(Sotheby's) **$396** **£200**

JAMES NOBLE – Still Life Of Spring Flowers, In A Vase On A Plinth – signed – 20 x 22in.
(Sotheby's) **$1,584** **£800**

ROBERT NOBLE – Preston Mill, Near East Linton – signed – on board – 21 x 13in.
(Sotheby's) **$437** **£220**

NOGARI – Portrait Of A Bearded Man, Half Length, In Oriental Dress – 26 x 21in.
(Sotheby's) **$2,716** **£1,400**

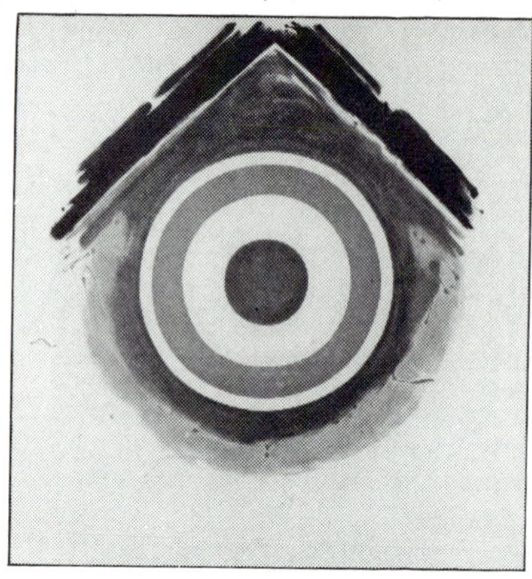

KENNETH NOLAND – Paint – dated 1959 on the reverse – acrylic on canvas – 72½ x 69¾in.
(Sotheby's) **$39,600** **£20,000**

PIETER NOLPE – A Dune Landscape With Peasants Outside A Cottage – on panel – 11¼ x 16¼in.
(Sotheby's) **$9,700** **£5,000**

ORLANDO NORIE – The Coldstream Guards Under Colonel George Upton, And Colonel Gordon Drummond Before Sebastopol, January And July 1855 – signed – heightened with bodycolour – 12½ x 18in.
(Sotheby's Belgravia) **$891** **£450 Pair**

O. NORIE – French Cavalry In Egypt – inscribed – 5 x 8in.
(Sotheby's Belgravia)
$59 **£30**

ORLANDO NORIE – The 6th Inniskilling Dragoons – signed – watercolour heightened with white – 7 x 11in.
(Christie's) **$330** **£170**

ORLANDO NORIE – The 3rd Hussars – signed – watercolour heightened with white – 7 x 11in.
(Christie's) **$310** **£160**

NORLONG – "Country Landscapes" – signed – watercolour drawings – 9¾ x 15¾in.
(J. Entwistle & Co.)
$15 **£8 Pair**

NORTH ITALIAN SCHOOL, circa 1500 – A Horse Near A Wall – pen and brown ink – 13.9 x 9.3cm.
(Christie's) **$672** **£350**

NORTH ITALIAN SCHOOL, early 19th century – Project For A Ceiling: The Court Of Psyche – pencil and watercolour, squared in pencil – 19.4 x 19.3cm.
(Christie's) **$268** **£140**

NORTHERN ITALIAN SCHOOL, 18th century – A Southern Landscape With Peasants Beside The Ruins Of An Antique Bridge – 24 x 18¼in.
(Sotheby's) **$1,746** **£900**

NORTH ITALIAN SCHOOL, circa 1600 – The Deposition – 53½ x 60in.
(Sotheby's) **$1,782** **£900**

NORTH ITALIAN SCHOOL, early 19th century – Design For A Pier Glass With A Consol Table – pen and brown ink and watercolour – 36.3 x 15.7cm.
(Christie's) **$460** **£240**

NORTH ITALIAN SCHOOL, late 17th century – A Romantic Landscape With Ruins, Figures And Animals – 32 x 46½in.
(Woolley & Wallis) **$1,370** **£700**

NORTH ITALIAN SCHOOL – Mountainous Landscape With Castle And Foreground Figures – 58 x 38in.
(Woolley & Wallis)
$574 **£290**

NORTH NETHERLANDISH SCHOOL, late 16th century, Follower of Cavaliere D'Arpino – The Crucifixion – 44 x 29¼in.
(Sotheby's) **$970** **£500**

BENJAMIN CAM NORTON – Hunters And A Spaniel Outside A Stable – signed and dated 1886 – 27 x 35in.
(Sotheby's) **$1,824** **£950**

CHARLES WILLIAM NORTON – 'Oh, Merry Goes The Time When The Heart is Young' – signed, inscribed on the reverse – 14 x 21in.
(Sotheby's Belgravia) **$440** **£220**

NORWICH SCHOOL – A Norfolk Wooded River Scene With Barges Unloading, Numerous Figures – oil – 11 x 7in.
(G. A. Key) **$693** **£350**

PIETRO ANTONIO NOVELLI – Frontispiece To Il Censimento Di Milano: Venice Enthroned With A Scribe, Justice And Attributes Of The Arts Below, And A View Of Milan Behind – signed – pen and brown ink on vellum – 37.2 x 23.7cm.
(Christie's) **$1,920** **£1,000**

J. NOTERMAN – Four Dogs Resting By An Open Fire Over Which Hangs A Cauldron – signed – oil – on panel – 17 x 22.5cm.
(Henry Spencer & Sons) **$950** **£480**

STEPHANO NOVO – Portrait Of A Pretty Girl – signed and dated 1893, inscribed – oil on canvas – 23¼ x 14½in.
(Bonham's) **$2,940** **£1,500**

J. NUTTER – On The Coast – signed, one dated 1917, the other 1924 – 7¾ x 11½in.
(Sotheby's Belgravia) **$108** **£55 Two**

WILLIAM HENRY NUTTER – A View Of Carlisle Abbey Ruins – signed and dated 1859 – 7 x 11¼in.
(Lawrence) **$380** **£200**

WILLIAM HENRY NUTTER – A Topographical View Of Carlisle – signed and dated 1859 – 7 x 11½in.
(Lawrence) **$520** **£260**

NUZZI – A Still Life Of Flowers, With A Peacock, All In A Landscape – 29 x 41¾in.
(Sotheby's) **$455** **£230**

M. NUZZI – Still Life Pictures Of Flowers In Gilt Vases, All On Stone Ledges – 21¼ x 54in.
(Sotheby's) **$3,564** **£1,800 Pair**

O

JOHN WRIGHT OAKES – A Coastal Scene With Beached Fishing Vessels At Sunset – signed and dated '78 – 34¼ x 49½in.
(Christie's) **$970** **£500**

JAMES ARTHUR O'CONNOR – An Angler On A Rock In A Wooded River Landscape; and Figures On A Woodland Path – one signed – 11¾ x 9½in.
(Sotheby's) **$6,138** **£3,100 Pair**

JAMES ARTHUR O'CONNOR – A Horseman Passing Queen Eleanor's Cross – on panel – 8 x 10in.
(Sotheby's) **$1,624** **£820**

JAMES ARTHUR O'CONNOR – A Woman Sitting By A Path In A Hilly Landscape – signed and dated 1832 – 9¾ x 13½in.
(Sotheby's) **$4,158** **£2,100**

JOHN O'CONNOR – A Mountainous Landscape With Groups Of Figures And Finely Detailed Trees – signed and dated – 14 x 18in.
(Russell, Baldwin & Bright)
$2,548 **£1,300**

H. R. ODDY – A Valley On The Moors – signed and dated '89 – watercolour heightened with white – 11½ x 18½in.
(Christie's) **$49** **£25**

PIXIE O'HARRIS – Midsummer Night's Dream – signed – watercolour – 30 x 43.5cm.
(Australian Art Auctions) **$220** **£112**

W. OLIVER – Girl With Basket Of Roses – 76 x 51cm.
(Edmiston's) **$349** **£180**

WILLIAM OLIVER – Reflections – signed, inscribed on a label on the reverse – 35 x 27in.
(Sotheby's Belgravia) **$3,622** **£1,800**

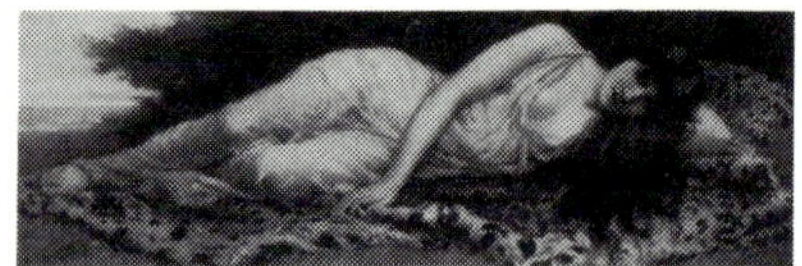

WILLIAM OLIVER – Exotic Thoughts – signed – 13 x 39in.
(Sotheby's Belgravia) **$5,231** **£2,600**

WILLIAM OLIVER – The Easter Bonnet – signed – 17½ x 13½in.
(Sotheby's Belgravia) **$317** **£160**

DAN O'NEILL – Portrait Of The Artist In His Studio – signed – 24 x 20in.
(Sotheby's) **$1,086** **£560**

GEORGE BERNARD O'NEILL – Market Day, Arrival Of The Hippodrome – signed – oil – 33 x 11in.
(Bonham's) **$20,790 £10,500**

GEORGE BERNARD O'NEILL – Family Treasures – signed and dated '86 – on panel – 13½ x 10in.
(Sotheby's Belgravia) **$9,054 £4,500**

C. ONOFRI – A View Near Tivoli – 51¾ x 37½in.
(Sotheby's) **$2,772 £1,400**

ONSLOW – The 'Russia', a three-masted barque, off the coast – 21½ x 31½in.
(Sotheby's Belgravia) **$134 £70**

ADRIAEN VAN OOLEN – An Evening Landscape – oil – 41½ x 64in.
(Bonham's) **$17,820 £9,000**

JAN FRANS VAN BLOEMEN, Called Orizzonte – A Classical Landscape With A River – 32 x 46¾in.
(Sotheby's) **$8,232 £4,200**

B. VAN ORLEY – Christ Bearing The Cross – on panel – 22 x 27½in.
(Sotheby's) **$75,660 £39,000**

SCHOOL OF BAREND VAN ORLEY – Figures In A Classical Interior – on panel – 38½ x 18½in.
(Sotheby's) **$3,960 £2,000**

W. ORMEA – A Still Life Of Fish, A Cod And A Crab On A Wooden Ledge – on panel – 22½ x 34¾in.
(Sotheby's) **$2,134 £1,100**

SIR WILLIAM ORPEN – The Letter – signed – 35½ x 33½in.
(Sotheby's) **$13,580** **£7,000**

SIR WILLIAM ORPEN – A Self Portrait Of The Artist Standing Before His Easel – signed – 29 x 21in.
(Sotheby's) **$4,850** **£2,500**

SIR WILLIAM ORPEN – Reflection, A Self Portrait – 29½ x 24½in.
(Sotheby's) **$17,460** **£9,000**

J. ORROCK – A Watermill – 8 x 11½in.
(Sotheby's Belgravia) **$76** **£40**

JAMES ORROCK – St. Andrews – signed, inscribed and dated 1888 – 11 x 16in.
(Sotheby's) **$230** **£120**

JAMES ORROCK – Near Askrigg Moor, Yorkshire – signed and dated 1877 – watercolour – 8¾ x 13¼in.
(Christie's) **$291** **£150**

JAMES ORROCK – Hindhead From The Hog's Back – signed, inscribed and dated 1910 – black chalk and watercolour heightened with white – 35¾ x 51¾in.
(Christie's) **$272** **£140**

MARTIN ORTHNER – A Trompe L'Oeil With A Drawing Of A Bird – signed and dated 1772 – pen and black ink and watercolour – 273 x 194mm.
(Christie's) **$114** **£60**

JAN VAN OS – Roses, Tulips, Convolvulus, Carnations And Other Flowers In A Sculpted Urn On A Plinth With A Bird's Nest In A Landscape – signed – on panel – 25¾ x 20¼in.
(Christie's) **$105,600** **£55,000**

JAN VAN OS – Roses And Other Flowers With Grapes, A Melon And Other Fruit, On A Stone Ledge In A Landscape – signed and dated 1774 – on panel – 29¾ x 22¾in.
(Christie's) **$96,000 £50,000**

JAN VAN OS – Roses, Tulips, Carnations And Other Flowers, In A Sculpted Urn On A Plinth, In A Landscape – signed – on panel – 29¾ x 22¾in.
(Christie's) **$172,800 £90,000**

VAN OS – Roses, Tulips, Carnations, Delphiniums And Other Flowers In A Terracotta urn; and Roses, Lilies, Narcissi, Irises And Other Flowers In A Terracotta Urn – 49 x 39½in.
(Christie's) **$3,686 £1,900 Pair**

VAN OS – Roses And Other Flowers In A Vase On A Stone Ledge – 13¾ x 11¼in.
(Christie's) **$4,074 £2,100**

WALTER FREDERICK OSBORNE – Scarecrows – signed and dated '88 – 10 x 6in.
(Sotheby's) **$1,649 £850**

WILLIAM OSBORNE – Two Terriers, Seated By A Step – signed with monogram – 24 x 28½in.
(Sotheby's) **$1,552 £800**

HENRY O'SHEA – By An Italian Lake – signed and dated 1892 – 14¾ x 25¾in.
(Sotheby's) **$155 £80**

OSTADE – Peasants Drinking In An Interior – 13 x 10¼in.
(Christie's) **$388** **£200**

OSTADE – An Allegorical Scene With Satyrs Around A Plant Sprouting Female's Head – signed and dated 1697 – oil on canvas – 13 x 17in.
(The Manchester Auction Mart.) **$604** **£300**

VAN OSTADE – The Interior Of A Tavern, Men Around A Barrel Drinking – on panel – 11 x 15in.
(Sotheby's) **$2,134** **£1,100**

ADRIAEN VAN OSTADE – Peasants Outside An Inn – on panel – 9½ x 12½in.
(Sotheby's) **$9,700** **£5,000**

ADRIAEN JANSZ. VAN OSTADE – Figures Outside An Inn – signed and indistinctly dated – 14 x 12¼in.
(Christie's) **$26,880** **£14,000**

I. VAN OSTADE – Peasants In An Interior – on panel – 10 x 8¼in.
(Christie's) **$1,649** **£850**

ISACK JANSZ. VAN OSTADE – A Frozen River Landscape, With Numerous Figures, Horse-Drawn Sleighs And Skaters By A Village Inn – signed – on panel – 23¼ x 31¼in.
(Christie's) **$518,400** **£270,000**

SEAN O'SULLIVAN – A Study Of A Nude Woman From The Back, Standing With Her Head Turned – inscribed on the reverse – black pencil – 12 x 4½in.
(Sotheby's) **$349** **£180**

C. W. OSWALD – Highland Cattle By A Loch – signed – 30 x 20in.
(Sotheby's Belgravia) **$106** **£55**

JOHN H. OSWALD – Florence From The Arno – signed, inscribed on the reverse – 8 x 12in.
(Sotheby's Belgravia) **$247** **£130**

JOHN H. OSWALD – West Wemyss Harbour, Low Water – signed and dated 1864, inscribed on the reverse – 15¼ x 27½in.
(Sotheby's) **$458** **£260**

JOHN H. OSWALD – Isola San Giorgio, Venice – signed, inscribed on the reverse – 11½ x 17½in.
(Sotheby's Belgravia) **$285** **£150**

PIERRE OUTIN – 'La Belle Modiste', An Interior Scene – signed and inscribed – oil on canvas – 67 x 90cm.
(King & Chasemore) **$17,028** **£8,600**

J. OVENS – The Death Of Sophonisba, Receiving The Cup Of Poison From A Messenger In Armour – on panel – 35 x 31½in.
(Sotheby's) **$1,358** **£700**

ERNEST OWEN – A View In The Country – signed and dated 1923 – 39 x 51½in.
(Sotheby's Belgravia)
$119 **£60**

J. OWEN – A Highland Loch – signed – 20 x 30in.
(Sotheby's Belgravia)
$48 **£25**

S. OWEN – 'A Seascape With Fishing Smacks And A Man-O'-War In The Distance – watercolour – 18 x 26cm.
(King & Chasemore)
$315 **£160**

P

FRANCESCO DE ROSA, Called Pacecco – Abraham And The Three Angels – 60 x 79½in.
(Christie's) **$6,208** **£3,200**

PAOLO PAGANI – Angels Hovering Above Gesturing Nude Figures (recto); Saint Francis Interceding For The Souls Of The Damned (verso) – black chalk, pen and brown ink, brown wash – 41.9 x 27.8cm.
(Christie's) **$2,880** **£1,500**

HENRY MAURICE PAGE – A Shepherd And His Flock – signed – 16 x 24in.
(Sotheby's Belgravia) **$238** **£120**

G. PAICE – 'The Camel', A Study Of A Hunter – signed and dated '07 – oil – 14 x 18in.
(Warner Sheppard & Wade)
$177 **£85**

GEORGE PAICE – A Grey Hunter – signed and dated '18 – 19¼ x 29½in.
(Sotheby's) **$757** **£390**

GEORGE PAICE – A Chestnut In A Stable – signed and dated '84 – 19¼ x 26¼in.
(Sotheby's Belgravia)
$218 **£110**

GEORGE PAICE – Portrait Of Brown Stout And Prince, Black And Bay Hunters Held By A Huntsman, In An Extensive Landscape – signed and dated '93 – on board – 25 x 35cm.
(Henry Spencer & Sons)
$554 **£280**

GEORGE PAICE – A Bay Hunter In His Stable – on board – 6½ x 9½in.
(Sotheby's Belgravia)
$238 **£120**

GEORGE PAICE – Laddie; A Harrier From The Gifford Pack – signed and inscribed – 10 x 12in.
(Sotheby's Belgravia)
$129 **£65 Two**

PAICE – A Solitude, The Woods At Sandhurst; Earlswood, Surrey – inscribed – 6 x 9in. and 9 x 6½in.
(Sotheby's Belgravia)
$139 **£70 Two**

ANTHONIE PALAMEDESZ. – A Musical Party In An Interior – on panel – 17¼ x 13¼in.
(Sotheby's) **$6,596** **£3,400**

HARRY SUTTON PALMER – A Wiltshire Stream – signed – 10 x 13¾in.
(Sotheby's Belgravia)
$1,067 **£550**

HARRY SUTTON PALMER – Summer Sunshine, Haslemere – signed and inscribed on the reverse – watercolour – 15½ x 24¼in.
(Christie's) **$1,552** **£800**

HARRY SUTTON PALMER – Study Of A Fawn – signed, inscribed and dated 1893 – heightened with white – 18½ x 25in.
(Sotheby's Belgravia)
$35 **£18**

HARRY SUTTON PALMER – Autumn In Surrey – signed – 21¾ x 30¼in.
(Sotheby's) **$2,079** **£1,050**

GIOVANNI PAOLO PANNINI *(ca. 1692-1765(?))* – Rome: The Piazza Navona – 20¾ x 42½in.
(Sotheby's) **$79,200** **£40,000**

PANNINI – A Capriccio View, With Figures Amongst Roman Ruins – 25½ x 39½in.
(Sotheby's) **$3,104** **£1,600**

PANNINI – The Colosseum, Rome, With Washerwomen – 39½ x 45in.
(Christie's) **$388** **£200**

G. P. PANNINI – An Architectural Capriccio With Figures In The Foreground And The Arch Of Constantine Beyond – 26¼ x 39¾in.
(Christie's) **$4,656** **£2,400**

G. P. PANNINI – Figures By Classical Ruins – 20¾ x 16½in.
(Christie's) **$2,134** **£1,100**

JACOPO DI PAOLO – St. John The Baptist – on panel – 29 x 10½in.
(Sotheby's) **$7,448** **£3,800**

G. J. PAPPAS – Mixed Flowers In Vase Resting In A Wall Niche With Butterfly – signed – oil – 23 x 18in.
(G. A. Key) **$72** **£36**

WALTER PARIS – The Forest Stream, Brockenhurst – signed and dated 1886 – watercolour – 10½ x 15in.
(Christie's) **$233** **£120**

PARISH – First View Of The Great Wall Of China, From The Pass Of Coope Koo – inscribed – from a sketch dated 1793 – watercolour – 7 x 10¼in.
(Sotheby's (Hong Kong) Ltd.) **$119** **£60**

JAMES STUART PARK – Still Life Of Red And White Roses – signed – 19 x 15in.
(Sotheby's) **$238** **£120**

JAMES STUART PARK – Still Life Of Geraniums – signed – 19½ x 15½in.
(Sotheby's) **$422** **£220**

J. STUART PARK – Pink And White Roses – circular – diameter 39cm.
(Edmiston's) **$679** **£350**

HENRY H. PARKER – A Surrey Cornfield Near Godalming – signed, inscribed on the reverse – 11½ x 17½in.
(Sotheby's Belgravia) **$2,213** **£1,100**

HENRY H. PARKER – The Mole, Dorking, Surrey – signed – 19¼ x 29¼in.
(Sotheby's Belgravia)
$6,036 £3,000

J. PARKER – 'Young Girl Before A Window' – oil on canvas – 18 x 15in.
(W. H. Lane & Son)
$388 £200

PARMIGIANINO – Portrait Of A Gentleman, Standing Three-Quarter Length, In An Interior Wearing Black And Brown Robes – 40¼ x 32½in.
(Christie's) **$1,287 £650**

EDMUND THOMAS PARRIS – Portrait Of William Aubrey De Vere Beauclerk, 9th Duke Of St. Albans, Grand Falconer Of England, With Elizabeth, Duchess Of St. Albans On Horseback, With Falconers – signed, inscribed and dated 1840 – 84 x 62in.
(Christie's) **$5,820 £3,000**

J. I. PARROCEL – An Extensive Southern Landscape With Cavaliers, Conversing Beneath A Tree To The Right, Bands Of Soldiers To The Left And Beyond – 20 x 29½in.
(Sotheby's) **$2,364 £1,200**

W. PARROTT – The Boulevard Des Italiens, Paris, After The Abdication Of Louis Philippe – 28 x 36in.
(Christie's) **$1,358 £700**

A. WILDE PARSONS – Fishing Boat Leaving Harbour – signed – oil on board – 11½ x 15½in.
(Morphets of Harrogate)
$109 £55

ARTHUR WILDE PARSONS – A Three-Masted Sailing Vessel Beats Up Portsmouth Harbour Before Three Dismasted Hulks On A Stormy Day – signed and dated 1904 – watercolour – 13 x 27¾in.
(Osmond, Tricks & Son)
$990 £500

ARTHUR WILDE PARSONS – A Dutch Sailing Barge Passing A Windmill On A Blustery Day; and A Dutch Sailing Barge Entering Port In A Fresh Breeze – signed and dated '83 – oil on canvas – 9½ x 13¾in.
(Osmond, Tricks & Son)
$1,782 £900 Pair

ARTHUR WILDE PARSONS – Busy Estuary Scene With Sailing Barges And Other Shipping On A Blustery Day – signed and dated 1904 – watercolour – 11¾ x 25½in.
(Osmond, Tricks & Son) **$535** **£270**

BEATRICE PARSONS – July Joyous – signed – 7 x 10in.
(Sotheby's Belgravia) **$129** **£65**

J. H. E. PARTINGTON – A Penny Whistle – signed – 15¼ x 21¼in.
(Sotheby's Belgravia) **$422** **£220**

ERNEST PARTON – On The Pang, Pangbourne; A Bit Of Surrey – signed – 15½ x 23½in.
(Sotheby's Belgravia) **$950** **£500 Pair**

JEAN BARTH PASCAL – An Extensive Wooded Landscape – signed, inscribed and dated 1828 on reverse – oil on canvas – 40 x 54in.
(Bonham's) **$6,336** **£3,200**

JULES PASCIN – Modele Couchee – 22¼ x 20in.
(Sotheby's) **$6,237** **£3,100**

JOHN F. PASMORE – The Fisherman And His Daughter – signed with monogram – 12 x 16in.
(Christie's) **$1,067** **£550**

JOHN F. PASMORE – A Merry Feast – signed – 21 x 36in.
(Christie's) **$1,164** **£600**

JOHN F. PASMORE – Gypsies – signed with monogram – on board – 14 x 18in
(Sotheby's Belgravia)
$554 **£280**

VICTOR PASMORE – Triangular Motif: The Indian Man, 1950 – signed with initals – 19¾ x 15½in.
(Sotheby's) **$1,386** **£700**

R. D. PASQUALL – A Busy Continental Port – signed – 17½ x 23½in.
(Sotheby's Belgravia) **$614** **£320**

BARTOLOMMEO PASSAROTTI, Attributed to – Head Of A Young Woman – inscribed and with an old inscription on the reverse – pen and brown ink – 19.4 x 15cm.
(Christie's) **$537** **£280**

P. PATEL – A Wooded River Landscape With Figures By A Classical Monument – bears signature and date – 18¼ x 22in.
(Christie's) **$634** **£320**

JEAN-BAPTISTE PATER *(1695-1736)* – 'L'Embarquement Pour Cythere' – 25 x 31½in.
(Sotheby's) **$128,700** **£65,000**

EMILY M. PATERSON – Fishing Boats, Venice – signed – 10½ x 15in.
(Sotheby's Belgravia) **$38** **£20**

TOM PATERSON – Summer Games – signed – heightened with white – 10 x 14in.
(Sotheby's Belgravia) **$34** **£18**

SIR JOSEPH NOEL PATON – The Madonna And Child – signed with monogram and dated 1876 – pen and sepia ink – circular – diameter 4½in.
(Sotheby's) **$89** **£45**

WALLER HUGH PATON – In Glen Moriston – signed – heightened with bodycolour – 9¾ x 14½in.
(Sotheby's) **$693** **£350**

WALLER HUGH PATON – A Beached Fishing Boat – signed – on panel – 11½ x 17½in.
(Sotheby's) **$652** **£340**

WALLER HUGH PATON – On A Highland Loch – signed – 16 x 21in.
(Sotheby's) **$365** **£190**

WALLER HUGH PATON – By A Loch – signed – 6½ x 14in.
(Sotheby's Belgravia) **$173** **£90**

W. H. PATON – An Extensive Highland Valley – heightened with white – 13½ x 21½in.
(Sotheby's Belgravia) **$124** **£65**

ALFRED FOWLER PATTEN – What Shall I Write? – signed and dated 1873 – 19¼ x 15¼in.
(Sotheby's Belgravia) **$887** **£450**

J. WILLIAM PATTISON – A Shepherd With His Daughter And Dog, And A Flock Of Sheep, In An Orchard – signed – watercolour – 16 x 20¼in.
(Geering & Colyer) **$376** **£190**

JAMES PATTERSON – Lilies Of France – signed, inscribed and dated 1918 on the reverse – 36 x 27½in.
(Sotheby's) **$614** **£320**

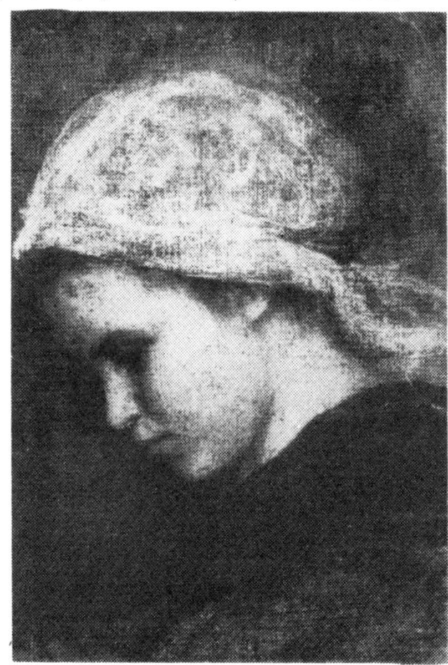

FRITZ PAULSEN – Portrait Of A Small Girl – signed, inscribed on the reverse – 7½ x 5½in.
(Sotheby's Belgravia) **$355** **£180**

PAYNE – Country Pastimes – 13½ x 20½in.
(Sotheby's Belgravia) **$247** **£130**

FRANK PAYNE – Childhood – signed – oil on board – 43 x 30cm.
(Australian Art Auctions)
$116 **£59**

WILLIAM PAYNE – Chepstow Castle On The River Wye, The Bristol Channel In The Distance – 17¼ x 24in.
(Sotheby's) **$1,513** **£780**

WILLIAM PAYNE – Rocks And Trees With A Hilltop Monastery, Monks Walking By The Water – 11¼ x 16½in.
(Sotheby's) **$293** **£150**

BRYAN PEARCE – 'St. Ives Harbour' – oil on canvas – 20 x 24in.
(W. H. Lane & Son) **$538** **£280**

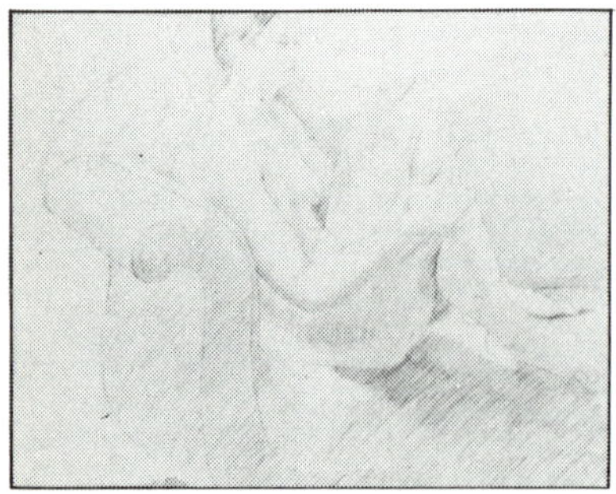

PHILIP PEARLSTEIN – Seated Female Nude – signed and dated 1971 – pencil on paper on canvas – 18¾ x 23½in.
(Sotheby's) **$891** **£450**

P. PEARS – A 'Vanitas' Still Life, Bubbles In A Dish, An Expiring Candle, A Celestial Globe, A Book Open On A Table Covered By A Pink Cloth With A Gold Fringe – signed and dated 1674 – on panel – 7¾ x 7in.
(Sotheby's) **$13,192** **£6,800**

CORNELIUS PEARSON – An Afternoon's Fishing – signed and dated 1865 – heightened with bodycolour – 11 x 21in.
(Sotheby's Belgravia)
$175 **£90**

HARRY JOHN PEARSON – Pleasantries – signed, inscribed on the reverse – on panel – 11 x 9in.
(Sotheby's Belgravia)
$106 **£55**

W. H. PEARSON – Trawlers Off Shoreham; and Beating To Windward – signed and inscribed – heightened with white – 16 x 27in.
(Sotheby's Belgravia)
$433 **£220 Pair**

JOHN PEDDER – Fetching Water – signed – heightened with bodycolour – 10½ x 14½in.
(Sotheby's Belgravia) **$69** **£35**

JOHN PEDDER – A Border Landscape – signed and dated 1886, and inscribed on a label on the reverse – 29 x 49½in.
(Sotheby's Belgravia) **$594** **£300**

J. PEEL – In A Valley – 11½ x 15½in.
(Sotheby's Belgravia)
$304 **£160**

JAMES PEEL – An Extensive Summer Landscape With Figures And A Horse And Cart Near Hazlemere, Surrey – signed on a label on reverse and inscribed – oil on canvas – 18 x 30in.
(Bonham's) **$2,548** **£1,300**

JAMES PEEL – On The Ribble Near Walton – circular – diameter 10½in.
(Christie's) **$737** **£380**

JAMES PEEL – Near Swaledale, Yorkshire – inscribed on an old label on the reverse – 15½ x 23¼in.
(Christie's) **$1,649** **£850**

B. PEETERS – A Shipwreck Off A Rocky Coast – 35¼ x 48½in.
(Sotheby's) **$1,584** **£800**

BONAVENTURA PEETERS – The Port Of Copenhagen, With Numerous Dutch, Danish, And Swedish Ships – signed with initials – on panel – 28½ x 40in.
(Sotheby's) **$20,370** **£10,400**

BONAVENTURA PEETERS – The Battle Of Lepanto – 31¾ x 51¾in.
(Christie's) **$21,120** **£11,000**

GILLIS PEETERS – A Coastal Landscape With A Sailing Vessel In A Choppy Sea – on panel – 5 x 7½in.
(Christie's) **$621** **£320**

THOMAS KENT PELHAM – In A Spanish Street – signed – 23½ x 17½in.
(Sotheby's Belgravia) **$760** **£400**

GIOVANNI ANTONIO PELLEGRINI, Attributed to – The Drunken Silenus – black and red chalk, pen and brown ink, brown wash – 18.2 x 26.2cm.
(Christie's) **$499 £260**

AARON EDWIN PENLEY – An Italian Farmhouse With A Tower – signed and dated 1857 – watercolour – 9 x 12½in.
(Christie's) **$97 £50**

ANDREW M. PENNEY – Upland Landscapes – signed and dated 1913 – one heightened with bodycolour – 9½ x 13½in.
(Sotheby's Belgravia) **$58 £30 Pair**

EDWIN PENNY – Study Of A White Sulphur Crested Cockatoo Perched Upon A Branch Upon Which Is Impaled An Orange – signed – watercolour heightened with bodycolour – 14¼ x 9¾in.
(Osmond, Tricks & Son) **$554 £280**

ALBERT JOSEPH PENOT – 'Female Nude' – signed – oil on canvas – 21¾ x 15in.
(Lalonde Bros. & Parham) **$1,188 £600**

SAMUEL JOHN PEPLOE – The White Sands, Iona – on panel – 5¾ x 9in.
(Sotheby's) **$1,728 £900**

JOHN PERCEVAL – Swy Game – 71 x 92cm.
(Australian Art Auctions) **$234 £122**

SIDNEY RICHARD PERCY – An Approaching Storm In The Hills – signed and dated 1850 – 39 x 59in.
(Sotheby's Belgravia) **$3,420 £1,700**

SIDNEY RICHARD PERCY – A Rest On The Road, Summer Noon – signed and dated '53 – 15 x 24in.
(Sotheby's Belgravia) **$5,231 £2,600**

SIDNEY RICHARD PERCY – A Wooded River Landscape With A Boatman – signed with initials – 9½ x 14¾in.
(Christie's) **$1,746** **£900**

SIDNEY RICHARD PERCY – The Haymakers – signed and dated '59 – 23½ x 37½in.
(Sotheby's Belgravia) **$9,658** **£4,800**

SIDNEY RICHARD PERCY – Llyn Ddinas, North Wales – inscribed and dated 1872 – 23¼ x 39½in.
(Sotheby's Belgravia) **$1,408** **£700**

SIDNEY RICHARD PERCY – Cattle In The Heather – signed and dated '85 – 29 x 49½in.
(Sotheby's Belgravia) **$2,414** **£1,200**

SIDNEY RICHARD PERCY – Near Dolgelly, North Wales – signed and dated 1855 – 39½ x 71in.
(Sotheby's Belgravia)
$2,616 **£1,300**

SIDNEY RICHARD PERCY – Near Barmouth, North Wales – signed – paper on board – 9½ x 14½in.
(Christie's) **$621** **£320**

SIDNEY RICHARD WILLIAMS PERCY – Ullswater – signed and dated 1872 – oil on canvas – 24 x 36in.
(Bonham's) **$10,890** **£5,500**

S. R. PERCY – A View In The Mountains – inscribed – 11½ x 23½in.
(Sotheby's Belgravia) **$326** **£170**

PEREDA – A Still Life Of Books On A Draped Table – 33½ x 43½in.
(Christie's) **$3,492** **£1,800**

ARTHUR PERIGAL – Mountain Scenery In Sutherland Near Laxford, Showing Foinavon, Arkle And Ben Stack – signed and dated 1869, inscribed on a label – 37 x 62in.
(Sotheby's) **$1,344** **£700**

ARTHUR PERIGAL – Trout Fishing – signed – 20¼ x 30in.
(Sotheby's) **$806** **£420**

L. E. PERMAN – Pink Roses – 35 x 44cm.
(Edmiston's) **$194** **£100**

FRANCOIS PERRIER – The Triumph Of Amphitrite, Neptune And Amphitrite On A Fantastic Chariot Drawn By Sea-Horses – 44½ x 65in.
(Sotheby's) **$3,528** **£1,800**

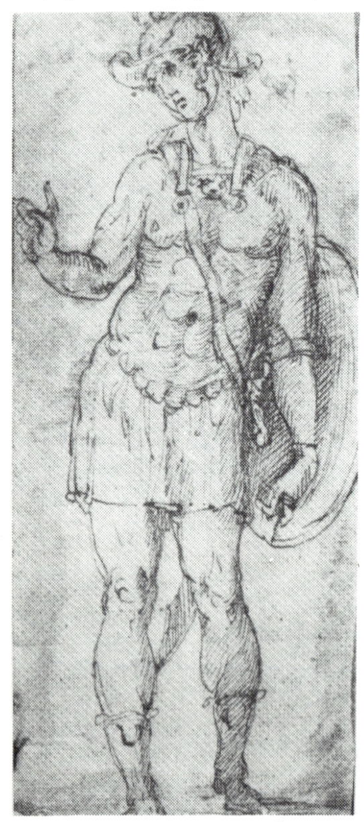

BALDASSARE PERUZZI, Circle of – A Classical Warrior With A Shield – pen and brown ink – 20.5 x 8.4cm.
(Christie's) **$307** **£160**

PERUGINO – Saint John The Evangelist – on panel – 21½ x 8¾in.
(Christie's) **$1,746** **£900**

ANTOINE PESNE – The Dancer Santina Olivieri, Called La Reggiana, As Leda – 38½ x 46in.
(Christie's) **$8,640** **£4,500**

PETHER – Windsor Castle By Moonlight – 44 x 59cm.
(Edmiston's) **$679** **£350**

HENRY PETHER – The Bridge Of The Rialto, Venice – signed and inscribed – 33½ x 54½in.
(Sotheby's Belgravia) **$5,231** **£2,600**

HENRY PETHER – Abingdon By Moonlight – signed – 23 x 35in.
(Sotheby's Belgravia) **$6,336** **£3,200**

HENRY PETHER – The Rialto Bridge – 21 x 29in.
(Sotheby's Belgravia) **$515** **£260**

SEBASTIAN PETHER – A Moonlit Estuary With Fishermen In The Foreground And A Bridge Beyond – 29 x 43in.
(Christie's) **$776** **£400**

ANTOINE BAPTISTE PETIT – Mosquee De Tayloun, Le Caire – inscribed 1848 – oil on paper – 11¼ x 8½in.
(Sotheby's) **$119** **£60**

JAMES PETRIE – Portrait Of The Rt. Hon. John Philpot Curran, The Irish Judge, Politician, And Orator, Half Length, Wearing A Black Coat – 29 x 24in.
(Sotheby's) **$1,164** **£600**

JOSEPH PAUL PETTITT – A Mountain Path, North Wales – signed and dated '65, inscribed on the reverse – 15 x 23½in.
(Sotheby's Belgravia) **$633** **£320**

LUDWIG PFLEGER – Apfel Und Biern Mispel – inscribed – watercolour – 477 x 315mm.
(Christie's) **$380** **£200**

J. PHILLIP – A Spanish Fruit-Seller – inscribed with monogram – 17½ x 13½in.
(Sotheby's Belgravia)
$148 **£75**

J. PHILLIP – Portrait Of A Girl With Long Dark Hair Wearing A Flower-Trimmed Hat, Brown Dress And Green Kerchief, Standing Against A Background Of Trees – monogramed and dated 1858 – oil on canvas – 72.5 x 62cm.
(Henry Spencer & Sons)
$281 **£145**

JOHN PHILLIP – Study Of An Eastern Interior – watercolour – 32 x 48cm.
(Edmiston's) **$70** **£36**

A. PHILLIPS – On Deck – signed – on metal – 19 x 21½in.
(Sotheby's Belgravia)
$148 **£75 Two**

PHILPOT – A Chinese Street Scene – signed – watercolour – 11¾ x 8in.
(Sotheby's (Hong Kong) Ltd.) **$216** **£109**

G. B. PIAZZETTA – A Young Woman Holding A Basket – black and white chalk on grey paper – 38.5 x 28.8cm.
(Christie's) **$499** **£260**

PABLO PICASSO – Femme Au Chapeau a Fleurs – signed and dated '44 – 32 x 25½in.
(Sotheby's) **$118,800** **£60,000**

PABLO PICASSO – Nature Morte, Fruits, Compotier, Carafe Sur Une Table – signed and dated '38 – 23¾ x 28¾in.
(Sotheby's) **$114,840** **£58,000**

FREDERICK RICHARD PICKERSGILL – The Duke Orsino And Viola – signed with initials – on panel – 17¾ x 13¼in.
(Christie's) **$776** **£400**

FREDERICK RICHARD PICKERSGILL – The Dance To Colin's Melody; an illustration to Spenser's 'Faerie Queene' – on panel – 27 x 54in.
(Christie's) **$15,520** **£8,000**

FREDERICK RICHARD PICKERSGILL – A Mother's Love – signed with monogram and dated 1862 – 19½ x 23½in.
(Sotheby's Belgravia) **$4,426 £2,200**

FREDERICK RICHARD PICKERSGILL – Phaedra And Cymocles, A Study – 6½ x 7½in.
(Sotheby's Belgravia) **$27 £14**

FREDERICK RICHARD PICKERSGILL – The Coronation Of Joan Of Arc – pencil heightened with bodycolour and coloured washes – 5¾ x 3¾in.
(Sotheby's Belgravia) **$57 £30**

PIEDMONT SCHOOL, early 18th century – Portrait Of A Little Girl – 25 x 18¾in.
(Sotheby's) **$1,764 £900**

NICOLAES PIEMONT – An Extensive Rocky River Landscape With An Angler In The Foreground – 21 x 28½in.
(Christie's) **$1,746 £900**

ARNOLD PIENNE – Highland Cattle On The Moor – signed with initials – on board – 14 x 18in.
(Sotheby's Belgravia) **$73 £38**

GEORGE PIENNE – Fishing Boats On The Beach – signed and dated '98 – 11½ x 23in.
(Sotheby's Belgravia) **$171 £90**

G. DE PIENNE – The River Teith, Doune – signed, inscribed on the reverse – 17¼ x 29½in.
(Sotheby's Belgravia) **$250 £130**

JACOB HENDRIK PIERNEEF – Trees In The Eastern Transvaal – signed – pen and red crayon, on brown paper – 10¾ x 14½in.
(Sotheby's) **$168 £85**

PIETER PIETERSZ. – The Prodigal Son In A Black Doublet With Violet Sleeves – 41¾ x 55in.
(Sotheby's) **$11,252 £5,800**

SANO DI PIETRO *(1406-1481)* – The Madonna And Child With Saints And Angels – gold ground – on panel – 26¼ x 18½in.
(Sotheby's) **$47,520 £24,000**

SANO DI PIETRO *(1406-1481)* – The Madonna And Child – gold ground – on panel – 13½ x 10¾in.
(Sotheby's) **$43,560 £22,000**

H. PIFFARD – 'The Proposal' – signed – on canvas – 60 x 50cm.
(King & Chasemore) **$806 £420**

ADALBERT PILCH – The Collector, An Elderly Gentleman Seated At A Table Studying Drawings, A Young Gentleman Wearing A Fur-Trimmed Robe Looks Over His Shoulder – signed – oil on canvas – 50 x 61cm.
(Henry Spencer & Sons) **$851 £430**

PILLEMENT – An Extensive Southern Landscape With Travellers Beside A Stream; A Mounted Figure And A Traveller In A Wooded Landscape – 19¼ x 23¼in.
(Sotheby's) **$4,950 £2,500 Pair**

JEAN PILLEMENT – A Coastal Landscape, With A Sailing Vessel In A Stormy Sea And Fishermen On The Rocks In The Foreground – signed and dated 1785 – 21 x 31in.
(Christie's) **$17,200 £9,000**

JEAN BAPTISTE PILLEMENT – A Winter Scene With A Cottage By A River – signed and dated 1805 – pastel – 45.8 x 57.5cm.
(Christie's) **$729** **£380**

JEAN BAPTISTE PILLEMENT – A Goatherd On A River Bank Opposite A Cabin; and Herdsmen Near A Cottage – both signed – black and white pastel – 29.2 x 31.8cm.
(Christie's) **$2,304** **£1,200 Pair**

D. PIOLA – A Peasant Girl Milking A Goat – 58½ x 43½in.
(Christie's) **$2,328** **£1,200**

JOHN PIPER – Connemara Landscape – signed – 47¾ x 59½in.
(Sotheby's) **$1,552** **£800**

JOHN PIPER – Construction, 1935 – oil, sand and wood on board – 21 x 24¾in.
(Sotheby's) **$1,881** **£950**

JOHN PIPER – Bullslaughter Bay, Near Portmadoc – signed – ink and watercolour, heightened with bodycolour – 11 x 14in.
(Sotheby's) **$594** **£300**

CAMILLE PISSARRO – L'Hermitage A Pontoise – signed and dated '81 – 23¾ x 29in.
(Sotheby's) **$108,900** **£55,000**

CAMILLE PISSARRO – Paysage Avec Deux Paysannes – signed – gouache on silk – 10½ x 22in.
(Sotheby's) **$31,680** **£16,000**

LUCIEN PISSARRO – Rosemount, Coldharbour, 1916 – black chalk, pen and ink and watercolour – 9¾ x 7¾in.
(Sotheby's) **$752** **£380**

LUCIEN PISSARRO – The Park – stamped with monogram – black chalk and watercolour – 10¾ x 8½in.
(Sotheby's) **$495** **£250**

WILLIAM PITT – Ancient Cottages, Childs Wickham, Worcestershire – signed and dated 1881, inscribed on the reverse – 9½ x 14½in.
(Sotheby's Belgravia)
$1,143 **£580**

WILLIAM PITT – An Estuary Scene With Numerous Shipping And Figures – signed and dated 1863 – oil – 12 x 22in.
(G. A. Key) **$792** **£400**

OSMUND PITTMAN – Loch Lubnaig – watercolour – 24 x 34cm.
(Edmiston's) **$66** **£34**

PITTONI – Christ On The Road To Calvary – canvas on panel – 14¼ x 7½in.
(Christie's) **$97** **£50**

GIAMBATTISTA PITTONI – Hamilcar Making Hannibal Swear Enmity To The Romans – 17¾ x 32¼in.
(Christie's) **$10,560** **£5,500**

JAMES CHARLES PLAYFAIR – Reading The News; Drinking Tea – signed and dated '72 – heightened with white – 12 x 8½in.
(Sotheby's Belgravia)
$247 **£130 Pair**

ROWLANDE PLUMBE – Shipping Off The Coast – signed and dated 1884 – 18 x 31in.
(Sotheby's Belgravia)
$591 **£300 Two**

BERNARDINO BARBATELLI, IL POCCETTI – Design For A Frieze With A Putto, A Dog And Floral Motifs – inscribed – pen and brown ink – 6.2 x 22.2cm.
(Christie's) **$250** **£130**

E. VAN DER POEL – A Village Fire At Night – bears initials – on panel – 11½ x 16in.
(Christie's) **$1,067** **£550**

EGBERT VAN DER POEL – Figures Outside A Burning Church At Night – signed and dated 1665(?) – on copper – 5½ x 7¼in.
(Christie's) **$1,649** **£850**

C. VAN POELENBURGH – A Southern Landscape With Herdsmen – on panel – 6 x 8in.
(Sotheby's) **$1,485** **£750**

C. VAN POELENBURGH – Nymphs Bathing – signed with initials – on panel – 8½ x 10in.
(Christie's) **$1,455** **£750**

CHARLES H. POINGDESTRE – A View In The Campagna – signed, inscribed and dated 1864 – 22½ x 35in.
(Sotheby's Belgravia)
$4,426 **£2,200**

SERGE POLIAKOFF – Untitled Composition – signed – oil and sand on canvas – 23 x 28in.
(Sotheby's) **$10,296 £5,200**

POLISH SCHOOL, circa 1700 – The Madonna And Child, Wearing Elaborate Gold Crowns – on panel – 13 x 10in.
(Sotheby's) **$369 £190**

JAMES POLLARD – Stage Coach Passengers At Breakfast – pencil and watercolour – 12 x 17¾in.
(Sotheby's) **$4,268 £2,200**

ALFRED POLLENTINE – San Giorgio Maggiore – signed – 19½ x 29½in.
(Sotheby's Belgravia) **$956 £480**

ALFRED POLLENTINE – The Grand Canal Venice – signed and dated '81, inscribed on the reverse – 29½ x 49½in.
(Sotheby's Belgravia) **$3,018 £1,500**

EDWIN A. POLLITT – 'The Swallow Falls, Bettys-y-Coed, North Wales' – signed and dated 1874 on the reverse – oil on canvas – 35½ x 47½in.
(Lalonde Bros. & Parham) **$745 £380**

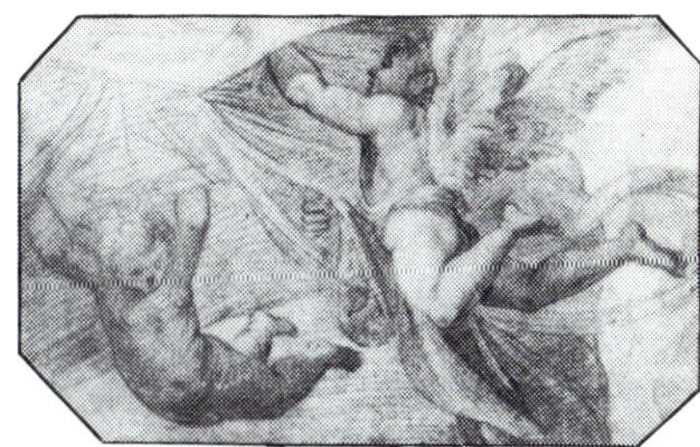

CRISTOFORO RONCALLI, IL POMARANCIO – An Angel And A Putto Holding An Awning – red chalk – 17 x 24.2cm.
(Christie's) **$288 £150**

CRISTOFORO RONCALLI, IL POMARANCIO, Attributed to – Study Of Christ – inscribed – red chalk – 20.2 x 17.2cm.
(Christie's) **$384 £200**

POOLE – At The Spring – bears signature and date – 27 x 35in.
(Sotheby's Belgravia)
$296 £150

POOLE – Asleep – 23½ x 19½in.
(Sotheby's Belgravia)
$86 £45

JAMES POOLE – Glencoe – signed, inscribed and dated 1851 on the reverse – 15 x 21in.
(Sotheby's) **$576 £300**

PAUL FALCONER POOLE – Pick-A-Back – inscribed on a label on the reverse – canvas – on panel – 14 x 11in.
(Sotheby's Belgravia) **$307** **£160**

PORPORO – A Basket Of Fruit On A Stone Ledge – 17½ x 20¾in.
(Christie's) **$1,455** **£750**

GUGLIELMO DELLA PORTA, Attributed to – Project For A Fountain, With Subsidiary Studies Of Birds, A Dog, And Part Of An Ewer – pen and brown ink – 17.6 x 14.9cm.
(Christie's) **$1,728** **£900**

D. PORTER – The Minstrel – signed – on board – 11½ x 9½in.
(Sotheby's Belgravia) **$480** **£250**

ALVARO PORTOGHESE – The Annunciation With Saints Catherine Of Alexandria And John The Baptist, James The Great And Justina Of Padua – on gold ground – 18½ x 5in.
(Christie's) **$21,120** **£11,000 Pair**

H. POT – Portrait Of A Lady, Bust Length, In Black, With A White Ruff And Cap – on panel – 10 x 8in.
(Sotheby's) **$1,584** **£800**

H. G. POT – Portrait Of A Woman, Small Three-Quarter Length, Wearing A Black Fur-Trimmed Dress And White Cap – inscribed and dated 1631 – on panel – 10½ x 7½in.
(Christie's) **$1,552** **£800**

LASLETT JOHN POTT – Hardwick Hall, Interior Of Mansion With Family Group – signed and dated 1874 – oil on canvas – 20½ x 27½in.
(Lalonde Bros. & Parham) **$871** **£440**

BEATRIX POTTER – Study Of Pelargoniums – monogrammed and dated 1886 – 10 x 13in.
(G. A. Key) **$119** **£60**

BEATRIX POTTER – Study Of Magnolias – monogrammed and dated 1886 – watercolour – 11 x 14in.
(G. A. Key) **$83** **£42**

PIETER SYMONSZ. POTTER – A Guardroom, A Man In A Buff Jerkin And Half Armour Standing Beside A Seated Woman In Yellow And A Soldier With Red Breeches – remains of a signature and dated 1633 – on panel – 16¼ x 21¼in.
(Sotheby's) **$11,760** **£6,000**

POURBUS – The Crucifixion – on panel – 23½ x 13½in.
(Christie's) **$291** **£150**

F. POURBUS – Portrait Of A Bearded Man, Bust Length, Wearing A Black Coat And A Ruff – inscribed and dated 1616 – on panel – 25½ x 20¼in.
(Christie's) **$388** **£200**

POUSSIN – An Italianate Rocky Wooded River Landscape With Peasants On A Path – 26½ x 35¼in.
(Christie's) **$1,455** **£750**

POUSSIN, After – The Annunciation – 28½ x 34in.
(Christie's) **$582** **£300**

POUSSIN, After, Early 19th century – 'Extensive Continental Classical River Landscape On A Stormy Day, A Woman With Young Child And A Drover With Animals' – oil on canvas – 26 x 36in.
(Lalonde Bros. & Parham) **$1,372** **£700**

JOSEPH POWELL – Gray's Monument At Stoke Poges, Stoke Poges' House In The Distance – signed – 6 x 9½in.
(Sotheby's) **$233** **£120**

W. E. POWELL – Teal And Mallard – signed and dated 1928 – watercolour heightened with white – 10¼ x 13¾in.
(Christie's) **$213** **£110**

W. E. POWELL – Canada And Greenland Geese – signed and dated 1928 – watercolour heightened with white – 9½ x 13½in.
(Christie's) **$213** **£110**

W. E. POWELL – Shelduck And Curlew Sandpipers – signed and dated 1928 – watercolour heightened with white – 10¼ x 14in.
(Christie's) **$213** **£110**

HAROLD SEPTIMUS POWER – Huntsman And Hounds – signed – watercolour heightened with bodycolour on linen – 14½ x 15¼in.
(Sotheby's) **$832** **£420**

HAROLD SEPTIMUS POWER – Early Morning Farm Scene – signed – oil on canvas – 43 x 34cm.
(Australian Art Auctions) **$375** **£195**

SIR EDWARD JOHN POYNTER – A Sibyl – signed with initials and dated '71 – recto; Two Studies Of Classical Figures – dated '71 – verso – 17 x 12in.
(Sotheby's Belgravia) **$181** **£90**

SIR EDWARD JOHN POYNTER – Study Of A Classical Lady – signed with initials and dated '78 – red chalk – 12¼ x 5¾in.
(Sotheby's Belgravia) **$241** **£120**

STEFANO POZZO – Antiochus Yearning For Stratonice – 38 x 52½in.
(Christie's) **$1,920** **£1,000**

STEFANO POZZO – Christ's Charge To Saint Peter – black and white chalk on blue paper – 29.2 x 30.1cm.
(Christie's) **$422** **£220**

POZZOSERRATO – An Elegantly Dressed Couple, Making Music – on panel – 14½ x 10½in.
(Sotheby's) **$126** **£65**

MAGNUS PRASCH – A German Hunting Party – signed – oil on canvas – 32 x 46in.
(Bonham's) **$9,408** **£4,800**

JONATHAN PRATT – 'The Flower Girl' – oil on canvas – 13½ x 9½in.
(W. H. Lane & Son)
$659 **£340**

WILLIAM PRATT – Returning From The Fields – signed and dated '19 – 29¼ x 19½in.
(Sotheby's) **$998** **£520**

WILLIAM PRATT – On The Shore At St. Andrews – signed and dated 1914 – 11¾ x 15½in.
(Sotheby's) **$614** **£320**

E. R. PREYBURG – 'Landscape With Sheep' – oil on canvas – 29 x 39in.
(W. H. Lane & Son) **$873** **£450**

AMADEO COUNT PREZIOSI – Constantinople – signed and dated 1865 – pencil and watercolour heightened with white and gold – 276 x 414mm.
(Christie's) **$181** **£95**

JANET PRICE – Landscape – signed – oil on board – 29 x 29cm.
(Australian Art Auctions) **$127** **£65**

JANET PRICE – Country Cottage – signed – oil on board – 30 x 30cm.
(Australian Art Auctions) **$125** **£64**

B. PRIESTMAN – Friesian Cattle In Pasture – signed and dated 1914 – 18 x 24in.
(Morphets of Harrogate) **$543** **£280**

BERTRAM PRIESTMAN – Ducks By A Pond – signed and dated '98 – on board – 15 x 19½in.
(Sotheby's Belgravia) **$748** **£380**

BERTRAM PRIESTMAN – A Local Farmstead With Horse And Cart – inscribed – oil on board – 7 x 10in.
(Anarew Sharpe & Partners) **$138** **£70**

BERTRAM PRIESTMAN – Cattle By Cornish River – signed and dated '17 – on panel – 10 x 13½in.
(Sotheby's Belgravia) **$431** **£220**

BERTRAM PRIESTMAN – Cattle By The Coast – signed and dated '13 – 17 x 23½in.
(Sotheby's Belgravia) **$480** **£250**

VALENTINE CAMERON PRINSEP – Phyllida – inscribed on the stretcher – 22½ x 18½in.
(Sotheby's Belgravia) **$614** **£320**

PAOLO PRIOLO – Saint Paul Preaching At Syracuse – signed, dated 1867 and inscribed – pencil and watercolour – 573 x 854mm.
(Christie's) **$380** **£200**

EDWARD PRITCHETT – The Molo – signed – oil – 26 x 39¼in.
(Bonham's) **$13,860** **£7,000**

EDWARD PRITCHETT – In The Piazza, San Marco, Venice – signed – 9½ x 13½in.
(Sotheby's Belgravia)
$3,621 **£1,800 Pair**

EDWARD PRITCHETT – A View On The Grand Canal, Venice With Santa Maria Della Salute; and The Bacino Di San Marco, Venice With San Giorgio Maggiore – signed – 11¾ x 17½in.
(Christie's) **$5,432** **£2,800 Pair**

EDWARD PRITCHETT – Santa Maria Della Salute; Rialto Bridge, Grand Canal – signed – 9½ x 13½in.
(Sotheby's Belgravia)
$2,816 **£1,400 Pair**

EDWARD PRITCHETT – The Piazzetta, Venice; and The Bridge Of Sighs And The Doge's Palace, Venice – 17½ x 13½in.
(Christie's) **$5,820 £3,000 Pair**

E. PRITCHETT – A Fishing Boat On An Italian Lake – inscribed on a label on the reverse – on board – 5 x 6½in.
(Sotheby's Belgravia)
$468 £240

ALBERT PROCTOR – Extensive River Scene With Figure In Punt – signed – watercolour – 10 x 31in.
(G. A. Key) **$107 £54**

ADAM EDWIN PROCTOR – On A Country Lane – signed and dated '99 – 9¼ x 17½in.
(Sotheby's Belgravia)
$335 £170

CORNELIS PRONK – A View Of Schloss Heemstede – pencil and grey wash – 171 x 194mm.
(Christie's) **$456 £240**

JOHN SKINNER PROUT – Children Near The Walls Of A Ruined Abbey – signed – watercolour heightened with white on buff paper – 11 x 7¾in.
(Christie's) **$310 £160**

SAM PROUT – Continental Cathedral – watercolour – on paper on panel – 14 x 10in.
(Andrew, Hilditch & Son)
$58 £28

SAMUEL PROUT – Dutch Fishing Boat With Other Ships At Sea – 18½ x 25½in.
(Sotheby's) **$1,649 £850**

SAMUEL PROUT – A Fountain At Ulm – watercolour – 28 x 20¾in.
(Sotheby's) **$1,261** **£650**

SAMUEL PROUT – The Fountain Of Louis XII, Blois – signed – pen and grey ink, watercolour, heightened with white – 12½ x 8¾in.
(Sotheby's) **$683** **£350**

SAMUEL PROUT – The Rialto, Venice – watercolour, heightened with bodycolour – 17 x 23½in.
(Sotheby's) **$4,074** **£2,100**

SAMUEL PROUT – Fishing In The Harbour By Moored Hulks – signed – 13¾ x 20¼in.
(Sotheby's) **$1,455** **£750**

SAMUEL PROUT – Fisherfolk On A Beach Beside Moored Vessels – signed – 13½ x 20¼in.
(Sotheby's) **$1,455** **£750**

SAMUEL PROUT – A Seated Figure On A Moored Boat In A Lake Landscape – signed – watercolour – 7 x 10¼in.
(Christie's) **$621** **£320**

SAMUEL PROUT – Old Spanish Courtyard – signed – watercolour – 14 x 10in.
(Richard Baker & Baker) **$242** **£125**

ALFRED PROVIS – A Woman Sewing By A Hearth – signed and dated 1876 – 10¼ x 14¼in.
(Christie's) **$1,164 £600**

JAN PROVOST – The Madonna And Child With Saint John The Baptist And A Donor, A Landscape Beyond – on panel – 22 x 17¼in.
(Christie's) **$57,600 £30,000**

G. WILLIS PRYCE – 'The Avon Gorge With The Clifton Suspension Bridge In The Far Distance'; and 'Wooded River Landscape' – signed – oil on canvas – 8 x 12in.
(Lalonde Bros. & Parham) **$235 £120 Pair**

G. PULIAN – A Flemish Town Scene With Figures In A Square – signed and dated 1841 – 14 x 18in.
(Russell, Baldwin & Bright) **$2,548 £1,300**

D. PULIGO – The Madonna And Child With The Infant Saint John The Baptist – on panel – 28 x 21½in.
(Christie's) **$2,328 £1,200**

JOHN ANTHONY PULLER – Extensive Swiss Mountainous Landscape With Numerous Figures And A Hay Laden Cart Being Driven Along A Country Road – oil on canvas – 21 x 28¼in.
(Lalonde Bros. & Parham) **$2,970 £1,500**

JOHN ANTHONY PULLER – Gipsies Crossing A Brook – 8½ x 11½in.
(Sotheby's Belgravia) **$966 £480**

T. G. PURVIS – The 'Islamount', In Heavy Seas – bears signature and inscription – 15 x 23¼in.
(Sotheby's Belgravia) **$55 £28**

JEAN PUY – La Rade De Lorient – signed, signed and dated 1919 on the reverse – 14¾ x 20in.
(Sotheby's) **$2,400 £1,200**

WILLIAM PYE – Running Out Of The Gale – signed – on panel – 9 x 14½in.
(Sotheby's Belgravia) **$422 £220**

A. PYNAKER, After, N. Verkolye – Coastal Landscape, With Figures Loading A Cutter, Moored By Ruins, Another Boat With Sail Hoisted In A Cove Beyond – bears signature – 32 x 39cm.
(Henry Spencer & Sons) **$520 £260**

GEORGE PYNE – The Great Gate, Trinity College, Cambridge – signed and dated 1850 – 8¾ x 11¾in.
(Sotheby's) **$1,086 £560**

GEORGE PYNE – Magdalen Bridge, Oxford; and Magdalen College – signed and dated 1870 and 1871 – watercolour – 5¾ x 8¼in.
(Christie's) **$310 £160 Pair**

JAMES BAKER PYNE – Lake Garda – signed, inscribed and dated 1864 – 23 x 32in.
(Sotheby's Belgravia) **$3,564** **£1,800**

JAMES BAKER PYNE – An Extensive Landscape At Sunset With Sightseers In The Foreground – signed and dated 1862 – 15¼ x 20in.
(Christie's) **$1,746** **£900**

JAMES BAKER PYNE – Trees Over A Rocky Gorge – signed and dated 1841 – heightened with bodycolour – 13¼ x 19¼in.
(Sotheby's) **$776** **£400**

JAMES BAKER PYNE – An Italian Lake Scene – signed and dated 1852 – heightened with white – 11½ x 19in.
(Sotheby's) **$582** **£300**

JAMES BAKER PYNE – River In The Mountains – 11¼ x 16½in.
(Sotheby's) **$931** **£480**

JAMES BAKER PYNE – A View Of Lake Maggiore – indistinctly signed and dated 1850 – 25 x 35¼in.
(Christie's) **$1,940** **£1,000**

JAMES BAKER PYNE – Dover – signed and dated '39 – 11 x 17in.
(Christie's) **$2,716** **£1,400**

W. B. PYNE – Windsor Castle From The Thames – signed – 22 x 40in.
(Sotheby's Belgravia) **$1,240** **£620**

MARTIN FERDINAND QUADAL – Portrait Of A Gentleman Seated, Three-Quarter Length Wearing A Black Coat – signed and dated 1778 – 51 x 40½in.
(Christie's) **$1,067 £550**

QUAST – A Cavalier Standing, Small Full Length – on panel – 15½ x 9in.
(Christie's) **$931 £480**

P. QUAST – Masqueraders Performing Before Elegant Figures At A Feast – on panel – 11 x 16¼in.
(Christie's) **$3,880 £2,000**

QUELLINUS – A Cavalry Skirmish – a grisaille – 20¾ x 37½in.
(Christie's) **$330 £170**

QUERFURT – A Hawking Party By A Ruin – 17 x 21in.
(Christie's) **$3,104 £1,600**

FRANCESCO DELLA QUESTA – Flowers In A Blue And White Vase With Figures; Flowers In A Blue And White Vase On A Table – one signed – 15¼ x 20½in.
(Sotheby's) **$5,880 £3,000 Two**

FRANCOIS QUESNEL – Portrait Of A Boy, In Red Slashed Doublet And Hose With Black Embroidery, One Hand On His Dagger, The Other On The Hilt Of His Sword – inscribed – on panel – 25¾ x 18¾in.
(Sotheby's) **$5,880 £3,000**

ALFRED ROBERT QUINTON – Chiddington – signed indistinctly with monogram – 16½ x 20½in.
(Sotheby's Belgravia)
$220 £110

ARTHUR RACKHAM – A Girl With A Warming Pan Approaching A Bed – signed and dated '08 – pen and black ink and watercolour – 8 x 6¼in.
(Christie's) **$1,843** **£950**

ARTHUR RACKHAM – A Girl Hovering In Diaphanous Draperies – signed – watercolour heightened with white on dark grey paper – 10½ x 5½in.
(Christie's) **$213** **£110**

ARTHUR RACKHAM – Nord Fjord, Utvik; and A Norwegian Village In The Mountains – signed with monogram and one inscribed – watercolour – 6½ x 9in.
(Christie's) **$175** **£90 Pair**

ARTHUR RACKHAM – Bruges – signed, inscribed and dated 1891 – watercolour – 6¼ x 10in.
(Christie's) **$194** **£100**

ARTHUR RACKHAM – Logs Beside A Lake – signed with monogram and dated '93 – watercolour – 11 x 9in.
(Christie's) **$252** **£130**

EDWARD RADFORD – 'Ga'Riyeh Bey'Da' – signed, inscribed on a label on the reverse – 13 x 9¼in.
(Sotheby's Belgravia) **$460** **£240**

R. RAIMONDI – 'The Musicians', A Middle Eastern Street Scene – signed – watercolour – 21¼ x 15in.
(Sotheby Bearne)
$892 **£460**

WILLIAM RAINEY – Laying It On The Line – heightened with bodycolour – 13¼ x 19in.
(Sotheby's Belgravia) **$119** **£60**

RAMSAY – Portrait Of George Buchanan, the Scottish historian – in a painted oval – 13 x 11in.
(Sotheby's Belgravia) **$249** **£130**

ALLAN RAMSAY – Invermark Castle, Moonrise – signed, inscribed and dated 1904 – 17 x 13in.
(Sotheby's) **$198** **£100**

ALLAN RAMSAY – A Highland River – signed and dated '85 – 19 x 29½in.
(Sotheby's) **$495** **£250**

AUBREY RAMUS – Loch Etive; In The Highlands – signed – 19 x 29in.
(Sotheby's) **$238** **£120** Two

AUBREY RAMUS – Blue Skies After A Storm – signed – 19½ x 29½in.
(Sotheby's Belgravia) **$149** **£75**

AUBREY RAMUS – Sailing Boats On A Lake – signed with initials – heightened with white – 9½ x 21in.
(Sotheby's Belgravia) **$34** **£18**

RAPHAEL, After – 'The Madonna del Granduca' – 2½ x 2in.
(Christie's) **$209** **£100**

RAPHAEL, After – The Holy Family – 19 x 15in.
(Sotheby's) **$146** **£75**

RAPHAEL, After – The Madonna Della Sedia – circular – diameter 20½in.
(Sotheby's) **$330** **£170**

RAFFAELLO SANZIO, Called Raphael, Follower of – Three Figures From The Disputa – pen and brown ink – 27.6 x 17.2cm.
(Christie's) **$480** **£250**

ALEXANDER WELLWOOD RATTRAY – On A Coastal Road – signed – 7 x 23in.
(Sotheby's) **$238** **£120**

ALEXANDER WELLWOOD RATTRAY – A Country Cottage – signed – 7½ x 10½in.
(Sotheby's Belgravia) **$28** **£15**

WILLIAM HENRY RAWORTH – A Lake In South Island, New Zealand – signed and dated 1895 – watercolour – 14½ x 26in.
(Sotheby's) **$335** **£170**

WILLIAM HENRY RAWORTH – At The Bend In The River, South Island, New Zealand – signed and dated 1895 – watercolour – 13¼ x 26¼in.
(Sotheby's) **$296** **£150**

LOUIS RAYNER – Steps In The Front Garden At Haddon Hall, Derbyshire – signed – watercolour heightened with white – 9¾ x 6¾in.
(Sotheby's) **$815** **£420**

LOUIS F. RAYNER – St. John's St. To Canongate, Edinburgh – signed – heightened with bodycolour – 18½ x 13½in.
(Sotheby's) **$3,168** **£1,600**

MARGARET RAYNER – In The Crypt – signed – gouache – 19 x 14½in.
(Sotheby's Belgravia) **$48** **£25**

F. READ, JNR., After N. Maes – 'A Dutch Family' – signed and inscribed on the reverse – watercolour – 52 x 41cm.
(King & Chasemore) **$392** **£200**

G. RECCO – A Fritallaria Imperials, Roses. Tulips And Other Flowers In A Vase – 24¾ x 19½in.
(Christie's) **$9,216** **£4,800**

GIUSEPPE RECCO – A Fishmonger – 47¼ x 67¼in.
(Christie's) **$9,700** **£5,000**

REDGRAVE – Washday – 15½ x 20½in.
(Sotheby's Belgravia) **$1,006** **£500**

HENRY REDMORE – Shipping Vessels Off The Coast In Choppy Seas – signed and dated 1866 – on panel – 7½ x 12½in.
(Christie's) **$3,492** **£1,800 Pair**

HENRY REDMORE – Shipping Offshore In A Choppy Sea; and A Coastal Landscape With Men-O'-War In A Calm – signed with initials and dated 1861 – 6½ x 10½in.
(Christie's) **$9,700** **£5,000 Pair**

H. REDMORE – Shipwreck With Seamen On Raft In Foreground, Sailing Ship In Distance – signed and dated 1876 – 18 x 10in.
(Dee & Atkinson) **$1,980** **£1,000**

C. REEVES – A Bit Cagey – signed – 10 x 14in.
(Sotheby's Belgravia) **£960** **£500**

FLORA MACDONALD REID – At The Flower Stall – signed and dated 1924 – 10¼ x 14¼in.
(Sotheby's) **$1,056** **£550**

SIR G. REID – Portrait Of A Young Lady In Evening Dress – inscribed with monogram and dated 1898 – 23 x 19in.
(Sotheby's Belgravia) **$356** **£180**

GEORGE OGILVY REID – Buying Sweets – on board – 8½ x 11½in.
(Sotheby's) **$288** **£150**

GEORGE OGILVY REID – The Fallen Star – signed – 15½ x 17½in.
(Sotheby's) **$384** **£200**

JOHN ROBERTSON REID – Toilers Of The Deep – signed, inscribed on the reverse – heightened with white – 20 x 28in.
(Sotheby's Belgravia) **$554** **£280**

ROBERT PAYTON REID – A Siesta – signed and dated 1909 – 15 x 23¼in.
(Sotheby's Belgravia)
$537 **£280**

STEPHEN REID – Ye Odds And Ends Shop – signed and dated '37 – 15½ x 19in.
(Sotheby's) **$576** **£300**

JOHANN CHRISTIAN REINHART – Monte Circello, Frontiere Des Etats Du Pape Entre Rome Et Naples – signed and dated 1828 – pencil, pen and grey ink and watercolour – 196 x 260mm.
(Christie's) **$1,520** **£800**

G. RENI – Ecce Homo – 23½ x 19¼in.
(Christie's) **$543** **£280**

G. RENI – A Woman, Half Length, Wearing A Mauve And White Dress – 32 x 27¼in.
(Christie's) **$1,455** **£750**

PIERRE-AUGUSTE RENOIR – Jeune Femme Assise – signed with initials – 28 x 23in.
(Sotheby's) **$132,660 £67,000**

PIERRE-AUGUSTE RENOIR – Baigneuse – signed – oil on canvas – 32 x 20in.
(Sotheby's) **$291,060 £147,000**

PIERRE-AUGUSTE RENOIR – Paysage La Gaude – stamped with the signature – – oil on canvas – 11½ x 18in.
(Sotheby's) **$39,600 £20,000**

PIERRE-AUGUSTE RENOIR – La Prairie – stamped with the signature – 7¾ x 12¼in.
(Sotheby's) **$25,740 £13,000**

ALICE RENSHAW – Dressed For Spring And Winter – signed – heightened with bodycolour – oval – 11¾ x 9¾in. and 12¾ x 10½in.
(Sotheby's Belgravia) **$129 £65 Pair**

PANDOLFO RESCHI – A Southern Landscape With A Waterfall – 70½ x 92in.
(Sotheby's) **$15,520 £8,000**

PANDOLFO RESCHI – A Southern Landscape With A Hunting Party, A Lady And Gentleman On Horseback, Followed By A Huntsman With Dogs – 78 x 117in.
(Sotheby's) **$29,100 £15,000**

M. VAN REYMERSWAELE – The Money-Lenders, Seated In An Interior – on panel – 36¾ x 32¾in.
(Sotheby's) **$8,118** **£4,100**

M. VAN REYMERSWAELE – The Calling Of Saint Matthew – on panel – 36¾ x 43½in.
(Christie's) **$4,224** **£2,200**

ALAN REYNOLDS – Brown Landscape – signed and dated '52 – watercolour – 10½ x 14½in.
(Sotheby's) **$594** **£300**

SIR J. REYNOLDS – Half Length Portrait Of Mary Palmer, Marchioness Of Thomond, Niece Of The Artist, Wearing A Black Feathered Hat – oil – 30 x 24in.
(James Harrison) **$2,142** **£1,025**

HENRY MEYNELL RHEAM – A Sweet Scent – signed with monogram and dated 1908 – 11¼ x 9in.
(Sotheby's Belgravia) **$630** **£320**

H. TANGYE REYNOLDS – Still Life Of Summer Roses And A Silver Ewer – signed – stencilled on the reverse – 21½ x 18½in.
(Sotheby's Belgravia) **$326** **£170**

OLIVER RHYS – 'Who Will Buy?' – signed – 35½ x 27¼in.
(Sotheby's Belgravia) **$1,308** **£650**

RIBERA – Saint Jerome – 45 x 29½in.
(Christie's) **$388** **£200**

GIUSEPPE DE RIBERA – The Penitent Magdalen – inscribed – pen and brown ink – 8.6 x 6.7cm.
(Christie's) **$499** **£260**

MARCO RICCI – Peasants Near A Ruined Castle With A Machicolated Tower – pen and brown ink – 25.2 x 37.2cm.
(Christie's) **$422** **£220**

M. RICCI – A Stormy Coastal Landscape With Fleeing Figures – 28¾ x 35¾in.
(Sotheby's) **$2,037** **£1,050**

M. RICCI – A Rocky River Landscape With Huntsmen, Beneath Trees To The Left, A Ruined Tower To The Right Beyond – 8¾ x 14¾in.
(Sotheby's) **$891** **£450**

M. RICCI – A Mountainous River Landscape With Travellers; and A Southern Landscape With Fisherman In A Small Boat And On Shore, A Town And Mountains Beyond – 19 x 19in.
(Sotheby's) **$6,930** **£3,500 Two**

S. RICCI – Moses Defending The Daughters Of Jethro – 18½ x 41in.
(Christie's) **$9,700** **£5,000**

SEBASTIANO RICCI – Study Of A Bearded Man, Half Length, Looking Down To The Left – inscribed – black chalk – 22 x 16cm.
(Christie's) **$3,840 £2,000**

WILLIAM TROST RICHARDS – A Summer Afternoon In A Garden In Philadelphia – signed, inscribed and dated 1859 – oil on canvas – 11½ x 15in.
(Sotheby's) **$1,773 £900**

W. RICHARDS, SNR. – Bridge Over The Derwent, Belper – signed and dated 1880 and inscribed on the reverse – 11 x 17in.
(Sotheby's Belgravia)
$456 £240

W. RICHARDS, SNR. – Cattle Resting – signed – 12¼ x 17½in.
(Sotheby's Belgravia)
$230 £120

W. RICHARDS – Country Views – signed – 15½ x 23¼in.
(Sotheby's Belgravia)
$277 £140 Pair

EDWARD M. RICHARDSON – A Swiss Village By A Lake – heightened with white – 17¼ x 35¾in.
(Sotheby's) **$877 £450**

JOHN ISAAC RICHARDSON – A Horseman Towing A Barge – signed – watercolour – 8¾ x 12¾in.
(Christie's) **$136 £70**

THOMAS MILES RICHARDSON – By The Falls – inscribed on the reverse – 9½ x 13in.
(Sotheby's Belgravia)
$144 £75

THOMAS MILES RICHARDSON – Lueno, Lago Maggiore – inscribed and dated 1837 – pencil and watercolour heightened with white on grey paper – 9½ x 13¾in.
(Christie's) **$291 £150**

THOMAS MILES RICHARDSON, SNR. – Sun Setting Over A Valley, Travellers On A Road – signed and dated 1836 – 12¾ x 19¾in.
(Sotheby's) **$543 £280**

THOMAS MILES RICHARDSON, SNR. – A Wreck On The Black Middens, A Cluster Of Dangerous Rocks At The Mouth Of The Tyne, Northumberland – signed and dated 1828 – heightened with bodycolour – 21 x 34¾in.
(Sotheby's) **$2,619** **£1,350**

THOMAS MILES RICHARDSON, SNR. – A Sunny Evening Near A Village, Travellers Passing Down A Road – 13 x 19½in.
(Sotheby's) **$543** **£280**

THOMAS MILES RICHARDSON, JNR. – A Castle On A Lake, Probably Dolbadarn – signed and dated 1855 – pencil and watercolour heightened with white on buff paper – 9½ x 13½in.
(Christie's) **$621** **£320**

THOMAS MILES RICHARDSON, JNR. – Returning From Labour – signed and inscribed on an old label on the reverse – on panel – 12¼ x 17½in.
(Christie's) **$2,328** **£1,200**

T. MILES RICHARDSON, JNR. – "Looking Up Strath Tay, Ben-y-Glo And Ben-y-Mackie, Perthshire", With Two Figures In Highland Dress – signed and dated 1854 – watercolour – 35 x 14½in.
(Richard Baker & Baker)
$1,649 **£850**

C. RICHMOND – Salvaging A Wreck – indistinctly signed – 11½ x 23½in.
(Sotheby's Belgravia)
$162 **£85**

GEORGE RICHMOND – The Hon. Thomas Ashburnham, Half Length, Seated – signed and dated 1842 – watercolour heightened with white; and The Lady Jane Swinburne, Half Length, Seated – signed and dated 1836 – pencil and watercolour – 12½ x 9in. and 16½ x 13in.
(Sotheby's) **$388** **£200 Pair**

GEORGE RICHMOND – A Sheet Of Studies Of A Young Lady – signed – pen and ink.
(Lawrence) **$114** **£60**

SIR WILLIAM BLAKE RICHMOND – Another Study For 'Music And Dancing', A Female Nude Plucking Her Harp – inscribed in pencil – red and black crayon on buff paper – 19 x 15¾in.
(Sotheby's) **$512** **£260**

HERBERT DAVIS RICHTER – Joy – signed and inscribed – 58½ x 78in.
(Sotheby's Belgravia) **$345** **£180**

HENRY JAMES RICHTER – A Woman At Her Toilet, Dreaming Of Marriage – signed – watercolour heightened with white – 19 x 15½in.
(Christie's) **$165** **£85**

JAMES RIDDEL – Goats – signed – 19½ x 24in.
(Sotheby's) **$652** **£340**

PHILIP H. RIDEOUT – Coaching In The Snow – signed and dated 1893 – 9 x 13in.
(Sotheby's Belgravia) **$188** **£95**

CISSIE RIDINGS – Mountainous Lakeland Landscape, With A Boat Off The Shore; and A Well-Wooded River Landscape, With A Stone Bridge – signed and dated 1896 – oil on canvas – 29 x 59cm.
(Henry Spencer & Sons) **$203** **£105 Pair**

LEON RIESENER – Vieillard Dans La Campagne – watercolour and gouache – 8 x 6½in.
(Sotheby's) **$158** **£80**

H. RIGAUD – A Portrait Of A Gentleman, Bust Length – 28¾ x 24¼in.
(Sotheby's) **$1,649** **£850**

HYACINTHE RIGAUD – A Youth Leaning On A Parapet, With A Subsidiary Study Of His Hand – black and white chalk on blue paper – 38.4 x 24.3cm.
(Christie's) **$1,248** **£650**

ERNEST HIGGINS RIGG – Beach And Field – signed – canvas on panel – 12¼ x 15½in.
(Sotheby's Belgravia) **$800** **£400 Pair**

LUDGER TOM RING – Flowers In A Jug – signed – on panel – 13¾ x 6¼in.
(Sotheby's) **$46,560** **£24,000**

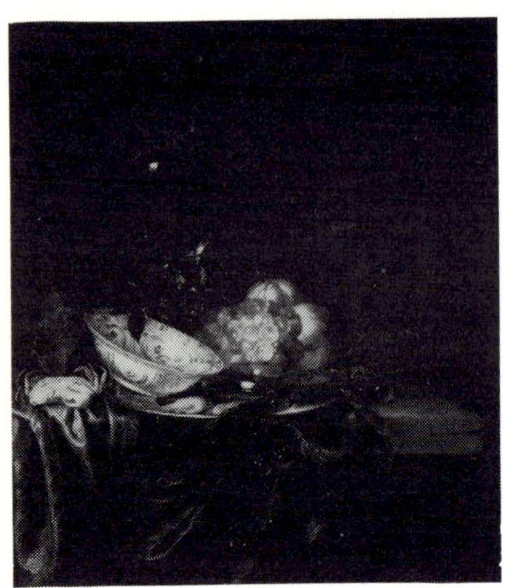

PIETER DE RING – A Still Life With A Roemer, With Foliage Entwined About It, A Flute-Glass, Grapes, Peaches And A Sprig Of Cherries Beside A Pewter Dish, On A Wooden Table Partly Covered By A Green Cloth – signed – 23 x 20in.
(Sotheby's) **$46,680** **£22,000**

PIETER DE RING – A Still Life Of A Bunch Of Grapes, Wild Strawberries In A Chinese Porcelain Bowl On A Pewter Dish, And A Half-Peeled Lemon On A Draped Table – 22¼ x 19in.
(Christie's) **$14,400** **£7,500**

JEAN-PAUL RIOPELLE – L'Heure Feu Follet – signed, signed and dated '56 on the reverse – oil on canvas – 17¾ x 21¼in.
(Sotheby's) **$3,762** **£1,900**

JEAN-PAUL RIOPELLE – Bruyeres – signed on the reverse – oil on canvas – 12½ x 17¾in.
(Sotheby's) **$3,762** **£1,900**

LEOPOLD RIVERS – The Village – signed – 5½ x 7½in.
(Sotheby's Belgravia) **$48** **£25**

LEOPOLD RIVERS – The Ploughman's Return – signed – 7½ x 11in.
(Sotheby's Belgravia) **$115** **£60**

HENRY PARSONS RIVIERE – 'Pets' – signed – watercolour – 20 x 15in.
(Christie's) **$402** **£200**

BRITON RIVIERE – Pigs In Clover – signed and dated 1871 – 11 x 17in.
(Sotheby's Belgravia) **$704** **£350**

BRITON RIVIERE – Necessity Is The Mother Of Invention – signed with monogram and dated 1885, inscribed on a label – 11½ x 13½in.
(Sotheby's Belgravia) **$2,012 £1,000**

BRITON RIVIERE – 'Dog Outside A Kennel' – 24 x 30in.
(Elliott & Green) **$594 £300**

H. P. RIVIERE – Rome View – signed – watercolour – 16 x 30½in.
(Richard Baker & Baker) **$582 £300**

ROBB – A Bacchanal – 17 x 23in.
(Sotheby's Belgravia) **$190 £100**

W. G. ROBB – Garden Scene With Figures – 43 x 61cm.
(Edmiston's) **$116 £60**

HUBERT ROBERT – An Italianate Wooded River Landscape, With Fishermen In A Boat And Figures By A Ruined Bridge – signed and dated 1778 – 15½ x 20½in.
(Christie's) **$34,560 £18,000**

HUBERT ROBERT – A Standing Female Martyr – inscribed – red chalk – 30.7 x 22cm.
(Christie's) **$345 £180**

HUBERT ROBERT *(1733-1808)* – A Caprice With A Villa In A Park – signed; A Caprice With The Temple Of The Sibyl – signed 1795 – 31¼ x 24¾in.
(Sotheby's) **$118,800 £60,000 Pair**

HUBERT ROBERT – A Man Reading A Broadsheet – red chalk, pen and brown ink – 11.1 x 7.7cm.
(Christie's) **$217 £70**

H. ROBERT – A Caprice View Of Rome With The Colosseum And The Arch Of Constantine – 32½ x 42in.
(Sotheby's) **$3,104** **£1,600**

BENJAMIN ROBERTS – Still Life Of Fruit By A Bank – signed and dated '69 – 9½ x 13¼in.
(Sotheby's Belgravia) **$634** **£320**

DAVID ROBERTS – The Shrine Of The Annunciation At Nazareth – signed – pencil and watercolour and bodycolour – 7¾ x 10½in.
(Sotheby's) **$776** **£400**

EDWIN ROBERTS – 'The Hornet' – oil on panel – 14 x 11½in.
(W. H. Lane & Son)
$1,843 **£950**

EDWIN ROBERTS – Wild Thyme – signed – 23½ x 19¾in.
(Sotheby's Belgravia)
$3,622 **£1,800**

EDWIN ROBERTS – A Warming Brew – signed – 23¼ x 19¼in.
(Sotheby's Belgravia)
$1,911 **£950**

EDWIN ROBERTS – 'Freeing The Lark' – oil on panel – 14 x 12in.
(W. H. Lane & Son)
$1,455 **£750**

HENRY BENJAMIN ROBERTS – Snatching Forty Winks – signed – on board – 11½ x 9½in.
(Sotheby's Belgravia)
$911 £460

I. L. ROBERTS – Pickering Castle, Yorkshire – signed and dated 1850 – 35½ x 47¼in.
(Sotheby's Belgravia)
$1,710 £850

TOM ROBERTS – The Formal Garden – signed – oil on canvas – 35 x 44cm.
(Australian Art Auctions)
$3,219 £1,677

CECIL ROBERTSON – A Chinese Waterway – 58 x 45cm.
(Edmiston's) **$27 £14**

CHARLES KAY ROBERTSON – Still Life Of Wallflowers In A Jug – signed – 15½ x 12½in.
(Sotheby's Belgravia)
$134 £70

CHARLES ROBERTSON – "The Carpet Seller" – signed and dated '81 – 48½ x 33½in.
(Phillips) **$9,700 £5,000**

GEORGE ROBERTSON – A View Of Wanstead House In The County Of Middlesex With Group Of People On The Lawn – pen and black ink, grey and brown washes – 14 x 30in.
(Sotheby's) **$624 £320**

STRUAN ROBERTSON – Unloading The Catch On The Beach – signed – coloured chalks, heightened with white – on buff paper – 10 x 13½in.
(Sotheby's) **$422 £220**

TOM ROBERTSON – Loch Linnie – signed, inscribed on a label on the reverse - 20½ x 28in.
(Sotheby's) **$495** **£250**

TOM ROBERTSON – Springtime, Killin – signed – on panel – 7¼ x 9¼in.
(Sotheby's) **$144** **£75**

CHARLES ROBINSON – Peek-A-Boo – signed – pen and ink, heightened with bodycolour – 12 x 6in.
(Sotheby's Belgravia) **$268** **£140**

FREDERICK CAYLEY ROBINSON – St. Francis In Meditation – signed – heightened with bodycolour – 14 x 7¼in.
(Sotheby's Belgravia) **$307** **£160**

JOAN ROBINSON – Still Life Of Flowers – signed with monogram and dated 1948 – 23½ x 19½in.
(Sotheby's Belgravia) **$211** **£110**

WILLIAM HEATH ROBINSON – Disturbed Rest; Late Breakfast; I Thank You, Sir Walter; A Time For All Things; He Loves Me, Loves Me Not; The Other Way Out – five signed and inscribed, the other inscribed – pen and ink – 9½ x 7in.
(Sotheby's Belgravia) **$134** **£70 Six**

WILLIAM HEATH ROBINSON – The Last Man In The Queue – signed and inscribed – pen and ink – 14½ x 10¼in.
(Sotheby's Belgravia) **$58** **£30**

WILLIAM HEATH ROBINSON – Putting The Shoe On The Wrong Foot; Possible But Not Probable; The Water Dance; Paul Jones On Holiday; Dejeuner, Deauville – signed and inscribed – pen and ink – 10 x 7in.
(Sotheby's Belgravia) **$106** **£55 Five**

WILLIAM HEATH ROBINSON – Round The Night Clubs – signed and inscribed – pen and ink – 14 x 10½in.
(Sotheby's Belgravia) **$86** **£45**

GEORGE FENNEL ROBSON – Grasmere With A Fisherman In A Boat – 6 x 11in.
(Sotheby's) **$546** **£280**

ALEXANDER IGNATIUS ROCHE – The Mill – signed – 19½ x 29½in.
(Sotheby's) **$921** **£480**

C. H. RODNEY – 'On The Scheldt' – signed – oil on canvas – 17½ x 27½in.
(Morton's Auction Exchange, Inc.) **$600** **£303**

CLARENCE ROE – Ilfracombe – signed and inscribed – 19½ x 29½in.
(Sotheby's Belgravia) **$494** **£260**

ROBERT ERNEST ROE – Shipping Outside Harbour; Coming Into Port – signed – 8½ x 12½in.
(Sotheby's Belgravia) **$1,425** **£750 Pair**

ROBERT HENRY ROE – A Stag And Two Hind In A Highland Landscape – signed and dated 1870 – 50 x 39½in.
(Sotheby's) **$693** **£350**

JUAN DE LAS ROELAS – The Immaculate Conception – 45½ x 34½in.
(Christie's) **$1,164** **£600**

FRANZ ROESLER – Landschaft Am See – signed and inscribed – watercolour – 14 x 21in.
(Sotheby's) **$67** **£35**

ROGERS – Off The Wreck – 14½ x 19½in.
(Sotheby's Belgravia) **$154** **£80**

W. ROGERS – Young Anglers On The Sussex Coast – signed, inscribed and dated 1850 on the reverse – heightened with white – 6¾ x 9¾in.
(Sotheby's Belgravia) **$67** **£35**

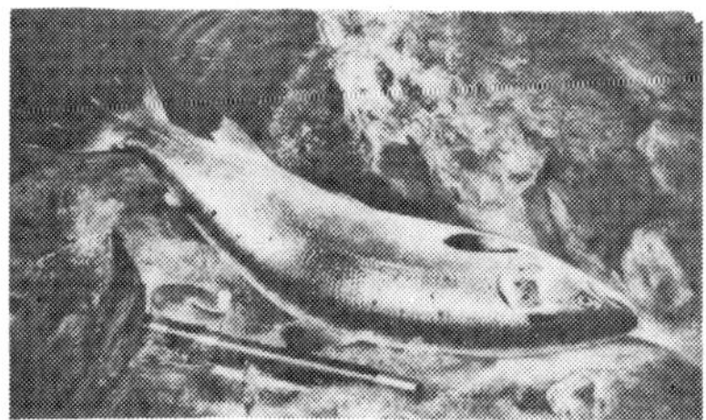

HENRY LEONIDAS ROLFE – A Fine Catch – signed and dated 1864 – 17 x 29in.
(Sotheby's) **$614** **£320**

HENRY LEONIDAS ROLFE – Fresh From The River – signed and dated 1864 – 23½ x 33½in.
(Sotheby's) **$1,344** **£700**

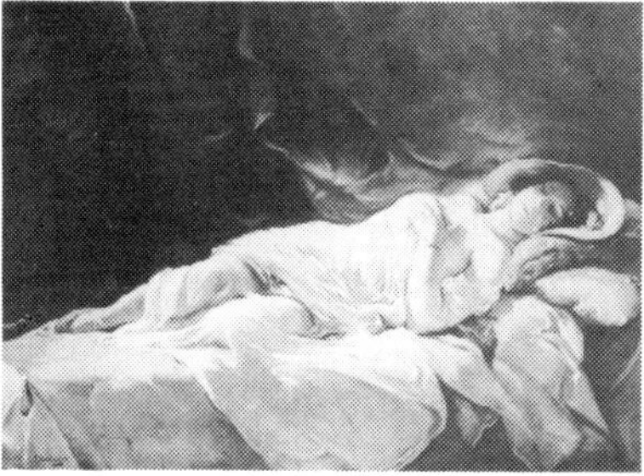

JULIUS ROLSHOVEN – 'Intermezzo' – signed – oil on canvas – 32 x 46in.
(Morton's Auction Exchange, Inc.) **$1,650** **£838**

JULIUS ROLSHOVEN – Fairies In A Twilight Glade – signed and inscribed – pastel and grease crayon on canvas – 20¾ x 36½in.
(Sotheby's) **$296** **£150**

ROMAN SCHOOL, 17th century – The Holy Family, In An Extensive Southern Landscape – on metal – 10 x 8in.
(Sotheby's) **$2,134** **£1,100**

ROMAN SCHOOL, circa 1720 – Saint Philip Neri Witnessing Saint Ignatius Loyola Blessing A Child, As The Madonna And Child Appear Above – 54¼ x 30¾in.
(Christie's) **$768** **£400**

ROMAN SCHOOL, circa 1790 – Tempio Di Vesta; and Avanzi Del Tempio Della Concordia – inscribed on the reverse – bodycolour – 98 x 135mm.
(Christie's) **$209** **£110 Pair**

ROMAN SCHOOL, early 18th century – Saint Catherine Of Siena Adorning Madonna And Child – oil – 34 x 43in.
(Phillips) **$1,307** **£660**

ROMAN OR BOLOGNESE SCHOOL, circa 1710 – The Triumph Of Saint Ursula – a modello – 20¼ x 11¼in.
(Christie's) **$806** **£420**

S. ROMBOUTS – A River Landscape With Herdsmen By A Stream, A Cottage Beneath A Clump Of Trees To The Left – on panel – 16¼ x 21¾in.
(Sotheby's) **$3,492** **£1,800**

W. ROMEYN – Cattle And Sheep Near A Byre – 15 x 19in.
(Christie's) **$514** **£260**

HENRIETTA RONNER – A Taste Of Mustard – signed, inscribed and dated 1881 on the reverse – watercolour – 10¾ x 17¾in.
(Christie's) **$504** **£260**

ROMNEY – Portrait Of A Lady Said To Be Lady Hamilton, Seated Half Length, By A Red Draped Curtain – 29½ x 24in.
(Christie's) **$369** **£190**

HERBERT KERR ROOKE – Bembridge, Isle Of Wight – signed with initials – on panel – 5 x 7in.
(Sotheby's) **$119** **£60**

THOMAS MATTHEWS ROOKE – The Confessors Screen – signed and dated 1924 – 15½ x 19in.
(Sotheby's Belgravia) **$69** **£35**

ROOS – A Wooded Landscape With Cattle And A Shepherd – on panel – 6½ x 8½in.
(Christie's) **$310** **£160**

P. P. ROOS – Herdsmen With Their Flocks, In Southern Landscapes – 18 x 24in.
(Sotheby's) **$3,168** **£1,600 Pair**

E. ROPER – On The Beach, South Durham – signed and dated 1881 – indistinctly inscribed on a label on the reverse – 17½ x 35½in.
(Sotheby's Belgravia)
$133 **£70**

ROSA – Studies Of Heads, Two In Helmets – brown and grey wash – 167 x 233mm.
(Christie's) **$105** **£55**

ROSA – An Italianate Wooded River Landscape With Fishermen In The Foreground – 18½ x 23¾in.
(Christie's) **$679** **£350**

SALVATOR ROSA – The Magdalen In The Wilderness (recto) – pen and brown ink; Alexander And Diogenes (verso) – red chalk – 36.8 x 27.5cm.
(Christie's) **$2,688** **£1,400**

SALVATOR ROSA – A Rocky Landscape With Figures By A Stream – 24¾ x 18½in.
(Christie's) **$1,843** **£950**

A. ROSE – Country Cottages – both signed – 11½ x 16in.
(Sotheby's Belgravia)
$1,248 **£650 Pair**

WILLIAM S. ROSE – Hay Time – signed with initials – 24½ x 34in.
(Christie's) **$970** **£500**

J. ROSIERSE – 'Goodnight Mama' Mother And Child In Candle Lit Room Viewed Through A Window – oil on panel – 13 x 10in.
(G. A. Key) **$4,257** **£2,150**

ALEXANDRE ROSLIN – Charlotte-Suzanne, Baronne D'Holbach, In A Pale Blue Dress Decorated With Large Pink Bows And With Wide Lace Sleeves – 28½ x 23¼in.
(Sotheby's) **$39,200** **£20,000**

ALEXANDER ROSLIN – Portrait Of The Empress Catherine The Great, Half Length, Wearing Imperial Robes And The Order Of St. Andrew – 30¼ x 25¾in.
(Christie's) **$3,840** **£2,000**

A. ROSLIN – A Self-Portrait Of The Artist, Seated, Wearing A Floral Patterned Silk Dressing Gown Over A White Shirt – on paper on canvas – pastel – 28 x 22¾in.
(Sotheby's) **$1,089** **£550**

ROSS – A Highlander In His Tartan – heightened with white – oval – 19½ x 15in.
(Sotheby's Belgravia) **$96** **£50**

ELEANOR M. ROSS – A Purrfect Friendship – signed – 23¼ x 7¼in.
(Sotheby's Belgravia) **$217** **£110**

DANTE GABRIEL ROSSETTI – My Lady Greensleeves – inscribed on the reverse – pencil – 14½ x 12½in.
(Sotheby's Belgravia) **$9,255** **£4,600**

MARIANO ROSSI – Minerva And The Three Fates – a sketch for a ceiling decoration – oil on paper on canvas – 11½ x 8in.
(Christie's) **$576** **£300**

SIR WILLIAM ROTHENSTEIN – The Storm – 29½ x 39½in.
(Sotheby's) **$2,376** **£1,200**

SIR WILLIAM ROTHENSTEIN – Firth – signed with initials, inscribed and dated '94 – on panel – 12½ x 15¾in.
(Sotheby's) **$594** **£300**

ROTTENHAMMER – An Allegory Of Plenty – pen and grey ink, grey wash heightened with white – 146 x 96mm.
(Christie's) **$95** **£50**

HANS ROTTENHAMMER – A Wooded Landscape With Diana And Callisto – on metal – 9¾ x 14¼in.
(Sotheby's) **$11,484** **£5,800**

J. ROTTENHAMMER – The Nativity – on metal – 11 x 9in.
(Sotheby's) **$1,261** **£650**

GEORGES ROUAULT – Cirque De L'Etoile Filante: Etude Pour Le Jongleur – oil and gouache on paper on canvas – 14¾ x 10¾in.
(Sotheby's) **$39,600** **£20,000**

GEORGES ROUAULT – Fille De Cirque A La Grosse Caisse – signed and dated 1929 – oil on paper – 12¼ x 8in.
(Sotheby's) **$41,580** **£21,000**

ROBERT WILLIAM ARTHUR ROUSE – A Gleam Of Sunshine – signed – 29½ x 49½in.
(Sotheby's Belgravia) **$950** **£480**

LOUIS EUGENE LE ROUX – Paysan Labourant – signed – watercolour – 12¼ x 18in.
(Sotheby's) **$418** **£220**

LOUIS EUGENE LE ROUX – Batiments De Ferme, L'Hiver – signed – watercolour – 9 x 12in.
(Sotheby's) **$323 £170**

G. B. DELLA ROVERE – The Charity Of A Saint – inscribed 1512-1572 – pen and brown ink, brown wash on brown paper – 227 x 272mm.
(Christie's) **$91 £48**

CHARLES ROWBOTHAM – Near Monte Carlo; Bay Of Naples – signed – heightened with bodycolour – 7¼ x 4¾in.
(Sotheby's Belgravia)
$310 £160 Pair

CHARLES ROWBOTHAM – 'Nice From Mount Bouron' – signed – watercolour – 16 x 30cm.
(King & Chasemore)
$392 £200

CHARLES ROWBOTHAM – 'At Ghiffa Lake, Maggiore' – signed – watercolour – 16 x 30cm.
(King & Chasemore) **$431 £220**

CHARLES LEESON ROWBOTHAM – The Adur, Sussex – signed and inscribed on the reverse – 5½ x 11½in.
(Sotheby's Belgravia) **$63 £32**

CHARLES ROWBOTHAM – Castle Of La Batiaz, Martigny, Switzerland; Messina, Sicily – signed and dated 1881, inscribed on the reverse – heightened with bodycolour – 9¼ x 7in.
(Sotheby's Belgravia)
$346 £180 Pair

CHARLES LEESON ROWBOTHAM – Lake Mergozzo, Nr. Pallanza – signed, inscribed and dated 1894 – heightened with bodycolour – 5 x 7½in.
(Sotheby's Belgravia)
$158 £80

CHARLES LEESON ROWBOTHAM – At Brighton – signed with initials, inscribed and dated '99 – heightened with white – 5½ x 11½in.
(Sotheby's Belgravia)
$89 £45

CLAUDE H. ROWBOTHAM – An Italian Lake; Flushing From Green Bank; A Rough Day, Falmouth – signed – two dated 1896, one dated 1897 – one heightened with white – 9 x 18in.
(Sotheby's Belgravia)
$114 £60 Three

THOMAS LEESON ROWBOTHAM – 'Caernarvon Castle' – watercolour – 8 x 11in.
(W. H. Lane & Son)
$307 £160

THOMAS LEESON SCARSE ROWBOTHAM, 19th century – The River Avon At Hotwells, Bristol With Shipping Before Clifton – sepia watercolour – 4¾ x 6¾in.
(Osmond, Tricks & Son)
$871 £440

THOMAS ROWDEN – Cattle On Dartmoor – signed – heightened with white – 9 x 20in.
(Sotheby's Belgravia)
$89 £45

GEORGE DERVILLE ROWLANDSON – The Leap; The Fall – signed with initials – 9 x 13in.
(Sotheby's Belgravia)
$139 £70 Pair

THOMAS ROWLANDSON – Buying Fish At The Cottage Door – pencil, pen with grey and brown ink, watercolour – on wove paper – 7 x 10½in.
(Sotheby's) **$2,340** **£1,200**

THOMAS ROWLANDSON – Leaping A Five-Barred Gate – pen and grey ink and watercolour – 7½ x 14¼in.
(Sotheby's) **$1,552** **£800**

THOMAS ROWLANDSON – The Mirror Of Fashion; and Vanity Worn Out, Or The Last Gasp Of Lady Archer – inscribed – pen and brown ink, watercolour – 8¾ x 7in. and 8¾ x 7½in.
(Sotheby's) **$780** **£400 Pair**

THOMAS ROWLANDSON – In The Pillory – signed and dated 1806 – pen and brown ink and watercolour – 12¼ x 10in.
(Sotheby's) **$1,358** **£700**

THOMAS ROWLANDSON – 'Stand And Deliver' – Highwaymen Holding Up A Couple In A Chaise – pen and black ink and watercolour – 9¼ x 13¼in.
(Sotheby's) **$970** **£500**

THOMAS ROWLANDSON – Hounds Resting By A Horse, A Barn Nearby – pencil, pen and brown ink, watercolour – 4¾ x 8¼in.
(Sotheby's) **$936** **£480**

THOMAS ROWLANDSON – Going To A New Home – pencil, pen and brown ink and watercolour – 6 x 9in.
(Sotheby's) **$2,056** **£1,060**

THOMAS ROWLANDSON – Refreshment For The Carter – pen and brown ink, watercolour – 6 x 9½in.
(Sotheby's) **$1,658** **£850**

THOMAS ROWLANDSON – The College Foundling – signed and dated 1821, inscribed on the reverse – pen and brown ink, watercolour – 10¾ x 8¼in.
(Sotheby's) **$1,658** **£850**

THOMAS ROWLANDSON – Rustic Lovers – pencil and red chalk on paper – 8 x 6¾in.
(Sotheby's) **$815** **£420**

THOMAS ROWLANDSON – Magna Carta Island From Runnymede – pencil, pen with brown and grey inks, watercolour – 8½ x 13in.
(Sotheby's) **$4,462** **£2,300**

THOMAS ROWLANDSON – A Debate At The Sheldonian, Oxford – pencil, pen with brown and grey inks and watercolour – 9 x 12¼in.
(Sotheby's) **$7,566** **£3,900**

THOMAS ROWLANDSON – Travellers On A Road, With Horseman Outside An Inn – pen and brown ink and watercolour – recto; An Artist Sketching Three Naked Girls – pencil – verso – 4¾ x 6in.
(Sotheby's) **$741** **£380**

THOMAS ROWLANDSON – A Girl Restraining Her Drunken Father – pen and brown ink and watercolour – 10¾ x 9½in.
(Christie's) **$485 £250**

THOMAS ROWLANDSON – Bad News – pen and sepia ink and watercolour; and Expelling An Intruder – pen and brown ink and watercolour; and Sensitive – inscribed – pen and brown ink and watercolour – 5 x 3½in.; 4¾ x 3¼in. and 4¼ x 5¾in.
(Sotheby's) **$683 £350 Three**

T. ROWLANDSON – The Quaker's Courtship – bears signature – pen and ink and watercolour – 9¼ x 7¾in.
(Christie's) **$107 £55**

JANET P. ROWLISTON – Snow Scene At Pitlochry, Scotland – signed, inscribed and dated 1894 – 17½ x 23½in.
(Sotheby's Belgravia) **$67 £35**

DE ROY – A Cow And Sheep In A Landscape – on panel – 6½ x 8in.
(Christie's) **$129 £65**

FERDINAND ROYBET – Scene De Tournoi – pencil, pen and brown ink – 5½ x 7in.
(Sotheby's) **$114 £60**

RUBENS – Bacchus – on panel – 18¾ x 25in.
(Christie's) **$369 £190**

RUBENS – Portrait Head Of A Woman – red and white chalk – 285 x 258mm.
(Christie's) **$608 £320**

RUBENS – The Lions' Den – inscribed – pen and brown ink, brown wash – 92 x 140mm.
(Christie's) **$124 £65**

RUBENS – The Mocking Of Christ – 31½ x 25in.
(Sotheby's) **$87 £45**

P. P. RUBENS – Apparition Of The Infant Christ And Saint John The Baptist To Saint Francis Of Assisi, In A Landscape – 49¾ x 39½in.
(Sotheby's) **$1,746 £900**

SIR P. P. RUBENS – A Young Woman, Bust Length – on panel – 14½ x 11½in.
(Christie's) **$11,520 £6,000**

SIR PETER PAUL RUBENS – Head Of A Satyr, After The Antique – inscribed – black and white chalk on light grey paper – 29 x 19.6cm.
(Christie's) **$2,688 £1,400**

SIR PETER PAUL RUBENS – Study Of A Franciscan Friar, Three-Quarter Length, In Profile To The Left – black chalk – 41.5 x 25cm.
(Christie's) **$9,600 £5,000**

SCHOOL OF SIR P. P. RUBENS – The Investiture Of A Cleric – 72½ x 58in.
(Sotheby's) **$1,881 £950**

RUBENS, Studio of – Diana Returning From The Chase – 53 x 87in.
(Christie's) **$4,268 £2,200**

RUBENS AND SNYDERS – A Bear Hunt, In A Clearing, A Wooded Landscape To The Right – on panel – 23¼ x 32in.
(Sotheby's) **$1,455 £750**

PIETER JANSZ. VAN RUIJVEN – A Greyhound Snapping At A Dove, Seen Through An Archway – signed – 31½ x 30¾in.
(Sotheby's) **$2,328 £1,200**

JACOB VAN RUISDAEL – A Wooded River Landscape With A Waterfall And A Cottage Beyond – signed – 15 x 13in.
(Christie's) **$11,640 £6,000**

JACOB VAN RUISDAEL – A Pool At The Edge Of A Wood – inscribed – 21 x 26in.
(Sotheby's) **$37,240 £19,000**

RUISDAEL – An Extensive View Of A Bay, On Which Are Numerous Sailing Boats – 35½ x 34¼in.
(Sotheby's) **$1,649 £850**

RUIZ – A Galley Ship Entering A Southern Port – 16½ x 22¼in.
(Sotheby's) **$1,940 £1,000**

H. RUMERS – 'Number Two' Off Poole, Commander J. T. Hart, 1866 – signed and inscribed – 18 x 26in.
(Sotheby's Belgravia) **$515 £260**

RUOPPOLO – A Still Life Of Fruit On A Ledge – 22¾ x 20in.
(Christie's) **$427 £220**

JOHN RUSKIN – Study Of A Footbridge – grisaille, heightened with white – 8 x 13in.
(Sotheby's Belgravia) **$402 £200**

CHARLES RUSSELL – Repose – signed and dated 1909 – 35½ x 27in.
(Sotheby's) **$1,746 £900**

CHARLES MARION RUSSELL – After His First Hunt – A Young Indian Boy Shows The Rabbit He Has Shot To His Father And Mother – signed and inscribed – pencil and watercolour, heightened with bodycolour – 18¼ x 22¼in.
(Sotheby's) **$59,100 £30,000**

GEORGE HORNE RUSSELL – In The Rockies – signed and dated '91 – watercolour – 10½ x 16¾in.
(Sotheby's) **$473 £240 Pair**

JOHN RUSSELL – The Favourite Rabbit – inscribed – pencil heightened with pink wash on vellum – 10¼ x 14in.
(Sotheby's) **$931 £480**

JOHN RUSSELL – Sheep Sheltering From A Thunderstorm – signed – 23 x 40½in.
(Sotheby's Belgravia) **$144 £75**

JOHN RUSSELL – A Jack Russell Terrier – signed – 28½ x 36½in.
(Sotheby's) **$1,056** **£550**

JOHN RUSSELL – A Lady In A Gothick Chamber – signed and dated 1799 – pastel – 23½ x 17½in.
(Sotheby's) **$1,164** **£600**

JOHN RUSSELL – Salmon – signed – 17½ x 38in.
(Sotheby's) **$230** **£120**

JOHN RUSSELL – Salmon – signed – 17 x 35in.
(Sotheby's) **$288** **£150**

JOHN RUSSELL – Portrait Of Miss Darby, In A White Dress, With A Child Holding A Sheet Of Music, In A Landscape – signed and dated 1793 – pastel – 31 x 39½in.
(Sotheby's) **$1,358** **£700**

JOHN RUSSELL – A Young Boy Holding A Cricket Ball Teasing A Dog – pastel – 24 x 18in.
(Sotheby's) **$2,716** **£1,400**

JOHN RUSSELL – A Young Girl Wearing A White Muslin Shawl Over A Silvery White Dress – signed and dated 1788 – pastel – 23 x 17¼in.
(Sotheby's) **$1,746** **£900**

HENRY RUSHBURY – Borghese Gardens, Rome – watercolour drawing – 29 x 44cm.
(Edmiston's) **$330** **£170**

R. RUYSCH – Roses, Poppies And Other Flowers In A Vase On A Stone Ledge – 29¾ x 24¼in.
(Christie's) **$6,208** **£3,200**

SALOMON JACOBSZ. VAN RUYSDAEL – A Wooded River Landscape With Fishermen In Boats, And Travellers In A Horsedrawn Cart Near A Church Beyond – signed with initials and dated 1644 – on panel – 20¾ x 33¼in.
(Christie's) **$230,400** **£120,000**

M. RYCKAERT – An Extensive Italianate Landscape With A Hunting Party In The Foreground And A Village By A River Beyond – on panel – 27½ x 61in.
(Christie's) **$17,280** **£9,000**

FRANS RYCKHALS – A Still Life Of Fruit, Vegetables And Game – inscribed – on panel – 18½ x 25in.
(Sotheby's) **$6,272** **£3,200**

HENRY RYLAND – A Word Of Advice – signed – watercolour – 14¾ x 10½in.
(Sotheby's Belgravia) **$765** **£380**

HENRY RYLAND – Roman Grace – signed – 14 x 9½in.
(Sotheby's Belgravia) **$335** **£170**

JOHN MICHAEL RYSBRACK – The Assumption Of The Virgin – pen and brown ink, brown wash heightened with white on buff paper – 38.8 x 30.2cm.
(Christie's) **$422** **£220**

LORENZO SABATINI, Attributed to – Saint Michael Triumphant Over Satan – inscribed – pen and brown ink, brown wash heightened with white – 39.2 x 23.8cm.
(Christie's) **$230** **£120**

SACCHI – Saint Francis Preaching To The Fishes – red chalk – 314 x 264mm.
(Christie's) **$38** **£20**

WALTER DENDY SADLER – Head Study Of A Girl – signed and dated 1919 – pencil and coloured crayon – 6½ x 4¾in.
(Sotheby's Belgravia)
$38 **£20**

WALTER DENDY SADLER – The Old And The Young – signed – 37 x 49in.
(Christie's) **$6,984** **£3,600**

H. SAFTLEVEN – A Rhineland Landscape – on panel – 13½ x 17½in.
(Sotheby's) **$12,740** **£6,500**

JOHN CUTHBERT SALMON – An Angler – signed and dated 1878 – 11½ x 17¾in.
(Sotheby's Belgravia)
$230 **£120**

A. SALUCCI – Christ And The Woman Taken In Adultery, Outside A Fantastic Temple With A Row Of Niches Containing Roman Busts – 38½ x 49½in.
(Sotheby's) **$3,762** **£1,900**

PAUL SANDBY – Londonderry Church – watercolour – 5½ x 7½in.
(W. H. Lane & Son)
$518 **£270**

PAUL SANDBY – Mr. Sandby Of Windsor Great Park And His Daughter Maria Frederica – inscribed on the reverse – pen and grey ink, watercolour – on paper – 6¼ x 4¾in.
(Sotheby's) **$1,164** **£600**

PAUL SANDBY – Bothwell Castle On The Clyde, Lanarkshire – gouache – 6½ x 10in.
(Sotheby's) **$4,074** **£2,100**

PAUL SANDBY – Bridge Over A River With A Church On A Cliff – gouache – 6½ x 10in.
(Sotheby's) **$1,067** **£550**

PAUL SANDBY – The Artist's Wife And Children Beneath A Tree – 7 x 4½in.
(Sotheby's) **$1,358** **£700**

ROBERT SANDERSON – 'You Have Me' – signed and dated 1897 – 20 x 30in.
(Sotheby's) **$1,287** **£650**

SAN GAGGIO, The Master of – A Triptych: The Madonna And Child With Saints And Scenes From The Passion – on panel – centre 12½ x 17½in., each wing 6½ x 18½in.
(Sotheby's) **$49,000** **£25,000**

ALESSANDRO SANQUIRICO – A Woman Before A Tribunal In A Gothic Hall – signed – pen and grey ink, grey wash – 28.7 x 36.9cm.
(Christie's) **$384** **£200**

PIETER VAN SANTVOORT – A Winter Landscape – on panel – 15¾ x 21¾in.
(Sotheby's) **$26,190** **£13,500**

HENRI-VERGE-SARRAT – Marine – signed, inscribed and dated 1922 – pencil, pen and ink and grey wash – 8 x 11¾in.
(Sotheby's) **$396** **£200**

JOHN NOST SARTORIUS – A Huntsman With Hound – oil – 14½ x 18in.
(Andrew Sharpe & Partners)
$1,231 **£625**

WILLIAM SARTORIUS – A Still Life Of Fruit And A Roemer Of White Wine – 24¾ x 30¼in.
(Sotheby's) **$2,167** **£1,100**

W. SARTORIUS – A Still Life Of Flowers And Fruit – 27 x 28in.
(Sotheby's) **$3,492** **£1,800**

GIOVANNI BATTISTA SALVI, Called Il Sassoferrato – The Madonna In Prayer, In Red, With A Blue Mantle And White Kerchief – 19 x 14¾in.
(Sotheby's) **$6,208** **£3,200**

GIOVANNI BATTISTA SALVI, Called Il Sassoferrato – The Madonna And Child With Cherubs – 23¼ x 29in.
(Sotheby's) **$8,820** **£4,500**

G. B. SALVI, IL SASSOFERRATO – The Holy Family – 27½ x 36½in.
(Christie's) **$3,298** **£1,700**

SAUVAGE – Classical Figures In Chariots – grisaille – 16½ x 68in.
(Christie's) **$582** **£300**

SAVERY – A Still Life Of Flowers In A Glass, On A Wooden Ledge – on metal – 11¾ x 8in.
(Sotheby's) **$3,960** **£2,000**

J. SAVERY – Autumn, A Landscape With Peasants Feasting And Drinking To Celebrate The Corn Harvest – on copper – 3½ x 4¼in.
(Sotheby's) **$9,100** **£4,600**

HUGH SAWREY – Bar Room Scene – signed – oil on canvas – 30 x 35cm.
(Australian Art Auctions) **$760** **£396**

HUGH SAWREY – Horseman Of The Flaming Dawn – signed – oil on board – 29 x 39cm.
(Australian Art Auctions) **$692** **£353**

AMY SAWYER – Goblin Market – signed and inscribed – heightened with bodycolour – 23½ x 38in.
(Sotheby's Belgravia) **$844** **£440**

AMY SAWYER – The Procession Of Beggars, "Hark!! Hark!! the dogs do bark" – signed and inscribed – pen and ink, heightened with bodycolour – 27 x 37in.
(Sotheby's Belgravia) **$268** **£140**

T. SAYER – A Walk Through The Woods – signed and dated 1891 – 13 x 16½in.
(Sotheby's Belgravia) **$115** **£60**

REUBEN SAYERS, After Sir Edwin Landseer – Alexander And Diogenes – signed and dated 1861, and signed, inscribed and dated on the reverse – 43½ x 56¼in.
(Christie's) **$1,746** **£900**

EDITH M. S. SCANNELL – In Fairyland – signed – circular – diameter 20¼in.
(Sotheby's Belgravia) **$689** **£350**

F. W. SCARBOROUGH – Return From Fishing – signed, inscribed on a label on the reverse – 13 x 18½in.
(Sotheby's Belgravia) **$126** **£65**

SCARSELLINO – Saint George And The Dragon – 15½ x 19in.
(Christie's) **$1,358** **£700**

SCARSELLINO – The Adoration Of The Shepherds; and The Adoration Of The Magi – on marble – 9 x 17in.
(Christie's) **$2,522** **£1,300 Pair**

GODFRIED SCHALCKEN – An Old Man Writing By Candlelight In A Landscape – on panel – 14 x 10in.
(Christie's) **$1,261** **£650**

JEAN-FREDERIC SCHALL – 'La Resistance Inutile' – 12½ x 9½in.
(Sotheby's) **$15,520** **£8,000**

H. SCHAUFFLEIN – Portrait Of A Young Man, Bust Length, In A Red Shirt Covered With A Fur-Trimmed Green Coat And A Black Hat – on panel – 11¾ x 8¾in.
(Sotheby's) **$3,564** **£1,800**

PIETER VAN SCHAYENBORGH – A Still Life Of Fish – signed – on panel – 23¾ x 31in.
(Sotheby's) **$4,268** **£2,200**

WILLEM SCHELLINKS – A Frozen River Landscape, With A Capriccio View Of The Ponte Molle, Rome – signed – 32¾ x 44¾in.
(Christie's) **$24,960** **£13,000**

BERNARD VAN SCHENDEL – The Interior Of A Cottage With Peasants Playing A Game – signed – on panel – 12¾ x 15¾in.
(Sotheby's) **$5,148** **£2,600**

JOHN CHRISTIAN SCHETKY – A View Of Belvoir Castle – signed and dated 1855 – 27¼ x 41¼in.
(Christie's) **$1,940** **£1,000**

SCHIAVONE – Saint John The Baptist And The Pharisees – on panel – 8½ x 14in.
(Christie's) **$621** **£320**

J. M. H. SCHLINGOMANN – Sandberg – signed and inscribed on the reverse – watercolour – 15 x 16in.
(Sotheby's) **$247** **£130**

JOHANNES SCHOEFF – Sailing Vessels In A Choppy Sea, A View Of The Harbour Of Haarlem Beyond – bears signature and dated 1645 – on panel – 14 x 18¼in.
(Sotheby's) **$7,372 £3,800**

SCHOEVARDTS – A River Landscape With A Horse-Drawn Cart On A Winding Path – on panel – 9½ x 13½in.
(Sotheby's) **$3,762 £1,900**

MATTHYS SCHOEVAERDTS – A Capriccio Harbour Scene With Figures By Classical Ruins – on copper – 10½ x 15in.
(Christie's) **$5,820 £3,000**

MATTHYS SCHOEVAERDTS – A Town Scene With Numerous Figures By A Church With An Obelisk Nearby – on panel – 11¾ x 16¾in.
(Christie's) **$6,790 £3,500**

FLORIS VAN SCHOOTEN – A Pewter Plate Of Strawberries, A Bowl Of Gooseberries, A Loaf Of Bread And A Silver Beaker On A Draped Table – signed with initials – on panel – 15 x 21½in.
(Christie's) **$18,240 £9,500**

PIETER SCHOUBROECK – Capriccio Coastal Landscapes With Fisherfolk And Other Figures – one signed with monogram – on panel – 19¾ x 24½in.
(Christie's) **$10,560 £5,500 Pair**

AERT SCHOUMAN – A Peacock And Other Birds In A Landscape – signed – 34½ x 31¼in.
(Christie's) **$2,910 £1,500**

A. H. SCHRAM – 'The Gardener's Daughter'; and 'Wild Roses' – signed and dated 1903 – oil – 19½ x 15½in.
(Dacre, Son & Hartley) **$2,112** **£1,050 Pair**

A. SCHRANZ – A Mediterranean Coastal Scene With A Dutch Trading Vessel At Anchor – on panel – 5¼ x 11¾in.
(Christie's) **$660** **£340**

O. M. VAN SCHRIECK, Called Snuffalaer – A Woodland Scene, Snakes And A Lizard On The Ground In A Forest – 15¾ x 17¾in.
(Sotheby's) **$13,580** **£7,000**

SCHUETZ – Italianate Wooded River Landscape With Figures – on panel – 2¾ x 3¾in.
(Christie's) **$737** **£380 Pair**

C. SCHUT – The Triumph Of Amphitrite – on copper – 20½ x 29in.
(Christie's) **$2,328** **£1,200**

SCHWEICKART – An Extensive Wooded River Landscape With Peasants, Cattle And Sheep In The Foreground And A Town Beyond – on panel – 13 x 17in.
(Christie's) **$1,940** **£1,000**

C. L. VAN SCHYNDEL – Peasants Merrymaking Outside An Inn – signed and dated 1704 – on panel – 10¾ x 13½in.
(Christie's) **$6,208** **£3,200**

DAVID SCOTT – Study For Figure Of Patriarch In Picture Of 'Family Discord' – inscribed – paper on canvas – 31¼ x 25¼in.
(Sotheby's) **$192** **£100**

GEORGES SCOTT – The Surrender Of General Kronje To General Roberts Of Kandaha At Padabourgh, With A Guard Of The Gordon Highlanders – signed – 44 x 69in.
(Sotheby's) **$1,584** **£800**

TOM SCOTT – Selkirk After Rain – signed and dated 1918 – 10 x 13¾in.
(Sotheby's) **$515** **£260**

TOM SCOTT – On A River Bank; A Farmstead – signed, one dated 1913, the other dated 1915 – 6 x 10in.
(Sotheby's Belgravia) **$149** **£75**

WILLIAM SCOTT OF BRIGHTON – Old Hove – watercolour – 11 x 16¼in.
(Christie's) **$87** **£45**

WILLIAM SCOTT – Dark Blue And White Still Life, 1963 – 14 x 12in.
(Sotheby's) **$1,089** **£550**

SCOTTISH SCHOOL, circa 1850 – A Piper – on panel – 12 x 10in.
(Sotheby's Belgravia) **$181** **£95**

EDWARD SEAGO – Winter Sunshine, Ludham Lane, Norfolk – signed and dated '50 – on board – 11½ x 15½in.
(Sotheby's) **$4,356** **£2,200**

EDWARD SEAGO – The Mill, Gouda – signed – 17½ x 23½in.
(Sotheby's) **$4,950** **£2,500**

EDWARD SEAGO – Honfleur – signed – on board – 16 x 24in.
(Sotheby's) **$11,088** **£5,600**

SEBASTIANO – Portrait Of A Young Man, Half Length, Before A Parapet Holding A Bow – bears date 1518 – on panel – 26¾ x 20½in.
(Christie's) **$2,910** **£1,500**

SEGHERS – A Still Life Of Flowers In A Crystal Vase – on panel – 17¾ x 14¼in.
(Sotheby's) **$4,268** **£2,200**

CARL SEILER – An Interior Scene With A Figure In 18th century Costume – signed – oil on panel – 24 x 18cm.
(King & Chasemore) **$4,356** **£2,200**

JACOPO DEL SELLAIO – The Rest On The Flight Into Egypt – on panel – circular – diameter 26½in.
(Christie's) **$15,360** **£8,000**

CHARLES A. SELLAR – The Start Of The Day – signed – 15½ x 23in.
(Sotheby's Belgravia) **$192** **£100**

SERANGELI – Portrait Of Erminia Ruffini With A Musical Score, A Score Of A Song Below – inscribed – pencil and pink wash – 177 x 105mm.
(Christie's) **$105** **£55**

SERBIAN SCHOOL, 17th century – Saint John The Baptist In The Wilderness – canvas on panel – 12¼ x 8¼in.
(Sotheby's) **$396** **£200**

J. T. SERRES – British Frigates In Heavy Weather – bears indistinct signature – watercolour – on Whatman paper – 10½ x 16¼in.
(Christie's) **$466** **£240**

DA SESTO – The Holy Family With The Infant Saint John The Baptist – on panel – 11 x 10¼in.
(Christie's) **$1,455** **£750**

SCHOOL OF SEVILLE, 17th century – Saint Thomas Villanueva Giving Alms To Children And Cripples, Beneath A Classical Archway – 48 x 37in.
(Sotheby's) **$1,089** **£550**

TOM SEYMOUR – At Avelea On Severn, Shropshire; Near Loughborough, Leicestershire – both signed – 16 x 12in.
(Sotheby's Belgravia)
$614 **£320 Pair**

TOM SEYMOUR – Waterfall On The River Tees, County Durham – signed, inscribed on the reverse – 13½ x 9½in.
(Sotheby's Belgravia)
$105 **£55**

TOM SEYMOUR – "Country Scene With Farmer And Cattle In Foreground" – signed – oil – 7½ x 15½in.
(J. Entwistle & Co.) **$130** **£68**

TOM SEYMOUR – "Lake And Country Scenes" – signed – oil – 7½ x 15½in.
(J. Entwistle & Co.) **$288** **£150 Pair**

TOM SEYMOUR – The Manse Burn, Arrochan – signed – 14 x 9½in.
(Sotheby's Belgravia) **$187** **£95**

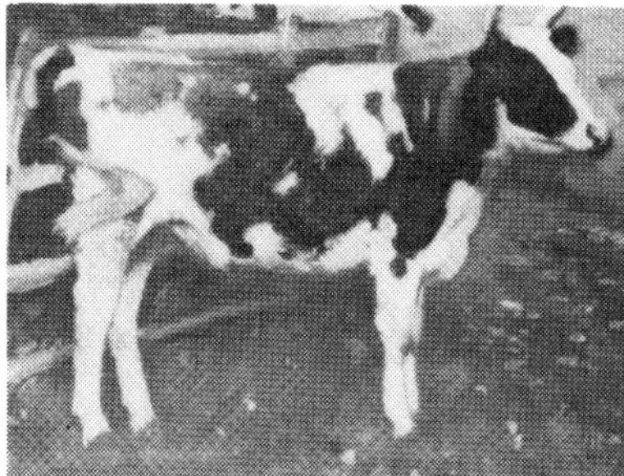

WILLIAM SOMERVILLE SHANKS – Study Of A Cow – signed – 11½ x 15¼in.
(Sotheby's) **$250** **£130**

JOHN BYAM LISTON SHAW – 'Now Is The Pilgrim Year Fair Autumn's Charge' – signed – 33½ x 47in.
(Sotheby's Belgravia) **$26,156** **£13,000**

SHAYER – Barges With Figures, Horses And Dog On A River Bank – bears signature and dated 1840 – watercolour – 11½ x 16in.
(Neales of Nottingham) **$154** **£79**

SHAYER – Fisherfolk – 24½ x 29in.
(Sotheby's Belgravia) **$499** **£260**

W. SHAYER – Coastal Scene, With Coasters And Sailing Barges Off The Shore In A Heavy Swell, With Figures On The Beach Under A Stormy Sky – on panel – 42 x 60cm.
(Henry Spencer & Sons) **$3,069** **£1,550**

W. SHAYER – A Coastal Landscape With Fisherfolk – 13½ x 17¼in.
(Christie's) **$543** **£280**

W. SHAYER – Fisherman And Wife Selling Early Morning Catch To Horseman – signed and dated 1835 – oil on panel – 17 x 23in.
(Manchester Auction Mart) **$707** **£350**

W. SHAYER – A Coastal Scene With Fisherfolk And A Beached Fishing Vessel – 23½ x 19½in.
(Christie's) **$1,358** **£700**

W. SHAYER, SNR. – The Fisherman's Family On The Isle Of Wight – inscribed and dated – 27½ x 35½in.
(Sotheby's Belgravia) **$3,400** **£1,700**

SHAYER

WILLIAM SHAYER – A Gypsy Camp In A Wooded Landscape – 27¼ x 35¾in.
(Christie's) **$1,067** **£550**

WILLIAM SHAYER – A Rural Landscape With A Couple Attending Cows And Goats – signed – 17 x 23in.
(Russell, Baldwin & Bright) **$5,488** **£2,800**

WILLIAM SHAYER, SNR. – Travellers On A Woodland Path – on board – 7 x 8¾in.
(Christie's) **$3,104** **£1,600**

WILLIAM SHAYER, SNR. – Mill Bay, Isle Of Wight – signed and inscribed on the reverse – on panel – 10¼ x 14¼in.
(Christie's) **$4,268** **£2,200**

WILLIAM SHAYER, SNR. – Coastal Scene, Isle Of Wight, With Fisherfolk In The Foreground – signed and dated 1836 – 27¼ x 35¾in.
(Christie's) **$10,670** **£5,500**

WILLIAM SHAYER, SNR. – Sisters – signed – 23½ x 18½in.
(Sotheby's Belgravia) **$2,414** **£1,200**

WILLIAM SHAYER, SNR. – The Sailor's Home – signed, inscribed on a label on the reverse – on panel – 14 x 18in.
(Sotheby's Belgravia) **$9,054** **£4,500**

WILLIAM SHAYER, JNR. – A Ploughboy In A Field – canvas on panel – 11½ x 11½in.
(Christie's) **$776** **£400**

WILLIAM J. SHAYER – Coaching Scenes – signed and dated 1873 – on board – five in diamond-shaped frame – 16 x 16in.
(Christie's) **$1,261** **£650**

WILLIAM J. SHAYER – Hunting Scenes – on board – five in diamond-shaped frame – 16 x 16in.
(Christie's) **$8,730** **£4,500**

WILLIAM J. SHAYER – A Country Tavern – signed – on panel – 9 x 12½in.
(Sotheby's Belgravia) **$6,841 £3,400**

WILLIAM SHAYER, SNR. And EDWARD CHARLES WILLIAMS – Milking Time; A Wooded Landscape With Herdsmen, Cattle And Sheep On A Path, By A Pond And Cottages Beyond – signed by both Artists and dated 1851 – 38¾ x 46½in.
(Christie's) **$10,670 £5,500**

ANDREW SHEARBON – A Flower For Father – inscribed and dated 1869 – 20 x 16in.
(Sotheby's Belgravia) **$1,710 £850**

VINCENT SHELDON – Building Scene – signed – etching – 19 x 15cm.
(Australian Art Auctions)
$192 £98

F. H. S. SHEPHERD – Morning On Golgotha – signed – 11 x 21in.
(Sotheby's Belgravia)
$48 £25

T. H. SHEPHERD – Edinburgh Castle From The Grass Market – heightened with bodycolour – 10 x 9in.
(Sotheby's) **$192 £100**

D. SHERRIN – A Snowy Night – inscribed – on board – 6 x 8in.
(Sotheby's Belgravia)
$86 £45

DANIEL SHERRIN – A Flock Of Sheep On A Highland Track – signed – 19 x 29in.
(Sotheby's Belgravia)
$211 £110

DANIEL SHERRIN – Landscape With Church And Cottages And River In Foreground – signed – oil on canvas – 30 x 50in.
(Morphets of Harrogate)
$1,344 £700

DANIEL SHERRIN – River Landscape – signed – oil on canvas – 20 x 30in.
(Morphets of Harrogate)
$748 £390

JOHN SHERRIN – A Bird's Nest And A Branch Of Apple Blossom – signed – watercolour and bodycolour – 8½ x 10¼in.
(Christie's) **$466 £240**

FREDERICK JAMES SHIELDS – Rebellion: A Study Of A Child's Head – signed with monogram and inscribed – red chalk on grey paper – 7½ x 6¼in.
(Christie's) **$97 £50**

JAN SIBERECHTS – A Wooded Landscape With Peasants, Cattle And A Haycart In A Stream – 39½ x 45½in.
(Christie's) **$5,044 £2,600**

BERNHARD SICKERT – Fiery Evening, Le Croesic – signed and dated 1905 – on panel – 12¾ x 15¾in.
(Sotheby's) **$198** **£100**

WALTER RICHARD SICKERT – Portrait Of A Lady – signed – 23½ x 17¾in.
(Sotheby's) **$792** **£400**

WALTER RICHARD SICKERT – Study for 'The Soldiers Of King Albert The Ready' – signed and dated 1914 – pen and sepia ink and black chalk – 12½ x 9¾in.
(Sotheby's) **$693** **£350**

WALTER RICHARD SICKERT – Street Scene, Dieppe – signed – pen and sepia ink – 7¼ x 3¾in.
(Sotheby's) **$832** **£420**

WALTER RICHARD SICKERT – The Cycle Shop – signed – on panel – 6 x 9in.
(Sotheby's) **$2,178** **£1,100**

WALTER RICHARD SICKERT – The Country House – signed – pen and sepia ink – 6 x 7¼in.
(Sotheby's) **$752** **£380**

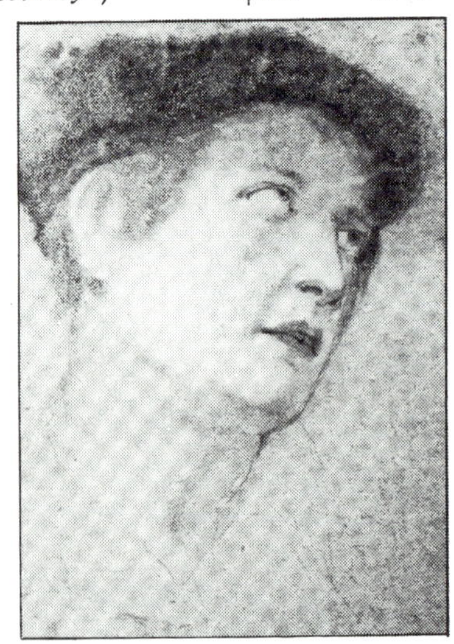

SIENESE SCHOOL, late 16th century – Head Of A Man – red and black and coloured chalk on blue paper – 26.7 x 20cm.
(Christie's) **$365** **£190**

PAUL SIGNAC – Anvers – signed, signed on the reverse – on panel – 8½ x 6¼in.
(Sotheby's) **$5,544** **£2,800**

OLIVER SILK – An Arab – signed and dated 1913 – heightened with bodycolour – 12½ x 10in.
(Sotheby's Belgravia) **$42** **£22**

ADAM SILO – Dutch Smallships In A Choppy Sea – 19½ x 27¾in.
(Christie's) **$9,700** **£5,000**

A. SILO – A Dutch Indiaman With Whalers In The Foreground – 31½ x 42in.
(Christie's) **$5,044** **£2,600**

SILO – Dutch Men-O'-War And Other Shipping In A Choppy Sea – 24½ x 31in.
(Christie's) **$582** **£300**

RICHARD SIMKIN – Colonel Lord Cavendish's Regiment Of Horse, 1688 – signed and inscribed – watercolour heightened with white – 13¾ x 9¾in.
(Christie's) **$68** **£35**

SIMMONS – Nymphs By A Lily Pond – oval – 12¼ x 16in.
(Sotheby's Belgravia)
$172 **£90**

EYRES SIMMONS – A Windmill – signed – 13½ x 9½in.
(Sotheby's Belgravia)
$96 **£50**

M. SIMON – Coastal Scene, Figures On Beach – signed – oil on canvas – 20 x 24in.
(Morphets of Harrogate)
$853 **£440**

M. SIMON – Moorland Scene – signed – oil on canvas – 20 x 24in.
(Morphets of Harrogate) **$194** **£100**

DE SIMONE – The 'Isleworth', a steam launch – 16½ x 22½in.
(Sotheby's Belgravia) **$77** **£40**

DE SIMONE – 'Ellen Anne', Captain Jones Master – signed and inscribed – gouache – 18½ x 23½in.
(Sotheby's Belgravia) **$44** **£22**

AUGUSTINE SIMONET – La Promenade En Caleche – signed and dated 1861 – pencil, pen, ink and watercolour – 8¾ x 13½in.
(Sotheby's) **$418** **£220**

ATTILIO SIMONETTI – Two Old Women By A Church Door – signed and dated 1870 – watercolour – 260 x 178mm.
(Christie's) **$114** **£60**

GUSTAVO SIMONI – Ladies On Terraces – one signed and dated '74 – watercolour – 352 x 242mm.
(Christie's) **$124** **£65 Pair**

F. SIMONINI – A Battle Skirmish Between Christians And Turks – 50 x 75¼in.
(Sotheby's) **$9,504** **£4,800**

CHARLES WALTER SIMPSON – Seagulls And Waves – signed with initials – on board – 7¼ x 9¼in.
(Sotheby's Belgravia) **$129** **£65**

WILLIAM SIMPSON – The Bombardment Of Sebastopol – signed and dated 1856 – pencil and watercolour heightened with white – 10¼ x 14in.
(Christie's) **$504** **£260**

CHARLES SIMS – The Three Graces – signed – 11¾ x 9½in.
(Sotheby's Belgravia) **$1,267** **£660**

HENRY SINGLETON – The Angel Expelling Adam And Eve From The Garden Of Eden – pencil – 12¼ x 10in.
(Sotheby's) **$127** **£65**

G. E. SINTZENICH – 'The Landslip At Rowsdon' – signed and dated 1877 – 24 x 30in.
(Husseys) **$252** **£130**

PETER SION – A Classical Battle Scene – signed – on copper – 23½ x 30in.
(Christie's) **$1,067** **£550**

VICTOR SIRONVAL – Vase De Lilas – signed – oil on canvas – 21½ x 18in.
(Sotheby's) **$297** **£150**

G. F. SLATER – Tugs At South Shields – signed and dated 1913 – 16 x 20in.
(Sotheby's Belgravia) **$396** **£200**

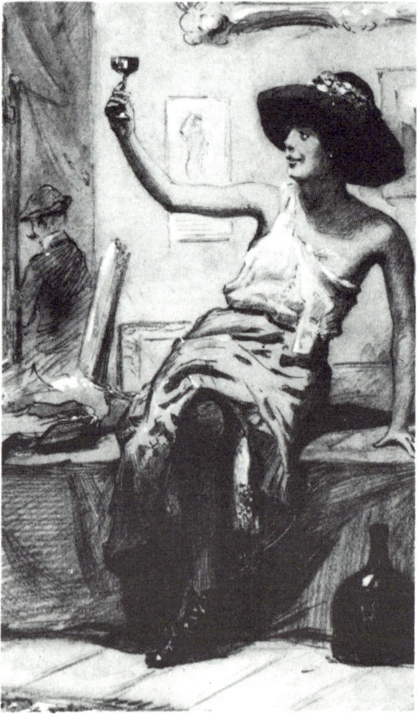

WILLY SLUITER – The Model's Toast – signed – black and white crayon and watercolour – 11¼ x 8¾in.
(Sotheby's) **$198** **£100**

FREDERICK SMALLFIELD – Sunset: Playing A Lute With A Peacock Feather – signed, indistinctly inscribed and dated 1863 – watercolour and bodycolour – 16½ x 21¾in.
(Christie's) **$271** **£140**

FREDERICK SMALLFIELD – Portrait Of A Lady Arranging Flowers – signed with monogram and dated 1854 – 11 x 11in.
(Sotheby's Belgravia)
$1,811 £900

D. I. SMART – View Of Yarmouth – signed – watercolour – 10 x 14in.
(G. A. Key) **$59 £30**

DOUGLAS ION SMART – Abraham Rydberg And Herzogin Cecile In Millwall Dock – signed and inscribed on the reverse – watercolour – 14¼ x 10in.
(Christie's) **$107 £55**

JOHN SMART – A Highland Drover – signed and dated 1890 – canvas on panel – 26½ x 21½in.
(Sotheby's) **$307 £160**

JOHN SMART – Near Callander, Perthshire – signed, inscribed on a label on the reverse – 38 x 56½in.
(Sotheby's) **$1,824 £950**

A. REGINALD SMITH – Springtime, Buckden – signed – watercolour – 14½ x 21in.
(Dacre, Son & Hartley) **$644 £320**

CARLTON ALFRED SMITH – Going For A Walk – signed – 21½ x 15in.
(Sotheby's Belgravia) **$690 £350**

CARLTON ALFRED SMITH – The Gardener's Brew – signed – 16 x 12in.
(Sotheby's Belgravia) **$912** **£480**

DENZIL SMITH – Two Frigates In Harbour – signed – canvas – on board – 13½ x 28in.
(Sotheby's Belgravia) **$173** **£90**

EDWIN D. SMITH – Portrait Of Rachel, Full Length, In A Cream Dress – signed and dated 1841 – pencil and watercolour – 18½ x 13in.
(Christie's) **$427** **£220**

GEORGE SMITH – Collecting Seaweed – signed – 28 x 36in.
(Sotheby's) **$950** **£480**

GEORGE SMITH – Ruminating – signed – on board – 11 x 15in.
(Sotheby's) **$257** **£130**

GEORGE SMITH – The Haycart – signed – on board – 15½ x 19in.
(Sotheby's) **$883** **£460**

J. SMITH – An Afternoon On A Lake; Washing Day – one signed and dated 1878 – 12 x 17in.
(Sotheby's Belgravia) **$155** **£80 Pair**

JAMES BURRELL SMITH – A Wooded River Landscape With A Figure On A Bridge – signed and dated 1876 – 20 x 26½in.
(Christie's) **$931** **£480**

JAMES BURRELL SMITH – On A Wooded River Bank – signed with monogram – 12 x 24in.
(Sotheby's Belgravia) **$304** **£160**

JAMES BURRELL SMITH – On The Shore Of An Italian Lake – signed and dated 1864 – heightened with bodycolour – 9¼ x 23in.
(Sotheby's Belgravia) **$768** **£400**

JOHN RAPHAEL SMITH – Mrs. Boisragon Of Bath – pastel – 8¾ x 7¼in.
(Sotheby's) **$827** **£420**

JOHN 'WARWICK' SMITH – Environs Of Geneva From The Banks Of The Rhone – signed and dated 1788 – 6¾ x 9¾in.
(Sotheby's) **$776** **£400**

JOHN 'WARWICK' SMITH – Carclaise Tin Mine, Cornwall – signed and inscribed on the reverse – watercolour – 5½ x 8¾in.
(Christie's) **$310** **£160**

JOHN 'WARWICK' SMITH – Boulders And Trees Near A Stream – signed and inscribed on the reverse – pen and grey ink, grey wash – 12¼ x 19in.
(Christie's) **$107** **£55**

SIR MATTHEW SMITH – St. Cyr, 1930 – signed and inscribed on the reverse – on panel – 5½ x 7in.
(Sotheby's) **$1,386** **£700**

SIR MATTHEW SMITH – Green Landscape – signed with initials – 20¾ x 28in.
(Sotheby's) **$5,940** **£3,000**

SIR MATTHEW SMITH – Girl With Flowers – 35½ x 27½in.
(Sotheby's) **$2,772** **£1,400**

ROBERT SMITH – An Indian Scene With Elephants, Soldiers etc. – signed and dated 1828 – oil on canvas – 62 x 105cm.
(King & Chasemore)
$2,940 **£1,500**

WILLIAM COLLINGWOOD SMITH – Figures On A Track By A River – signed – watercolour heightened with white – 13¼ x 19¼in.
(Christie's) **$165** **£85**

WILLIAM COLLINGWOOD SMITH – A Coastal View With A Distant Town, Probably In Italy – signed – watercolour – 6¾ x 9¾in.
(Christie's) **$107** **£55**

W. H. SMITH – Still Life Of Mixed Fruit On A Bench – signed and dated 1831 – oil – 16 x 21in.
(G. A. Key) **$297** **£150**

SMITH – The 'Assel', A British Ship In Arctic Waters – 22½ x 37½in.
(Sotheby's Belgravia) $317 £160

SMYTHE – Resting – 11 x 15½in.
(Sotheby's Belgravia) $277 £140

E. R. SMYTHE – A Wooded Landscape, With Donkeys And A Sleeping Boy – initialled and dated 1825 – 11½ x 17¾in.
(Christie's) $679 £350

EDWARD ROBERT SMYTHE – Horses And Sheep In A Stable – on panel – 14 x 18in.
(Christie's) $582 £300

EDWARD ROBERT SMYTHE – A Wooded Landscape With A Donkey – 11¾ x 15¼in.
(Christie's) $2,134 £1,100

T. SMYTHE – Gamekeeper's Bay Pony Standing Beneath A Tree With Two Rabbits Attached To His Saddle, A Dog At His Feet – signed – on panel – 25 x 35.5cm.
(Henry Spencer & Sons) $455 £230

T. SMYTHE – Off To Market – on panel – 5¼ x 6½in.
(Sotheby's Belgravia) $394 £200

T. E. SMYTHE – Summer; Winter – both signed and dated 1879 – 11¾ x 8¼in.
(Sotheby's Belgravia) $365 £190 Pair

THOMAS SMYTHE – The Plough Team Returning – signed – on panel – oval – 11 x 14in.
(Sotheby's Belgravia) $2,758 £1,400

THOMAS SMYTHE – Returning From Market – signed – oil on panel – 9¼ x 14½in.
(Bonham's) $6,860 £3,500

SNAFFLES – An Irish Point-To-Point – signed – coloured lithograph – 562 x 758mm.
(Sotheby's) **$1,591** **£820**

SNAYERS – A Cavalry Engagement – 29¾ x 44in.
(Christie's) **$2,716** **£1,400**

SNAYERS – A Wooded Landscape, With A Waggon Train – canvas on panel – 14½ x 18in.
(Christie's) **$679** **£350**

PEETER SNAYERS – A Skirmish In A Wooded River Landscape – bears monogram and dated 1670 – on panel – 9¾ x 7in.
(Christie's) **$4,656** **£2,400**

PEETER SNAYERS – Villagers Repelling An Attack By Marauders – signed in monogram and dated 1631 – on panel – 14¾ x 20¼in.
(Sotheby's) **$19,400** **£10,000**

OTTO SNYDE – A Fisher Boy – signed – 21 x 14¾in.
(Sotheby's Belgravia) **$61** **£32**

SNYDERS – A Still Life With Lobster On A Blue And White Platter, On A Wooden Ledge – 35½ x 48in.
(Sotheby's) **$5,148** **£2,600**

SNYDERS – Peaches, Grapes, A Melon And A Squirrel In A Basket, A Porcelain Dish, Grapes And Dead Birds On A Table – 33¼ x 47in.
(Christie's) **$3,104** **£1,600**

F. SNYDERS – Figs, Grapes, Plums And Other Fruit With A Parrot And A Squirrel On A Stone Ledge – on panel – 20 x 29¼in.
(Christie's) **$7,372** **£3,800**

F. SNYDERS – Eagles Fighting Over A Dead Stag – 57¼ x 77¾in.
(Christie's) **$1,455** **£750**

F. SNYDERS – A Still Life Of Fruit With A Macaw, And A Monkey, On A Wooden Ledge Covered By A Red Cloth – 27 x 37in.
(Sotheby's) **$8,316** **£4,200**

SOEST – Portrait Of A Commander, Bust Length, Wearing Armour With A Red Sash – 29¾ x 24¼in.
(Christie's) **$330** **£170**

G. A. SOGLIANI – The Holy Family With St. John – on panel – 30¾ x 23in.
(Sotheby's) **$3,880 £2,000**

A. SOLARIO – Cleopatra In A Red Dress, Wearing A Jewelled Blue Diadem, A Speckled Snake In Her Hands – on panel transferred to canvas – 21¾ x 16¼in.
(Sotheby's) **$5,626 £2,900**

G. G. DEL SOLE – The Penitent Mary Magdalene, Seated In A Landscape – monochrome – 18 x 13in.
(Sotheby's) **$911 £460**

FRANCESCO SOLIMENA – The Tribute Money – 30 x 40½in.
(Christie's) **$9,216 £4,800**

FRANCESCO SOLIMENA – The Judgment Of Midas – black chalk, pen and grey ink, grey wash, squared in black chalk – 18.5 x 25.8cm.
(Christie's) **$576 £300**

SIMEON SOLOMON – Damon And Aglae – 35 x 23½in.
(Sotheby's Belgravia) **$10,060 £5,000**

SOLOMON JOSEPH SOLOMON – Portrait Of A Lady – signed with monogram and dated 1901 – coloured chalks – oval 20 x 18in.
(Sotheby's Belgravia) **$96 £50**

JOHN VAN SOMER – The Israelites Captive In Babylon – signed and dated 1719, and inscribed – on paper – 10¼ x 14in.
(Sotheby's) **$585 £300**

F. SOMERSET – On The Italian Coast – inscribed and dated 1890, indistinctly inscribed on the reverse – on panel – 10½ x 13¾in.
(Sotheby's Belgravia) **$79** **£40**

RICHARD GAY SOMERSET – Extensive Autumnal Hilly Landscape With A Small Flock Of Sheep Grazing Among Bracken And Trees – signed – oil on canvas – 74 x 110cm.
(Henry Spencer & Sons) **$515** **£260**

EDITH OE SOMERVILLE – A Patrick's Day Hunt – inscribed – black ink and watercolour – 10 x 13½in.
(Sotheby's) **$213** **£110**

HENRI SOMM – Un Vieillard – signed – pen and indian ink – 6 x 4¾in.
(Sotheby's) **$79** **£40**

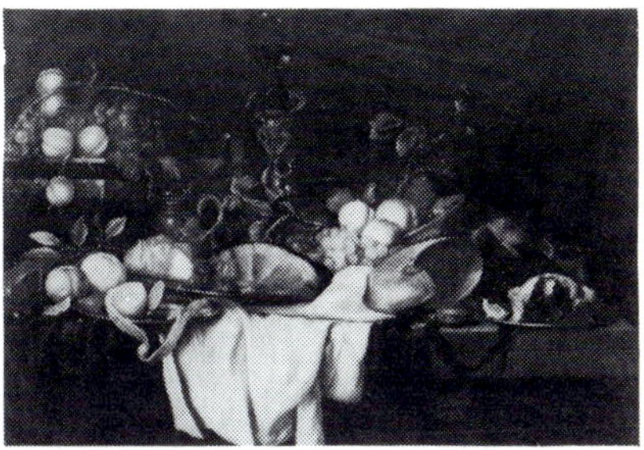

JORIS VAN SON – A Vanitas Still Life On A Wooden Ledge Covered By A Green Cloth – dated 1651 – 30¼ x 43½in.
(Sotheby's) **$15,520** **£8,000**

JORIS VAN SON – A Garland Of Fruit – 27½ x 24in.
(Sotheby's) **$10,780** **£5,500**

JORIS VAN SON – A Banquet Still Life Of Fruit, And Glasses, A Lobster And Shrimps On A Draped Table – 28¼ x 39¾in.
(Christie's) **$32,640** **£17,000**

ELISABETH SONREL – Jeune Femme Aux Hortensias – signed – pencil and watercolour – 16½ x 19½in.
(Sotheby's) **$3,990 £2,100**

A. VIVIANI, Called Il Sordo – The Rest On The Flight Into Egypt – on copper – 6½ x 5¼in.
(Christie's) **$864 £450**

SORGH – Peasants Eating In An Interior – 10¾ x 12¾in.
(Christie's) **$1,067 £550**

HENDRIK MARTENSZ. SORGH – The Interior Of A Stable – signed – on panel – 17¾ x 20in.
(Sotheby's) **$3,168 £1,600**

SORGH – Peasants Regaling In An Interior – on panel – 10½ x 14½in.
(Christie's)• **$1,843 £950**

JOHN B. SOUTER – Yellow Roses And Pink Roses – signed and dated 1953 on the reverse – oil on board – 11½ x 15½in.
(Geering & Colyer) **$194 £100 Pair**

SOUTH AFRICAN SCHOOL, mid 19th century – A South African Cottage Near Stellenbosch; A South African Farm House – inscribed – collage with engraved work, wood and dried grasses – 13 x 18½in.
(Sotheby's) **$394 £200 Pair**

SOUTH AMERICAN SCHOOL, circa 1850 - The Proprietors Accepting Hospitality On Their Estate Near Rio De Janeiro – watercolour – 17 x 11½in.
(Sotheby's) **$1,065 £540**

SOUTH AMERICAN SCHOOL, circa 1840 – Rio De Janeiro With The Prais De Botafogo; and The Sugar Loaf From The Shore, Fishing Boats In The Foreground – oil on canvas – 16¼ x 25¼in.
(Sotheby's) **$27,580 £14,000 Two**

J. M. SOUTHERN – An Autumn Afternoon – signed – 23¾ x 37½in.
(Sotheby's Belgravia) **$288 £150**

FRANK SOUTHGATE – Ducks On The Seashore – signed – heightened with white – 11½ x 23½in.
(Sotheby's Belgravia) **$730 £380**

SPANISH SCHOOL, 17th century – The Princess Isabella As A Child – oil on canvas – 24½ x 17½in.
(Morton's Auction Exchange, Inc.)
$1,050 £530

SPANISH SCHOOL, 17th century – Portrait Of A Conquistidor, Full Length – inscribed – oil on canvas – 77 x 46in.
(Morton's Auction Exchange, Inc.)
$1,600 £808

SPANISH SCHOOL – Portrait Of A Nobleman, Full Length – inscribed and dated 1657 – 77 x 47½in.
(Morton's Auction Exchange, Inc.)
$1,600 £808

DOMENICO GARGIULO, Called Mico Spadaro – The Adoration Of The Shepherds – 29 x 39in.
(Christie's) **$42,240 £22,000**

HARRY SPENCE – A View In Shropshire – signed – 19½ x 23½in.
(Sotheby's) **$396 £200**

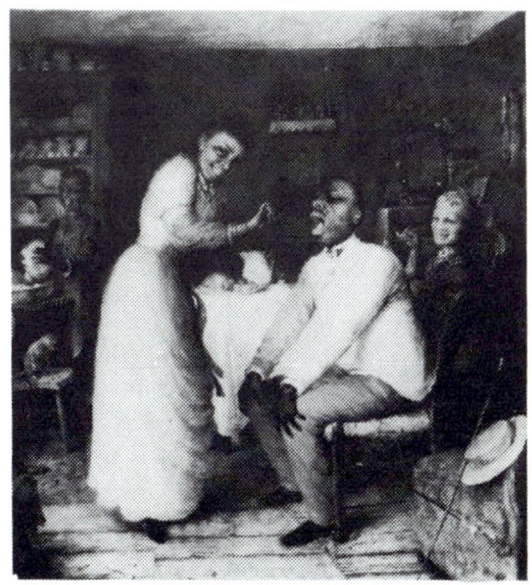

LILLY MARTIN SPENCER – 'Blind Faith' – signed and dated 1896 – oil on canvas – 36 x 29in.
(Morton's Auction Exchange, Inc.)
$5,500 £2,792

PERCY FREDERICK SEATON SPENCE – Egyptian Reggae; An Exotic Perfume, advertisements for 'The Flamingo' lipstick – one signed and dated 1926 – gouache – one oval – 21½ x 15¼in. and 27¼ x 18in.
(Sotheby's Belgravia)
$608 £320 Pair

VERA SPENCER – Japanese Child In National Dress In Interior – oil – 19 x 13in.
(G. A. Key) **$127 £64**

THOMAS SPINKS – On The Conway, North Wales; Cattle By A River – signed with monogram, one dated 1871, the other inscribed on the reverse – 7½ x 15½in.
(Sotheby's Belgravia)
$418 £220 Pair

THOMAS SPINKS – Pont-Y-Caen, On The Llugwy, Near Capel Curig – signed and dated 1883, inscribed on the reverse – 28 x 36in.
(Sotheby's Belgravia)
$437 £220

B. SPRANGER – Apollo And Marsyas – grisaille – 14¾ x 19¾in.
(Christie's) **$1,455 £750**

B. SPRANGER – A Wooded Glade With The Toilette Of Diana And Her Nymphs, Acteon With His Hunting Dogs Approaching From The Left – on metal – 15¾ x 20¼in.
(Sotheby's) **$5,940 £3,000**

ALPHONS SPRING – An Interior With Three Men Around A Table, Drinking And Smoking – signed – on wood panel – 9 x 12in.
(Russell, Baldwin & Bright)
$4,900 £2,500

L. VAN STAATEN – Canal Scenes – watercolour – 17 x 12in.
(Bracketts) **$585 £280 Pair**

JOHANN LUDWIG STAHL – Portrait Of A Woman – signed and dated 1782 – black and red chalk – 251 x 182mm.
(Christie's) **$67 £35**

C. STANFIELD – An Italian Town – on panel - 10 x 12in.
(Sotheby's Belgravia)
$172 £90

CLARKSON STANFIELD – A Ruined Bridge And Old House On The River At Angers – signed with monogram, inscribed and dated 1851 – pencil, watercolour and bodycolour – 9¼ x 20¼in.
(Christie's) **$1,746 £900**

CLARKSON STANFIELD – A Figure And A Dog Outside By A Bridge – signed – brown and grey wash heightened with white – 11¾ x 16¾in.
(Christie's) **$116 £60**

W. CLARKSON STANFIELD – 'Off Calais', Men In A Small Boat Collecting Wreckage In A Heavy Swell, Other Boats Near The Pier – signed – 70 x 90cm.
(Henry Spencer & Sons)
$574 £290

G. H. STANLEY – Shipping Off The Coast – signed and dated 1884 and '81 – 19½ x 15½in.
(Sotheby's Belgravia)
$218 £110 Pair

ALFRED STANNARD – A View Of Canterbury Cathedral – signed and dated 1828 – canvas on panel – 17 x 25½in.
(Christie's) **$2,522 £1,300**

ALFRED STANNARD – A Coastal Scene With Fisherfolk And Fishing Vessels Beyond – signed and dated 1865 – 10 x 16½in.
(Christie's) **$2,522 £1,300**

ELOISE HARRIET STANNARD – A Still Life Of Melons, Grapes, Currants And Plums On A Ledge – signed and dated 1878 – circular – diameter 19½in.
(Christie's) **$6,208 £3,200**

ELOISE HARRIET STANNARD – A Bunch Of Grapes And An Apple In A Basket, On A Grassy Bank – signed and dated 1866 – oval – 10½ x 13½in.
(Christie's) **$3,880 £2,000**

ELOISE HARRIET STANNARD – Strawberries On A Cabbage Leaf, With A Branch Of Honeysuckle On A Bank – signed and dated 1866 – oval – 10½ x 13½in.
(Christie's) **$4,268 £2,200**

ELOISE HARRIET STANNARD – Apricots And White Currants – signed and dated 1900 – 8¼ x 11½in.
(Sotheby's Belgravia) **$1,920 £1,000**

HENRY JOHN SYLVESTER STANNARD – August Scenes – signed – 9 x 13in.
(Sotheby's Belgravia) **$349 £180 Pair**

HENRY SYLVESTER STANNARD – A Cottage Near Warwick: Rural Scene, With A Small Girl Holding A Cat And Standing By The Gate Of The Thatched Cottage – signed – watercolour – 34.5 x 24.5cm.
(Henry Spencer & Sons) **$310** **£160**

THERESA SYLVESTER STANNARD – Summer Blooms – signed – 9 x 14½in.
(Sotheby's Belgravia) **$109** **£55**

HUGHES STANTON – Picking Turnips – bears signature – 17½ x 23½in.
(Sotheby's Belgravia) **$57** **£30**

STANZIONE – A Young Woman, Bust Length – 17 x 14in.
(Christie's) **$310** **£160**

MASSIMO STANZIONE, Attributed to – Studies Of The Pieta And A Saint Bound To A Tree – black chalk, pen and brown ink, brown wash – 8.3 x 17.8cm.
(Christie's) **$365** **£190**

J. STARK – Figures And Cattle In A Wood – on panel – 14½ x 11½in.
(Christie's) **$2,716** **£1,400**

JAMES STARK – A Wooded Landscape With Figures On A Path And Cattle Beyond – 21½ x 29¼in.
(Christie's) **$1,940** **£1,000**

JAN ADRIAENSZ. VAN STAVEREN – A Hermit Monk At Prayer In A Rocky Wooded Landscape – on panel – 14 x 17¾in.
(Christie's) **$1,261** **£650**

JAN VAN STAVEREN – A Hermit At Prayer In A Crypt – bears signature and date 1642 – on panel – 24½ x 18½in.
(Sotheby's) **$1,940** **£1,000**

KENNETH STEEL – The Square, Salisbury – watercolour drawing – 31 x 37cm.
(Edmiston's) **$252** **£130**

J. STEEN – Peasants Brawling In An Interior – bears signature – on panel – 7½ x 9in.
(Christie's) **$3,104** **£1,600**

JAN STEEN – Interior With A Sleeping Woman – bears signature and dated 1664 – 15 x 12½in.
(Sotheby's) **$19,600** **£10,000**

JAN STEEN – Outside The 'Three Owls' Inn – inscribed, bears signature – on panel – 11¾ x 9½in.
(Christie's) **$15,360** **£8,000**

JAN HAVICSZ. STEEN – The Backgammon Players – signed – on panel – 14¾ x 12½in.
(Christie's) **$61,440 £32,000**

HENDRICK VAN STEENWYCK – The Liberation Of Saint Peter – signed and dated 1635 – 28¼ x 40½in.
(Christie's) **$5,820 £3,000**

HENDRICK VAN STEENWYCK – The Interior Of A Gothic Church – signed and dated 1609 – 5½ x 7½in.
(Sotheby's) **$19,400 £10,000**

PHILIP WILSON STEER – Knaresborough – signed and dated 1900 – coloured chalk and watercolour – 9½ x 14¼in.
(Sotheby's) **$1,188 £600**

PHILIP WILSON STEER – On The Severn – signed and dated 1925 – watercolour – 8¼ x 11½in.
(Sotheby's) **$495 £250**

GEORGES STEIN – 'Quai Aux Fleurs' – signed and inscribed – watercolour – 11 x 15in.
(Morton's Auction Exchange, Inc.) **$750 £379**

GEORGES STEIN – Scene Outside The Moulin Rouge – signed and inscribed – watercolour – 11 x 15in.
(Morton's Auction Exchange, Inc.) **$650 £328**

STEPHANOFF – Amorous Dalliance – watercolour – 19½ x 15¼in.
(Christie's) **$97 £50**

A. STEPHENS – Figures In An 18th Century French Interior – signed – oil on panel – 10½ x 14½in.
(Morton's Auction Exchange, Inc.) **$3,500 £1,767**

ETHEL ANNA STEPHENS – Ocean Beach, Manly – signed and dated '13 – oil on board – 16 x 21.5cm.
(Australian Art Auctions) **$304 £158**

JULIUS STERCK – A Square In A French Town With A Brightly Lit Fun Fair At Night – signed – oil on canvas – 19½ x 15½in.
(Osmond, Tricks & Son) **$792 £400**

PALAMEDES PALAMEDESZ., Called Stevaerts – A Cavalry Skirmish, Mounted Figures In Close Combat In The Foreground Of A Landscape, Another Melee To The Left, And Beyond – signed – on panel – 21 x 29½in.
(Sotheby's) **$7,128 £3,600**

ALFRED STEVENS – Dans Le Salon – signed and inscribed – watercolour – 21½ x 14¾in.
(Sotheby's) **$1,140 £600**

GEORGE STEVENSON – Bond Church, Pool; Outside A Cottage, Isle Of Wight – signed, one dated '90 – 13 x 20in.
(Sotheby's Belgravia) **$304 £160 Pair**

MACAULAY STEVENSON – At The End Of The Day, A Farmer Leading His Horses Homeward – oil on board – 11½ x 13¾in.
(Neales of Nottingham) **$166 £84**

RICHARD MACAULEY STEVENSON – Montreuil – signed – 25½ x 39in.
(Sotheby's) **$499 £260**

CHARLES EDWARD STEWART – Tired Out – signed – 19¼ x 15¼in.
(Sotheby's Belgravia) **$752 £380**

JOHN STEWART – Adam And Eve – 27 x 36in.
(Sotheby's Belgravia) **$218 £110**

JAMES STEWART – Highland Cattle In A Glen – signed and dated 1903 – 50½ x 40¾in.
(Sotheby's) **$792 £400**

W. STEWART – Threshing Grain – inscribed – 13 x 17in.
(Sotheby's Belgravia) **$19 £10**

ST. IVES SCHOOL, late 19th century – 'St. Ives Under Snow, From The Harbour' – oil on canvas – 20 x 26in.
(W. H. Lane & Son) **$310 £160**

BERNARD O. STOCKS – Kentish Views – signed and dated 1891 – 9 x 11in.
(Sotheby's Belgravia) **$86 £45 Pair**

WALTER FRYER STOCKS – Warkworth Castle – signed and dated 1887 – heightened with bodycolour – 21 x 37in.
(Sotheby's Belgravia) **$277 £140**

WALTER FRYER STOCKS – Peace And Plenty – signed and dated 1882, inscribed on the reverse – heightened with bodycolour – 16 x 22in.
(Sotheby's Belgravia) **$108 £55**

WALTER FRYER STOCKS – An Ancient Bridge – inscribed on the reverse – heightened with white – 13 x 18in.
(Sotheby's Belgravia) **$69 £35**

WALTER FRYER STOCKS – Illustrations To Dryden's Poems – signed, all inscribed with verses – watercolour – 8½ x 5½in.
(Christie's) **$194 £100 Four**

EDWIN STOCQUELER – At The Gold Diggings, Australia – signed and dated 1877 – oil on canvas – 24 x 20in.
(Sotheby's) **$2,069** **£1,050**

JAN VAN DER STOFFE – A Cavalry Skirmish, Horsemen Armed With Swords And Pistols In Combat – signed and dated 1637 – on panel – 18½ x 38in.
(Sotheby's) **$3,960** **£2,000**

JAN VAN DER STOFFE – A Cavalry Attack, A Body Of Cavalry Galloping From A Wood To Attack A Mounted Force On A Slope – on panel – 15¾ x 26¼in.
(Sotheby's) **$4,268** **£2,200**

MARTIN BOELEMA DE STOMME – A Still Life Of A Pie On A Pewter Dish, A Nautilus Cup, Wine Glasses, An Overturned Tazza And A Peeled Lemon On A Draped Table – on panel – 21 x 28¼in.
(Christie's) **$14,400** **£7,500**

STONE – Portrait Of King Charles I, Bust Length, Wearing Armour – 29 x 24in.
(Christie's) **$291** **£150**

STONE – Portrait Of King Charles I, Bust Length, Wearing Armour – 23½ x 18¾in.
(Christie's) **$388** **£200**

MARCUS STONE – 'Reverie' – oil on canvas – 7½ x 5½in.
(W. H. Lane & Son)
$863 **£445**

MARCUS STONE – African Violets – signed – 13½ x 17¼in.
(Sotheby's Belgravia) **$162** **£85**

MARCUS STONE – Bullfinch And Blossom; Greenfinch And Apple Blossom – signed – on panel – 13½ x 9½in.
(Sotheby's Belgravia)
$228 **£120 Pair**

R. STONE – The Meet; Full Cry – both signed – on panel – 6½ x 12½in.
(Sotheby's Belgravia)
$1,056 **£550 Pair**

STOOP – A Sportsman With His Dog – on panel – 5¾ x 1¾in.
(Christie's) **$310** **£160**

D. STOOP – A Wooded River Landscape With A Milkmaid, Cattle And Sheep – on panel – 17¾ x 24½in.
(Christie's) **$1,940** **£1,000**

DIRCK STOOP, Attributed to – Studies Of Three Hounds – black and white chalk on grey paper – 152 x 250mm.
(Christie's) **$190** **£100**

ABRAHAM STORCK – Czar Peter The Great Welcomed By The Dutch East India Company Off Amsterdam – 30 x 38in.
(Sotheby's) **$12,740** **£6,500**

ABRAHAM STORCK – Peter The Great Visiting The 'Peter And Paul' In The Ij Off Amsterdam – 27¼ x 34in.
(Sotheby's) **$29,100 £15,000**

ABRAHAM JANSZ. STORCK – A Capriccio Mediterranean Port Scene – 32 x 38in.
(Christie's) **$11,640 £6,000**

ABRAHAM JANSZ. STORCK – A Capriccio Mediterranean Harbour Scene – signed and indistinctly dated – 24 x 29¼in.
(Christie's) **$21,120 £11,000**

ABRAHAM JANSZ. STORCK – A Capriccio Harbour Scene With Figures By A Monument – signed – 33 x 26½in.
(Christie's) **$5,376 £2,800**

ABRAHAM JANSZ. STORCK – A Capriccio Mediterranean Harbour Scene – signed – 30¾ x 25¾in.
(Christie's) **$9,600 £5,000**

A. STORCK – A Harbour With Sailing And Rowing Vessels In A Choppy Sea – 26 x 33¼in.
(Sotheby's) **$4,850 £2,500**

JACOB STORCK – A Caprice View Of Amsterdam, A Barge Carrying A Dignitary Arriving In Port, A Man-O'-War And Several Sailing Vessels Beyond – signed – 31½ x 42¼in.
(Sotheby's) **$21,780 £11,000**

THOMAS STOTHARD – A Chinese Carpenter – signed – watercolour – 8½ x 6¾in.
(Christie's) **$63 £32**

WILLIAM STRANG – The Supper At Emmaus – 23¾ x 19½in.
(Sotheby's) **$396 £200**

WILLIAM STRANG – Portrait Of A Girl With Green Jacket – 64 x 49cm.
(Edmiston's) **$107 £55**

JOHN MELHUISH STRUDWICK – An Angel – signed with initials and dated 1895 – on panel – 28 x 10½in.
(Christie's) **$29,100 £15,000**

ARTHUR JOHN STRUTT – At An Italian Spring – signed, inscribed and dated 1862 – 15 x 12in.
(Sotheby's Belgravia) **$49 £25**

WILLIAM STRUTT – Studies: Reindeer; and A Reindeer Pulling A Sledge – one signed, inscribed and dated 1877 – pencil and watercolour, one heightened with white – 9¼ x 11¾in. and smaller.
(Christie's) **$146 £75 Pair**

VAN STRY – A Wooded River Landscape With A Peasant And Cattle – on panel – 7½ x 9½in.
(Christie's) **$554** **£280**

J. VAN STRY – Barn Interiors With Figures And Cattle – on panel – 16¾ x 15¼in.
(Christie's) **$3,298** **£1,700 Pair**

JAN VAN STRY – A River Landscape With Sailing Barges And Shepherds And Cattle – on panel – 19½ x 23½in.
(Christie's) **$6,208** **£3,200**

C. E. GORDON STUART – A Knitting Lesson – signed, indistinctly inscribed – 35¼ x 23¼in.
(Sotheby's) **$1,113** **£580**

L. STUART – Autumn Near Sutton – signed, inscribed on the reverse – oval – 8½ x 10½in.
(Sotheby's Belgravia) **$39** **£20**

ROBERT EASTON STUART – Study Of A Workshop – signed – 19½ x 15½in.
(Sotheby's Belgravia) **$63** **£32**

W. E. D. STUART – Peaches, Plums, Grapes And Pineapples On A Ledge – signed and dated 1851 – on board – circular – diameter 22½in.
(Christie's) **$582** **£300**

J. WOODHOUSE STUBBS – On The Way Home – signed – 71 x 58in.
(Sotheby's Belgravia) **$345** **£180**

FRANZ VON STUCK – Bildnis Eines Madchens – signed – pencil, black chalk and gouache – on board – 21¼ x 18¾in.
(Sotheby's) **$4,180** **£2,200**

PIERRE SUBLEYRAS – The Mass Of Saint Basil – 53 x 29½in.
(Christie's) **$11,520** **£6,000**

PIERRE SUBLEYRAS – The Infant Christ In Glory -- 11½ x 8¾in.
(Christie's) **$3,072** **£1,600**

ROWLAND SUDDABY – Still Life And Jasmine – signed and dated '38 – 25 x 30in.
(Sotheby's) **$178** **£90**

H. SUMMERS – The Woodmen's Rest – signed and dated 1901 – 31½ x 45in.
(Sotheby's Belgravia) **$570** **£300**

GRAHAM SUTHERLAND – Falling Bird – signed and dated 1942 – pen and ink, coloured chalk and watercolour heightened with bodycolour – 9¼ x 12in.
(Sotheby's) **$2,376** **£1,200**

GRAHAM SUTHERLAND – Landscape With Estuary, 1945 – watercolour heightened with bodycolour – 15¼ x 28¾in.
(Sotheby's) **$3,960** **£2,000**

CORNELIS VAN SWANENBURGH – An Italianate Wooded River Landscape With Horsemen And Cattle On A Path – signed – 23 x 28½in.
(Christie's) **$2,328** **£1,200**

SWANEVELT – Tobias And The Angel – on panel – 9½ x 13½in.
(Christie's) **$1,164 £600**

HERMAN VAN SWANEVELT – An Italianate Wooded River Landscape With A Fisherman And Travellers In The Foreground – signed, inscribed and dated 1642(?) – 13¾ x 19½in.
(Christie's) **$2,522 £1,300**

HERMAN VAN SWANEVELT – A Scene Outside An Inn – inscribed indistinctly – on panel – circular – diameter 10½in.
(Sotheby's) **$3,492 £1,800**

SWART – The Resurrection – pen and brown ink, brown wash – 206 x 144mm.
(Christie's) **$86 £45**

SWEBACH – Company In A Boat By A Diving Board – pencil and watercolour – 107 x 146mm.
(Christie's) **$285 £150**

GEORGE HILLIARD SWINSTEAD – 'A Happy Family' – signed – oil – 34 x 44½in.
(Bonham's) **$9,900 £5,000**

SWISS SCHOOL, 19th century – Views On Swiss Lakes – bodycolour – 850 x 1080mm.
(Christie's) **$1,425 £750 Three**

JOHN SYER – Seascape With A Lifeboat Being Launched Into A Stormy Sea From A Horse Drawn Wagon – signed – watercolour heightened with bodycolour – 15¼ x 22½in.
(Osmond, Tricks & Son) **$594 £300**

JOHN SYER – A River Landscape With A Herdsman And Cattle On A Bridge – signed – on panel – 12 x 18½in.
(Christie's) **$873 £450**

JOHN SYER, JNR. – In The Lakes – signed and dated 1875 – 30 x 50½in.
(Sotheby's Belgravia) **$1,006 £500**

DORCIE SYKES – Still Lives Of Roses And Wallflowers – signed – 11½ x 15½in.
(Sotheby's Belgravia) **$38 £20 Pair**

HENRY SYKES – Fishing On A River; Fisherfolk On A Beach – signed – 11 x 23½in.
(Sotheby's Belgravia) **$494 £260 Pair**

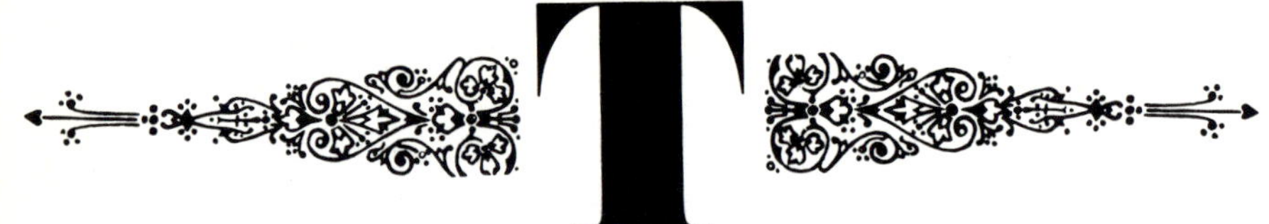

ANTONI TAPIES – Untitled Composition – signed and dated '62 – sand and paint on cardboard on canvas – 42½ x 59in.
(Sotheby's) **$16,236 £8,200**

C. H. TARAVAL – A Pagan Sacrifice – black chalk, pen and brown ink, brown wash heightened with white on brown paper – 425 x 582mm.
(Christie's) **$162 £85**

J. A. HENDERSON TARBET – A Scottish Loch – signed and inscribed – 11¼ x 19½in.
(Sotheby's Belgravia) **$139 £70**

WILLIAM H. TASKER – The Finish – signed with initials and dated 1849 – 6 x 12½in.
(Christie's) **$737 £380**

TASSEL – The Triumph Of The Church Over Idolatry – 26 x 34½in.
(Christie's) **$1,552 £800**

TASSI – A Capriccio Mediterranean Coastal Scene With A Ferry By Classical Ruins – 32¾ x 44in.
(Christie's) **$1,455 £750**

AGOSTINO TASSI, Attributed to – An Italian Landscape With A Castle Above The Sea And A Man Shooting Duck – black chalk, pen and brown ink – 19.5 x 26.7cm.
(Christie's) **$422 £220**

C. A. TAVELLA – A Southern Landscape With Figures Crossing A Bridge – 28 x 35½in.
(Sotheby's) **$2,328 £1,200**

C. A. TAVELLA – A Wooded Italianate Landscape, With Figures By A Stream – oil on cardboard on board – 5¾ x 4¾in.
(Christie's) **$614 £320**

EDWARD TAYLER – Memories; Sweet Seventeen – one signed with monogram – one heightened with bodycolour – 14½ x 11½in.
(Sotheby's Belgravia) **$827 £420 Two**

JOHN FREDERICK TAYLER – Full Cry – Huntsmen And Hounds Streaming Down A Hillside – signed with initials and dated 1867 – 8¾ x 7in.
(Sotheby's) **$388 £200**

E. TAYLOR – An Extensive Highland Landscape With A Figure And His Dog In The Foreground, Cattle Grazing Beyond – signed – oil on board – 7½ x 14¾in.
(Neales of Nottingham) **$194 £98**

J. TAYLOR – Henry VIII And Ann Boleyn – signed – oil on canvas – 26½ x 20½in.
(Morton's Auction Exchange, Inc.) **$300 £156**

RICHARD TAYLOR, Attributed to – An Ancient Building At Kingston In Surrey Called The Rolly – inscribed and dated 1767 – pen and ink and watercolour – 10¾ x 14¾in.
(Christie's) **$194 £100**

TEAGUE – Loch Achray – bears signature, date and inscription – 5½ x 21¼in.
(Sotheby's Belgravia) **$80 £42**

TEMPESTA – The Creation Of Eve – 16½ x 19½in.
(Christie's) **$194 £100**

E. G. TENCH – 'Lowestoft Fishing Vessel Under Sail In Choppy Seas' – signed and dated 1912 – oil on board – 21¼ x 34½in.
(J. W. Hilham) **$201 £100**

TENIERS – A Smoker In An Interior, Other Peasants Seated Gaming Around A Table – on panel – 9½ x 11¾in.
(Sotheby's) **$7,524 £3,800**

TENIERS – Peasants Eating Outside An Inn – bears monogram – on copper – 6½ x 8½in.
(Christie's) **$1,746 £900**

TENIERS – Peasants Merrymaking Outside An Inn – on panel – 10¼ x 14in.
(Christie's) **$1,067 £550**

TENIERS – Peasants Music-Making In An Interior – on panel – 14 x 12in.
(Christie's) **$815 £420**

TENIERS – An Interior With A Man And Woman With Other Figures Before An Open Fire – on panel – 7¾ x 9¾in.
(Messenger May Baverstock) **$744 £370**

TENIERS – An Interior With Peasants Playing Backgammon, Other Figures To The Right Beyond – 20 x 25½in.
(Sotheby's) **$931 £480**

D. TENIERS The Elder – The Raising Of Lazarus – 28¼ x 23in.
(Christie's) **$4,656 £2,400**

DAVID TENIERS The Elder – Minerva And The Nine Muses – signed – on panel – 19½ x 30¼in.
(Sotheby's) **$12,610 £6,500**

DAVID TENIERS The Younger – A Peasant Eating In An Interior – signed – on panel – oval – 9½ x 12½in.
(Christie's) **$26,880 £14,000**

DAVID TENIERS The Younger – A Hurdy Gurdy Player On The Outskirts Of A Town – signed – on panel – 7½ x 5½in.
(Sotheby's) **$8,148** **£4,200**

DAVID TENIERS The Younger – A Wooded River Landscape With Cattle, A Shepherd And Sheep – signed – 21¼ x 27½in.
(Christie's) **$5,820** **£3,000**

D. TENIERS The Younger – Peasants Merry-making Outside An Inn By A Stream – bears monogram – on panel – 9½ x 16¼in.
(Christie's) **$3,104** **£1,600**

D. TENIERS The Younger – The Personification Of Winter – bears monogram – on panel – 8 x 6¼in.
(Christie's) **$1,261** **£650**

DAVID TENIERS The Younger – Peasants Playing Cards In An Interior – signed – on panel – 13½ x 17½in.
(Christie's) **$57,600** **£30,000**

DAVID TENIERS The Younger, After Guido Reni – The Penitent Saint Peter – canvas on panel – 6½ x 4¾in.
(Christie's) **$3,104** **£1,600**

DAVID TENIERS The Younger – A Prisoner Being Sentenced, Surrounded By Armed Soldiers, A Cannon And Armour On The Ground To The Left – bears signature – on metal – 24¾ x 35in.
(Sotheby's) **$9,504** **£4,800**

DAVID TENIERS The Younger, After Jacopo Tintoretto – Portrait Of An Old Man, Seated With A Boy – on panel – 8¼ x 6¼in.
(Christie's) **$1,843 £950**

D. TENIERS, The Younger, Titian, After – The Entombment – on panel – 13½ x 17¼in.
(Christie's) **$621 £320**

TENIERS – A Merry Party Outside An Inn – 27¼ x 34¾in.
(Sotheby's) **$7,920 £4,000**

TENIERS – Peasants Outside An Inn, A Wooded Landscape Beyond – bears monogram – 19½ x 22½in.
(Sotheby's) **$712 £360**

TENIERS – An Interior, A Peasant Lighting His Pipe In The Foreground, Others Drinking And Smoking Around A Table Beyond – on panel – 9½ x 12in.
(Sotheby's) **$752 £380**

JOHN TENNANT – A View Of Hastings From The Coast – signed and dated 1826 – 23¼ x 38in.
(Christie's) **$2,910 £1,500**

JOHN TENNANT – A View Near Lymington, Hampshire – signed and dated 1851 – 15 x 26in.
(Christie's) **$950 £500**

JOHN F. TENNANT – Travellers With A Pony On A Sunlit Country Road – signed and dated 1839 – oil on canvas – 35 x 49in.
(Bonham's) **$3,332 £1,700**

W. G. TENNICK – Staithes, Yorkshire – signed and dated 1880 – 19 x 27½in.
(Sotheby's Belgravia) **$307 £160**

SIR JOHN TENNIEL – How Gil Blas Arrayed Himself In The Blue Velvet – signed with monogram, signed, inscribed and dated 1881 on an artist's label on the reverse – watercolour – 15 x 10¾in.
(Christie's) **$388 £200**

TERBORCH, After – An Interior, With A Lady Drinking – on panel – 22½ x 18in.
(Sotheby's) **$1,008 £520**

HENRY JOHN TERRY – 'The Sabbath' – signed – watercolour – 16 x 11in.
(Christie's) **$271 £130**

HENRY HERBERT LA THANGUE – Cutting Bracken – signed, inscribed on a label on reverse – 57 x 50in.
(Sotheby's Belgravia) **$7,646 £3,800**

HENRY HERBERT LA THANGUE – Winter In Liguria – signed – 41 x 35in.
(Sotheby's Belgravia) **$14,084 £7,000**

HENRY HERBERT LA THANGUE – Carrara Mountains – signed, inscribed on a label on the reverse – 13½ x 19in.
(Sotheby's Belgravia)
$345 £180

THIELE – A River Landscape With Travellers, Mountains Beyond; A Southern Landscape With Herdsmen, A Town Beyond – on metal – 4¾ x 6¼in.
(Sotheby's) **$1,552 £800 Pair**

J. P. VAN THIELEN – Flowers In A Glass Vase – on panel – 23½ x 17½in.
(Sotheby's) **$6,336 £3,200**

THOB – 'Taffy' And 'Clyde', Border Collies – both signed, inscribed and dated Feb. 1885 – on board – 9 x 7in. and 7 x 9in.
(Sotheby's Belgravia)
$172 £90 Pair

JAMES CRAWFORD THOM – In Time Of Need – signed and dated '70 – 23¼ x 43¼in.
(Sotheby's Belgravia) **$247 £130**

JAMES CRAWFORD THOM – 'Feeding The Chicks' – signed and dated 1868 – oil on panel – 30 x 45cm.
(King & Chasemore)
$1,773 £900

HANS THOMA – Der Kampf – signed with initials and dated '90 – pastel – 16½ x 22in.
(Sotheby's) **$570 £300**

G. THOMAS – The Interior Of An Alchemist's Workshop – 22¼ x 31in.
(Sotheby's) **$7,920 £4,000**

THORNBERY – Moonlight Seascape, With Fishing Smacks In A Heavy Swell Off The Coast – oil on board – 13.5 x 20.5cm.
(Henry Spencer & Sons)
$291 £150

THORBURN – The Flushing Point – bears signature and date – 14 x 23½in.
(Sotheby's) **$672** **£350**

ARCHIBALD THORBURN – Grouse – signed with initials – heightened with bodycolour – 6½ x 5in.
(Sotheby's) **$422** **£220**

ARCHIBALD THORBURN – A Covey Of Grouse – signed and dated 1882 – 17½ x 27in.
(Sotheby's) **$2,772** **£1,400**

ARCHIBALD THORBURN – A Woodcock – signed and dated 1887 – on panel – 5½ x 7½in.
(Christie's) **$970** **£500**

ARCHIBALD THORBURN – Studies Of Jackdaws' Heads – one signed with initials – all heightened with bodycolour – two 3¼ x 4½in. and one 3½ x 3¾in.
(Sotheby's) **$499** **£260 Three**

ARCHIBALD THORBURN – Gulls – signed and dated 1885 – heightened with white – 4 x 5in.
(Sotheby's) **$576** **£300**

ARCHIBALD THORBURN – Marsh Harriers, Adult And Immature Male – signed and dated 1924 – heightened with white – 7¼ x 10¾in.
(Sotheby's) **$1,188** **£600**

ARCHIBALD THORBURN – A Ruddy Shelduck – signed and dated 1919 – heightened with bodycolour – 7 x 10½in.
(Sotheby's) **$1,920** **£1,000**

ARCHIBALD THORBURN – Sand Pipers – watercolour – 18½ x 14½in.
(Messenger May Baverstock)
$3,923 **£1,950**

ARCHIBALD THORBURN – A Liver And White Pointer – heightened with white – on buff paper – 7 x 9½in.
(Sotheby's) **$326** **£170**

ARCHIBALD THORBURN – Golden Eagles – initialled – wash – 16 x 14cm.
(Australian Art Auctions)
$86 **£44**

ARCHIBALD THORBURN – The Last Chance Before Dark – signed and dated 1904 – heightened with bodycolour – 10½ x 14¾in.
(Sotheby's) **$1,536** **£800**

ARCHIBALD THORBURN – A Mountain Hare (Autumn) And An Irish Hare – signed and dated 1919 – watercolour and bodycolour on pale green paper – 11¾ x 14¾in.
(Christie's) **$9,312** **£4,800**

ARCHIBALD THORBURN – The Highlands In Winter – signed – heightened with white – on buff paper – 15 x 21in.
(Sotheby's) **$230** **£120**

ARCHIBALD THORBURN – Study Of Two Spaniels – heightened with white – on buff paper – 7 x 9½in.
(Sotheby's) **$307** **£160**

ARCHIBALD THORBURN – A Mallard Drake Brought Down By A Peregrine Falcon – signed and dated 1906 – watercolour heightened with white – 19½ x 30¾in.
(Christie's) **$4,268** **£2,200**

ARCHIBALD THORBURN – Stalking Country, Poolewe – dated 1893 – heightened with bodycolour – 14½ x 21¼in.
(Sotheby's) **$691** **£360**

ARCHIBALD THORBURN – Studies Of Bittern – pencil, watercolour and bodycolour on yellowish brown paper – 6½ x 10¼in.
(Christie's) **$310** **£160**

ARCHIBALD THORBURN – Study Of Mallard Taking Off – signed with initials – heightened with bodycolour – 7 x 4½in.
(Sotheby's) **$537** **£280**

ARCHIBALD THORBURN – A Golden Eagle And Mate – signed with initials – heightened with bodycolour – 4½ x 6¼in.
(Sotheby's) **$480** **£250**

ARCHIBALD THORBURN – An Owl With A Dead Bird On A Branch – signed with initials and dated 'Christmas 1915' – watercolour heightened with white on grey paper – 4¼ x 3¼in.
(Christie's) **$427** **£220**

ARCHIBALD THORBURN – A Dormouse On A Tree Stump – signed and dated 1908 – watercolour heightened with white on grey paper – 7 x 5in.
(Christie's) **$582** **£300**

ARCHIBALD THORBURN – A Covey Of Partridges – inscribed and dated 1886 – 14 x 21in.
(Sotheby's) **$9,600 £5,000**

ARCHIBALD THORBURN – Chaffinch Bird – signed – wash – 12 x 15cm.
(Australian Art Auctions) **$69 £35**

PHILIP J. THORNHILL – Golden Threads – 49½ x 71¾in.
(Christie's) **$2,716 £1,400**

THORNLEY – 'Fishing Boats' – bears signature – 15 x 12in.
(Gribble Booth & Taylor) **$1,006 £500**

WILLIAM THORNLEY – Harbour Scene With Small Boats In A Stormy Sea – oil on canvas – 24 x 44.5cm.
(Henry Spencer & Sons) **$307 £155**

WILLIAM THORNLEY – Coming Up The Thames; and Evening On The Shore – one indistinctly signed – 14 x 12in.
(Sotheby's Belgravia) **$1,544 £780 Pair**

WILLIAM THORNLEY – 'Wreck Of A Brig At Whitby', With A View Of The Abbey Over The Town Under A Dawn Sky; and 'Low Tide, Scarborough', With A View Of The Castle And Shipping – signed and inscribed on verso – 39 x 59.5cm.
(Henry Spencer & Sons) **$4,554 £2,300 Pair**

THORS – After A Day's Fishing – 12 x 18in.
(Sotheby's Belgravia) **$277 £140**

JOSEPH THORS – Extensive Rural Landscapes, With Cottages Among Trees, With Figures And Hens On A Track And By A Pond – signed – 49 x 60cm.
(Henry Spencer & Sons) **$6,534 £3,300**

JOSEPH THORS – Wooded Landscapes With Figures – both bear Nasmyth signatures – 7½ x 11½in.
(Christie's) **$3,492 £1,800 Pair**

JOSEPH THORS – A View Near Cobham, Surrey – signed, inscribed on the reverse – 15½ x 23½in.
(Sotheby's Belgravia) **$1,536 £800**

JOSEPH THORS – Wooded Landscapes With Peasants On Paths – signed – on panel – 8¼ x 7¼in.
(Christie's) **$1,940 £1,000 Pair**

JOSEPH THORS – A Landscape With A Windmill And A Pond In The Foreground – signed – on canvas – 41 x 62cm.
(King & Chasemore) **$1,536 £800**

JOSEPH THORS – Wooded Landscapes With Peasants On Paths – signed – on panel – 8¼ x 7¼in.
(Christie's) **$1,940 £1,000 Pair**

A. TIARINI – Samson And Delilah, She Assisted By An Armoured Philistine Holds A Pair Of Shears And A Lock Of Hair – 84 x 67in.
(Sotheby's) **$4,268 £2,200**

TIEPOLO – An Oriental, Bust Length – 24½ x 19in.
(Christie's) **$427** **£220**

GIANDOMENICO TIEPOLO – An Ex-Voto: The Virgin In Glory, With The Kneeling Saint Anthony Of Padua, Appearing Above The Sickbed Of A Lady Surrounded By Members Of Her Family – 14¼ x 17¼in.
(Christie's) **$36,480** **£19,000**

GIOVANNI BATTISTA TIEPOLO – The Madonna Of Loreto Appearing To Three Saints – inscribed on the reverse – pen and brown ink, brown wash – 27.9 x 17.6cm.
(Christie's) **$4,800** **£2,500**

GIOVANNI BATTISTA TIEPOLO, Circle of – The Temptation Of Saint Anthony – red chalk, pen and brown ink, brown wash heightened with white – 287 x 401mm.
(Christie's) **$570** **£300**

G. B. TIEPOLO – Ariadne On Clouds – a fragment – 10 x 12¼in.
(Christie's) **$5,820** **£3,000**

GIOVANNI DOMENICO TIEPOLO – Cupid And A Group Of Putti In The Clouds – signed – pen and brown ink, brown wash – 18.7 x 25.3cm.
(Christie's) **$2,496** **£1,300**

GILLIS VAN TILBORCH – A Family Group In A Courtyard, Around A Laden Table Outside A House Are Two Men And Two Women, One With A Baby, And A Maidservant Bringing A Glass Of Wine; In Front Of Them A Boy With A Falcon – 32¼ x 45¼in.
(Sotheby's) **$15,520** **£8,000**

GILLIS VAN TILBORCH – Peasants Outside An Inn – inscribed – 14½ x 11½in.
(Sotheby's) **$8,730** **£4,500**

G. VAN TILBORCH – A Woman Feeding A Monkey – on panel – 15¾ x 13½in.
(Christie's) **$634** **£320**

O. TILCHE – A Scene In The Egyptian Desert, With Arab Figures On Camels – signed – watercolour – 11¼ x 18¾in.
(Geering & Colyer) **$126** **£65**

TINGQUA, Style of – A View Of Hong Kong And The Harbour, 1858; A View Of Macao, 1858; and A Joss House, Canton – watercolour – gouache – 6¾ x 9½in.
(Sotheby's (Hong Kong) Ltd.)
$1,622 **£819 Three**

D. TINTORETTO – Portrait Of A Nobleman, Half Length, Wearing A Black Coat – 24 x 19½in.
(Christie's) **$970** **£500**

DOMENICO TINTORETTO – Portrait Of A Bearded Elderly Man, Head And Shoulders, Turned Towards The Left – paper on canvas – 14¾ x 11¼in.
(Sotheby's) **$1,980** **£1,000**

W. V. TIPPET – Wooded River Landscape With Herd Of Deer – signed and dated '83 – oil on canvas – 24 x 36in.
(Lalonde Bros. & Parham)
$277 **£140**

TISCHBEIN – An Oriental, Bust Length, Wearing A Turban – 22 x 17½in.
(Christie's) **$543** **£280**

JOHANN HEINRICH TISCHBEIN The Elder – The Angel Staying Abraham's Hand – signed and dated 1784 – 31¾ x 29in.
(Sotheby's) **$1,455** **£750**

JACQUES JOSEPH TISSOT – Les Adieux – signed – black chalk and grey wash, heightened with white, on buff paper – 39 x 24in.
(Sotheby's Belgravia)
$22,132 **£11,000**

TITIAN, After – Saint Anthony, The Miracle Of The Jealous Husband – 23¼ x 11¾in.
(Christie's) **$504** **£260**

TITIAN, After – The Blinding Of Cupid – 43 x 34½in.
(Sotheby's) **$388** **£200**

PHILIPP PETER ROOS Called Rosa Da Tivoli – An Italianate Landscape With A Shepherd And Sheep – 23¼ x 28in.
(Christie's) **$1,552** **£800**

PHILIPP PETER ROOS, Called Rosa Da Tivoli – Italianate Landscapes With Shepherds And Animals – 35½ x 48in.
(Christie's) **$5,432** **£2,800 Pair**

LOUIS TOCQUE – Portrait Of Count Kirill Grigorievitch Razumovsky Standing, Three-Quarter Length, On A Battlefield Wearing The Uniform Of The Polish Order Of The White Eagle – 54½ x 43½in.
(Christie's) **$7,372** **£3,800**

TOEPUT – A Hawking Party In A Landscape; A River Landscape With Figures In A Rowing Boat – 12¼ x 19in.
(Sotheby's) **$2,328** **£1,200 Pair**

HENRY G. TODD – Still Life Of Grapes And A Peach – signed and dated 1889 – 9 x 7½in.
(Sotheby's Belgravia) **$990** **£500**

HENRY GEORGE TODD – Still Life Of Fruit On A Ledge – signed and dated 1879 – 11¼ x 9½in.
(Sotheby's Belgravia) **$1,440** **£750**

DOMENICUS VAN TOL – A Philosopher In His Study – signed with initials – on panel – 12¼ x 9½in.
(Sotheby's) **$2,813** **£1,450**

ROBERT TONGE – Luxore – signed, inscribed and dated 1855 – heightened with white on buff paper – 13 x 19½in.
(Sotheby's) **$741** **£380**

FRANK W. W. TOPHAM – 'The Reaper', Peasant Girl With Scythe With Sea Behind – signed and dated 1885 – oil on canvas – 10½ x 13½in.
(Manchester Auction Mart)
$848 **£420**

PATRICK JOSEPH TOUHY – Sunshine And Rain Over An Extensive Landscape – signed and inscribed on the reverse – canvas on board – 9¾ x 12¼in.
(Sotheby's) **$1,358** **£700**

HENRI DE TOULOUSE-LAUTREC – Monsieur – signed with initials and inscribed – on panel – 13 x 9in.
(Sotheby's) **$39,600 £20,000**

HENRI DE TOULOUSE-LAUTREC – Piqueur Et Bucheron – on panel – 13¾ x 10¾in.
(Sotheby's) **$41,580 £21,000**

GEORGES DE LA TOUR, Attributed to – The Denial Of St. Peter, To The Left A Man In Armour With A Red Coat, Drawing His Sword With One Hand And The Other Holding The Wrist Of St. Peter – 35¼ x 46in.
(Sotheby's) **$8,232 £4,200**

A. M. DE TOVAR – A Peasant Girl, Holding A Basket of Fruit; and A Peasant Girl Holding A Basket Of Pottery – 26¾ x 22½in.
(Christie's) **$4,656 £2,400 Pair**

G. K. TOWNSHEND – On The Hawkesbury – signed – oil – 22 x 28cm.
(Australian Art Auctions) $257 £134

H. S. TOZER – Village Gossip – signed and dated 1929 – 9 x 13in.
(Sotheby's Belgravia) $307 £160

FRANCESCO TRABALLESI – A Muse, Bust Length, In A Rose Drapery – on panel – 17¼ x 12¼in.
(Sotheby's) $1,683 £850

EDWARD TRAIN – A Salvage Operation – signed and dated 1854 – 12 x 17¼in.
(Sotheby's Belgravia) $457 £130

CHRISTIAN TREIL – The Temptation Of Saint Anthony, In His Study Reading An Open Manuscript – signed and dated 1772 – on panel – 9¾ x 12½in.
(Sotheby's) $1,591 £820

PIERRE CHARLES TREMOLIERE – Two Putti With A Looking Glass – inscribed on the reverse – black and white chalk, pen and brown ink on blue-grey paper – 268 x 203mm.
(Christie's) $143 £75

F. TREVISANI – The Madonna Fainting At The Foot Of The Cross – 37¾ x 28½in.
(Christie's) $921 £480

PIERRE CHARLES TREMOLIERE – Music, Seated On A Cloud, Crowned With Laurel Playing A Golden Lyre; Poetry, Seated On A Cloud, Crowned With Laurel, A Pen In Her Hand – signed – 44½ x 53½in.
(Sotheby's) $13,580 £7,000 Pair

FRANCESCO TREVISANI – Portrait Of Cardinal Pietro Ottoboni, Bust Length, Holding A Letter – 28½ x 23¾in.
(Christie's) $1,536 £800

TREVISANI – The Madonna In Prayer, In Rose And Blue, With A Yellow Shawl Covering Her Head And Shoulders – 24¼ x 18¾in.
(Sotheby's) **$2,211** **£1,100**

SARA TROOST – Portrait Of An Elderly Lady, Wearing A Blue Silk Dress, A White Silk Shawl Trimmed With Fur And A White Cap – signed and dated 1762 – pastel on paper – 27¼ x 22¼in.
(Sotheby's) **$1,188** **£600**

JEAN FRANCOIS DE TROY – Group Portrait Of The Comtesse Du Lys And The Marquises De La Baume And Franqueville – signed and dated 1712 – 54½ x 65¼in.
(Christie's) **$28,800** **£15,000**

PETRONELLA TRUMP – Still Life Of Roses – signed – 11½ x 35½in.
(Sotheby's Belgravia)
$228 **£120**

A. TUCKER – 'Carthorses And Dray In Rural Landscape' – signed and dated 1893 – 32 x 18in.
(Gribble Booth & Taylor)
$162 **£80**

ARTHUR TUCKER – Glen Affraie, Ross-shire; Kilchurn Castle, Loch Awe; Rydal Water; and Autumnal River Landscape With Trees – signed – watercolour – 25 x 35cm.
(Henry Spencer & Sons)
$297 **£150 Four**

ARTHUR TUCKER – A Westmorland Farm – signed – watercolour – 10½ x 6¾in.
(Geering & Colyer) **$91** **£50**

EDWARD TUCKER – An Alpine Chalet – signed – heightened with white – 20 x 26in
(Sotheby's Belgravia) **$182** **£95**

JOHN WALLACE TUCKER – The Newton Passage Boat, Near Exeter, Devon – signed and inscribed on reverse and dated 1829 – oil on panel – 7 x 10in.
(Lalonde Bros. & Parham)
$1,485 **£750**

RAYMOND TUCKER – A Fisherman And His Daughter By A House At Clovelly, N. Devon – signed and dated 1863 – watercolour heightened with white – 13¼ x 17¼in
(Christie's) **$776** **£400**

HENRY SCOTT TUKE – Going Afloat – signed and dated 1900 – 21¾ x 15¾in.
(Sotheby's) **$832** **£420**

HENRY SCOTT TUKE – The Cavern – signed – on panel – 10¼ x 13¾in.
(Sotheby's) **$1,485** **£750**

HENRY SCOTT TUKE – 'Lowestoft Drifters In Falmouth Bay' – watercolour – 12 x 18in.
(W. H. Lane & Son)
$446 **£230**

JOHN TUNNARD – Take Off – signed – on board – 19¾ x 23½in.
(Sotheby's) **$990** **£500**

TURNER – Lady With A Fan – signed – on panel – 11 x 6½in.
(Sotheby's Belgravia) **$149** **£75**

TURNER – Highland Cattle On A Wet Day – 19 x 29in.
(Sotheby's Belgravia) **$288** **£150**

GEORGE TURNER – Near Kirk Treton, Derbyshire – signed, inscribed and dated 1901 on the reverse – 15½ x 24in.
(Sotheby's Belgravia) **$3,168** **£1,600**

GEORGE TURNER – Watching A Flock – signed – 23 x 35in.
(Sotheby's Belgravia) **$1,305** **£680**

GEORGE TURNER – 'Lane Near Kirk Ireton', Well-Wooded Rural Landscape With A Shepherd, His Dog And Sheep Resting On A Track By A Gate – signed, inscribed on verso, and dated 1902 – oil – on board – 29 x 39cm.
(Henry Spencer & Sons) **$1,385** **£700**

GEORGE TURNER – A Cottage Near The Wood – inscribed on the reverse of the original canvas – 11½ x 19½in.
(Sotheby's Belgravia) **$864** **£450**

JOSEPH MALLORD WILLIAM TURNER – Glastonbury Abbey, Somerset – signed with monogram and dated 1792 – 7½ x 9¾in.
(Sotheby's) **$2,716** **£1,400**

JOSEPH MALLORD WILLIAM TURNER, late 18th century – A View Of The Avon Gorge At Bristol With A View Of A Sailing Vessel Before The Old Hotwells House – signed – pen and ink and watercolour drawing – 10¼ x 13in.
(Osmond, Tricks & Son) **$6,138** **£3,100**

W. TURNER – Study Of A Group Of Cattle In A Landscape – bears signature – oil on canvas – 12 x 20in.
(Neales of Nottingham) **$91** **£46**

WILLIAM TURNER – On The River By Christchurch Meadow, Oxford, With Sailing And Rowing Boats – pencil and watercolour heightened with white – 9 x 15½in.
(Sotheby's) **$975** **£500**

W. H. TURNER – Horses In A Field – signed with initials and dated 1849 – 11 x 14in.
(Christie's) **$427** **£220**

WALTER FREDERICK ROOFE TYNDALE – The Sermon – signed and dated '88 – 17½ x 39½in.
(Sotheby's Belgravia) **$10,060** **£5,000**

THE REV. MICHAEL TYSON – The Chapel At Guy's Cliff, Warwickshire - inscribed on the reverse – pen and grey ink and watercolour – 4¾ x 6¾in.
(Christie's) **$107** **£55**

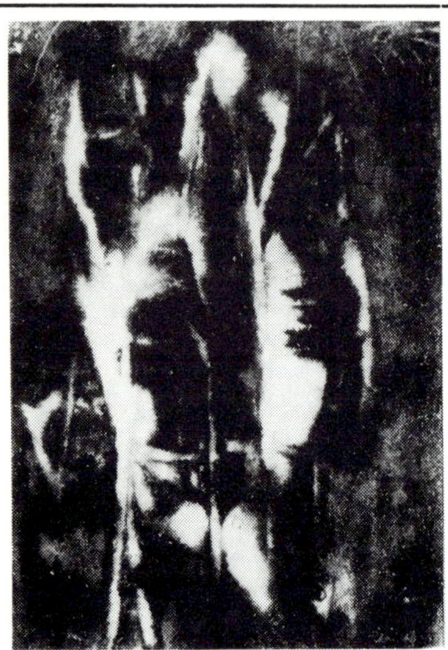

RAOUL UBAC – Au Fond Ombre Et Bleu – signed with initials – coloured crayons – 12¼ x 8½in.
(Sotheby's) **$317** **£160**

RAOUL UBAC – Au Fond Noir – pastel – 10½ x 7¾in.
(Sotheby's) **$198** **£100**

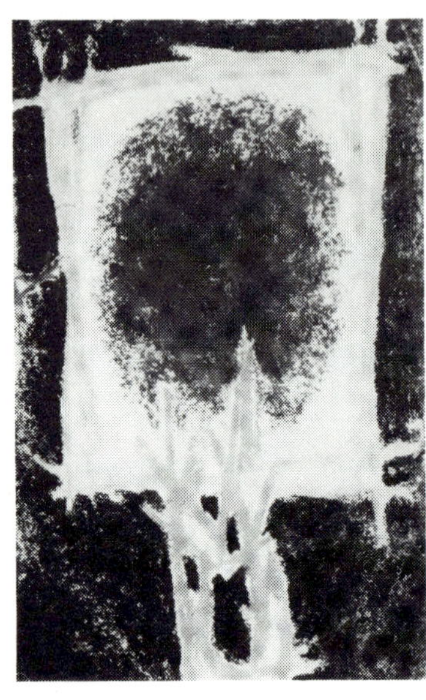

RAOUL UBAC – Lumieres La Nuit – signed with initials – pastel – 12¼ x 7¾in.
(Sotheby's) **$257** **£130**

LUCAS VAN UDEN – A Wooded River Landscape, With Shepherds, And Sheep And A Manor House Beyond – 30 x 37in.
(Christie's) **$5,760** **£3,000**

LUCAS VAN UDEN – A Wooded River Landscape With Travellers On A Road – on panel – 6¼ x 11½in.
(Christie's) **$8,148** **£4,200**

VAN UDEN – A Wooded Landscape With A Herdsman And Traveller – on panel – 9¼ x 13¾in.
(Sotheby's) **$1,707** **£880**

UHLMAAN – Le Coin De Rue – oil on canvas board – signed – 10¼ x 10¾in.
(Sotheby's) **$168** **£85**

JACOB VAN DER ULFT – A Roman View: To The Right A Statue Of A Female On A Plinth And A Temple With Corinthian Columns – signed – on panel – 15¾ x 22¼in.
(Sotheby's) **$20,370** **£10,500**

F. T. UNDERHILL – Still Life With Three Plums – watercolour – signed – 7 x 11in. and 10¼ x 15in.
(Sotheby Bearne) **$118** **£60 two**

FREDERICK THOMAS UNDERHILL – The Last Piece – signed and dated 1818 – heightened with white – 10½ x 8¼in.
(Sotheby's Belgravia) **$297** **£150**

WILLIAM UNDERHILL – The Fruits Of Summer – signed and dated 1869 – 29½ x 24in.
(Sotheby's Belgravia)
$1,440 **£750**

WILLIAM UNDERHILL – Young Poachers – 28 x 36in.
(Sotheby's) **$1,920** **£1,000**

A. URICHI – View Of Lake Como – oil on board – signed – 39 x 54¾in.
(Sotheby's) **$40** **£20**

THE MASTER OF THE SAINT URSULA LEGEND, Circle of – The Madonna And Child – on panel – oval – 14½ x 14in.
(Christie's) **$16,320** **£8,500**

ADRIAEN VAN UTRECHT – A Still Life With Fish And Vegetables – signed – 45 x 56¾in.
(Sotheby's) **$8,924** **£4,600**

SCHOOL OF UTRECHT, 17th century – Pan In A Leopard's Skin, A Wreath Of Reeds On His Head, Holding Reed Pipes And A Shepherd's Staff – 34¼ x 31¾in.
(Sotheby's) **$3,528** **£1,800**

SCHOOL OF UTRECHT – A Vanitas, A Putto Draped In Rose Silk, Blowing Bubbles In A Landscape – inscribed and dated 1651 – on panel – 12½ x 8¼in.
(Sotheby's) **$776** **£400**

MAURICE UTRILLO – Place De Village – signed – 13 x 16¼in.
(Sotheby's) **$13,860** **£7,000**

MAURICE UTRILLO – La Maison De Mimi Pinson, Rue Du Mont-Cenis – signed, signed and inscribed on the reverse – on board – 24 x 30¾in.
(Sotheby's) **$49,500** **£25,000**

MAURICE UTRILLO – Le Lapin Agile A Montmartre – signed and inscribed – on board – 23½ x 31½in.
(Sotheby's) **$39,600** **£20,000**

MAURICE UTRILLO – La Place Emile Zola – signed – board on panel – 10 x 21¼in.
(Sotheby's) **$19,800** **£10,000**

MAURICE UTRILLO – Rue A Montmartre – signed and inscribed – 9 x 7in.
(Sotheby's) **$16,830** **£8,500**

MAURICE UTRILLO – Une Ecole Aux Environs D'Hautmont (Nord) – signed – 20½ x 26½in.
(Sotheby's) **$31,680** **£16,000**

ANDRE UTTER – Les Collines Bearnaises – oil on canvas – signed and dated 1923; signed, titled and dated on the reverse – 21 x 25¼in.
(Sotheby's) **$831** **£420**

THOMAS UWINS – Neapolitan Peasants – 19¾ x 24¼in.
(Christie's) **$990** **£500**

LODEWYCK DE VADDER – An Extensive Wooded Landscape With Peasants On A Path – signed with initials – on panel – 19 x 23¾in.
(Christie's) **$11,640** **£6,000**

WALLERANT VAILLANT – Portrait Of A Man, Bust Length, Wearing An Embroidered Collar Over Armour – black and white chalk on blue paper – 40.5 x 34.3cm.
(Christie's) **$960** **£500**

VALENCIENNES – A Landscape With A Town With Smoking Chimneys – oil on paper – 252 x 312mm.
(Christie's) **$105** **£55**

VALENCIENNES – An Extensive Evening Landscape – oil on brown paper – 298 x 432mm.
(Christie's) **$209** **£110**

VALENCIENNES – A Mountain Ridge Above The Sea – oil on brown paper – 212 x 307mm.
(Christie's) **$209** **£110**

PIERRE HENRI DE VALENCIENNES – Mount Athos, Extensive Mountainous Landscape With Groups Of Figures Looking Towards The Mountain; and Military Encampment Among Classical Buildings With The Soldiery Holding The Maggi In Chains – one signed and dated 1796 – oil on canvas – 40 x 90.5cm.
(Henry Spencer & Sons) **$57,420** **£29,000 Pair**

JACOPO DA VALENZA – The Madonna And Child, In An Interior – on panel – 33½ x 24½in.
(Sotheby's) **$13,860** **£7,000**

JACOPO DA VALENZA – The Madonna And Child – on panel – 22 x 17in.
(Christie's) **$9,216** **£4,800**

WILLIAM FLEMING VALLANCE – Autumn In Argyllshire – signed and dated 1877 – heightened with white – 14 x 21in.
(Sotheby's Belgravia) **$59** **£30**

FREDERICK F. VALTER – Sheep In A Pasture; Sheep And A Cow By A Fence – one signed and dated '99 – one on panel, one on board – 11 x 9in.
(Sotheby's Belgravia) **$228** **£120 Pair**

SCIPIONE VANNUTELLI – Matadors – signed and inscribed – watercolour – 410 x 255mm.
(Christie's) **$247** **£130 Two**

VANVITELLI – A View Of The Ponte Rotto, Rome – 28½ x 37½in.
(Christie's) **$3,686** **£1,900**

GASPAR VAN WITTEL, Called Vanvittelli – A View Of The Campo Vaccino, Rome, With Various Travellers And Herdsmen – 14¾ x 28in.
(Sotheby's) **$19,700** **£10,000**

VARLEY – Cattle Watering By Ruins – watercolour – 5½ x 8¼in.
(Christie's) **$194** **£100**

C. VARLEY – Boats Drawn Up On A River Bank Near A Town – pencil and watercolour – 7¼ x 10½in.
(Christie's) **$39** **£20**

CORNELIUS VARLEY – Cattle By A Cottage With Woman Washing Clothes By A Windswept Tree – signed and dated 1828, and inscribed – pen and brown ink and wash – 9¼ x 13½in.
(Sotheby's) **$291** **£150**

JOHN VARLEY – Tintern Abbey At Dusk – signed and dated 1840 – heightened with gum arabic – 7 x 14in.
(Sotheby's) **$815** **£420**

JOHN VARLEY – London From Greenwich With The Royal Observatory On Flamsteed Hill – signed and dated 1835 – 5¾ x 9in.
(Sotheby's) **$2,716** **£1,400**

JOHN VARLEY – Fir Trees And Pool – signed – 7½ x 12¼in.
(Sotheby's) **$931** **£480**

JOHN VARLEY – Eton – signed – watercolour – 3½ x 5¼in.
(Christie's) **$427** **£220**

JOHN VARLEY – At A Pool At Dusk – watercolour, crayon, partially heightened with gum arabic, on buff paper – 11½ x 16½in.
(Sotheby's) **$485** **£250**

JOHN VARLEY – Battersea Seen From The River At Chelsea – signed – pencil and watercolour – 4½ x 6¾in.
(Sotheby's) **$582** **£300**

JOHN VARLEY – An Extensive View Over A Lake – signed and signed, inscribed and dated 1833 on the reverse – watercolour – 5 x 6¾in.
(Christie's) **$349** **£180**

VICTOR VASARELY – Garam II – signed, signed and dated 1949/58 on the reverse – oil on board mounted on wood – 17 x 12¼in.
(Sotheby's) **$5,148** **£2,600**

VICTOR VASARELY – Piet – signed, signed and dated 1972 on the reverse – oil on board – 36¼ x 24½in.
(Sotheby's) **$7,524** **£3,800**

VICTOR VASARELY – Aiala – signed, signed and dated 1950 on the reverse – oil on board mounted on wood – 19¾ x 21¼in.
(Sotheby's) **$4,752** **£2,400**

KEITH VAUGHAN – Apple Pickers – coloured chalk and watercolour, heightened with bodycolour – 12 x 14¾in.
(Sotheby's) **$436** **£220**

SIMON HARMON VEDDER – A Mammoth Attack – signed – 24 x 16½in.
(Sotheby's Belgravia) **$230** **£120**

O. VAN VEEN – The Triumph Of Claudius Civilis – on panel – 20 x 30¼in.
(Christie's) **$621** **£320**

NICOLAES VAN VEERENDAEL – A Swag Of Roses, Hydrangeas, Poppies And Other Flowers Hanging In A Niche – signed – 24½ x 18¾in.
(Christie's) **$23,040** **£12,000**

A. VAN DE VELDE – Sheep And A Peasant In A Landscape – bears signature and the date 1667 – on panel – 8 x 6½in.
(Christie's) **$16,490 £8,500**

C. E. M. VAN DE VELDE – A Town By The Sea In The South Of France – watercolour – 10¼ x 14¾in.
(Christie's) **$62 £32**

CORNELIS VAN DE VELDE – The 'Royal Sovereign' Firing A Salute – 26 x 20½in.
(Christie's) **$1,455 £750**

JANSZ. VAN DE VELDE – A Still Life Of A Blue And White Chinese Porcelain Mug And Bowl, A Roemer, A Clay Pipe, Tobacco And A Smouldering Taper On A Draped Ledge – signed and indistinctly dated 16-6 – on panel – 23¼ x 18½in.
(Christie's) **$19,200 £10,000**

PIETER VAN DE VELDE – Dutch Men-O-War And Other Shipping Off Flushing – on panel – 28¼ x 41¼in.
(Christie's) **$3,880 £2,000**

WILLEM VAN DE VELDE II, Attributed to – Shipping In A Choppy Sea Offshore – inscribed – black chalk, pen and black ink, grey wash heightened with white on faded blue paper – 14.5 x 22.5cm.
(Christie's) **$537 £280**

VENETIAN SCHOOL OF VERDU PAINTERS, early 19th century – The Grand Canal Looking Towards The Lagoon With Many Figures In Front Of The Church Of The Carita – oil on canvas – 75 x 126cm.
(Henry Spencer & Sons)
$5,940 £3,000

VENETIAN SCHOOL, circa 1520 – A Statue Of A Nude Seen From The Back In A Niche – inscribed on the reverse – black chalk, heightened with white on blue paper – 40 x 18.9cm.
(Christie's) **$3,840 £2,000**

VENETIAN SCHOOL, 18th century – A Rustic Scene, A Woman And Child In The Foreground Of A Landscape – 16½ x 22in.
(Sotheby's) **$1,148 £580**

VENETIAN SCHOOL, late 18th century – The Triumph Of David, The Young Warrior In Yellow Holding The Head Of Goliath, Offered A Cloak Of Victory By Israelite Warriors – 33¾ x 58in.
(Sotheby's) **$1,485 £750**

ADRIAEN VAN DE VENNE – A Peasant Dance In A Landscape, Illustrating A Dutch Proverb – signed and inscribed – en grisaille – on panel – 10½ x 14in.
(Sotheby's) **$3,880 £2,000**

ARTHUR VENTNOR – At Sunset – signed – on board – 19½ x 15¼in.
(Sotheby's Belgravia) **$95 £48**

CORNELIS VERBEECK – Frigates And Other Vessels In A Choppy Sea – on panel – 22 x 29in.
(Christie's) **$6,144 £3,200**

EUGENE VERBOECKHOVEN – Sheep With Hen; and Sheep With Shepherd – signed – wood panels – 7 x 9in.
(Morphets of Harrogate) **$1,228 £620 Pair**

EMILE VERBRUGGE – Pont de Bergrunage, Bruges, Le Matin – signed – oil on board – 9¼ x 13in.
(Sotheby's) **$436 £220**

VERBRUGGEN – Mixed Flowers In An Urn – on panel – 55 x 45cm.
(Edmiston's) **$1,666 £850**

VERBRUGGEN – A Still Life Of Flowers In A Gilt Urn, On A Wooden Ledge – 34 x 17½in.
(Sotheby's Belgravia) **$1,485 £750**

G. P. VERBRUGGEN – Flowers In A Vase – 36 x 24in.
(Sotheby's) **$6,060 £3,000 Two**

G. P. VERBRUGGEN The Younger – A Still Life Of Flowers In A Sculptured Urn On A Ledge With A Bird's Nest – 45½ x 36in.
(Lawrence) **$1,980 £1,000**

VERBRUGGEN – A Still Life Of Flowers In A Sculptured Urn, Within A Stone Niche on metal – 26 x 21in.
(Sotheby's) **$1,782 £900**

GASPER PIETER VERBRUGGEN II – 'Still Life' – signed – oil – 44½ x 36½in.
(Bonham's) **$5,544 £2,800**

GASPAR PIETER VERBRUGGEN The Younger – An Ornamental Urn Decorated With Fruit And Flowers, With A Parrot And Other Birds – signed – 74 x 49in.
(Christie's) **$28,800 £15,000**

J. P. VERBRUGGEN – A Still Life Of Flowers and Birds – 41 x 30¾in.
(Sotheby's) **$3,880 £2,000**

RUTGER VERBURGH – A Merry Party Outside An Inn, A Peasant Plays A Bagpipe While Others Dance – signed – on panel – 21¼ x 25¾in.
(Sotheby's) **$5,820** **£3,000**

FRANCOIS VERDIER – The Angels Appearing To Balaam And The Ass – black and white chalk, grey wash on grey paper – 13.6 x 23.8cm.
(Christie's) **$57** **£30**

JAN PEETER VERDUSSEN – Italianate Wooded Landscapes With Horsemen And Peasants By Ruins – signed – 6¼ x 5¼in.
(Christie's) **$2,910** **£1,500 Pair**

VERELST – A Still Life Of Flowers In A Gilt Urn, On A Wooden Ledge – 29¼ x 24¼in.
(Sotheby's) **$11,880** **£6,000**

VERELST – A Still Life Of Flowers In A Crystal Vase, On A Wooden Ledge – 15 x 10¾in.
(Sotheby's) **$2,970** **£1,500**

S. P. VERELEST – A Still Life Study Of Peonies And Tulips In An Urn – oil on canvas – 78 x 82cm.
(King & Chasemore) **$1,281** **£650**

DIRK VERHAERT – An Italianate Estuary With Ruins, Figures And Shipping – 29 x 38in.
(Christie's) **$2,910** **£1,500**

VERKOLJE – A Music Lesson In An Interior, A Lady And Two Gentlemen Around A Table Covered By A Turkey Carpet, A Parrot In A Cage Above – bears monogram – on panel – 23½ x 20½in.
(Sotheby's) **$14,850** **£7,500**

VERMEULEN – Mercury And Argus – black chalk, pen and brown ink, brown wash – 202 x 165mm.
(Christie's) **$133** **£70**

ANDRIES VERMEULEN – An Extensive Winter Landscape, With Woodmen And A Horse-Drawn Sledge – 12¾ x 16in.
(Christie's) **$10,560** **£5,500**

FREDERICK ARTHUR VERNER – Buffalo Charging Across The Prairie – signed and dated 1893 – watercolour – 24¾ x 39in.
(Sotheby's) **$7,092** **£3,600**

VERNET – A Stormy Coastal Scene With A Wreck – 26½ x 37in.
(Christie's) **$198** **£100**

C. J. VERNET – A Mediterranean Coastal Scene At Sunset With Fishermen Putting To Sea – signed and dated 1776 – 44 x 63in.
(Christie's) **$6,208** **£3,200**

CLAUDE-JOSEPH VERNET – A Southern Harbour Scene – signed and dated 1745 – 34½ x 47¼in.
(Sotheby's) **$46,560 £24,000**

HORACE VERNET – XIX Brumaire De L'An VIII, Bonaparte A L'Orangerie De Saint-Cloud – signed with initials – pen and brown ink and wash, heightened with white – 11¼ x 15¼in.
(Sotheby's) **$2,079 £1,050**

R. W. VERNON – New Brighton Battery And Seashore – watercolour – 8¾ x 13¾in.
(Outhwaite & Litherland) **$141 £70**

WILLIAM HENRY VERNON – A Forest Glade; and Fishing In A Pond – one indistinctly signed with initials and dated – 13¼ x 19¼in.
(Sotheby's) **$634 £320** Two

WILLIAM H. VERNON – A Coastal Scene – inscribed on a label on the reverse – heightened with white – 13 x 18in.
(Sotheby's Belgravia) **$28 £15**

VERONESE SCHOOL, circa 1600 – The Mystic Marriage Of Saint Catherine, In A Wooded Landscape – on metal – 9½ x 12in.
(Sotheby's) **$1,386 £700**

VERONESE SCHOOL, 16th century – The Annunciation To The Virgin – on panel – 27¼ x 17in.
(Sotheby's) **$1,188 £600**

VERONESE SCHOOL – Saint Catherine – 10 x 7½in.
(Sotheby's) **$317** **£160**

LIEVE VERSCHUIER – A Harbour At Sunset – signed – on panel – 14 x 19in.
(Sotheby's) **$14,550** **£7,500**

VERSCHURING – A Halt Outside An Inn, Cavaliers Offered Refreshment By A Serving Maid – bears signature – on panel – 12 x 9½in.
(Sotheby's) **$3,152** **£1,600**

H. VERSCHURING – Studies Of Horsemen And A Dog – red chalk, pen and brown ink, brown wash – 156 x 199mm.
(Christie's) **$95** **£50**

WOUTER VERSCHUUR, JNR. – Two Horses With A Cart On The Banks Of A River By A Moored Rowing Boat And Ferry – signed and inscribed – oil on canvas – 37 x 45cm.
(Henry Spencer & Sons) **$1,227** **£620**

WOUTER VERSCHUUR, JNR. – Two Horses Feeding From A Manger In A Stable Interior – oil – on paper – 32 x 41cm.
(Henry Spencer & Sons) **$297** **£150**

WOUTER VERSCHUUR And MARTHE LANJALLEY – Horses And A Stable Boy – signed – watercolour – 5½ x 8in.
(Sotheby's) **$684** **£360**

J. VERSPRONCK – Portrait Of A Man In A Black Hat, Half Length, Turned Towards The Left – on panel – 29¾ x 24in.
(Sotheby's) **$6,336** **£3,200**

JOHANNES CORNELISZ. VERSPRONCK – Portrait Of A Gentleman, Small Half Length, Wearing Black Costume – on panel – 9½ x 7¼in.
(Christie's) **$17,280** **£9,000**

VERSTRAELEN – A Winter Scene With Figures On A Frozen Lake, A Group In The Foreground On A Horsedrawn Sled, Others Around A Fire To The Left – on panel – 11 x 14¾in.
(Sotheby's) **$3,366** **£1,700**

DANIEL VERTANGEN – The Rape Of Cloelia, A Capriccio View Of Rome Beyond – on panel – 15¼ x 20¾in.
(Christie's) **$10,670** **£5,500**

W. VESTER – Extensive Dutch Landscape With Figures – signed and dated 1870 – oil on canvas – 32 x 49in.
(Bonham's) **$7,840** **£4,000**

ACHILLE VIANELLI – Fishermen On The Outskirts Of Naples With Capri In The Distance – signed – watercolour – 146 x 212mm.
(Christie's) **$494** **£260**

PAULUS VAN VIANEN The Younger – The Temptation Of Saint Anthony – signed and dated – on panel – 21 x 27½in.
(Sotheby's) **$1,940** **£1,000**

A. VICKERS – A River Landscape With A Coach Crossing A Bridge – watercolour – 9¼ x 13¼in.
(Christie's) **$136** **£70**

A. VICKERS – Returning Home – inscribed and dated – 7½ x 15½in.
(Sotheby's Belgravia) **$266** **£140**

ALFRED VICKERS – Windsor From The Brocas Meadows – signed and dated 1854, and signed, inscribed and dated 1854 on the reverse – 24¼ x 37¼in.
(Christie's) **$18,430** **£9,500**

ALFRED VICKERS – An Extensive Landscape, With Cottages By A River – signed – on panel – 9½ x 13¾in.
(Christie's) **$1,552** **£800**

A. H. VICKERS – An Extensive River Landscape With Fishermen; and A Coastal Landscape With Fisherfolk – signed and one dated '07 – 7½ x 15¾in.
(Christie's) **$1,164** **£600 Pair**

A. H. VICKERS – A Wooded Vale – bears a monogram and dated – on board – 10 x 14in.
(Sotheby's) **$277** **£140**

ALFRED H. VICKERS – A View Near Connemara, Ireland; and A Lakeside View – signed, one dated '08 – heightened with bodycolour – 7 x 14in.
(Sotheby's) **$504** **£260 Two**

ALFRED H. VICKERS – A Riverside Town – signed and dated 1894 – 8 x 12in.
(Sotheby's Belgravia) **$576** **£300**

ALFRED H. VICKERS – On A Canal – signed – 8 x 11½in.
(Sotheby's) **$514** **£260**

ALFRED GOMERSAL VICKERS – A River In A Rocky Landscape – watercolour with touches of bodycolour – 9¾ x 13½in.
(Christie's) **$175** **£90**

ALFRED VICKERS, SNR. – An Estuary, The Isle Of Wight – 15½ x 27in.
(Sotheby's Belgravia) **$8,048** **£4,000**

ALFRED VICKERS And THOMAS SIDNEY COOPER – Cattle And Sheep On A Road – signed by both artists and dated 1841 – on panel – 16¾ x 13½in.
(Christie's) **$4,268** **£2,200**

VICTORIAN SCHOOL – Portrait Of A Young Lady, Bust Length, Wearing A Black Gown With White Lawn Collar And Floral Bonnet – indistinctly signed – oil on canvas – 63 x 49cm.
(Henry Spencer & Sons) **$396** **£200**

VICTORIAN SCHOOL – Portrait Of A Young Lady, Seated, Full Length, On A Rock, Wearing A White Dress With Brown Cloak And Straw Bonnet, A Dog And A Basket Of Fruit At Her Feet – oil on canvas – 73 x 58cm.
(Henry Spencer & Sons) **$515** **£260**

VICTORIAN SCHOOL – Young Woman Wearing A Striped Brown Coat, Green Dress And A Red Underskirt, Standing In A Rocky Landscape – on board – 40 x 29cm.
(Henry Spencer & Sons) **$792** **£400**

VICTORIAN SCHOOL – Portrait Of Two Young Girls Wearing White Gowns With Pink Ribbons, Their Hair In Ringlets, A Hilly Landscape Beyond – oil – in circle – 83 x 69cm.
(Henry Spencer & Sons) **$368** **£190**

JAN VICTORS – A Dutch Village Square With Travellers Halting At An Inn – bears signature – 31¾ x 41¾in.
(Sotheby's) **$7,760** **£4,000**

E. VIGEE-LEBRUN – Portrait Of A Lady, Said To Be Madame De Toullemonde, Seated, Wearing An Aquamarine Silk Dress – 58¼ x 44½in.
(Sotheby's) **$3,762** **£1,900**

C. VIGNALI – A Young Man, Bust Length, Wearing Dark Red Costume – 17½ x 14in.
(Christie's) **$460** **£240**

FREDERICK VILLIERS – Scything – signed and dated 1886 – 13½ x 11in.
(Sotheby's Belgravia) **$168** **£85**

G. VINCENT – A Shady Lane – bears initials – 10¼ x 8in.
(Sotheby's Belgravia) **$307** **£160**

W. VINCENT – Still Lives Of Fruit And Flowers – both signed – 15 x 19½in.
(Sotheby's Belgravia) **$422** **£220 Pair**

DA VINCI, After – Study Of An Angel's Head From 'The Holy Family' – inscribed on a label on the reverse – heightened with white – circular – diameter 10½in.
(Sotheby's Belgravia) **$105** **£55**

LEONARDO DA VINCI, Follower of – Caricature Head Of An Old Woman – pen and brown ink – 11.7 x 6.7cm.
(Christie's) **$1,344** **£700**

JAN VINCK – A Dutch Landscape With Figures On A Path Beside A Town, Various Travellers Walking And Conversing Beside A Stream – signed with monogram and dated 1665 – on panel – 30½ x 47in.
(Sotheby's) **$2,522** **£1,300**

DAVID VINCKBOONS – A Gallant Company At A Banquet, Young People In A Garden Enclosed By Arbours – 18¾ x 34¼in.
(Sotheby's) **$13,580** **£7,000**

BAMBINO VISPO, Master of the, *(Active in early XV century)* – The Madonna And Child With Saints And Angels – gold ground – on panel – 37½ x 18in.
(Sotheby's) **$83,160 £42,000**

JAN CORNELISZ. VISSCHER – Portrait Of A Young Woman, Half Length, In An Oval Frame – signed – black chalk on vellum – 18.8 x 16.7cm.
(Christie's) **$3,072 £1,600**

MAURICE DE VLAMINCK – Pont Et Riviere – signed – 13 x 16¼in.
(Sotheby's) **$67,320 £34,000**

S. DE VLIEGER – A Rowing Boat Approaching Men-O'-War – grey and brown wash – 150 x 125mm.
(Christie's) **$228 £120**

WILLEM VAN DER VLIET – Willem De Lange Of Delft, In Black, Standing Before A Table With A Yellow Cloth; Maria Pijnacker In Black Silk, Standing By A Table – signed and dated 1626 and inscribed – on panel – 44¾ x 34¼in.
(Sotheby's) **$9,800 £5,000 Pair**

VOET – Apollo And Daphne – on panel – 13¼ x 17¼in.
(Christie's) **$277** **£140**

LUDWIG VOGEL – A Swiss Historical Scene – pen and grey ink, brown and yellow wash heightened with white – 221 x 197mm.
(Christie's) **$152** **£80**

CAREL VAN VOGELAER – A Lady With A Garland Of Flowers – 38½ x 51¾in.
(Christie's) **$3,880** **£2,000**

LEON-JOSEPH VOIRIN – La Loge De Theatre – signed and dated 1883 – pencil and watercolour – 11 x 8in.
(Sotheby's) **$1,292** **£680**

J. F. VOLK – Giuseppe Garibaldi, Head And Shoulders, Inclined To Left – signed – pencil and watercolour – 6½ x 4¾in.
(Sotheby's) **$129** **£65**

VOLLERDT – A Mountainous Wooded Landscape, Figures In The Foreground, A Town Beyond – on panel – 18 x 23½in.
(Sotheby's) **$388** **£200**

J. C. VOLLERDT – An Extensive Rhenish Landscape With Figures Beside A Lake – inscribed on the reverse – on panel – 11¾ x 17¼in.
(Sotheby's) **$2,970** **£1,500**

JOHANN CHRISTIAN VOLLERDT – A Hilly Wooded Landscape – 24¼ x 29¼in.
(Sotheby's) **$2,522** **£1,300**

JOHAN CHRISTIAN VOLLERDT – A Winter Scene With Reed-Cutters, Numerous Figures On A Frozen River, With Peasants Cutting Reeds – signed – on panel – 8½ x 12in.
(Sotheby's) **$15,680** **£8,000**

JOHANN CHRISTIAN VOLLERDT – River Landscape With Travellers And A Fisherman – 16¾ x 22in.
(Sotheby's) **$8,316** **£4,200**

JAN VOLSCHENK – A Mountainous Landscape Near Oudtshorrn – signed and dated 1913, inscribed on the reverse – oil on canvas – 8¾ x 4¼in.
(Sotheby's) **$197** **£100**

BALDASSARE FRANCESCHINI, IL VOLTERRANO – Studies Of A Saint Holding A Book – inscribed – red chalk on grey paper – 272 x 379mm.
(Christie's) **$143** **£75**

DE VOS – Time And Envy Carrying Off Beauty – pen and brown ink, brown wash heightened with white – 216 x 157mm.
(Christie's) **$53** **£28**

DE VOS – The Feast Of Herod – on panel – 12½ x 21in.
(Christie's) **$679** **£350**

E. VOS – A Frozen River Landscape With Figures On Ice And Buildings Behind – signed – pen and brown ink, brown wash on vellum – 19.4 x 27.4cm.
(Christie's) **$396** **£200**

P. DE VOS – An Assembly Of Birds And Animals In An Extensive Landscape – 67¾ x 103in.
(Sotheby's) **$14,850** **£7,500**

PAUL DE VOS – Coursing In An Extensive Landscape – 45 x 73¾in.
(Christie's) **$4,224** **£2,200**

PAUL DE VOS – Hounds Attacking A Bear – 64 x 93½in.
(Sotheby's) **$2,522** **£1,300**

D. VOSMAER – A Dutch Canal View, Figures Crossing A Bridge To The Right – on panel – 30¾ x 43¾in.
(Sotheby's) **$2,178** **£1,100**

DANIEL VOSMAER – The Gunpowder Explosion At Delft, 1654 – signed and inscribed – 33¼ x 40in.
(Sotheby's) **$12,610** **£6,500**

VRANCX – The Execution Of A Saint In A Piazza – inscribed on the reverse – black chalk, pen and brown ink, brown wash, the reverse inscribed – 258 x 222mm.
(Christie's) **$114** **£60**

SEBASTIAEN VRANCX – A Winter Landscape With Soldiers – on panel – 14½ x 24in.
(Sotheby's) **$38,800** **£20,000**

SEBASTIAN VRANCX – Elegant Figures On The Terrace Of A Palazzo With A Formal Garden Beyond – on panel – 13¼ x 18¾in.
(Christie's) **$17,280 £9,000**

VRIES – A Biblical Subject In A Wooded Landscape – on panel – 10¼ x 13½in.
(Sotheby's) **$673 £340**

ROELOF VAN VRIES – A Canal Scene With A Round Tower, Surmounted By A Dove-Cote – signed – 21¼ x 17½in.
(Sotheby's) **$8,924 £4,600**

ROELOF VAN VRIES – A Wooded Landscape Near Haarlem With Figures On A Path By A Cottage – bears indistinct initials – on panel – 29½ x 36½in.
(Christie's) **$7,296 £3,800**

GERRIT VAN VUCHT – A Vanitas Still Life – on panel – 9¾ x 13¾in.
(Sotheby's) **$6,208 £3,200**

JAN VAN DER VUCHT – The Interior Of A Church, With Figures – signed – on panel – 20 x 29¾in.
(Christie's) **$10,560 £5,500**

J. L. VYCHAN – Off Boulogne – signed and inscribed on the reverse – on board – 10 x 16in.
(Sotheby's Belgravia) **$194 £100**

W

A. WAAGEN – Italian Coastal Scenes – signed – oil on canvas – 10½ x 4½in.
(Manchester Auction Mart) **$768** **£380 Pair**

EDWARD WADSWORTH – Still Life, Dungeness – tempera on panel – 15 x 21in.
(Sotheby's) **$1,485** **£750**

LOUIS WILLIAM WAIN – Christmas Pud – signed and inscribed – grisaille – 17¾ x 27in.
(Sotheby's Belgravia) **$171** **£90**

THOMAS FRANCIS WAINEWRIGHT – Sheep In An Extensive Landscape – signed and dated 1871 – on panel – 8 x 12in.
(Christie's) **$1,067** **£550**

HAROLD WAITE – Cattle Grazing; A Quarry – both signed – 9 x 13½in. and 14¼ x 13in.
(Sotheby's Belgravia) **$115** **£60 Two**

HAROLD WAITE – The Moors, Sunset – signed – 18¼ x 24in.
(Sotheby's Belgravia) **$163** **£85**

ROBERT THORNE WAITE – Cattle On A Road Near A Cottage – signed – watercolour – 14¾ x 21¾in.
(Christie's) **$369** **£190**

L. CHELTENHAM WAKE – Summer Roses – signed and dated 1881 – 23½ x 17½in.
(Sotheby's Belgravia) **$630** **£320**

ROLAND WAKELIN – Still Life, Jug Of Flowers – signed and dated 1933 – watercolour and pencil – 30 x 23cm.
(Australian Art Auctions) **$321** **£164**

ERNEST WALBOURN – Butterflies – 23½ x 17½in.
(Sotheby's Belgravia) **$1,710** **£850**

ERNEST WALBOURN – The Miller's Daughter – inscribed – 23½ x 35½in.
(Sotheby's Belgravia) **$1,911** **£950**

ERNEST WALBOURN – Primroses – signed – 18½ x 28½in.
(Sotheby's Belgravia) **$1,650** **£820**

WILLIAM WALCOT – St. Paul's Cathedral – signed and dated 1907 – pencil and watercolour heightened with bodycolour – 28½ x 17¾in.
(Sotheby's) **$1,584** **£800**

HOWARD WALFORD – A Country Cottage – signed – 15 x 10in.
(Sotheby's Belgravia)
$99 **£50**

DAME ETHEL WALKER – A Nude Study – signed – on board – 13¾ x 9½in.
(Sotheby's Belgravia)
$230 **£120**

HARRY WALLACE – By A Woodland Stream – signed and dated 1877 – 19½ x 29½in.
(Sotheby's Belgravia)
$436 **£220**

HUGH R. WALLACE – Teeing Off – signed with initials and dated '97 – heightened with white – on grey paper – 21½ x 15½in.
(Sotheby's) **$230** **£120**

JAMES WALLACE – A Perthshire Farm – signed – 19½ x 39½in.
(Sotheby's Belgravia) **$99** **£50**

JOHN WALLACE – On The Nidd, Below Knaresborough – signed and dated 1899 – 16 x 20in.
(Sotheby's Belgravia) **$86** **£45**

JOHN WALLACE – Country Cottages – signed and dated '98 – 19½ x 29½in.
(Sotheby's Belgravia) **$230** **£120**

WILLIAM WALLS – 'A Man's A Man For A'That' – signed – canvas laid on board – inscribed on the mount 'Antwerp 1885' – circular – diameter 15in.
(Sotheby's Belgravia) **$172** **£90**

WILLIAM WALLS – A Jolly Angler – signed – canvas laid on board – 19¼ x 15in.
(Sotheby's Belgravia) **$307** **£160**

WILLIAM WALLS – A Jaguar Resting In A Tree – 19¼ x 29¼in.
(Sotheby's) **$238** **£120**

WILLIAM WALLS – The Horse Fair – signed – 36 x 48½in.
(Sotheby's) **$326** **£170**

J. WALTER – Coastal Landscape With Two Fisherwomen On The Shore As Seamen Set Out In A Rowing Boat, Buildings And Hills Beyond – signed – 60 x 105cm.
(Henry Spencer & Sons) **$871** **£440**

GEORGE STANDFIELD WALTERS – River Scene – watercolour – 12½ x 19¼in.
(Outhwaite & Litherland) **$212** **£105**

GEORGE STANFIELD WALTERS – Lowestoft Fishing Boats Coming Into Harbour – signed – heightened with white – 9 x 15in.
(Sotheby's Belgravia) **$119** **£60**

GEORGE STANFIELD WALTERS – On The Stour Near Harwich; Yarmouth Boats On The River At Gorleston – signed and dated 1898 and 1906 – heightened with white – 7 x 10in.
(Sotheby's Belgravia) **$356** **£180 Pair**

CECILE WALTON – The River Maiden – signed – 8½ x 8½in.
(Sotheby's) **$594** **£300**

EDWARD ARTHUR WALTON – On The Moors – signed and dated '79 – 19¾ x 29½in.
(Sotheby's) **$576** **£300**

ELIJAH WALTON – In The Alps, Near Chamonix – 13½ x 9½in.
(Sotheby's) **$291** **£150**

EDWARD MATTHEW WARD – Alice Lisle – signed – 13 x 17in.
(Christie's) **$776** **£400**

EDWARD MATTHEW WARD – The King's Daughter – signed and dated '86 – 33½ x 25½in.
(Christie's) **$1,455** **£750**

EDWARD MATTHEW WARD – The South Sea Bubble, A Scene In Change Alley In 1720 – signed, inscribed and dated 1846 on the reverse – 16¾ x 23¾in.
(Christie's) **$1,455** **£750**

WARD OF HULL – The Northern Whale Fleet With The Whaler Harmony Of Hull Attacking And Killing The Whale In Davis Straits – inscribed on a label on the reverse – oil on board – 17¾ x 25½in.
(Sotheby's) **$2,069** **£1,050**

J. WARD – A Portrait Of Mrs McNab Spinning – signed with initials – pencil drawing – 6 x 9in.
(Andrew, Hilditch & Son)
$146 **£70**

JAMES WARD – A Bulldog Sitting – signed with initials and dated 1796, inscribed on the reverse – black and white chalks on buff paper – 7½ x 7¾in.
(Sotheby's) **$390** **£200**

JAMES CHARLES WARD – View On The Coast, Isle Of Arran – signed and dated 1869, inscribed on a label on the reverse – 17½ x 36in.
(Sotheby's) **$475** **£240**

MARTIN THEODORE WARD – A Sportsman With Dogs Shooting In A Landscape – on board – 6¾ x 8½in.
(Christie's) **$1,164** **£600**

WILLIAM H. And JAMES CHARLES WARD – A Mallard, Bunches Of Grapes, Peaches And Plums, In A Landscape – signed and dated 1852 – 7¾ x 9¾in.
(Christie's) **$582** **£300**

ARTHUR WARDLE – Head Studies Of A Mare And Foal – signed – 21 x 14in.
(Sotheby's Belgravia) **$960** **£500**

ARTHUR WARDLE – Three Terriers After A Rabbit – signed – 19 x 24in.
(Sotheby's Belgravia) **$1,881** **£950**

ARTHUR WARDLE – Head Studies Of Horses – signed – 21 x 14in.
(Sotheby's Belgravia) **$806** **£420**

J. L. WARDLEWORTH – Shakespeare Reciting Before Queen Elizabeth – signed – 39½ x 29½in.
(Sotheby's Belgravia) **$228** **$120**

J. WARE – Landscape With Four Sheep – signed and dated 1905 – oil on canvas – 10½ x 15½in.
(Butler & Hatch Waterman) **$262** **£130**

W. H. WARING – Haymakers At Rest – signed – 13½ x 17½in.
(Sotheby's Belgravia) **$722** **£380**

ANDY WARHOL – Coloured Campbell's Soup Can – signed and dated '65 on the reverse – silk-screen and acrylic on canvas – 36¼ x 24¼in.
(Sotheby's) **$16,830** **£8,500**

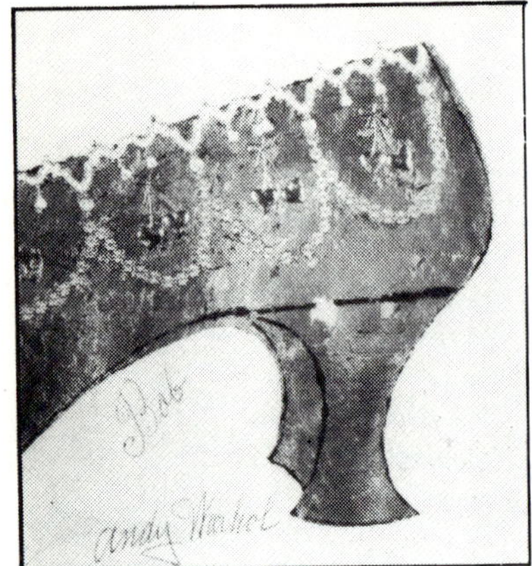

ANDY WARHOL – Shoe – Bob – signed and inscribed – gold-leaf, indian ink and collage on paper – 13 x 10in.
(Sotheby's) **$1,782** **£900**

ANDY WARHOL – James Cagney – signed and dated 1964 on the reverse – silk-screen on paper – 30 x 40in.
(Sotheby's) **$3,960** **£2,000**

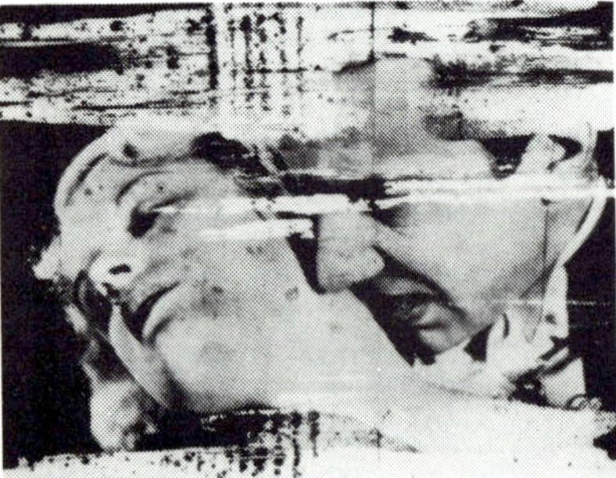

ANDY WARHOL – The Kiss (Bela Lugosi) – signed and dated 1963 on the reverse – silk-screen on paper – 30 x 40in.
(Sotheby's) **$5,940** **£3,000**

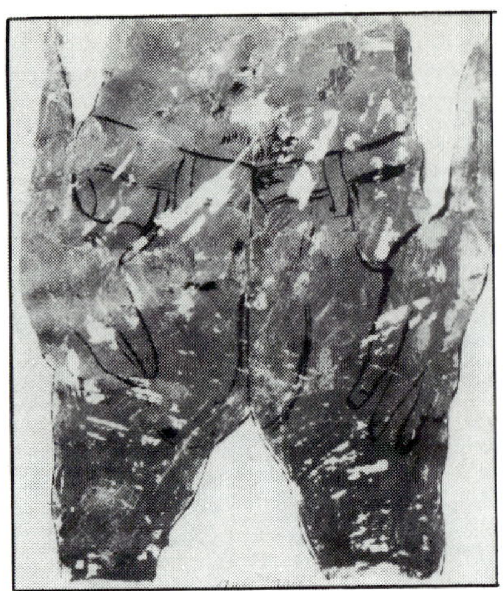

ANDY WARHOL – Golden Boy – Torso In Jeans – signed – gold-leaf and indian ink on paper - 19 x 16in.
(Sotheby's) **$4,356** **£2,200**

BONOMI WARREN – 'Extensive Country Landscape, Harvest Scene With Two Young Girls Resting Under A Tree – signed and dated 1886 – watercolour – 31 x 53in.
(Lalonde Bros. & Parham) **$314** **£160**

EDMUND P. WARREN – 'River Meadows' – watercolour – 19 x 25in.
(W. H. Lane & Son) **$291** **£150**

ANTHONIE WATERLOO – A View Of A Castle Overlooking The Bend Of A River, With Trees In The Foreground – inscribed - black chalk, brown wash and watercolour heightened with yellow and green – 22.3 x 18.8cm.
(Christie's) **$960** **£500**

WATERLOW – Feeding Poultry – bears signature and date – 22 x 15½in.
(Sotheby's Belgravia) **$192** **£100**

W. R. WATERS – Fisherwives – signed and dated 1877 – 29½ x 25in.
(Sotheby's Belgravia) **$1,089** **£550**

AMOS WATMOUGH – Cattle In A Pasture – signed – 15 x 24in.
(Sotheby's Belgravia) **$499** **£260**

CHARLES WATSON – Misty Mountainous Landscape With Highland Cattle Drinking At A Stream – signed, dated 1895 – oil on canvas – 59 x 90cm.
(Henry Spencer & Sons) **$634** **£320**

CHARLES WATSON – Highland Cattle; Mountain Sheep – signed and dated 1899 – 9½ x 13½in.
(Sotheby's Belgravia) **$475** **£240 Pair**

J. DAWSON WATSON – The Faggot Gatherers – signed with initials, and dated 1886 – 12½ x 8in.
(Sotheby's Belgravia) **$49** **£25**

ROBERT WATSON – Highland Cattle Watering – signed and dated 1910 – 24 x 36in.
(Sotheby's) **$864** **£450**

ROBERT WATSON – Mountainous Lakeland Landscape, With A Shepherd, His Dog And Flock Resting On The Bank – signed and dated 1891 – 18 x 28cm.
(Henry Spencer & Sons) **$582** **£300**

WALTER J. WATSON – Loch Lyon, Perthshire; A Highland River – signed and dated 1931 – 16 x 26in.
(Sotheby's) **$3,840** **£2,000 Pair**

WILLIAM STEWART WATSON – The Wounded Jacobite – signed and dated 1835 – on panel – 22½ x 32in.
(Sotheby's) **$672** **£350**

WATTS – Spring Fever – 23¼ x 17¼in.
(Sotheby's Belgravia) **$297** **£150**

FREDERICK WILLIAM WATTS – River Landscape, With A Man Fishing In The Foreground – 19 x 24½in.
(Christie's) **$11,640** **£6,000**

FREDERICK WILLIAM WATTS – Henley-On-Thames – signed with initials and dated '27 – 21¼ x 32in.
(Christie's) **$11,640** **£6,000**

FREDERICK WILLIAM WATTS – Tree Studies – on board – each 7 x 4½in.
(Sotheby's Belgravia) **$158** **£80 Three**

FREDERICK WILLIAM WATTS – Wooded River Landscape, With A Cottage, And A Horse-Drawn Cart On A Road – 39¾ x 53¾in.
(Christie's) **$31,040** **£16,000**

FREDERICK WILLIAM WATTS – Eton College From The River – 19½ x 27in.
(Sotheby's Belgravia) **$8,450** **£4,200**

FREDERICK WILLIAM WATTS – A Wooded Landscape, With Figures By Cottages And Ducks On A Pond – 19¼ x 28¼in.
(Christie's) **$16,490** **£8,500**

FREDERICK WILLIAM WATTS – A Wooded River Landscape, With A Lock And A Village Beyond – 19¼ x 28¼in.
(Christie's) **$7,372** **£3,800**

GEORGE FREDERICK WATTS – Love And Death – 52¼ x 30½in.
(Sotheby's Belgravia) **$11,066** **£5,500**

GEORGE FREDERICK WATTS – The Creation Of Eve – 34 x 13¾in.
(Sotheby's Belgravia) **$5,030** **£2,500**

CHARLES JONES WAY – Florence – signed and inscribed – heightened with bodycolour – 9 x 13½in.
(Sotheby's Belgravia) **$81** **£42**

CHARLES M. WEBB – A Glass Of Claret – signed and dated 1895 – 19½ x 23½in.
(Sotheby's Belgravia) **$1,810** **£900**

JAMES WEBB – Arabs Outside A Mosque In Cairo – 23½ x 39½in.
(Christie's) **$1,261** **£650**

JAMES WEBB – A View Of St. Paul's From The Thames – indistinctly signed – 29 x 49in.
(Sotheby's Belgravia) **$9,658** **£4,800**

JAMES WEBB – A Salvage Operation – bears signature – 7½ x 15½in.
(Sotheby's Belgravia) **$380** **£200**

W. WEBB – Peel Harbour With Shipping – dated 1895 – 54 x 95cm.
(Edmiston's) **$1,785** **£920**

WILLIAM WEBB – Douglas Harbour – signed and inscribed – 21¾ x 38in.
(Christie's) **$1,940** **£1,000**

WILLIAM EDWARD WEBB – Castletown, Isle Of Man – signed – 10 x 15in.
(Sotheby's Belgravia) **$3,219** **£1,600**

WILLIAM EDWARD WEBB – Port St. Mary, Isle Of Man – signed – 15½ x 19½in.
(Sotheby's Belgravia) **$3,018** **£1,500**

WEBB – Hauling In The Nets, Rough Seas - 14¼ x 20in.
(Sotheby's Belgravia) **$495** **£250**

DAVID WEBER – A Swiss Villa, With Outbuildings, Carriage, Horseman And Walkers On Road – signed and dated 1814 – pen and brown ink and watercolour heightened with white – 11¾ x 18¼in.
(Sotheby's) **$832** **£420**

G. DE WEDIG – Portrait Of A Lady, Standing Three-Quarter Length, Wearing A Black Gown And White Ruff – inscribed – on panel – 35 x 25½in.
(Christie's) **$2,328** **£1,200**

FREDERICK WEEKES – Siegfried – 46½ x 29½in.
(Sotheby's Belgravia)
$297 **£150**

HENRY WEEKES – A Dog Worrying Donkeys – signed and dated 1877 – 27¼ x 38½in.
(Christie's) **$4,656 £2,400**

WEENIX – A Wooded Landscape With The Spoils Of The Hunt – 43½ x 59in.
(Sotheby's) **$3,168 £1,600**

ARTHUR H. WEIGALL – The Fan – signed – 14 x 11in.
(Christie's) **$1,188 £600**

CAREL WEIGHT – Fright – signed – on board – 40½ x 38in.
(Sotheby's) **$436 £220**

LOUIS WEIRTER – A Street In Etaples, Brittany – signed and dated 1913 – 23 x 18¼in.
(Sotheby's Belgravia)
$62 £32

JOHANNES WEISSENBRUCH – River Landscape With Rowing Boat – signed – watercolour and gouache – 15½ x 10in.
(Sotheby's) **$3,610 £1,900**

GEORGE WELLS – Fern Gatherers, North Devon Coast – signed and dated 1860, inscribed on a label on the reverse – 12½ x 18in.
(Sotheby's Belgravia) **$1,089 £550**

J. SANDERSON WELLS – The Challenge, Depicting Four Figures With Three Horses At Main Gate Of Residence – signed – oil – 11½ x 15½in.
(Richard Baker & Baker) **$1,843 £950**

JOHN S. SANDERSON WELLS – The Edinburgh Academy – signed – 24½ x 30in.
(Sotheby's) **$6,144 £3,200**

WILLIAM WELLS – Haymaking – signed – 15½ x 19in.
(Sotheby's) **$1,248 £650**

PIETER VAN DER WERFF – Portrait Of A Gentleman, Bust Length, In A Red Cloak – signed and dated 1709 – oval – 30¾ x 25¾in.
(Sotheby's) **$1,746 £900**

CARL WERNER – The Pomegranate Girl – signed and dated 1860 – heightened with bodycolour – 18 x 12in.
(Sotheby's Belgravia) **$230 £120**

ADOLF ULRIK WERTMULLER – Portrait Of A Lady, Bust Length, Wearing A Spotted Silk Dress, A White Neckerchief And A Large Mob Cap – signed and dated 1789 – 24½ x 20¼in.
(Christie's) **$2,134 £1,100**

BENJAMIN WEST – Alexander III, King Of Scotland, Rescued From The Fury Of A Stag By Colin Fitzgerald – signed and dated 1784 and inscribed – on paper – 13¾ x 20¼in.
(Sotheby's) **$10,670 £5,500**

DAVID WEST – Caithness Hill From Loch More – signed – 25 x 38in.
(Sotheby's) **$554 £280**

DAVID WEST – River Lossie; River Avon – signed – 8 x 10in.
(Sotheby's) **$652** **£340 Pair**

DAVID WEST – Fishing On A River Bank – signed – 18½ x 23½in.
(Sotheby's Belgravia)
$317 **£160**

WILLIAM WEST – A Norwegian Waterfall – bears signature – 35¼ x 47¼in.
(Sotheby's Belgravia)
$4,829 **£2,400**

J. WESTALL – Extensive Mountainous Lakeland Landscape With Many Small Boats And An Island On The Lake – signed – oil on canvas – 46.5 x 66cm.
(Henry Spencer & Sons)
$574 **£290**

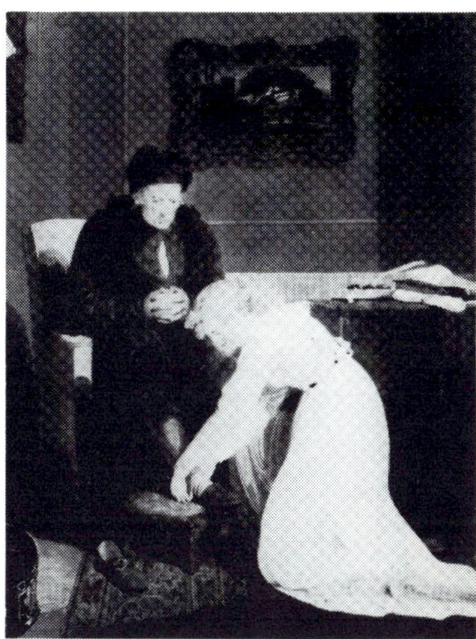

RICHARD WESTALL – Filial Duty – pencil and watercolour, heightened with white – 19½ x 16½in.
(Sotheby's) **$621** **£320**

WILLIAM WESTALL – The Hong Merchant's Garden – signed – 6¼ x 10¼in.
(Sotheby's) **$582** **£300**

T. WESTON – A Storm Blowing Up – 11½ x 16½in.
(Sotheby's Belgravia)
$1,006 **£500**

C. WESTON – Rustic Scene With Ploughman And Horse Returning Home Along Muddy Track, Sheep Grazing In Foreground, Farm Buildings In Background – signed – oil – 19 x 29in.
(G. A. Key) **$218** **£110**

J. DE WET – An Oriental Merchant Inspecting Cargo, Seated With Attendants In A Town Square – on panel – 24 x 33in.
(Sotheby's) **$2,376** **£1,200**

JACOB WILLEMSZ. DE WET The Elder – Christ Disputing With The Doctors In The Temple – signed – on panel – 17¼ x 21½in.
(Sotheby's) **$6,272** **£3,200**

ROGIER VAN DER WEYDEN, Follower of – The Deposition, The Virgin Embracing Christ Whose Body Is Borne By St. Joseph Of Arimathaea, Assisted By An Angel And St. Nicodemus – on panel – 23¼ x 38½in.
(Sotheby's) **$548,800** **£280,000**

JACOB WEYER – A Cavalry Skirmish – on panel – 12¼ x 24in.
(Christie's) **$2,910** **£1,500**

HENRY WHATLEY – Wooded Landscape With Watermill And Figures Seated On A Bridle Path – signed – watercolour – 30½ x 43¼in.
(Lalonde Bros. & Parham) **$475** **£240**

FRANCIS WHEATLEY – The Pet Magpie – signed and dated 1798 – 8¼ x 5¾in.
(Sotheby's) **$1,980** **£1,000**

FRANCIS WHEATLEY – Lismore Castle, Co. Waterford, With Bridge Over The Blackwater River, Peasants And Animals By Cottages – pen and black ink and watercolour – 14 x 20½in.
(Sotheby's) **$2,134** **£1,100**

WHEELER – Portrait Of A Gentleman With His Hunter – 36 x 28in.
(Sotheby's Belgravia) **$209** **£110**

ALFRED WHEELER – Terriers – signed – on board – 7 x 10in.
(Sotheby's Belgravia) **$634** **£320**

J. A. WHEELER – Fording A Stream – bears signature – on panel – 9¼ x 15¼in.
(Sotheby's Belgravia) **$228** **£120**

JOHN ARNOLD WHEELER – Study Of Two Jack Russell Heads – signed – on board – 9¼ x 12½in.
(Sotheby's Belgravia) **$228** **£120**

JOHN ARNOLD WHEELER – Over The Sticks – signed with monogram – on board – 7½ x 10in.
(Sotheby's Belgravia) **$396** **£200**

MARY V. WHEELHOUSE – The Lady Of The Lamp – signed – pen and black ink and watercolour – 9¼ x 6½in.
(Christie's) **$68** **£35**

WHEELWRIGHT – Returning From The Fields – indistinctly signed with monogram and dated 1904 – 15½ x 23¼in.
(Sotheby's Belgravia) **$356** **£180**

JOHN WHITE – Peeling Potatoes – signed and dated 1875 – 21½ x 16½in.
(Sotheby's Belgravia) **$576** **£300**

W. WHITE – A Pinch Of Snuff – signed – 29 x 39in.
(Sotheby's Belgravia) **$297** **£150**

BRETT WHITELEY – Lion – signed – etching – 51 x 50cm.
(Australian Art Auctions) **$161** **£82**

THOMAS WHITTLE, SNR. – Still Life Of Fruit – signed and dated 1866 – 25 x 30in.
(Sotheby's Belgravia) **$475** **£240**

THOMAS WHITTLE – A Rural Landscape With A Drover And Cattle In The Foreground – signed and dated 1879 – on canvas – 33 x 46cm.
(King & Chasemore) **$670** **£340**

CHARLES WHYMPER – Pheasants Feeding – signed with initials – heightened with bodycolour – 16 x 22in.
(Sotheby's) **$614** **£320**

CHARLES WHYMPER – Sheldrakes Breeding In Rabbit Holes On Sandringham Common, Norfolk – signed and dated '21 heightened with white – 19 x 27in.
(Sotheby's Belgravia) **$288** **£150**

CHARLES WHYMPER – A Cock Pheasant Rising – signed – heightened with bodycolour – 12¼ x 9in.
(Sotheby's Belgravia) **$105** **£55**

T. WICKSTEAD – A Lady And Gentleman Seated In A Formal Garden – 27½ x 33½in.
(Christie's) **$2,971** **£1,500**

F. J. WIDGERY – Dartmoor Scene – signed – watercolour – 12 x 17in.
(Husseys) **$146** **£74**

FREDERICK JOHN WIDGERY – An Extensive River Landscape – signed – 15 x 30in.
(Christie's) **$1,552** **£800**

FREDERICK JOHN WIDGERY – The Dorset Moors Near Corfe – signed and inscribed – bodycolour – 19½ x 29½in.
(Christie's) **$194** **£100**

FREDERICK JOHN WIDGERY – The Doone Valley, Exmoor – signed – heightened with bodycolour – 9½ x 13½in.
(Sotheby's Belgravia) **$192** **£100**

WIERIX – Christ On The Cross – pen and grey ink on vellum; and a drawing of The Lamentation – by another hand – 252 x 135mm.
(Christie's) **$76** **£40 Two**

H. W. WILATS – In Distress – signed and dated 1873, inscribed on the reverse – on board – 4½ x 6in.
(Sotheby's Belgravia) **$163** **£85**

CHARLES WILD – Screen Leading To The Choir Of Canterbury Cathedral – signed and inscribed – 22½ x 18in.
(Sotheby's) **$109** **£55**

H. WATKINS WILD – Whitby Sands – signed and dated '99 – heightened with white – 9½ x 14¼in.
(Sotheby's Belgravia) **$48** **£25 Pair**

WILLIAM WILDE – An Extensive River Landscape With Sheep Grazing By An Old Bridge – signed and dated '75 – watercolour – 14 x 20in.
(Neales of Nottingham) **$158** **£80**

WILLIAM WILDE – A Highland Landscape With Figure Walking Along A Pathway – signed and dated '76 – 9½ x 13¾in.
(Neales of Nottingham) **$55** **£28**

J. WILDENS – A Wooded Landscape With Travellers On A Path And A Castle Beyond – on panel – 9¾ x 13½in.
(Christie's) **$2,716** **£1,400**

J. WILDENS – A Landscape With Travellers; An Extensive Mountainous Landscape; Elegant Figures Outside A Castle; Herdsmen Beside A Stone Bridge; A Herdsman On A Forest Path; A River Landscape With Peasants Outside A Cottage – on panel – 3 x 8¾in.
(Sotheby's) **$4,752** **£2,400 Six**

SIR DAVID WILKIE – Idle Boys Detected – a sketch – 7 x 8½in.
(Sotheby's) **$499** **£260**

SIR DAVID WILKIE – A Sheet Of Studies Of A Group Of People Surrounding A Horseman; and A Landscape With A Cart Descending A Hill – pen and brown ink – 8 x 10in.
(Sotheby's) **$312** **£160**

E. WILKINSON – A View In Derbyshire – signed and dated 1870 – 23 x 40in.
(Sotheby's Belgravia) **$376** **£190**

HUGH WILKINSON – Study From Nature – inscribed on a label on the reverse – on panel – 12½ x 15½in.
(Sotheby's Belgravia) **$48** **£25**

NORMAN WILKINSON – Seascape With A Battle Cruiser – signed and dated 1907 – oil on canvas – 50 x 39in.
(Morphets of Harrogate) **$515** **£260**

MAURICE C. WILKS – Silver Morning, Roundstone, Co. Galway – signed and inscribed – 20 x 24in.
(Sotheby's) **$1,125** **£580**

GEORGE BARRELL WILLCOCK – An Extensive Wooded River Landscape With A Figure By A Cottage In The Foreground, And Hills Beyond – signed – 25¼ x 43½in.
(Christie's) **$4,268** **£2,200**

A. WILLETT – Wooded River Landscapes – signed – watercolour – 12 x 10in.
(Morphets of Harrogate)
$99 £50 Pair

ARTHUR WILLETT – Following The Scent; Crossing The Ford – signed – heightened with bodycolour – 5 x 17½in.
(Sotheby's Belgravia)
$238 £120 Pair

ADOLPHE WILLETTE – Le Remords De Mahomet – signed, inscribed and dated 1912 – pen and indian ink and blue crayon – 11¼ x 7½in.
(Sotheby's) $138 £70

HELEN WILLEY – A Peep Into The Greenhouse – signed and dated 1879, inscribed on a label on the reverse – 29¼ x 22in.
(Sotheby's Belgravia)
$380 £200

WILLIAMS – A Country Cottage – 16 x 24in.
(Sotheby's Belgravia) $384 £200

WILLIAMS – Fishing By A Stream – signed – 17½ x 25in.
(Sotheby's Belgravia)
$356 £180

WILLIAMS – A Wooded Pond – 20½ x 28½in.
(Sotheby's Belgravia)
$307 £160

WILLIAMS – A Gypsy Encampment – bears signature – 23½ x 42in.
(Sotheby's Belgravia)
$614 £320

ALEXANDER WILLIAMS – An Extensive View Of The Lower Lake, Killarney – signed, inscribed on the reverse – canvas on board – 10 x 17in.
(Sotheby's) $737 £380

ALEXANDER WILLIAMS – A View Of Lough Caragh Co. Kerry; and A View Of Lough Guitane Near Killarney – signed and inscribed – 10¼ x 18¼in.
(Sotheby's) $698 £360 Two

ALEXANDER WILLIAMS – On A River – signed – on board – 4½ x 11½in.
(Sotheby's) $272 £140

A. S. WILLIAMS – A View Of A Sea Lough On The West Coast Of Ireland, A Steam Launch In The Centre Against A Mountainous Background – signed – on board – 11 x 18½in.
(Sotheby's) $698 £360

A. W. WILLIAMS – Figures By A Wood – bears signature and date – 15½ x 23in.
(Sotheby's Belgravia)
$570 £300

E. C. WILLIAMS – By An Overshot Mill – 19 x 29in.
(Sotheby's Belgravia) **$1,089** **£550**

EDWARD CHARLES WILLIAMS – 'The Gleaners' – oil on canvas – 32 x 48cm.
(King & Chasemore)
$2,079 **£1,050**

E. RICARDO WILLIAMS – Fishing Boats, Santa Margherita, Italy – signed, inscribed and dated 1933 – 10½ x 13in.
(Sotheby's Belgravia) **$15** **£8**

GILBERT T. WILLIAMS – A North Italian Town – signed and dated '08 – 5½ x 13½in.
(Sotheby's Belgravia) **$178** **£90**

HARRY P. WILLIAMS – On The Devon Coast – 9¼ x 15¼in.
(Sotheby's Belgravia) **$238** **£120**

HENRY WILLIAMS – Country Scenes – signed – 7½ x 15½in.
(Sotheby's Belgravia)
$192 **£100 Four**

HUGH WILLIAM WILLIAMS – Kilchurn Castle, Loch Awe, Argyll – 7¾ x 10¼in.
(Sotheby's) **$679** **£350**

HUGH WILLIAM 'GRECIAN' WILLIAMS – A Wooded Landscape With A Bridge Over A River – watercolour – 8½ x 11½in.
(Christie's) **$194** **£100**

JOHN WILLIAMS – Gypsies On The Road; and A Gypsy Encampment – signed with initials and dated 1842 – 9½ x 11½in.
(Sotheby's Belgravia)
$4,426 **£2,200 Pair**

JOHN HAYNES WILLIAMS – Salle Du Trone – signed – 19 x 29in.
(Sotheby's Belgravia)
$1,980 £1,000

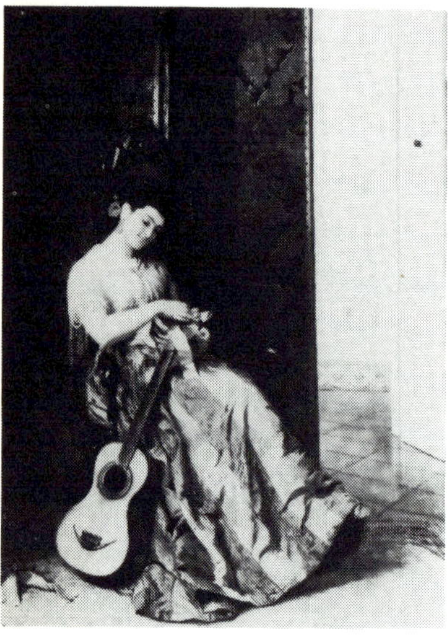

JOHN HAYNES WILLIAMS – A Bow For Her Beau – signed and dated 1874 – 35 x 26in.
(Sotheby's Belgravia)
$2,012 £1,000

PENRY WILLIAMS – At The Spring – signed, inscribed and dated 1883 – 30 x 21½in.
(Sotheby's Belgravia) **$3,762 £1,900**

TERRICK WILLIAMS – Normandy – signed – heightened with bodycolour – 9½ x 14in.
(Sotheby's Belgravia)
$105 £55

W. WILLIAMS – A Windmill On The Coast – 9½ x 13½in.
(Sotheby's Belgravia)
$576 £300

W. D. WILLIAMS – A Bay Hunter In A Stable – signed and dated 1872 – 19½ x 25½in.
(Sotheby's Belgravia)
$194 £100

WALTER WILLIAMS – A Snowstorm On Ben Lomond – signed, inscribed on a label on the reverse – 24 x 36in.
(Sotheby's Belgravia)
$845 £420

WALTER WILLIAMS – Bolton Abbey – signed with initials and dated 1874, inscribed on the reverse – 6¼ x 4½in.
(Sotheby's Belgravia)
$356 £180

WALTER HEATH WILLIAMS – A Summer Afternoon – 26 x 40in.
(Sotheby's Belgravia)
$2,616 £1,300

WILLIAM WILLIAMS – A Gentleman On A Bay Hunter In A Landscape – signed with initials – on panel – 9 x 12½in.
(Christie's) $737 £380

WILLIAM WILLIAMS – On A Hilltop – signed, inscribed and dated 1850 – 14 x 22¾in.
(Sotheby's Belgravia) $722 £380

WALTER HEATH WILLIAMS – Noonday Rest – 17¼ x 25¼in.
(Sotheby's Belgravia) $1,386 £700

WILLIAM WILLIAMS – A Fine Day In An Estuary – signed and inscribed – 29½ x 49½in.
(Sotheby's Belgravia) $14,084 £7,000

DANIEL ALEXANDER WILLIAMSON – Cattle Grazing In The Highlands – signed with monogram – 13 x 19½in.
(Sotheby's Belgravia) $30 £16

FREDERICK WILLIAMSON – Cattle Watering – signed and dated 1872 – coloured washes – 8 x 13½in.
(Phillips) $337 £170

J. WILLIAMSON – Silver Birches, Burnham And Burnham Beeches, Near Windsor – signed – oil – 29 x 19in.
(G. A. Key) $475 £240 Pair

J. WILLIAMSON – Dancing At Otaheite Before Captain Cook; Taking Up Ice For A Supply Of Fresh Water – both signed and dated '03, inscribed on the reverse – 10 x 14in.
(Sotheby's Belgravia) $77 £40 Pair

W. H. WILLIAMSON – Fishing Boats In Heavy Seas Off A Harbour Mouth, A Large Sailing Ship At Anchor Beyond – indistinctly signed – oil on canvas – 15½ x 21½in.
(Neales of Nottingham) $1,465 £740 Pair

W. H. WILLIAMSON – A Squall Off Scarborough – signed and dated 1870 – 23 x 35in.
(Sotheby's Belgravia) $1,330 £700

WILLIS – Going Out To Pasture – 7 x 9½in.
(Sotheby's Belgravia) $58 £30

H. B. WILLIS – Cattle And A Donkey In A Landscape – 12 x 16in.
(Sotheby's Belgravia) $144 £75

NORTON WILLIS – 'Seascape With Boats' – signed – watercolour – 24 x 14in.
(Gribble Booth & Taylor) $162 £80

VERA WILLOUGHBY – Scheherazade – signed with monogram – 36 x 28in.
(Sotheby's) **$1,782** **£900**

JOHN RILEY WILMER – Dardamians View The Monster Dead, One Of The Myths From The Story Of Perseus – signed and dated 1906, inscribed on the reverse – heightened with bodycolour – 14¾ x 21in.
(Sotheby's Belgravia) **$2,970** **£1,500**

JOHN RILEY WILMER – A Thracian Maiden – signed and dated 1923 – 12 x 9in.
(Sotheby's Belgravia) **$76** **£40**

ANDREW WILSON – A Road Through The Woods – signed and dated 1820 – 13½ x 17½in.
(Sotheby's) **$3,564** **£1,800**

B. WILSON – A Ruined Abbey – signed and dated 1905 – 25½ x 37½in.
(Sotheby's Belgravia)
$125 **£65**

CECIL WILSON – Portrait Of Coronach With J. Childs Up – signed and dated 1926 – 29½ x 39¼in.
(Sotheby's Belgravia)
$713 **£360**

H. WILSON – Meeting The Fishing Boats – signed and dated 1881 – on board – 5 x 7in.
(Sotheby's Belgravia)
$42 **£22**

J. WILSON – Marine Scenes Off Isle Of Wight – signed – oil on canvas – 7 x 14in.
(D. M. Nesbit & Co.)
$1,086 **£560 Pair**

JOHN WILSON – Off Tynemouth – signed – 11 x 19½in.
(Sotheby's Belgravia)
$1,148 **£580**

J. J. WILSON – Shipping Off A Harbour – bears initials – 16½ x 32½in.
(Sotheby's Belgravia) **$475** **£240**

JOHN JAMES WILSON – A Coastal Landscape, With Fisherfolk In The Foreground And Fishing Vessels Offshore – signed with initials and dated 1852 – 17½ x 29½in.
(Christie's) **$3,104** **£1,600**

P. MacGREGOR WILSON – Cottage By A Loch – watercolour – 29 x 49cm.
(Edmiston's) **$27** **£14**

W. WILSON – Becalmed Fishing Boats – signed and dated '88 – 20 x 30in.
(Sotheby's Belgravia) **$376** **£190**

H. B. WIMBUSH – Loch And Mountains – watercolour – 51 x 74cm.
(Edmiston's) **$261** **£135**

HENRY B. WIMBUSH – Trafalgar Square; The Royal Exchange – signed – heightened with white – 7½ x 11in.
(Sotheby's Belgravia) **$556** **£290 Pair**

EDMUND MORISON WIMPERIS – A Mill On The West Okement River – signed with initials – watercolour heightened with white – 9½ x 13½in.
(Christie's) **$466** **£240**

SIR JAMES LAWTON WINGATE – Rain Cloud, Loch Fyne – signed – 10 x 14in.
(Sotheby's) **$729** **£380**

FREDERICK WINKFIELD – Tower Bridge From The River – signed – 17½ x 29½in.
(Sotheby's) **$713** **£360**

P. DE WINT – Ploughing Near Croxford, Extensive Rural Landscape With Five Two-Horse Ploughing Teams – watercolour – 31 x 56cm.
(Henry Spencer & Sons) **$417** **£210**

PETER DE WINT – The Vale Of Gwent – recto; An Open Beach Bordered By Sand Dunes – verso – 4½ x 8¼in.
(Sotheby's) **$873** **£450**

PETER DE WINT – Figures And Cattle By Cottages In A Summer Landscape – 11½ x 17¾in.
(Sotheby's) **$2,910** **£1,500**

PETER DE WINT – Horses Watering At A Pool At Evening – 20½ x 28½in.
(Sotheby's) **$1,940** **£1,000**

PETER DE WINT – An Old Building With Horses Resting – 6¼ x 11in.
(Sotheby's) **$815** **£420**

CHARLES WINTER – In A Woodland Clearing – signed – 13 x 17in.
(Sotheby's Belgravia) **$554** **£280**

WILLIAM TATTON WINTER – The Shepherdess – signed, inscribed and dated 1909 on the reverse – 11½ x 14¾in.
(Sotheby's Belgravia)
$614 **£320**

WINTERHALTER – A Lady Of Fashion – 11 x 9in.
(Sotheby's Belgravia)
$295 **£150**

F. X. WINTERHALTER – Portrait Of A Lady – oval – 35 x 26in.
(Sotheby's Belgravia)
$805 **£400**

F. X. WINTERHALTER – A La Mode – inscribed on the reverse – 4½ x 3in.
(Sotheby's Belgravia) **$198 £100**

WINTERHALTER – Portrait Of A Boy – 23½ x 20in.
(Sotheby's Belgravia) **$158 £80**

WINTERHALTER – Portrait Of A Young Girl – on board – 11 x 9in.
(Sotheby's Belgravia) **$119 £60**

J. C. WINTOUR – Castle Grounds – 15 x 23½in.
(Sotheby's Belgravia) **$211 £110**

W. H. WISE – H.M.S. Galliorpees Standing Out Of Port Hardy, Cook Straits, New Zealand – signed and dated 1865, indistinctly inscribed on the reverse – oil on board – 8½ x 13in.
(Sotheby's) **$19 £10**

J. DE WIT – Putti Fishing, In A Landscape – bears signature – en grisaille – 29½ x 40½in.
(Sotheby's) **$1,584 £866**

J. DE WIT – The Judgment Of Solomon – on panel – oval – 16½ x 22in.
(Christie's) **$475 £240**

MATTHIAS WITHOOS – An Italianate Wooded River Landscape With Travellers On A Road – signed – on panel – 15 x 19¾in.
(Christie's) **$4,850 £2,500**

HEEREMAN WITMONT – A Coastal Landscape With A Man-O'-War And Other Vessels In A Choppy Sea – grisaille – on panel – 19½ x 28in.
(Christie's) **$21,120 £11,000**

ALFRED WOLMARK – Flowers In A Jug – signed with initials – on panel – 12¾ x 8½in.
(Sotheby's) **$238 £120**

ALFRED WOLMARK – Portrait Of Mrs. Cyril Ross – signed and dated 1950 – canvas on board – 19½ x 15½in.
(Sotheby's) **$238 £120**

ALFRED WOLMARK – The Concertina Player – signed and dated '04 – 40¼ x 23in.
(Sotheby's) **$990 £500**

ALFRED WOLMARK – The Flower Seller – signed – on panel – 18 x 14¾in.
(Sotheby's) **$634 £320**

WILLIAM CLARK WONTNER – Adeline – signed, inscribed – 24½ x 20½in.
(Sotheby's Belgravia) **$5,544** **£2,800**

CHARLES HAIGH WOOD – His Latest Ode – inscribed – 19½ x 15½in.
(Sotheby's Belgravia) **$864** **£450**

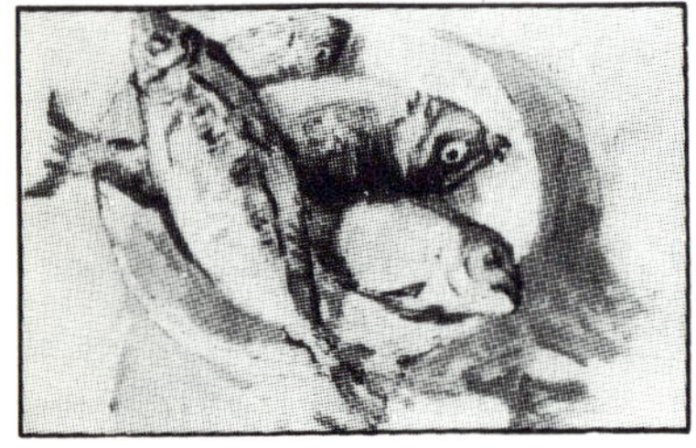

CHRISTOPHER WOOD – Fish On A Plate – dated 1922 – 10¼ x 15½in.
(Sotheby's) **$1,485** **£750**

CHRISTOPHER WOOD – Portrait Of A Woman – dated 1926 – on board – 13¾ x 10½in.
(Sotheby's) **$990** **£500**

CHRISTOPHER WOOD – La Blonde Qui Posait, 1925 – pencil – 18½ x 11¼in.
(Sotheby's) **$238** **£120**

E. WOOD – The River Thames Near Pangbourne; The River Thames Near Goring – signed – heightened with white – 7½ x 11in.
(Sotheby's Belgravia) **$188** **£95 Pair**

FRANK W. WOOD – The Old And The New – signed and dated 1902, inscribed on a label on the reverse – 13½ x 19½in.
(Sotheby's Belgravia) **$209** **£110**

LAWSON WOOD – The Despatch – signed, inscribed and dated 1907 – heightened with white – 10½ x 8½in.
(Sotheby's Belgravia) **$168** **£85**

LEWIS JOHN WOOD – View On The Great Holyhead Road Near Penmachno-Moel Siabod Mountain In The Distance, North Wales – oil on panel – 9½ x 10½in.
(W. H. Lane & Son) **$288** **£150**

RICHARD CATON WOODVILLE – The Parley – signed and dated 1892 – watercolour – 14½ x 10¼in.
(Christie's) **$168** **£85**

GEORGE MOUTARD WOODWARD – Smokers In A Tavern; and Figures Drinking – signed – pen and grey ink, grey wash – 7 x 4½in.
(Christie's) **$97** **£50 Pair**

H. S. WOODWARD – Salmon Fishing In Norway – signed and dated 1910, inscribed on the reverse – 22 x 14in.
(Sotheby's) **$211** **£110**

THOMAS WOODWARD – 'The Farmer's Boy', A Boy Seated On A Sack At The Feet Of A Harnessed Horse, As A Small Dog Looks On, A Man And Two Horses Harrowing In The Field Beyond Under A Cloudy Summer Sky – panel – 30 x 41cm.
(Henry Spencer & Sons) **$1,782** **£900**

WILLIAM WOOLARD – A Buchan Coast Fisherman – signed, inscribed and inscribed on the reverse – heightened with bodycolour – 21½ x 13½in.
(Sotheby's) **$537** **£280**

WILLIAM WOOLARD – The Herring Fleet Leaving Tarbet, Loch Fyne – signed, inscribed and dated 1897 – 11 x 23in.
(Sotheby's Belgravia) **$67** **£35**

ALFRED JOSEPH WOOLMER – The Captive In The Castle – signed and dated 1875 – 33½ x 18in.
(Christie's) **$873** **£450**

CHARLES N. WOOLNOOTH – A Mountain Waterfall – signed – heightened with body-colour – 10½ x 17in.
(Sotheby's Belgravia) **$163** **£85**

FRANCIS WORMLEIGHTON – The Knife Grinder, Wormingford, Essex – signed and dated 1875 – 16 x 22½in.
(Sotheby's Belgravia) **$1,102** **£580**

THOMAS WORSEY – Spring Flowers By A Mossy Bank – signed and dated 1864 – 15¼ x 12½in.
(Sotheby's Belgravia) **$806** **£420**

H. V. WORTH – A Secret – signed and dated 1873 – 49 x 36½in.
(Sotheby's Belgravia) **$495** **£250**

ARCHIBALD JAMES STUART WORTLEY – Portrait Of Miss Tombs – signed with monogram and dated 1889 – 40¼ x 26¾in.
(Sotheby's Belgravia)
$6,336 **£3,200**

CLAES CLAESZ. WOU – An Episode In The Battle Of The Downs, 21 October, 1629 – bears initials – on panel – 19½ x 38½in.
(Sotheby's) **$4,950** **£2,500**

WOUTERS – The Judgment Of Paris – on copper – 10¾ x 16in.
(Christie's) **$776** **£400**

F. WOUTERS – Diana And Her Nymphs Bathing – on panel – 16½ x 28in.
(Christie's) **$1,067** **£550**

JAN WOUTERSZ., Called Stap – A Money-lender And His Wife, Counting Gold At A Desk – signed in monogram – on panel – 48 x 35½in.
(Sotheby's) **$15,520** **£8,000**

WOUVERMAN – 'Battle Scene' – oil on metal – 33 x 39cm.
(King & Chasemore) **$950** **£480 Pair**

P. WOUWERMAN – A Cavalry Engagement – bears another signature – on panel – 15½ x 20in.
(Christie's) **$1,164** **£600**

P. WOUWERMAN – A Hawking Party Halted Outside An Inn – bears signature – 22¼ x 25½in.
(Christie's) **$6,208** **£3,200**

GEORGE WRIGHT – Setting Off; and Well Over – signed – 10 x 18in.
(Christie's) **$7,954** **£4,100 Pair**

GEORGE WRIGHT – Finding The Scent – signed – 19 x 29½in.
(Sotheby's Belgravia) **$7,920** **£4,000**

J. WRIGHT, 19th century – An Estuary Scene With Figures And Beached Boats, Distant Castle Against The Setting Sun – signed – 11 x 16in.
(Russell, Baldwin & Bright)
$2,352 **£1,200**

JAMES WRIGHT – Rosencath Woods – 49 x 60cm.
(Edmiston's) **$120** **£62**

MARIA OCTAVIA WRIGHT – Freshwater Cliffs, Isle Of Wight; and Stromness, Orkney Islands – one signed and dated 1829, the other inscribed – watercolour – 7¾ x 11¾in. and smaller.
(Christie's) **$388** **£200 Pair**

R. B. WRIGHT – 'Nr. Bangor' – signed – watercolour – 9¾ x 15in.
(Dacre, Son & Hartley) **$40** **£20**

ROBERT W. WRIGHT – The Search – signed and dated 1899 – on panel – 10½ x 12¾in.
(Sotheby's Belgravia)
$1,485 **£750**

ROBERT W. WRIGHT – Churning The Butter – signed and dated 1874 – 19¼ x 15½in.
(Sotheby's Belgravia) **$1,485** **£750**

ALEXANDER WUST – Cattle Watering At Dusk – signed and dated '62 – 19¾ x 31½in.
(Sotheby's) **$1,083** **£550**

WYCK – A Village Scene With Horsemen And Travellers In The Foreground – 24½ x 29½in.
(Christie's) **$1,164** **£600**

J. WYCK – An Italianate Wooded River Landscape With An Ambush – 22¾ x 30in.
(Christie's) **$1,843** **£950**

JAN WYCK – A Battle Between Christians And Turks – 42 x 74in.
(Sotheby's) **$3,880** **£2,000**

T. WYCK – A Capriccio Of A Mediterranean Harbour With Merchants And Other Figures – 23½ x 28in.
(Christie's) **$873** **£450**

THOMAS WYCK – An Italianate River Town With A Ferry In The Foreground – 21 x 36½in.
(Christie's) **$10,670** **£5,500**

VAN STEEN WYCK – Christ Crowned With Thorns – copper – on panel – 10 x 11½in.
(Christie's) **$970** **£500**

WILLIAM WYLD – A Street In Calais – signed and dated 1832 – 15¾ x 12in.
(Sotheby's) **$585** **£300**

WILLIAM WYLD – The Castle Of Steffelburg On The Danube – signed – watercolour – 7 x 10in.
(Christie's) **$582** **£300**

KATE WYLIE – Still Life Of Flowers In A Vase – signed – 19½ x 15½in.
(Sotheby's Belgravia) **$77** **£40**

W. L. WYLLIE – Boats Anchored In A River, Possibly The Thames – signed and dated 1883 – 19 x 12in.
(Andrew, Hilditch & Son) **$554** **£265**

WILLIAM LIONEL WYLLIE – An Estuary With Lighthouse, Fishing Boats And Fisherfolk – signed – watercolour – 9½ x 16in.
(Geering & Colyer) **$369** **£190**

WILLIAM LIONEL WYLLIE – An Estuary At Low Tide – signed and dated '71 – on board – 6½ x 10¼in.
(Sotheby's Belgravia) **$912** **£480**

WILLIAM LIONEL WYLLIE – Ayr Harbour – signed and inscribed – 8 x 13in.
(Sotheby's) **$652** **£340**

J. WYNANTS – Landscape, Figures Sheltering Below A Hill Before A Distant Landscape With River And Mountains – oil on canvas – 14 x 11½in.
(W. H. Lane & Son) **$2,400** **£1,250**

JAN WYNANTS – An Extensive Wooded Landscape With Mountains Beyond – signed – on panel – 11 x 15¼in.
(Christie's) **$12,480** **£6,500**

J. B. YARNOLD – Well-Wooded River Landscape, With A Figure Fishing By A Waterfall – signed – oil on canvas – 59 x 49cm.
(Henry Spencer & Sons) **$388** **£200**

JOSEPH W. YARNOLD – A Highland Torrent – signed – 28 x 35½in.
(Sotheby's Belgravia) **$277** **£140**

THOMAS YATES – A Cutter Near A British Frigate Off The Coast – watercolour – 4½ x 6¼in.
(Christie's) **$349** **£180**

W. YATES, SNR. – Young Anglers – signed – 19½ x 29½in.
(Sotheby's Belgravia) **$614** **£320**

WILLIAM FREDERICK YEAMES – On Bread And Water – signed and dated 1866 – 19¾ x 43¾in.
(Christie's) **$2,134** **£1,100**

JACK BUTLER YEATS – A Child's Window – signed – 13½ x 20½in.
(Sotheby's) **$12,610** **£6,500**

JACK BUTLER YEATS – A Lake Scene In The West Of Ireland, The Prow Of A Rowing Boat In The Foreground – signed – on panel – 9¼ x 14¼in.
(Sotheby's) **$3,880** **£2,000**

JACK BUTLER YEATS – Winter In Galway – signed – on panel – 9¼ x 14¾in.
(Sotheby's) **$11,252** **£5,800**

YEUQUA, Attributed to – A Junk In A Choppy Sea – 19¼ x 14½in.
(Sotheby's (Hong Kong) Ltd.)
$693 £350

CATERINA YKENS – Farmyard Fowl, Chickens And Ducklings Feeding Beside A Jewel Trinket Lying In The Foreground – signed – on metal – 29¼ x 21¾in.
(Sotheby's) **$4,356 £2,200**

W. H. YORK – The 'City Of York' Off The White Cliffs – 28 x 36in.
(Sotheby's Belgravia)
$713 £360

ALEXANDER YOUNG – Going Out To Graze – signed and dated '87 – on card – 17 x 11½in.
(Sotheby's) **$297 £150**

ALEXANDER YOUNG – A Quiet Dock – signed and dated '87 – on board – 13½ x 8¾in.
(Sotheby's) **$384 £200**

ARETTA YOUNG – An Indian Pulling His Sleigh Through Snow Covered Forest, The Sun Setting Over A Frozen Lake – signed, inscribed and dated '89 – oil on canvas – 12 x 18in.
(Sotheby's) **$315** **£160**

J. T. YOUNG – A Wooded Landscape, With Shepherds, Cattle And Sheep And Travellers On A Path By A Lake – signed and dated 1822 – 29½ x 36¾in.
(Christie's) **$1,843** **£950**

WILLIAM YOUNG – Stepping Stones Near Capel Curig – signed and dated '93 – 29½ x 49in.
(Sotheby's Belgravia) **$1,509** **£750**

A. YSENBRANDT – The Madonna And Child – on panel – 5 x 4in.
(Christie's) **$6,790** **£3,500**

ADRIAEN YSENBRANDT – The Adoration Of The Kings – on panel – 16 x 11½in.
(Sotheby's) **$18,620** **£9,500**

ZAIS – A Wooded Landscape With Peasants Outside A Barn – 16 x 24¼in.
(Christie's) **$466** **£240**

ZAIS – A Landscape, With Figures Gathered Under A Tree To The Left Foreground, Houses Beyond – 20 x 30in.
(Sotheby's) **$475** **£240**

GIUSEPPE ZAIS – An Italian Landscape With Sportsmen; An Italian Landscape With Peasants And A Cow – 17 x 24½in.
(Sotheby's) **$37,240** **£19,000 Pair**

D. ZAMPINI, After Domenichini – Portrait Of A Lady With Violin And Holding A Manuscript – oil on canvas – oval – 17½ x 13½in.
(Morphets of Harrogate) **$297** **£150**

REINIER NOOMS, Called Zeeman – Spanish Ships In Action With Barbary Pirates – signed – 19½ x 25¼in.
(Sotheby's) **$8,865** **£4,500**

ZICK – The Death Of Saint Joseph – 18½ x 14¼in.
(Christie's) **$109** **£55**

JANUARIUS ZICK – Christ On The Cross, A Skull At The Foot Of The Cross, Jerusalem To The Right Beyond – 18 x 9¼in.
(Sotheby's) **$1,980** **£1,000**

DORIS ZINKEISEN – Tattersall's – signed – 19½ x 29½in.
(Sotheby's) **$752** **£380**

G. ZOBOLI – The Vestal Virgins Performing A Sacrifice – 25¾ x 35¼in.
(Christie's) **$806** **£420**

GIUSEPPE ZOCCHI – The Bridge At Signa Seen From The West; and The Bridge At San Piero A Sieve – 19¾ x 39¼in.
(Sotheby's) **$50,440** **£26,000 Pair**

ZUCCARELLI – An Extensive Italian Landscape With Figures In The Foreground – bodycolour on buff paper – 323 x 442mm.
(Christie's) **$133** **£70**

ZUCCARELLI – A Wooded River Landscape With Figures In The Foreground And A Shepherd And His Flock Beyond – 30½ x 24in.
(Christie's) **$1,164** **£600**

ZUCCARELLI – Classical Figures By A Ruin – 23¼ x 30¼in.
(Christie's) **$737** **£380**

F. ZUCCARELLI – A Wooded Landscape, With A Beggar And Peasants Making Music – 16 x 26in.
(Christie's) **$1,940** **£1,000**

FRANCESCO ZUCCARELLI – Joseph Sold To The Ishmaelites – 24¾ x 33½in.
(Sotheby's) **$7,840** **£4,000**

FRANCESCO ZUCCARELLI – A Southern Landscape With Peasants By A Stream – 30½ x 46¾in.
(Sotheby's) **$29,100** **£15,000**

FRANCESCO ZUCCARELLI – A Southern River Landscape With A Distant Town By A River – 30½ x 46¾in.
(Sotheby's) **$34,920** **£18,000**

FEDERIGO ZUCCARO, Circle of – A Courtly Assembly Struck By Plague (recto) – black and red chalk, pen and brown ink, brown wash; A Biblical Scene (verso) – red chalk, pen and brown ink – 15.8 x 27.3cm.
(Christie's) **$499** **£260**

ZUCCHI – A Bacchante – canvas on panel – 19 x 13in.
(Sotheby's) **$634** **£320**

ZURBARAN – Saint Catherine Of Siena In Prayer, A Crown Of Thorns On Her Head – 48 x 37½in.
(Sotheby's) **$1,980** **£1,000**

CAMBRIDGE REFERENCE LIBRARY